The Ethos of Europe

Can the EU become a 'just' institution? Andrew Williams considers this highly charged political and moral question by examining the role of five salient values said to be influential in the governance and law of the Union: peace, the rule of law, respect for human rights, democracy, and liberty. He assesses each of these as elements of an apparent 'institutional ethos' and philosophy of EU law and finds that justice as a governing ideal has failed to be taken seriously in the EU. To remedy this condition, he proposes a new set of principles upon which justice might be brought more to the fore in the Union's governance. By focusing on the realisation of human rights as a core institutional value, Williams argues that the EU can better define its moral limits so as to evolve as a more just project.

Formerly a practising solicitor in London, Andrew Williams teaches EU and human rights law at the School of Law in the University of Warwick.

For a full list of titles published in the series, please see the end of the book.

The Ethos of Europe
Values, Law and Justice in the EU

Andrew Williams

CAMBRIDGE
UNIVERSITY PRESS

CAMBRIDGE UNIVERSITY PRESS
Cambridge, New York, Melbourne, Madrid, Cape Town, Singapore,
São Paulo, Delhi, Dubai, Tokyo

Cambridge University Press
The Edinburgh Building, Cambridge CB2 8RU, UK

Published in the United States of America by Cambridge University Press,
New York

www.cambridge.org
Information on this title: www.cambridge.org/9780521118286

First published 2010

Printed in the United Kingdom at the University Press, Cambridge

A catalogue record for this publication is available from the British Library

Library of Congress Cataloguing in Publication data
Williams, Andrew J., 1951–
　　The ethos of Europe : values, law and justice in the EU / Andrew Williams.
　　　　p.　cm. – (Cambridge studies in European law and policy)
　　Includes bibliographical references and index.
　　ISBN 978-0-521-11828-6 (hardback)
　　1. Law–European Union countries–Philosophy.　2. Law and
　　ethics.　3. Constitutional law–Moral and ethical aspects–European
　　Union countries.　I. Title.　II. Series.
　　KJE960.W55 2010
　　341.242′2–dc22　　　　2009050374

ISBN 978-0-521-11828-6 Hardback
ISBN 978-0-521-13404-0 Paperback
１００J９８&2０１

Contents

Preface

This book represents an investigation into the ethical terrain of the European Union. In the course of its enquiry, it reveals how the practice of the institutions, through law *and* policy, through adjudication and regulation, through rhetoric and action, has led to the adoption of a number of values, each of which possesses indeterminate substance and is highly ambiguous. It argues that an institutional ethos, composed in part by a philosophy of EU law, has developed that lacks any coherence *and*, ultimately, clear moral purpose. Most importantly, there has been a failure to take 'justice' seriously as a central, defining and governing theme. The EU's capacity to respond to crises and provide a focal point for vital decisions that will affect the lives of countless peoples inside and outside its domain is therefore diminished.

But my aim in this assessment is *not* simply to dismiss the Union as an 'unjust institution' or to argue that the evident failings make it worthy of dismantlement. Rather, the analysis is intended as a prelude to considering how change might be effected so as to make the EU *more* disposed to justice. Understanding the nature of the problem is the first step on this route. Believing that the trajectories of the ethos and the philosophy of law do not have to remain fixed, that they can be re-directed, is the second. But in order to achieve this, to make the EU a more just institution, a reconfiguration of values, law and the constitution of the EU is necessary. A fundamental reappraisal is required that will provide the Union with a clearer appreciation of its philosophical underpinnings and a more certain ethical framework. *That* is the ambition of this book. Having provided an evaluation of the salient values purportedly governing the EU, I look towards constructing *one* plausible account of justice based on a coherent set of principles that could provoke the change sought. This is a foundation upon which further work will build. Practical as well as philosophical effort will still be needed. But I believe starting this process in earnest is a worthwhile endeavour given the scale of the problem and the tasks required to remedy it.

In this respect the introduction of the Lisbon Treaty, reference to which I have incorporated into the text where relevant, is merely the latest moment in the EU's history. It does not reduce the overall problem or the remedial task I advocate. It does, however, make discussion about the future ethical direction of the Union more urgent. Any great constitutional change should provoke a sense of reflection.

There are people I wish to thank for helping me to complete this book. At Warwick Law School I have benefited over a number of years from the comments and insights of Upendra Baxi, Victor Tadros and Jayan Nayar. All of them have taken pains to read through early drafts of sections of the book and ask important questions of my arguments. I would also like to acknowledge the continuing support of Gráinne de Búrca who has been unstinting in her encouragement. On a more personal note, I am as always hugely grateful to my parents, Norman and Pauline Williams, for the positive attitude that they take to my work. But most of all I want to thank Kathy, Antonia and Claudia who have put up with so much in this book's gestation. Their enduring love and generosity have made it possible for me to undertake and complete this project. They have made it worthwhile.

1   The ethos of Europe: an introduction

Of course temporary agreements are possible between capitalists and between states. In this sense a United States of Europe is possible as an agreement between the European capitalists ... but to what end?

Lenin 1915

An uncertain 'soul'

Half a century after the EU was formed there is still doubt and angst about the nature of its constitution.[1] We are perhaps no nearer a clear understanding of what the European Union is *for* ('to what end' in Lenin's prescient terms) or the values that govern its development and practice than we were in 1957. Even though its success, if measured in terms of longevity, ubiquity and political importance, is incontrovertible it remains essentially contested,[2] an 'unresolved political problem' depending on perspective.[3] Indeed, the longer time has gone on the more complex the issue has become. As testimony to its extraordinary evolution there now seems to be so much the EU *could* be as we progress into the twenty-first century. From technocratic facilitator for the enrichment of its members to exemplar for global justice (and an expansive variety in between) the EU might be interpreted

---

[1] For convenience I use the term 'EU' or 'Union' throughout this book to signify the entity that has been in existence since 1957. Although it has gone through a number of designations, the EU is intended to capture its historical identity and institutional continuity. I do mention the EEC or the European Community where that particular term relates to a specific time and event.

[2] Zenon Bańkowski and Emilios Christodoulidis, 'The European Union as an Essentially Contested Project', *European Law Journal* 4:4 (1998) 341–54.

[3] Etienne Balibar, *We, The People of Europe: Reflections on Transnational Citizenship* (Princeton: Princeton University Press, 2004) at 2.

as a conceptual chameleon, shifting its purpose depending on the changing political, social, economic and legal environment as well as perspective.

Unsurprisingly, therefore, the EU has always defied easy categorisation. It seems to possess a floating character. One minute an international organisation, the next, a state in the making. Then again a regime that crosses traditional boundaries, an entity that hovers amidst and between different collective regime-types. We might be fairly certain about what it is not, however. It is not a state. Nor has it evolved in the way that nations of Western Europe have evolved. It has not emerged as a simple product of culture or popular uprising. It may have the initial appearance of an 'imagined community',[4] mimicking the construction of some European nations, but the imagination has invariably had to come from relatively few individuals. The EU was created by a closed agreement between a small number of states influenced by a similarly few 'founding fathers'. Since that creation it has developed both as a product of external intervention (through the influence and practices of Member State governments as well as other actors) and internal initiative (through its constructed institutions). But ambiguity has reigned. The EU remains a political conundrum both as to what it is about and what it should do.

The political uncertainty attached to the EU, sometimes referred to as a lack of *telos*, has been matched in a number of other realms. There has been and remains vagueness as to the Union's spatial limits. The Six became the Nine, became the Twelve, became the Fifteen, became the Twenty-four. Now we have twenty-seven Member States. Negotiations continue with particular Balkan countries. Turkey remains, at least for the present, committed to attaining membership. How is the Union thus confined? Where does 'Europe' end if Turkey is a potential member? What logic persists in limits imposed by geographical features such as the Carpathians, the Urals, the Caucasus, the Mediterranean? One only has to look at the map of modern-day Europe to ask; if Finland and the Baltic States, why not Ukraine and Belarus? If Cyprus, why not the southern shore of the Mediterranean? If Turkey, why not Georgia and Armenia? And if those, why not Russia? The limits are blurred. And the Treaty of European Union hardly helps when it allows for 'any European State', without supplying a definition in this regard,

---

[4] See Benedict Anderson, *Imagined Communities: Reflections on the Origin and Spread of Nationalism* (London: Verso, 1991).

to 'apply to become a member of the Union'.[5] Such uncertainty leaves open the door for an idea of Europe that can only vaguely assist with any process of self-constituting. There is a danger that 'Europe will become an incoherent collection of sub-unions lacking any historical, ethnic, psychic – or even geographical – reason to exist'.[6] Its borders are indeed neither defining nor defined as a project or projection.[7] Olli Rehn, the EU's enlargement commissioner may have said in 2006 that 'values make the borders of Europe'.[8] His colleague Vladimir Špidla echoed these words proclaiming 'Europe ends' where its values 'are not shared'.[9] But this only serves to increase the geographical uncertainty. Indeed, it suggests that any correlation between a scheme of values and 'Europe', as a geographical rather than political construct, is false. And that the link between the name 'Europe' and the EU is contradictory.

Culturally, too, uncertainty flows from the geographical and demographical mix of the EU's present as well as potential future territory and population. Some figures have questioned the ability of the Union to assimilate cultures radically different from those which have been perceived as centrally 'European'. Giscard d'Estaing's infamous comment that Turkey as an Islamic country, and therefore by extension all countries that possessed an Islamic religious majority, could not belong to the EU, is indicative of a certain Eurocentric, some would undoubtedly say racist, ideology.[10] But of course what it is to be 'European' is a subject of much debate. Can there be a totalising description without the imposition of a worldview that ultimately discriminates against those with different images? Does 'Europe' really possess a partial identity through 'shared traditions and heritages' such as 'Roman law, political democracy, parliamentary institutions, and Judaeo-Christian ethics' as A.D. Smith has claimed?[11] We must surely appreciate the

---

[5] Article 49 TEU.
[6] Philip Allott, 'The Crisis of European Constitutionalism: Reflections on the Revolution in Europe', *Common Market Law Review* 34 (1997) 439–90 at 487.
[7] Étienne Balibar has called this a 'borderland' that has no borders. See Balibar, *We, The People of Europe* at 220.
[8] See, www.guardian.co.uk/world/2006/nov/08/eu.worlddispatch and Olli Rehn, *Europe's Next Frontiers* (Baden-Baden: Nomos, 2006).
[9] Vladimir Špidla, 'Some Reflections on the European Social Model', in Detlev Albers, Stephen Haseler and Henning Meyer (eds.), *Social Europe: a Continent's Answer to Market Fundamentalism* (London: European Research Forum, 2006) 111–16, at 112.
[10] See *Le Monde*, 9 November 2002.
[11] Anthony D. Smith, 'National Identity and the Idea of European Unity', in Peter Gowan and Perry Anderson (eds.), *The Question of Europe* (London: Verso, 1997) 318–42 at 335.

perils that can attach to a project that fails to understand the importance of culture in the creation of a political enterprise intent on giving effect to some kind of integration.[12] Charges of neo-colonialism, exclusion, even xenophobia surface with varying degrees of persuasion.[13] At an extremely provocative level it might even give vent to Balibar's suggestion that a 'virtual *European apartheid*' has been constructed, based on a 'stigmatization and repression of populations whose presence within European societies is nonetheless increasingly massive and legitimate'.[14] But uncertainty of the EU regarding culture appears to result in its basic inability to address these dangers. The uncertainty that exists is a product of failure to provide any sense of inclusion. Exclusion emerges as an interpretation of its uncertain approach, suggesting for some that European unification is based more on hate and fear than on feelings of fraternity and hospitality.[15] Even the rhetoric of 'unity through diversity' has failed to address these issues other than superficially. In a belated attempt to take culture seriously as a vital component of integration the EU has demonstrated an inability to come to terms with the ever-changing complex terrain of this subject. It has left itself open to the critique that in seeking 'unity' it in fact undermines diversity.[16] Diversity is only acceptable, it has been

For a more recent attempt to advocate for a serious embrace of Christian values into the constituting texts of the EU, see Joseph Weiler, *Un'Europa Cristiana: un saggio esplorativo* (Milan: BUR, 2003).

[12] See, for instance, the critique of Edward Said, *Culture and Imperialism* (London: Vintage, 1994).

[13] See, variously, Verena Stolke, 'Talking Culture: New Boundaries, New Rhetorics of Exclusion in Europe', *Current Anthropology* 36:1 (1995) 1–24; Peter Fitzpatrick, 'New Europe, Old Story: Racism and the European Community', in Paddy Ireland and Per Laleng (eds.), *The Critical Lawyers' Handbook 2* (London: Pluto Press, 1997) 86–95; and Allott, 'The Crisis of European Constitutionalism' at 486–9 where he notes the 'collective neo-colonialism in central and eastern Europe' as a possible element of '[a]n imposed prussianizing of part of Europe'.

[14] Balibar, *We, The People of Europe* at x.

[15] Jean-Francois Lyotard famously claimed that 'unification of Europe means the unification of hatreds' and Conor Gearty has also adopted a similar tone when he suggested that 'at the centre of the plan for a new European landscape there is to be found a hard seed of hate'. See Jean-François Lyotard, *Europe, the Jews and the Book* (London: UCL Press, 1993) at 159 and Conor A. Gearty, 'The Internal and External "Other" in the Union Legal Order: Racism, Religious Intolerance and Xenophobia in Europe', in Philip Alston, Mara Bustelo and James Heenan (eds.), *The EU and Human Rights* (Oxford: Oxford University Press, 1999) 325–58 at 327.

[16] Cris Shore, 'The Cultural Policies of the European Union and Cultural Diversity', Research Position Paper 3 Council of Europe 2003, online, available at: www.coe.int/t/dg4/cultureheritage/Completed/Diversity/EN_Diversity_Bennett.pdf.

argued, in so far as it does not jeopardise unity. The cultural aspects of Europe thus remain steadfastly indeterminate, subject to 'a constant process of negotiation, exchange and syncretism'.[17]

But perhaps the greatest uncertainty is philosophical in nature. The coupling of a contested sense of purpose and a vague appreciation of form has provided an environment almost designed to undermine any consistent identity construction. Ambiguity on matters of what and how 'certain beliefs and values' have interacted within the 'distinct community' that the EU has come to represent has been fundamental.[18] Questions as to the nature of those values that have directed the EU during its development, the extent to which they have had effect and influence, and the relationship that exists between them in the resolution of conflicts have plagued the EU from even before it took institutional form. Although values were espoused rhetorically and constitutionally from the earliest moments in the EU's history, their scope and depth and inter-relationship have always been unclear. How, for instance, was the resolution to 'preserve peace and liberty' in the preamble to the 1957 EEC Treaty to be understood? To what extent were those 'cherished values' and shared 'attitudes to life', noted in the 1973 Declaration of a European Identity, to be applied? How, indeed, were 'the principles of representative democracy, of the rule of law, of social justice – which is the ultimate goal of economic progress – and of respect for human rights'[19] to be measured against each other and developed institutionally?

This philosophical uncertainty has been recognised within the EU from its beginnings. The response has often taken a metaphysical turn. Soon after it was created a search for its 'spirit' emerged as a means to express the ambitions for the entity beyond the Treaty text. At the end of the 1960s the need for an 'identity' *of* and *for* the Union became fashionable, the former for projection beyond the Community to the outside world, the latter to create some sense of belonging for citizens *within*. Then, the desire to complete the internal market in the 1990s was described as putting 'flesh on the bones'. It was not long before Jacques Delors began to speak of the search for a 'soul', recognising the importance of moving beyond the technical and economic advantages of the Union to attract the greater loyalty and commitment of

---

[17] *Ibid.*
[18] Jan Zielonka, *Europe as Empire: the Nature of the Enlarged European Union* (Oxford: Oxford University Press, 2006) at 133.
[19] EC Bull 12–1973 118–22.

the people of Europe to this elusive polity constructed in their name.[20] Delors said specifically that if 'in the next ten years we haven't managed to give a Soul to Europe, to give it spirituality and meaning the game will be up'.[21]

Of course, Delors was speaking at a time when Europe was entering a period of immense upheaval. The end of the Cold War had provoked a sense of ideological and political vacuum in Western Europe.[22] The perceived need to fix some kind of ethical framework for the EU, to provide an identity through espoused values, had become of vital concern. Ironically perhaps, the ubiquity of EU-sponsored initiatives that were self-consciously devoted to promulgating but also entrenching often repeated Western liberal values in post-communist states also gave added impetus to the advance of these same values *within* a Europe supposedly already constructed upon them. For, how could the EU require putative Member States to demonstrate their commitment and observance to a whole range of political criteria without at least maintaining that both existing members and European institutions were already abiding by them? A mirror had indeed been held up to the EU's face. The fact that the EU had up until then still satisfactorily to address those critiques focused on its democratic deficit, its ambivalent attitude towards human rights, and its inability to fashion a fully working single market, suggested that transition could be as much for domestic as it was external consumption. When enlargement became a possible political settlement for a Europe emerging from the fearful shadows of a schismatic continent, the self-interrogation as to what the new Europe might stand for intensified. A wholesale constitutional review, as it might now appear in retrospect, began in an attempt

---

[20] This prompted the 2004 Berlin Conference on 'A Soul for Europe' which managed to make the matter an almost exclusively cultural policy enterprise thereby missing the point of its own rhetoric. For brief conclusions of the conference see www.felix. meritis.nl/nieuws/berlin/declaration.html.

[21] President Delors, Speech to the churches, Brussels, 4 February 1992, online, available at: http://europa.eu.int/comm/dgs/policy_advisers/activities/ dialogue_religions_humanisms/issues/soul_for_Europe/index_En.htm.

[22] Tony Judt, in his recent history of post-war Europe, commented, '[w]hen Communism fell and the Soviet Union imploded, they took with them not just an ideological system but the political and geographical coordinates of an entire continent'. Judt, *Postwar: A History of Europe Since 1945* (London: Pimlico, 2007) at 749. Similarly, John Gray has been vociferous in remarking that this upheaval and 'the disappearance of familiar post-war political landmarks ... left Western thought and policy regarding the post-communist countries rudderless'. See *Enlightenment's Wake* (Abingdon: Routledge, 2007) at 56.

to make sense of the evolving EU without losing sight of its origins and history. So the Treaty on European Union (TEU), pronounced at Maastricht, attempted to grapple with some issues of institutional values by making the more specific claim in its Preamble that the Union was attached to the 'principles of liberty, democracy and respect for human rights and fundamental freedoms and of the rule of law'. The Treaty of Amsterdam incorporated these into the body of the TEU text and invested them with a certain mythic constitutional quality in the process. The Union was described, in Article 6(1), as 'founded on' these principles, an assertion that was not necessarily self-evident. And then the political decision to form a 'constitution', formalised through a Convention on the Future of Europe in 2001, gave institutional force to the 'soul-searching' that the EU had provoked.

The identification of a panoply of 'principles' and 'values' that should govern the Union was finally agreed within the context of a Constitutional Treaty. Although this Treaty became famously still-born, the attachment to a specified list of values, along with most of the provisions, was replicated in the replacement Lisbon Treaty. An apparent political will, or at least, intent, to represent constitutionally the EU's 'moral identity' to some degree has become entrenched.[23] The assertion is retained, presently in the new Article 2 of the TEU, that the EU is:

founded on the values of respect for human dignity, freedom, democracy, equality, the rule of law and respect for human rights, including the rights of persons belonging to minorities. These values are common to the Member States in a society in which pluralism, non-discrimination, tolerance, justice, solidarity and equality between women and men prevail.

This is complemented by the new Article 3 TEU, which maintains that the Union's aim is 'to promote peace, its values and the well-being of its peoples'. The EU will promote 'social justice and protection, equality between women and men, solidarity between generations and protection of the rights of the child' and 'economic, social and territorial cohesion, and solidarity among Member States'. Externally,

it shall contribute to peace, security, the sustainable development of the Earth, solidarity and mutual respect among peoples, free and fair trade, eradication of poverty and the protection of human rights, in particular the rights of the

---

[23] Takis Tridimas suggests this was the purpose of Article I-2 CT. See Tridimas, *The General Principles of EU Law*, 2nd edn (Oxford: Oxford University Press, 2006) at 16.

child, as well as to the strict observance and the development of international law, including respect for the principles of the United Nations Charter.

Identifying such a plethora of constitutional principles and values mixed with policy statements is a particularly inept way to construct, or even simply represent, a meaningful philosophical framework for the EU. There is little by way of definition here that might counter the uncertainty I have already highlighted. Nonetheless, with the Lisbon Treaty provisions coming into force, there is a clear and concerted attempt to enshrine constitutionally a notion of the 'good' for Europe that is sought through the EU.

Despite these valiant attempts to construct meaning for the EU, as Delors demanded, many commentators clearly remain to be convinced. There has been a tendency to contend that the EU simply does not possess any 'ethos'. Without adequately defining what this term means, a variety of figures or analysts have suggested that there is an 'absence' here that leaves the EU in an unresolved crisis. Vaclav Havel, for instance, wrote that Europe 'lacks an ethos; it lacks imagination … it lacks a genuine identification with the meaning and purpose of integration'.[24] Ian Ward has argued that attaining clear ethical coordinates from the discourses of 'unity in diversity' and subsidiarity is extremely problematic. Reconciling 'uniformity and diversity', he has suggested, 'demands an intellectual suppleness' that is currently lacking.[25] What is required and what is missing is a 'public philosophy which can inspire'.[26] Others claim that the 'public space' that has developed in the EU is 'fragmented and weak'.[27] In such an environment there can 'hardly be a single dominant identity, ethos, and demos'.[28] Rather, values appear contingent, malleable and ever changing. It follows that public and political attachment to, or identity with, the EU becomes increasingly difficult. Etienne Balibar has gone so far as to suggest that there has yet to be constructed an identity for the EU 'capable of becoming part of both objective institutions and individuals' imaginations'.[29] There has been a failure to bring 'to consciousness' the 'soul and person of Europe', if that were ever possible.[30] The absence of an

---

[24] Vaclev Havel as quoted by Ian Ward, 'A Decade of Europe? Some Reflections on an Aspiration', *Journal of Law and Society* 30 (2003) 236–57 at 257.

[25] *Ibid.* at 255.   [26] *Ibid.*

[27] Zielonka, *Europe as Empire* at 138.

[28] *Ibid.*   [29] Balibar, *We, The People of Europe* at 9.

[30] Allott, 'The Crisis of European Constitutionalism' at 469. Such critique is not new. Nearly fifty years ago, Stanley Hoffman diagnosed that 'Europe today has no clear

'ethos', therefore, appears as a prevalent and crucial criticism. People simply do not know what the EU stands for.

But is all this critique accurate? Does philosophical uncertainty, the uncertain 'soul', presuppose the absence of an ethos, that there is no ethical core to the European Union? Not if we see 'ethos' in a more defined light. And indeed, if we look deeper into the history of EU critique we can see this made evident.[31] In a seminal text produced some fifty years ago, Karl Deutsch and his fellow report writers, interpreted empirical observations of 'amalgamated security-communities' and spoke of the 'way of life' of selected regional integration projects.[32] This 'way of life' was defined as 'a set of socially accepted values and of institutional means for their pursuit and attainment, and a set of established or emerging habits of behaviour corresponding to them'.[33] By looking, in effect, to ideal, practical and legal forms of constitution, all of which together encompass a 'society's self-constituting',[34] Deutsch recognised the importance of action as much as ideas in constructing a community.[35] But the construction of norms has as much to do with the effect of cumulative practice and practices as it does with principles enshrined in any constitutional text. A 'political ethos'

identity, no profile other than that which a process of industrialisation and a process of economic integration have given it. Europe today has no sense of direction and purpose'. See, Hoffman, 'Europe's Identity Crisis: Between the Past and America', in Hoffman, *The European Sisyphus: Essays on Europe 1964–1994* (Boulder, CO: Westview Press, 1995) 9–50 at 9.

[31] This is in addition to that philosophical dimension related to 'Europe' as an historical idea as opposed to Europe in the guise of the EU. See for instance, Paul Ricoeur, 'Reflections on a New Ethos for Europe', in Richard Kearney (ed.), *The Hermeneutics of Action* (London: Sage, 1996) 3–13.

[32] Karl Deutsch, Sidney A. Burrell, Robert A. Kann et al. *Political Community and the North Atlantic Area: International Organization in the Light of Historical Experience* (Princeton: Princeton University Press, 1957).

[33] *Ibid.* at 48.

[34] See Philip Allott, *Eunomia; New Order for a New World* (Oxford: Oxford University Press, 1990). Allott's description is echoed by a number of EU commentators vis-à-vis its process of constitutionalism. See, for instance, Neil Walker, 'Europe's Constitutional Momentum and the Search for Polity Legitimacy', *International Journal of Constitutional Law* 3:2 (2005) 211–38 and Miguel Polares Maduro, 'The Importance of Being Called a Constitution: Constitutional Authority and the Authority of Constitutionalism', *International Journal of Constitutional Law* (2005) 332–56.

[35] More recently, Berthold Rittberger and Frank Schimmelfennig adopted the term 'ethos' to denote those 'constitutive norms that define the collective identity of the community – who "we" are, what we stand for and how we differ from other communities'. See Berthold Rittberger and Frank Schimmelfennig, 'The Constitutionalization of the European Union; Explaining the Parliamentarization and Institutionalization

or 'self-understanding' can emerge through transparent democratic processes, or through practical (communicative) action rather than some form of unarticulated and 'natural' social evolution.[36]

In this sense, we are *not* dealing with a concept of ethos that relates to individuals or some form of homogenous society. The overall uncertainty of form and purpose of the EU, which I have described, does not allow for strong claims to be made that a public ethos has emerged from a European society of peoples. It is common ground that there is no European *demos*, that there is no apparent ethos capable of emerging from some form of *volksgeist*. But this does not mean that the concept of 'ethos' has no relevance here. It does have specific application to the *institution* of the EU. We can therefore, I submit, talk usefully about an '*institutional ethos*'. But what do I mean by this?

Let me propose a working definition. 'Institutional ethos' should mean the collective disposition, character and fundamental values that capture the existent sense of the EU as an institution in terms of both its particular formally constructed arrangement *and* its 'general pattern of activity'.[37] It echoes, in part, G.A. Cohen's description of the ethos of a society as 'the set of sentiments and attitudes in virtue of which its normal practices, and informal pressures, are what they are'.[38] In other words, it is the EU's underlying and continuing ethical genius. It incorporates the sense in Greek of both *ēthos* (character) and *ethos* (custom), encompassing and reflecting the ethical nature of the EU as it has developed institutionally, and as that nature has informed, influenced and guided its law, its policy and its practices.[39] The philosopher Max Scheler's definition of ethos as 'the experiential structure of values and their immanent rules of preferring, which lie *behind* both the morality and ethics of a people' resonates here, although, of course,

---

of Human Rights', May 2005, Institution of Advanced Studies Vienna Political Science Series, online, available at: www.ihs.ac.at/publications/pol/pw_104.pdf at 19.

[36] Jürgen Habermas, 'Is the Development of a European Identity Necessary, and is it Possible?', in *The Divided West* (Cambridge: Polity Press, 2006) 67–82 at 80.

[37] I am using the dual definition of 'institution' provided by Robert Keohane, *International Institutions and State Power: Essays in International Relations Theory* (Boulder, CO: Westview Press, 1989) at 162.

[38] G.A. Cohen, 'Where the Action is: on the Site of Distributive Justice', *Philosophy and Public Affairs* 26 (1997) 3–30 at 28.

[39] This evokes Hans-Georg Gadamer's interpretation of Aristotle's use of 'ethos', which denoted a 'sphere' not of rigid laws alone nor of 'lawlessness' but rather institutions and attitudes. See Hans-Georg Gadamer, *Truth and Method* (London: Sheed and Ward, 1979) at 279.

I am *not* attempting to claim that a European *volk* exists.[40] Scheler used the concept of ethos to understand how practices were governed particularly over time, noting its historical adaptation, distinguishing it from fundamental 'moral change' that might take place through societal shifts. Similarly, I propose that this has as much relevance for the EU, as an instituted polity, analogous to other forms of 'community' without necessarily attaining that social status. Its very institutional existence and history determines that an institutional ethos has emerged over time, altering subtly as decisions and practices, whether political, legal, social or economic, evolve. Such an institutional ethos loosely structures and guides what is acceptable, setting parameters through rules (both formal and informal) and norms for such alterations to be subsumed within and by the institution. It also helps determine what the institution does or does not recognise as appropriate for its value preferences. It may not be 'primordial' or 'stable', but it is key to 'a political culture' necessary to sustain (putative) democratic institutions such as the EU pretends to be.[41]

None of the above is to suggest that individuals operating within the institutional environment of the EU, coming into contact with its structures and practices, do not bring with them their own ethical perspectives. Nor does it mean that change cannot occur through the actions of such individuals. But it *is* to suggest that the institutional ethos within the institutional setting, the structures and norms that have evolved, has the effect of shaping the acceptance and interpretation of individual actions, of shaping individual and institutional choices, and generally framing practices emerging from the institution. It follows that the older the institution the more entrenched the institutional ethos. The weight of past practices repeated over and again and past decisions affirmed across time lies heavily on the behaviour of those who come within its domain.

Such an appreciation and definition of institutional ethos provokes two observations for my study. First, the critique that the EU lacks an ethos is misleading if not blatantly incorrect. Merely through the EU's construction as a polity that attempts to impose order on the basis of espoused values or principles, an institutional ethos is created. We may not like its nature (assuming we can determine it) but we should not

---

[40] I am substituting 'institution' for 'people'. Max Scheler, *Formalism in Ethics and Non-Formal Ethics of Values* (Evanston: Northwestern University Press, 1973) at 302.
[41] Jan Zielonka, *Europe as Empire* at 133.

dismiss its presence and influence. Second, law occupies a hugely significant place within the construction of the institutional ethos. For a 'new legal order', such as the EU contends it has become, law as rules, as regulation, legislation *and* judicial interpretation, in both 'soft' and 'hard' formations, will not only reflect but will also help develop the institutional ethos' scope and character.[42] This is reinforced by the fact that law has been valorised for its quality of establishing some degree of reasonable 'certainty' and helping construct a supposedly well-considered ethical framework for the EU. It has been presented as 'a rational force towards the inevitable'[43] (whatever that inevitability might entail) providing a form of discipline or subtle surveillance to ensure commitment to the EU.[44] By some, it has even been viewed as a counterweight to the multiple dimensions of uncertainty I have already described. Eurocrats, from Walter Hallstein to José Barroso, have seen law as providing the necessary glue to keep the EU together, a natural consequence, one might suppose, of the lack of mass public mobilisation to give force to the Union. Law as an integral and integrating feature of 'community' has been the underlying theme. Barroso, indeed, went so far as to declare that 'assuring the coherence of the [European] project is *only* possible through the rule of law'.[45]

The reliance and emphasis placed on law has built on an unspoken acceptance of notions of modern Western law and its processes so as to establish order, clarity and a degree of certainty for the settlement of disputes and for planning by those constituents who are affected by its application. It enables expectations to be given some degree of shape. That is a common attribute ascribed to law across a range of legal philosophies. Even amongst legal pluralists or post-modern analysts there

---

[42] Tridimas has gone so far as to suggest that Article I-2 of the failed Constitutional Treaty, now replicated in the Lisbon Treaty, which attempts to fix the values for the Union, did no more than 'represent the EU legal order as it currently stands'. He maintains that this constitutional statement was 'to cultivate the emergence of a European demos by laying down the attributes of a moral identity and a political community', or institutional ethos in other terms. Tridimas, *The General Principles of EU Law* at 15 and 16.

[43] Deirdre Curtin, 'European Legal Integration: Paradise Lost?', in Deirdre Curtin, Jan M. Smits, André Klip and Joseph A. McCahery (eds.), *European Integration and Law* (Antwerp: Intersentia, 2006) 1–54 at 1.

[44] Several recent polemical texts emphasise this line of thought. See Mark Leonard, *Why Europe will Run the 21st Century* (London: Fourth Estate, 2005) and Parag Khanna, *The Second World: Empires and Influence in the New Global Order* (London: Penguin, 2008).

[45] José Manuel Barroso, 'Uniting in Peace: the Role of Law in the European Union', Jean Monnet Lecture, EUI Florence (2006) at 4.

is recognition that the force of law necessitates a degree of certainty within at least local or systemic parameters. Otherwise, the charge of arbitrary decision-making is raised to undermine the whole premise for a particular system of law and the political order over which it is supposed to rule.

But notwithstanding this necessary quality, law in the EU has had to evolve, as already suggested, within a geographical, political, philosophical and constitutional environment that remains steadfastly conditioned *by* uncertainty to the point of indeterminacy. It has had to respond to significant debate and shifting patterns in political direction, in perceived threat, in economic conditions, in geo-politics, in demographics, and in constitutional structure. So we have a law that has been provided with few constitutionally-fixed coordinates. How then can those values preferred politically and thus supposedly to be applied through law be protected so as not to go beyond reasonable uncertainty and become indeterminate in content and tone?[46]

All this implies that the study of the EU's institutional ethos, its potential component values, and EU law's vital role within it, is of huge importance. It is a surprise therefore, when we look closely, that the relationship between these matters remains something of uncharted territory. There has been some deeper reflection provoked by the rise of constitutionalism but such studies are embryonic in character.[47] All struggle with the difficulty of understanding the sources of EU values and EU law in the absence of any coherent form of 'consciousness of collective belonging' as Habermas terms it.[48] We appear to be no nearer a considered understanding of the contribution of law to the values and the make-up of the institutional ethos of the EU or vice versa. In particular, no captivating philosophy for the Union or of its law has emerged. And, more importantly, no developed discourse or established institution-specific theory of substantive justice has been evident.

---

[46] Little wonder then that Francis Jacobs, for one, suggests that 'many fundamental choices for society are now made, and probably have to be made, not by the legislature, not by the executive, but by the courts'. The implication is that judicial decision-making resolves political irresolution vis-à-vis values and any conflicts between them. See Francis G. Jacobs, *The Sovereignty of Law: The European Way* (Cambridge: Cambridge University Press, 2007) at 1.

[47] See, for instance, J.H.H. Weiler and Marlene Wind (eds.), *European Constitutionalism Beyond the State* (Cambridge: Cambridge University Press, 2003).

[48] Jürgen Habermas, 'What is a People?', in *The Postnational Constellation: Political Essays* (Cambridge: Polity Press,) 1–25 at 18.

The failure to provide such critique and perhaps resolve the pervading and debilitating sense of indeterminacy (emerging from the coalescence of the many dimensions of uncertainty reviewed above), intimates an analytical deficiency in respect of the EU's ethical character. The inability to excavate the nature of the institutional ethos and the vital relationship between law and values within the EU is one of the significant reasons, I suggest, why a coherent account of what the EU actually stands for and what it will withstand ethically remains largely absent. An assessment of the institutional ethos and its relationship with its stated values, its law and notions of justice is therefore of pre-eminent necessity. Such is the aim of this book. For if we cannot understand what either makes, or could make, the EU a *just* institution the prospects for its survival must surely be suspect. Indeed, would we want it to survive if it failed demonstrably as a just institution? As soon as crisis visits, as the economic depression that began in 2008 might well provoke, what hope is there for justice to be the determining factor in making decisions?

The objectives of the book

Within the context of the above overall aim my specific objectives are to address a series of basic questions. What is the nature of the EU's institutional ethos? What is the character of the predominant values that can be plausibly inferred as components of that ethos? What part has and does law play vis-à-vis the construction and promulgation of both these values and the institutional ethos? How does law cope with and respond to the indeterminacy of the EU's institutionally projected values? How can and how should it reflect or contribute to any ethical dimension with any degree of confidence? What philosophy of European law exists and what philosophy would be desirable? And where does, or should, justice find a place within this complex institutional site?

The book tackles these questions in two parts. First, it undertakes an assessment of those salient values that the EU has identified constitutionally as comprising its ethical presence. The way in which law reflects and interacts with these values is particularly relevant. This is necessary if we are to understand the institutional ethos of the EU and the role of EU law within it. The depth and scope of those values, which are at least expressed now as forming the ethical foundations of the Union, are the focus of my analysis. Respect for human rights, liberty, democracy and the rule of law represent those most forcefully and frequently cited values in this regard. As we have already seen, Article 6(1) TEU made them fundamental within the EU's legal order. After Lisbon, that is how they remain. Of course, one should not be so naïve as to suppose that these are either necessarily truly formative or a complete expression of influential values. But they have acquired a degree of pre-eminence through their reiteration over the years both politically and judicially. They have to be taken seriously, therefore, at least as a plausible point of departure for assessing the 'ethical convictions' voiced institutionally.

Nonetheless, these four foundational values do not and cannot, as I have said, provide a total expression of the perceived 'goods', the achievement of which may be the aim of the EU. The Constitutional and Lisbon Treaties attempted to expand the corpus of values to reflect a broader ethos. In particular, the intent to promote 'peace' in the new Article 3 TEU is a crucial reaffirmation of the EU's roots. Although we might be tempted to think of this concept as more related to *telos* than institutional ethos, peace has also been expressed consistently throughout the EU's history as a value to be pursued both internally and externally. It remains a powerful governing concept to the extent that there is good cause to suppose it represents one of those 'underlying values and principles' that inform, but are not necessarily reflected expressly in, the general principles as now traditionally ascribed to European law.[49] There is a strong argument, therefore, for peace to warrant individual examination.

On these initial premises, I have chosen to excavate the institutional ethos through separate chapters on peace, the rule of law, human rights, democracy and liberty. It will be apparent, naturally, that these values are not wholly separable. Each infects and is infected by the others. It would be nonsensical to consider them in complete isolation. Nonetheless, in the first instance, their constitutional nomination warrants separate analysis. However, to acknowledge that these are not all-consuming as operative values, I incorporate other prominent conceptions into their assessment. 'Well-being', which, like peace, is an aim expressed in the Lisbon Treaty that might encompass the general

---

[49] Tridimas notes the possible discovery of the general principles of EU law from this source. However, my sense of ethos is not restricted to EU law as an independent system. Unlike Tridimas, in this respect, I am referring to the underlying values that the whole institution of the EU might prefer. These may well overlap but not necessarily. See Tridimas, *The General Principles of EU Law*.

economic dimension and aim of the Union (although it remains a highly ambiguous notion in the EU's hands), 'security' (sometimes considered a value in its own right),[50] 'human dignity', 'solidarity' and 'equality', are all embraced at relevant points within my chapter-by-chapter analysis. Some would no doubt see these other values as necessitating chapters of their own. But that is not my choice.

Of course, this investigatory enterprise alone is an ambitious task. However, unless we begin to explore the dimensions of the institutional ethos through its value components it is difficult to see how the EU's adherence to those values can be assessed as a whole and in conjunction with one another. Even though whole books may be devoted to each and every value I have chosen to examine, there is still a need for a broader perspective to be applied. This is what I aim to provide, a sketch of the conceptual and practical field in each case. Given my definition of institutional ethos, this is bound to be contextual and textual, aware of the institutional narratives that have been constructed with regard to them both individually and collectively, and conscious of the practices that have developed in parallel. This is particularly the case when turning to the role of law. As Deirdre Curtin recommends, 'in the contemporary EU it is no longer advisable nor at times even possible to ignore the broader (political, economic) *context* within which the law operates'.[51]

So, to 'develop a more nuanced picture of European law'[52] and the EU's institutional ethos as a whole, I intend to undertake something of a genealogy of values within the institutional domain. The history of not only 'hard law', 'adjudicative law' and 'soft law' but also of legislation, regulation, decision and practices of ordering will fall within this task. It will also embrace policy and the rhetoric and political statements about values made across policy areas and over time.

Applying this basic approach, Chapter 2 will address the notion of peace in the context of the EU and Chapters 3 to 6 will do the same for the rule of law, human rights, democracy and liberty respectively. In each case, I will first try to provide a definitional spectrum against which we can assess the EU's approach. For, clearly all of these values could assume a variety of meanings that undeniably will be

---

[50] Zygmunt Bauman has called security a 'value that, in practice if not in theory, dwarfs and elbows out all other values'. See Bauman, *Europe: An Unfinished Adventure* (Cambridge: Polity Press, 2004) at 32.

[51] Curtin, 'European Legal Integration: Paradise Lost?' at 2.

[52] *Ibid.*

complicated by the peculiar position held by the EU. Its location as a polity that shifts from an intergovernmental arrangement to one which has direct impact on the lives of individuals means that each value-spectrum has to encompass both municipal and international features. That is one of the consequences of its *sui generis* position and indeed the uncertainty I have already outlined. Having provided some basis for assessment, each value chapter then looks at the history of the EU's institutional record. My question in every case is: what is the quality of the value reflected in the EU and its law?

The second part of the book then moves from the particular to the general. It draws on the genealogy of salient values and their relationship with EU law to consider how we can interpret the revealed character of the institutional ethos. This is a prelude to assessing how it might be reconfigured.

So, Chapter 7 first assesses the institutional ethos as a whole, reviewing each of the values examined as components of the EU's ethical framework. I construct an argument here that an overarching uncertainty that is reflected in the incoherent and contradictory ways in which specific values are identified, defined and applied, is evident. This is not, I maintain, a condition of healthy ambiguity, one which can make a virtue of indecision so as to allow multiple projects to co-exist without threatening the EU as a whole. Nor is it within the bounds of understandable systemic uncertainty that lies at the heart of any process of legal adjudication or political decision-making. Rather, it is a dis-abling and destabilising condition that provokes the continual critique of hypocrisy (or irony, as I have described it elsewhere),[53] undermining the EU, de-legitimising it, distancing its constituents from its institutions, and giving succour to dangerous practices of exclusion. In short, the current institutional ethos is antithetical to the EU becoming a 'just institution'.

This evaluation allows me to develop a critical perspective on what kind of philosophy of EU law has evolved within and as a vital part of this institutional ethos. The argument I advance is that EU law has become infected by the underlying indeterminacy of ideal that has deeply affected the appreciation and realisation of the more salient values. These values have been applied in a haphazard fashion and without an understanding of normative content. Focusing on the

---

[53] See Andrew Williams, *EU Human Rights Policies: a Study in Irony* (Oxford: Oxford University Press, 2004).

European Court of Justice's jurisprudence, I argue that a largely pragmatic approach has been adopted that has concentrated on principles or virtues of governance rather than attempting to offer a way of satisfactorily defining values or ensuring their realisation. The underlying philosophy thus appears to be based on a theory of interpretation (of original political will) rather than a theory of justice. What purpose the EU serves has become self-serving and self-referential and extremely unlikely to engender popular support for the EU as a whole. Indeed, in adhering to a philosophy so grounded in a theory of interpretation, the whole enterprise appears ethically vacuous if not duplicitous. Making a virtue of uncertainty through such notions as subsidiarity, respect for diversity, pluralism and multi-level governance, has done little to remedy this fundamental defect.

These claims lead me to argue that the salient values analysed, in particular as promoted through law, possess minimal substance and are highly ambiguous and indeterminate in the EU context. Weighed together they have helped construct an institutional ethos that lacks reasonable coherence *and* moral purpose. Ultimately its ethical lightness may help explain why the EU seems incapable of attracting the loyalty and support of its constituents, let alone any sense of 'constitutional patriotism'. Indeed, rather than establish a clear ethical framework, EU adjudicative law has contributed to this lack of clarity and purpose. Specifically, the failure to adopt 'justice' in its constitutional preference for values (it only appears as an ancillary matter, not in terms of foundational value) is both an indication and a symptom of this condition.[54] Law has become complicit in the masking of whatever political project has developed from time to time. Rather than acting as a counterbalance to a system that intends to preserve the power of capital and existing inequities, and global injustice, it offers a veneer of 'goodness' through its putative adherence to the list of first order values considered in this book. It even manages to bolster the apparent strength of this gloss with a second order of principles. Holding faith with a series of administrative virtues, EU law attempts to provide an unconvincing legitimacy of means in the absence of a clear legitimacy of ends.

[54] Michael Foley has suggested that constitutions have the quality of vagueness just so as to prevent changing values and principles from undermining their power to structure governance. This appears to be directly applicable to the EU where 'vagueness' has been something of an institutional trait. See M. Foley, *The Silence of Constitutions: Gaps, 'Abeyances' and Political Temperament in the Maintenance of Government* (Abingdon: Routledge, 1989).

But if the existing institutional ethos and philosophy of EU law is unsatisfactory, what alternative is possible? Is it conceivable that *another* ethos and philosophy can be entertained based on an account of justice more suited to the complex environment of the Union? Should we even attempt to provide any ethical framework? From a general theoretical perspective there *has* been a willingness to contemplate what kind of institutional philosophy might be adopted.[55] There has, indeed, been no shortage of commentary that sees in the EU the possibility of the application of some form of theory of justice. The list of intellectuals interested in the potential of the EU reads like a reference list of modern sociology and philosophy. From Benhabib to Beck, from Habermas to Todorov, from Bauman to de Sousa Santos, from Derrida to Balibar, varied attempts have been made to instil in the idea of European unification some foundation of justice dealing with its affairs.[56] These attempts have largely, although not exclusively, focused on the external dimension, particularly when trying to assess the promise of the EU to contribute to a regime of 'global justice'. But internally and particularly within the discipline of EU law little credence has been given to such a possibility. It is this general condition and reticence that I aim to challenge.

So, in Chapter 8 I begin to explore the possibility of reconfiguring justice at the core of the institutional ethos. I consider the groundwork for constructing a plausible account of justice for this uniquely placed polity, straddling attributes of statehood, federation and international organisation. This is achieved by setting out what I suggest are necessary fundamental assumptions. By outlining and justifying the key theoretical understandings required for justice to inform the governance of the EU as a particular, located institution, I aim to make more explicit the basis upon which it might begin to structure its development as a more *just* institution. No doubt the assumptions I make could be expanded, revised or replaced. But the

---

[55] See for instance Bauman, *Europe: An Unfinished Adventure*.

[56] Key texts include: Seyla Benhabib, *Another Cosmopolitanism* (Oxford: Oxford University Press, 2006); Ulrich Beck and Edgar Grande, *Cosmopolitan Europe* (Cambridge: Polity, 2007); Tzvetan Todorov, *The New World Disorder* (Cambridge: Polity, 2005); Bauman, *Europe: An Unfinished Adventure*; Boaventura de Sousa Santos, *Towards a New Legal Common Sense* (London: Butterworths, 2002); Jacques Derrida, *The Other Heading: Reflections on Today's Europe* (Indiana: Indiana University Press, 1992); and Etienne Balibar, *We, The People of Europe*.

purpose here is not to suggest that there is only one possible formulation. It is, rather, to begin to think more carefully about the way in which values, law, institutional form and processes should be considered in unison so as to forge a plausible theory of justice to govern such intersection.

That final overarching task is a significant one which I do not aim to fulfil in this book. But there is every reason to make some tentative proposals if only to provoke pointed discussion as to how the EU's institutional ethos might be developed to emphasise the need for justice as a core value. This I do in Chapter 9. My starting point is to suggest that a revised philosophy of EU law would be of central importance in this endeavour. This is in recognition of the crucial role played by law in the construction of an institutional ethos that is not, as I have said, the product of a *volksgeist* (nor likely to be so) but of a process of institutionalisation. My outline proposals relate to the way in which such a philosophy might be reconfigured so that it would have practical potential. I emphasise the desirability of aligning a specific constitutional settlement with an approach to adjudication by the European Court of Justice that builds on recent jurisprudence which promises a more serious approach to values. I will argue that the key provision of the draft Constitutional Treaty, replicated in the Lisbon Treaty, which sets the aim of the Union to 'promote peace, its values, and the well-being of its peoples' is an inspired although flawed amendment. I will argue that for justice to be more fully enshrined in the institutional ethos this provision should be interpreted in law so as to not only promote but *respect, protect* and *fulfil* the values to be constitutionally identified. I will argue that to reduce the indeterminacy of, to give greater substance to, and to frame the direction of, these salient values in the EU will require an expanded conception of *human* rights (as opposed to fundamental rights). And I will argue that this will require both a revised Bill of Rights for Europe *and* a revised institutional structure of principles capable of understanding, monitoring and enforcing such rights effectively. Whether this would result in the re-construction of the EU primarily as a human rights organisation is a moot point. However, I suggest that this revision in the philosophy of EU law would be a plausible and practical move to enhance the EU as an institution that takes justice more seriously as a governing ideal. This is the argument with which I will conclude the book although, of course, not the debate.

Conclusion

Philip Allott observed astutely some years ago that the EU represented a 'Europe seen darkly through a constitutional looking-glass, full of distorted images of familiar constitutional forms'.[57] He demanded, in response, that '*la grande âme de l'Europe*' had to be re-discovered. Without accepting that there is a soul awaiting some kind of reawakening, this book recognises Allott's coupled appreciations of method and ambition and is an attempt to respond to both. Overall, it is an exercise in holding the institution of the EU and its law to account. The method adopted is to excavate the values of the EU as they are espoused within the overall context of an institutional ethos. We can then better judge the depth and scope of influence of these values. This is by way of prelude to a deeper consideration of what the philosophy of EU law is and what it and the overall institutional ethos might become. Whether this can amount to creating a 'soul for Europe', which Delors with a flourish demanded for the EU, remains to be seen.

Such critique and analysis has been remarkably absent from the study of the EU since it came into being. Despite the fact that the defunct but resurrected Constitutional Treaty tried to capture the European imagination, its troubled implementation is a reflection of this philosophical condition. A change is warranted and necessary. It is also possible. Without it I do not think it is much of a prediction to say that the EU will continue to flounder, jerking from crisis to crisis. Who, after all, can put their trust in an institution that finds it so difficult to state with conviction those values for which it stands *and then to live up to a coherent form of them in practice*? A plausible account of justice underpinning a revised institutional ethos and philosophy of EU law would be a vital starting point for remedying this void. To misquote Carl Jung, the need for meaning is essential if we are to avoid being crushed by the awefulness of the EU's condition.

The EU is not about to be crushed but sooner or later its meaning has to be found. This book is a contribution to this end.

---

[57] Allott, 'The Crisis of European Constitutionalism' at 490.

2   Peace

Introduction

In 1984 Presidents Kohl and Mitterand provided one of those images that capture decades of rhetoric and history. Attending the annual commemorative service in Verdun, remembering the terrible battle that took place there in 1916, the two politicians held hands. They may have been close to arm's length when they did so, translating any sense of personal intimacy into one of state rapport, and it may have been stage-managed rather than an act of impulse, but the symbolism of that gesture was revelatory. The fact that the image has since been embraced by the first gay French TV channel as an advertising icon cannot diminish its enduring power. The gesture *and* its location remain significant. But what does it symbolise for the EU? The pursuit of peace is one answer to this question. But what kind of 'peace'? And might it form a plausible value that influences actions and decisions of the EU to any significant degree?

On the face of it, the relationship between peace and European integration might be viewed simply as negative in character. In other words, peace is the absence of war between or within states. It is less a statement of value and more a statement of fact. It represents a sense of inter-state stability 'as a balance of forces'.[1] Little in the way of ethical demand results for the EU except to commit Member States to avoid military engagement with each other. Mitterand and Kohl's gesture certainly reinforces such an assurance.

But this is surely too simplistic a reading of peace in the EU's context. It suggests that its possible formation and influence was limited to the maintenance of a sophisticated non-aggression pact. Most would

---

[1] John Rawls, *The Law of Peoples* (Cambridge, MA: Harvard University Press, 1999) at 44.

accept, however, that the settlement in Europe far surpasses such a purpose. One could argue that the existence of the EU has contributed not only to the 'reduction/elimination of direct violence' but also to the 'reduction/elimination of structural violence'.[2] More positive interpretations of peace, therefore, might be applicable. These could infer not just the 'absence of fighting' but 'peace-with-rights, a condition of liberty and security that can only exist in the absence of aggression'.[3] Notions of a 'just peace' that seek a form of relations, or process, between peoples as well as states (wishing to be part of some kind of 'community') might similarly be entertained as describing an approach towards politics and law that appreciated and responded to the rights and interests of all. In other words, peace *as a value* may have been instrumental in establishing not only a condition of the absence of war but also a sense of justice as the basis for living together.

When we contemplate the link between justice and peace, the former defining the latter, we open up a whole spectrum of value possibilities. Building on the absence of fighting as a primary condition (although conceivably not a necessary one – there may be a possibility of exercising selective military action for the purposes of preserving peace) varying degrees of peaceful co-existence could be anticipated. All manner of political arrangements on an inter-state scale might be contemplated, from a secure or stable peace to a peace that incorporated a substantive theory of justice within its construction. At one level, the appreciation of interdependence might be so strong that 'peace' would amount to a universal way of life that adopted mutually agreed values and principles of acting that gave no cause for war and managed conflict accordingly.

Law might be considered a plausible conduit for, and necessary component of, a just peace. Pierre Allan and Alexis Keller, indeed, defined the term as a 'process whereby peace and justice are reached together by two or more parties recognizing each others' identities, each renouncing some central demands, and each accepting to abide by common rules jointly developed'.[4] They pointed to the necessity of law

---

[2] The distinction is Johan Galtung's. See Galtung, 'Peace and the World as Inter-civilizational Interaction', in Raimo Väyrynen (ed.), *The Quest for Peace: Transcending Collective Violence and War among Societies, Cultures and States* (London: Sage, 1987) 330–47 at 330.

[3] Michael Walzer, *Just and Unjust Wars*, 3rd edn (New York: Basic Books, 2000) at 51.

[4] Pierre Allan and Alexis Keller, 'The Concept of Just Peace, or Achieving Peace Through Recognition, Renunciation, and Rule', in Allan and Keller (eds.), *What is a Just Peace?* (Oxford: Oxford University Press, 2006) 195–215 at 195.

as providing both rules of conduct and conventions for interpreting or altering those rules. Such qualities could provide the environment for the settlement of disputes and the development of justice through the recognition of 'the other'. The claim is that law can safeguard object-ive and independent solutions to problems in a mutually acceptable fashion, resolving conflict without recourse to violence and providing comprehensible and agreed rules by which states and peoples can see justice being done. Of course, law alone cannot fulfil all the aims of a just peace. Other public processes would have to contribute. But law that incorporates characteristics commensurate with the preservation of peace nonetheless provides an intelligible way in which principles of justice can be readily set and applied. This would be the case whether or not we are looking at 'hard' or 'soft' law. The former may well pro-vide a degree of clarity and certainty, subject always to the effects of unintended consequences, but the latter may also offer considerable scope for the development of peace as a condition and a process. By addressing problems and disputes in a way that is more diplomatic than forceful, more pluralistic than dictatorial, parties might accept more readily judgments that do not fully accord with their perceived interests. 'Renouncement' is a key partner to 'recognition' in this thicker concept of 'peace'.

All these possibilities need to be explored if we are to discover whether and to what extent peace represents any meaningful influ-ence as a value for the EU. Of course, there can be little doubt that an end to war in Western Europe was a primary motivation for the initial construction of the European Economic Community. The historical conflicts between France and Germany provided a clear focus of that movement in the 1940s and early 1950s. A *rapprochement* was of para-mount concern if Europe was to be resurrected. In this respect, Verdun provided a particularly strong image of shared suffering. Mitterand and Kohl's gesture, photographed outside the *Ossuaire*, one of the most pitiless war memorials amongst a whole legion of such places across Northern France and Belgium, reflects that appreciation. They were standing before a monument that houses the remains of 130,000 *unidentified* soldiers killed in the battle, a significant fraction of the 700,000 casualties in total. The holding of hands speaks of the fear and loathing conjured up by the sheer enormity of these figures. It is recog-nition of collective recoil from the horror and madness of war.

One might be driven to assert at the very least, therefore, that peace in the limited sense of an absence of inter-state war was one

of the founding ideals of European constitutionalism and a constituent part of the EU's institutional ethos. This has been confirmed by
the Treaty Establishing a Constitution for Europe and its successor
the Lisbon Treaty, which makes the promotion of 'peace' one of the
EU's fundamental aims. But peace might here also seem necessary for
the development of other values or principles that supposedly govern
the Union. It appears as one of essential *precondition*, an 'absolute' in
Hannah Arendt's terms,[5] upon which all other ideals and values are
constructed. Or at least they make little practical sense in its absence.
This in turn might indicate that peace as a value has some positive substance and influence. The scope and depth of the EU's activities over
the past fifty years might suggest that the gesture has had as much to
do with the governance of the EU as it has with remembering the dangers of conflict. It could be symbolic of a method of inter-state relations
that looked outwards as well as inwards, that turned its back on mili-
tarism and dictatorship and endorsed peace as a determining value,
not just a condition to be achieved.

An assessment of the plausibility of the value of peace as part of the
EU's institutional ethos is, therefore, the purpose of this chapter. Three
historical dimensions will be considered. First, there is what might be
termed the idea of 'original' peace. This was primarily for interior consumption, a response to the internecine conflicts most evident in the
two world wars, and which was evoked by the memories and images of
slaughter at Verdun and the First World War apocalypse. Still deployed
as enduring institutional rationale, peace in this sense has become a
condition precedent for EU politics. It is predicated in part on elements
of Immanuel Kant's design for the achievement of lasting 'peace' but
has been more currently defined in international political discourse
as 'democratic peace', a conception that is founded on the belief that
democratic states will not go to war with each other. In this guise, the
struggle for peace has justified economic and political integration, purportedly within a democratic framework. It is promoted specifically
through law. But in order to acquire credence, has peace in this sense
been viewed through a particular prism? In order to create a sense
of unity, or identity, from the experience of conflict, and to promote
a sense of interdependence from a history of warfare and mutually
inflicted suffering, has there been a process of selective institutional
memory to justify the rhetoric of self-satisfied and self-fulfilled peace?

---

[5] Hannah Arendt, *On Violence* (London: Allen Lane, 1970).

If so, what has been forgotten? And how does this affect the value of 'peace' that has been constructed over time?

Second, there is the concept of 'global peace' as a defining principle for the EU's *external* affairs. This dimension has been promulgated as a related but distinctly parallel concept to that of the 'internal peace'. By offering itself as an exemplar of a regime founded and governed by peace, it has instituted development, trade, environment and foreign policies with peace purportedly as an underlying value. But what has been the impact on the efficacy of this discourse of, first, the cacophony in response to the conflict in the former Yugoslavia and, second, the relative institutional silence accompanying the war against Iraq of 2003? Have these events and the EU's responses raised questions about the influence of this external 'peace' as an element of its institutional ethos? Or can more recent events point to a change in approach?

Third, there is the 'new peace', as I have coined it. This dimension reflects the increasing importance attached to the notion of 'security', potentially superseding the two previous strands as well as perhaps conflicting with other values purportedly fundamental to the Union. A significant question is whether this discourse of peace provokes a sense of a *pax europa* whereby the strategic deployment of violence, sanctioned by (and even delivered through) law, is considered a necessary 'evil' for a greater European or even global peace? Or does, perhaps, this dominance of security have only momentary weight?

Each of these dimensions is dealt with in the three succeeding sections. My aim is to determine the scope of peace as a value in the EU's hands. As befits my central thesis, the role of law is a key concern for me throughout this analysis. For although there is a strong association between law and 'peaceful integration', the relationship between law and peace is by no means uniform across the three strands.

The 'original peace'

The concept of peace in Europe has been of philosophical as well as political concern for centuries. A tradition of pan-European advocacy for the end of war between the region's states was well established through the writings of Abbé de Saint-Pierre, who first utilised the notion of a '*Projet de Paix Perpetuelle*', Jean-Jacques Rousseau, Immanuel Kant, Coudenhove-Kalergi and the intellectuals of the resistance movements during the Second World War.[6] Once the Second World War was over, a renewed determination to institute peace as a lasting condition became prominent. That was to be achieved, according to the thinking of Robert Schuman, Jean Monnet, Konrad Adenaeur and various others, through a European cooperative venture predicated on a process of economic, and then perhaps political and social, integration of states.

The narrative of this creation of the EU is a familiar one.[7] We need not rehearse it in great detail here. However, it is important to acquire a sense of how the concept of peace was approached in the EU's formative stage. The story is not as straightforward as it has been presented institutionally.

One of the first relevant constituting documents of the EU was, of course, the 1950 Schuman Declaration. This occupies a key position in the EU narrative. Its language has been repeated with metronomic frequency and the whole text retains iconic importance. However, when we revisit it we can see that the conflict that is the subject of such a momentous political response is peculiarly restricted. Although the Declaration attempts to deal with war as a phenomenon of human relations, its proposition that the 'pooling of coal and steel production' once established 'will make it plain that any war between France and Germany becomes not merely unthinkable, but materially impossible' indicates a specific narrative of violence in Europe. The Declaration may well speak of safeguarding 'world peace' and promoting through its achievement a 'wider and deeper community' but this is to be 'between countries long opposed to one another by sanguinary divisions'. The context is wholly Eurocentric. The focus is upon the 'age old opposition of France and Germany'. Indeed, Robert Schuman expressed the view that the key consideration of the Declaration was to 'disempoison relations' between these two countries and thereby to 'safeguard peace'.[8] This is hardly surprising given the particular perspectives of France and Germany at that time.

---

[6] A text of great significance was David Mitrany, *A Working Peace System* (Chicago: Quadrangle Books, 1966).

[7] For an account of the relationship between the search for peace and the early formation of the EU see Mette Eilstrup-Saniovanni and Daniel Verdier, 'European Integration as a Solution to War', *European Journal of International Relations* 11:1 (2005) 99–135.

[8] Quoted by Jacques Delors in the Closing Address of the 1990 Symposium, *Building the Future Together* organised by the European Commission to mark the Fortieth Anniversary of the Declaration of 9 May 1950 at 52.

The text, therefore, resonates with a political purpose acknowledging a destructive European history that includes, but is not confined to, the conflagrations of the twentieth century. A violent nexus between France and Germany is presented as indicative of a continental tendency stretching across centuries. This was the crucial concern for the establishment of the 'first concrete foundation of a European federation' as the Declaration describes. Violence in the form of inter-state war acted as the moral impetus for cooperation. The pursuit of peace and the notion of a union of European states were inextricably linked, the latter being a constitutional imperative ('indispensable to the preservation of peace') to prevent a repetition of war *in Europe*.

The specific nature of remembered violence was also redolent in the European Coal and Steel Community Treaty (ECSC) that followed the Declaration. The language was consistent. Its preamble resolved the parties,

to substitute for age old rivalries the merging of their essential interests; to create, by establishing an economic community, the basis for a broader and deeper community among peoples long divided by bloody conflicts.[9]

A sense of a history based on the *longue dureé*, perhaps, was redolent here. The core materials of war, held by those states historically intent on conflict, were to be captured by subjecting them to a common system of control.

The rhetoric of peace continued to be repeated throughout the EU's formative texts. The Preamble to the EEC Treaty in 1957 resolved to 'preserve and strengthen peace and liberty' by pooling Member States' resources. Various key institutional actors also drew on this language with great regularity. Walter Hallstein, President of the Commission in 1960, repeated 'the need to ensure the survival of Europe' through the EU based on the rule of law and economic integration.[10] Mario Scelba, President of the Parliament in 1969, also recalled the 'horrors of the last fratricidal war', which, 'spurred the exponents of the great democratic currents in Europe to find new ways of sparing [the youth of today] a repetition of these horrors'.[11] And Jean Rey, President of the Commission, referred, in 1968, to the antidote the EU offered for 'our old continent laid waste down the centuries by so many conflicts'.[12] Even today the message is reiterated on a regular basis, justifying the maintenance of

---

[9] Preamble, Treaty Establishing the European Coal and Steel Community.
[10] EC Bull 1–1960 at 9.   [11] EC Bull 5–1969 7.   [12] EC Bull 6–1968 12.

the Union and demonstrating its success.[13] The Preamble to the Treaty establishing a Constitution for Europe spoke of Europe 'reunited after bitter experiences' and the determination 'to transcend ... former divisions'. Without apparent embarrassment, it identified the EU as 'the great venture which makes it a special area of human hope'. Such claims rely on the evidence of the lack of conflict between nations in the EU over the past fifty years. The EU represents itself as an exemplar, where violence/war has been defeated by reason of the EU's very existence. It is, in other words, synonymous with peace.

Surely, none of this reading is controversial. Of course, one might speculate as to the 'real' motives lying behind the formation of the EU. But there can be little doubt that the pursuit of peace was a vital factor in its conception. Even so, there are hidden ambiguities here. The narrative is constrained. Although it might indicate the adoption of a value that determines institutional actions and activities, the definition of peace relies upon a very restricted understanding of conflict and its causes. It is premised upon a particular scheme of remembrance *and* forgetting.

This manifests itself, as I have already indicated, through the apparent institutional projection that the conflicts necessitating European integration were *historically uniform*. There was no real distinction made between the wars of the twentieth century and those of previous eras. Their effects may have been more horrific, the devastation wrought may have been more extreme but ultimately the two world wars were presented as part of a long line of continental disputes erupting into violence. They were surprising only in their scope rather than their novelty. Of course, there may have been a difference in the intensity and spread of the fighting and the technologies of destruction that were deployed. But the nature of conflict was presented as fundamentally indistinguishable. The First and Second World Wars were both of the same order, both 'classical wars' in Johan Galtung's words, 'intra-European tribal warfare between nation-states'.[14]

The preference for remembering this version of the history of conflict in Europe is perhaps symbolised by that photograph of Mitterand

---

[13] See, for instance, Commission, *Building the Future Together* at 39 where the President of the European Parliament referred to the EU as becoming 'a haven of peace' providing a 'shining example' to 'encourage all those throughout the world who share the same goals'.

[14] Johan Galtung, *The European Community: a Superpower in the Making* (London: George Allen & Unwin, 1973) at 13.

and Kohl. They were commemorating a specific battle of the First World War that represented the senseless infliction of suffering almost without distinction between the soldiers of Germany and France. Even though the war was reprehensible in nature, failing to qualify as a 'just war' for any of its parties, both sides could respond in retrospect with honour in its remembrance.[15] There was generally no dishonour attached to the combatants, at least after the event. Verdun was seen as an example of *la gloire* in some French history.[16] From the German perspective there was no need to see the fighting as in itself a crime, howsoever it may have been portrayed by the Allies during and after hostilities. The literature that emerged in both cultures bore similar hallmarks as a result.[17] The peoples of each country may have been betrayed by their leaders in being led to such slaughter but they had little for which to reproach themselves.[18] No wonder then that the two Presidents could safely hold hands in mutual remembrance of the dead. The shame was limited.

But could the Second World War be presented in a similar way? As we have seen, no distinction was raised constitutionally or rhetorically in the formative texts of the EU. But there is a moral unease connected to the Second World War. It does not offer the simple sense of honourable and noble participation in war. Constitutional memory of complicity with Nazism through collaboration, through Vichy, of extremism based on discrimination and de-humanisation, of complicity in the crimes that characterised the 1939–45 war, tended to be absent in the formative stage of the EU. There was even an ambivalence with regard to the Holocaust as a manifestation of the actual and potential violence of Europe, not only with regard to the horror of the camps but also as a signifier of those other genocides and pogroms perpetrated in Europe and elsewhere by Europeans over the centuries. The Holocaust may well *now* be the subject of institutional commemoration and the rhetoric of essential identity of the Union but this has not always been the case. Few references to the Holocaust were made in the early texts of

---

[15] Jonathan Glover has identified honour as one of the unifying aspects of the responses of the participant nations to the conflagration. See, Jonathan Glover, *Humanity: a Moral History of the Twentieth Century* (London: Pimlico, 2001) 196–8.

[16] See Alistair Horne, *The Price of Glory* (London: Penguin, 1993).

[17] See, for instance, the works of Frederic March, Ernst Jünger, Herman Hesse and others.

[18] Ernst Jünger's *Storm of Steel* (London: Penguin, 2004) even valorised the bravery and determination in the face of such extreme conditions.

the EU. Only relatively recently, through the adoption of Holocaust Day and the identification made between the racism and xenophobia of the 1980s and 1990s and previous anti-Semitic practices, has the EU begun to remember this aspect of internal violence. Certainly there was no initial institutional rush to deploy law to address the 'hatreds' that Jean-Francois Lyotard suggested underpinned European unification.[19] There was no attempt to condition the EU so as to confront the shame that Karl Jaspers attributed to the German nation.[20] Even the preambular statements of the Treaties failed to go beyond inter-state rivalry. It was hardly surprising then that the violence of colonialism practised by a number of original Member States both prior to and during the existence of the EU provoked little if any comment let alone criticism. France's exploits in Algeria, Belgium's residue of colonial rule in the Congo, merited no concern. The imperialist tendencies critiqued by Galtung were left to one side, with current and former colonies neatly enveloped into the European project as 'associated territories'.[21]

In all, therefore, the original notion of 'peace' was captured by a specific understanding of conflict and violence. By focusing on a very partial history of inter-state battles between France and Germany, as though they represented persistent and related antagonisms that stretched across the centuries, the EU was formed with a particular notion of peace in mind. It was a simplistic and *negative* perception, adopted to justify the construction of the EU and based on avoiding certain kinds of war amongst particular nations.

Was there a role for law in this restrained notion of peace? Certainly, law had the quality of antithesis to war that would appeal to those wishing to impose a 'working peace'.[22] But the focus was upon the economic dimension of inter-state relations. It was the 'pooling of resources' that would 'preserve and strengthen peace' all within a legally controlled economic design. To construct a single market would bind states together in a compact of mutual interest. If those interests conflicted, resort would be to law to solve disputes. This was a wholly rational response, which had its roots in Kant's philosophical identification of the qualities necessary for a 'perpetual peace'. To avoid war people must 'arrange the conflict of their unpeaceable dispositions' through constraining 'one another to submit to coercive law and so bring about

---

[19] Jean-François Lyotard, *Europe, the Jews and the Book* (London: UCL Press, 1993) at 159.
[20] Karl Jaspers, *The Question of German Guilt* (New York: Capricorn Books, 1961).
[21] See Galtung, *The European Community: A Superpower in the Making*.
[22] See David Mitrany, *A Working Peace System*.

a condition of peace in which laws have force'.[23] At the inter-state level this required not just a 'peace pact' but a 'pacific league'.[24] Law would act as facilitator for the resolution of disputes, providing the necessary framework of obligation in the limited field of economic cooperation whilst appearing to preserve the underlying sovereignty of nations.

The European Court of Justice uncovered some of the flavour of law's role fairly early on in the life of the EU. In *van Gend en Loos* the EEC Treaty was described as 'more than an agreement which merely creates mutual obligations between the contracting States'.[25] A 'new legal order of international law' had been constructed whereby 'States have limited their sovereign rights, albeit within limited fields'. In *Costa v. ENEL* the Court set out the fundamental organising principle:

The transfer by the States from their domestic legal system to the Community legal system of the rights and obligations arising under the Treaty carries with it a permanent limitation of their sovereign rights, against which a subsequent unilateral act incompatible with the concept of the Community cannot prevail.[26]

The concept of community (as opposed to '*the* Community') suggested the absence of internecine conflict and the resolution of disputes by lawful means. As such the EU as conceived was, and remains, a reasonable, albeit limited, legal response in the name of 'peace'. As José Barroso recalls, the EU was a 'creation of law' and it was this 'which has allowed the successful and peaceful unification of our continent, when all previous attempts to unite Europe by force have failed'.[27] Law was an alternative to force, an antithesis to a state of war, suggesting that regulation can instil unity and eradicate conflict.

But does the scheme of peace through law hold much influence when so heavily concentrated on the antagonisms between states that were already exhausted by the severity of their most recent wars? If the causes of war and conflict are more complex than simply inter-state antagonism, how does this preservation of peace guide and inform the development of European law?

---

[23] Immanuel Kant, 'Toward Perpetual Peace; A Philosophical Project', in Mary J. Gregor (trans. and ed.), *Immanuel Kant: Practical Philosophy* (Cambridge: Cambridge University Press, 1996) 315–51 at 335.

[24] *Ibid.* at 327.

[25] Case 26/62 *van Gend en Loos* [1963] ECR 1.

[26] Case 6/64 *Flaminio Costa* v. *ENEL* [1964] ECR 585.

[27] See José Manuel Barroso, 'Uniting in Peace: the Role of Law in the European Union', Jean Monnet Lecture, EUI Florence, 31 March 2006, available at: www.iue.it/PUB/ JeanMonnetLecturesPDF/JMLBarroso2006.pdf at 3.

As with Kant's proposals, the EU's original construction was predicated on the eradication of a particular and conveniently defined type of violence.[28] It focused on that most rational of conflict creators: economic interest. The irrational causes, the 'passions' and prejudices, were not so encompassed. A clean break with the attitudes of the past was sanctioned but without providing the explicit constitutional tools to address other causes of war or conflict.

This limited understanding of peace was the product of an equally limited understanding of the conflict that the EU was purported as addressing. It required a sanitisation and generalisation of the nature of that conflict. Sanitised, because it avoided any introspection related to complicity with the regimes of atrocity that prevailed in the Second World War. Generalised, because it presented war in Europe as all of a type. The restrictive notion of peace failed to consider what gave rise to conflict and could not have been predicated on addressing the *causes* of war. War and peace were treated simplistically, both concepts dealt with as opposites. What was missing was 'the complexity of the causes of war' which 'requires a conception that understands peace as a *process* accomplished by non-violent means'.[29] Joining previously conflictual parties into a restricted legal compact that tries to bind them to one another economically might deal with one particular manifestation of destructive violence. But would it necessarily assist in preventing other forms of violence both internal and external? '[A]symmetries of standards of living and economic power; powerful technologies of an unprecedented scale; the arms trade, especially the spread of atomic, biological, and chemical weapons', which Habermas identifies as 'obvious threats', were apparent in the 1950s as much as they are today.[30] So too were the hatreds that underscored the anti-Semitism and racism prevalent across Europe. These were not apparent in the understanding of challenges to peace for the EU in its original composition.[31]

---

[28] Jürgen Habermas identified a similar shortcoming in Kant's proposals for perpetual peace. In looking to the 'evil of war' as a form of relationship 'between regimes and states' he asserts that the perpetual 'peace in question is as limited as the war from which it arises'. See, Jürgen Habermas, 'Kant's Idea of Perpetual Peace', in Habermas, *The Inclusion of the Other: Studies in Political Theory* (Cambridge: Polity Press, 1998) 167.

[29] *Ibid.*   [30] *Ibid.*

[31] We will see later in this chapter how these causes of conflict have, however, been acknowledged by the institutions in their *external* dealings. See, in particular, Commission, 'Communication from the Commission on Conflict Prevention', COM/2001/0211 final.

Peace, therefore, had limited meaning, a meaning which still sought to preserve a state system premised on a Eurocentric understanding of the world that had been found deeply flawed. This was reflected in EU law. It may have appeared of immediate necessity to construct a partnership between states that would help remove the threat of war between them. But this failed to recognise the threats to peace from violence beyond the strict militaristic form. Ironically, it did not even structure any competence to deal with military matters within its own boundaries.[32] Institutional figures may continue to call upon the peace maintained through the EU as evidence of its success and necessity but such confidence is based upon amnesia as much as remembrance.

There are alternative readings, of course. Joseph Weiler suggested that the original injunction contained in the EEC Treaty to found 'an ever closer union among the *peoples* of Europe' was indicative of a 'civilizing strategy of dealing with the "other"'.[33] The whole enterprise was based, he maintained, on a 'willingness to accept a binding discipline which is rooted in and derives from a community of others'. Law's role reflects the value of peace through 'tolerance' by promoting and facilitating a community that brings peoples together. But to which 'peoples' does this refer? Can we say it included those who did not possess 'European' state citizenship? Did it include those who were within but outside the peoples of Europe? Was the 'alien', to whom Weiler refers, capable of including *non-Europeans* and those living in, but socially, economically and politically excluded from, European states? If peace-through-tolerance-through-law, a sequence one can infer from Weiler's analysis, was really a value-based construction for the EU, it was not otherwise apparent in its original formation. None of the rhetoric or practice addressed directly those causes of conflict that related to wider issues than inter-state rivalry. A reticence in relation to these matters, particularly when it came to the construction of a binding framework through law, represents a significant omission in the original construction of the European edifice.

All this suggests that the original peace has been of limited importance as a value within the EU's institutional ethos. It had more character as a *pre-condition*. And as such it is difficult to suggest that law has

---

[32] This remains the condition despite the debate over a European Army and European Defence policy.

[33] Joseph Weiler, 'In Defence of the Status Quo: Europe's Constitutional *Sonderweg*', in J. Weiler and M. Wind (eds.), *European Constitutionalism Beyond the State* (Cambridge: Cambridge University Press, 2003) 7–23 at 19.

been able to do anything other than reflect the requirement to construct a framework of bonds for limited purposes. It allows the charge to develop that law has been deployed as a means of deflection, enabling the discourse of peace to appear supported by the force of law when, in truth, it masks other aims. Those who might argue that the EU was an exercise in the retention of power, the rescue not only of the nation-state but also a capitalist system still reliant on a colonial mentality and unwilling to address directly the 'dark side' of European civilisation, will no doubt see law in this context as complicit in maintaining the seeds of conflict.[34] At the very least it might be interpreted as neutral in such matters, which might amount to the same thing.

It would be foolish to suggest this is the whole picture, however. It may be argued that the EU has gradually woken up to the demands of 'peace' as a constituting value. But has an understanding of peace been incorporated? And if so, has the EU been provided with the constitutional tools and law necessary for it to be effective in the pursuit of a wider-understood peace? Here we need to consider the development of the external ambitions associated with the EU over the last thirty years or more.

The external dimension: towards global peace

Intent on helping to regenerate internal economies and caught between the two superpowers of the USSR and the United States, the EU could not realistically provide the focus for any great influence for peace outside its borders when it was first instituted. In the 1960s, however, when the then Member States became intent on establishing the EU's place in the world, relying upon its economic success and its prospective enlargement to include the UK, peace as a wider objective began to be taken more seriously. The attitude was summed up at a Council meeting in 1968 when the French and German governments issued a joint declaration.

In affirming their position on the desired development and enlargement of the E.E.C. the two Governments have in view an essential aim of their policy, which is to enable a strong and united Europe to play its proper role, i.e. to be an organised, independent and active force for world equilibrium and consequently for peace.[35]

---

[34] The obscuring of this dark side forms a key subject for some analysis of the Holocaust. See in particular Zygmunt Bauman, *Modernity and the Holocaust* (Cambridge: Polity Press, 2000).

[35] Joint Franco-German Declaration, EC Bull 3–1968 at 20.

But what kind of contribution was envisaged? The institutional ambition was evident as early as 1963. Then, the European Parliament adopted a resolution that spoke of a Europe 'within an Atlantic partnership and on a footing of equality with the USA', able to 'play its part in the defence of the free West, in the maintenance of peace and general economic progress'.[36] But when Johan Galtung argued that the EU was a superpower in the making this depended on identifying the EU as a *separate* entity from the United States.[37] That was difficult to do in the 1960s and early 1970s when militarily the United States provided the only hope of realistic defence in the event of serious attack. Even so, some commentators felt able to suggest that Europe had been 'pacified' *because* of the role played by the two superpowers.[38] Despite Western Europe's clear preference to look westwards in all things, the US/USSR stalemate had ensured that peace was maintained. But any slippage in the equilibrium could still turn Europe into a final battleground of total destruction.

This was the shadow of Armageddon. Under it, the EU was seen as a means of providing the Member States with greater voice on the world stage. It, therefore, became of increasing political importance to forge some kind of distinctive identity for the EU to ensure it maintained and even increased its political presence. Promoting peace beyond its borders was one area where it might achieve some definition, particularly given the 'success' attributed to the original peace within the EU. Peace was therefore evolving as one of the unifying *values* in this process of identity manufacture. And, in a form of circular logic, it was seen as only possible through the creation of a recognisably forceful European polity. So, when the Commission made a declaration to coincide with the formal completion of a 'Customs Union' in 1968 it stated,

[p]olitical integration must facilitate a détente and co-operation between the East and the West, thus making an essential contribution to the establishment of a pacific order in Europe.[39]

The concern for peace had moved beyond the rhetoric of settling once and for all the enmity between France and Germany and now

---

[36] EC Bull 1–1963 at 19.   [37] Galtung, *The European Community: a Superpower in the Making*.

[38] See, François Duchêne, 'Europe's Role in World Peace', in Richard Mayne (ed.), *Europe Tomorrow* (London: Fontana, 1972) 32–47.

[39] Declaration by the Commission on the occasion of the achievement of the Customs Union on 1 July 1968, EC Bull 7–1968 at 6.

encompassed wider geo-political realities. New threats were to be countered through and by the Union. But still the bedrock of such an approach was seen as a successful union between peoples. The Commission went on.

The reconciliation of peoples has been first and foremost the reconciliation of European nations, ravaged by the two World Wars of 1914–18 and 1939–45, both born in Europe of the clash of nationalisms: for the peoples of Europe these were genuine civil wars. This time is now past. The moment has come to call the young and creative forces of Europe to union, action and hope.[40]

The changing circumstances of international relations during this period of the Cold War had ensured a move beyond the resolution of internal fears of conflict. The possibility of war between the then members of the EU was, by this stage, already remote. But this was palpably not the case between the West and the Soviet bloc. The threat of conflict was apprehended as very real and for good reason. How the region as a whole might be drawn into war was of the utmost political importance.

Inevitably, this provoked an external vision unbound by economic considerations alone. The creation of European Political Cooperation (EPC) at the end of the 1960s reflected the changing political sensitivities. Not only did it respond to the exigencies of the continental and global political environment but it also gave greater impetus for closer political ties between those members of the EU. The sentiment was expressed well by Mario Scelba, President of the European Parliament in 1969. He noted that the EU, based on its representation as a reunification of Europe, could be used as 'a civilising instrument' for the purpose of 'peace and civil and social progress'.[41] It appeared to be transforming its ethos from one of reconciliation to one with wider conflict resolution in mind.

A series of institutional pronouncements reinforced this new direction. In 1969 the Member States identified their 'common conviction' that the EU was 'conscious of the role it has to play in promoting the relaxation of international tension and the rapprochement among all peoples, and first and foremost amongst those of the entire European continent' in their Hague Summit Declaration.[42] Such a move would

---

[40] *Ibid.* at 8.
[41] Speech to the European Parliament March 1969, EC Bull 5–1969 at 7.
[42] Communiqué of the Conference of the Heads of State and Government of the Member States of the European Community, The Hague, 2 December 1969, para. 4.

be 'indispensable if ... world equilibrium and peace is to be preserved'. This was a conscious effort to invest the EU with a broader sense of political purpose. EPC was one manifestation, requiring an external dimension for the EU based fundamentally on the pursuit of peace. The Member States then issued the crucial Paris Declaration of 1972, which called for the developing EU to 'affirm its own views in international relations, as befits its mission to be open to the world and for progress, peace and co-operation'.[43] The Declaration on European Identity of 1973 followed, acknowledging that since the Member States had 'overcome their past enmities' it could be affirmed that 'unity is a basic European necessity to ensure the survival of the civilization which they have in common'.[44] Future progress and integration were inextricably linked with an exterior projection of the EU as well as a deepening of existing internal cooperation.

The notion of 'common responsibility' was crucial in this identity discourse.[45] An EU as a 'distinct entity', rather than simply individual Member States, needed to assume a sense of collective obligation to pursue peace on the international stage. This was not altogether altruistic. Given the EU's understood vulnerability between the two superpowers, peace was a goal that had practical benefits. Nonetheless, did this double equation of peace and identity, and of peace and responsibility, indicate a change in the value of peace in the EU's institutional ethos?

The main areas of external activity to fulfil the newly embraced 'responsibility' were development cooperation, the 'harmonious development of world trade', a common commercial policy towards the countries of Eastern Europe (so as to promote détente) and greater involvement with the Conference on Security and Co-operation in Europe (CSCE). A general trend was developing towards interpreting peace in a regional *and* global context. Over the succeeding two decades, however, EPC was more of symbolic value in relation to the pursuit of peace than it was of real practical achievement. World peace was an ideal unaccompanied by any serious united political activity on

---

[43] Statement of the Conference of the Heads of State and Government of the Member States of the European Union, Paris, 21 October 1972, preamble.

[44] Declaration on European Identity by the Nine Foreign Ministers, Copenhagen, 14 December 1973.

[45] See the 'Copenhagen Report' being the Second Report of the Foreign Ministers to the Heads of State and Government of the Member States of the European Community, Copenhagen, 23 July 1973, Part 1.

the part of the EU. Of course, a language of peace was adopted in the EU's institutional rhetoric. But it would be difficult to maintain that 'peace' as a value had developed in practice significantly beyond the internal concept already discussed. The commitment to cement peace by creating stronger bonds through law and technocratic operation may have continued to be pursued with some enthusiasm internally, enhanced by successive enlargements, but it was not applied to the wider conception of peace. Law and a functioning central bureaucracy were deliberately kept at a distance from the external dimension. With no permanent secretariat, marginal Commission involvement, limited powers assigned and an absence of legal constraint regarding decisions reached and enacted under EPC, the system more closely evoked a working agreement between independent states than a radical enforcement of the ideal of union.[46] The character of EPC from its inception to the beginning of the 1980s was a 'selective delegation of powers in the field of diplomatic declaratory policy and only marginally in tangible operational terms'.[47]

Alfred Pijpers has suggested that 'the peculiar structure and policies of EPC' were 'induced by the idea and mechanisms of the balance of power'.[48] But even though identified as 'one of the most classical, and well-tried *Realpolitische* instruments for peace and security in world politics' the notion of balance of power was always based on a narrow understanding of 'peace'. It attested more to the parochial premises of the 'original peace' I have already described. Peace was once more equated with the absence of war in Europe. Little consideration was given to the possibility that the maintenance of the so-called balance of power would re-direct conflict, and the misery accompanying it, to other parts of the world. The wars, civil or otherwise, experienced in Asia, Africa and the Middle East did not attract a principled positive reaction that would support a claim that the pursuit of peace was an effective governing standard.[49] Sometimes condemned, sometimes ignored, sometimes supported in practice through arms supplies, these

---

[46] For a review of the nature of European Political Co-operation see Panayiotis Ifestos, *European Political Co-operation: Towards a Framework of Supranational Diplomacy* (Aldershot: Avebury, 1987).

[47] *Ibid.* 235.

[48] Alfred E. Pijpers, 'European Political Co-operation and the Realist Paradigm', in Martin Holland (ed.), *The Future of European Political Co-operation* (London: Macmillan, 1991) 8–35 at 24–5.

[49] See John Lewis Gaddis, *The Cold War* (London: Penguin, 2007).

conflicts in 'far-away places' provoked little coherent peace strategies in the EU. Although there is evidence that some common positions taken brought a degree of uniformity to Member States' external attitudes during this period it would be difficult to contend that a consistent pursuit of 'peace' was a determining factor. The approach to problems was ad hoc and often difficult to decipher. Undoubtedly there is little if any evidence of where and when the EU institutions operated directly *against* peace but that is hardly confirmation that a determined and focused understanding of how peace might command operations was embraced. The EU's attitude was at best ambiguous.

The ambiguity became more pronounced in those reactions through EPC to particular conflicts during the 1970s and early 1980s. The Iran–Iraq war, for instance, failed to provoke any meaningful response to end the conflict. The European Council became concerned by reports of the use of chemical weapons in the war by Iraq (and against its own citizens) but could only muster a 'statement' recording the Member States' 'distress at the allegations'.[50] Otherwise, the EU took a collective stance of neutrality.[51] Perhaps this was inevitable given that France provided a substantial percentage of conventional weapons exports to Iraq between 1973 and 1990.[52] The UK had also been a supplier, albeit covert, as became evident following the Scott Inquiry in 1993.[53] Given the scale of the war and its ferocity, the lack of consistency displayed between Member States and the EU, and the lack of coherence in the EU's institutional response, it was hard to detect a serious pursuit of peace here.

Some indication that peace *could* frame the EU's external affairs was, however, evident in relation to the problems in the Middle East. Although initially characterised by lack of coordination and 'contradictions and fragmentation, internally and externally',[54] the EU gradually produced a collective response worthy of the name. From a position at the end of the 1960s where it seemed no two Member States

---

[50] Statement by the European Council on the Iran-Iraq Conflict, Brussels, 27 March 1984.

[51] See Christopher Hill and Karen Smith (eds.), *European Foreign Policy: Key Documents* (London: Routledge, 2000) 328–30.

[52] See David Styan, *France and Iraq: Oil, Arms and French Policy Making in the Middle East* (London: I.B. Tauris & Company, 2006).

[53] See, for instance, J. Radcliffe, 'The Scott Inquiry, Constitutional Conventions and Accountability in British Government', *Crime, Law and Social Change* 26:3 (1997) 239–52.

[54] Ifestos, *European Political Co-operation* at 564.

could agree about how the ongoing conflict might be addressed, EPC was able to fashion a commitment to become involved for peace. The 1980 Venice Declaration that recognised the right of the Palestinians to self-determination was perhaps emblematic of a more concerted approach.[55] Whether or not the policy was effective is neither here nor there. The cooperative efforts made by the Member States indicated the potential for developing an institutional strategy.

From a constitutional perspective the general potential was further developed with the entry into force of the Single European Act in 1987 (SEA). This purported to bring together the provisions dealing with economic integration already at work in the Communities and the solely intergovernmental agreement of EPC. It provided for the Commission to be 'fully associated with the proceedings' of EPC,[56] and for the Parliament to be informed of relevant issues addressed and its views to be 'taken into consideration'.[57] It also demanded consistency between the external policies of the Community and the decisions made under EPC.[58]

But even though the SEA codified the processes of cooperation, the language adopted contradicted the perception of convergence when it came to the *purpose* of external action. Wolfgang Wessels may have been correct in interpreting the SEA as providing EU foreign policy with a 'new *esprit de corps,* a new set of principles, rules and decision making procedures',[59] but the nature of those values underpinning the text remained obscure. Was the objective of EPC, as incorporated into the Treaty structure, so clear that it did not require articulation? Did it incorporate a principle of peace? The only reference appeared in the SEA Preamble where the parties declared themselves to be,

AWARE of the responsibility incumbent upon Europe to aim at speaking ever increasingly with one voice and to act with consistency and solidarity in order … to display the principles of democracy and compliance with the law and with human rights to which they are attached, so that together they may make their own contribution to the preservation of international peace and security in accordance with the undertaking entered into by them within the framework of the United Nations Charter.

[55] Hill and Smith, *European Foreign Policy* 297–316.
[56] Article 30(3)(b) SEA.   [57] Article 30(4) SEA.
[58] Article 30(5) SEA.
[59] Wolfgang Wessels, 'EPC after the Single European Act: Towards a European Foreign Policy via Treaty Obligations', in Martin Holland (ed.), *The Future of European Political Co-operation* (London: Macmillan, 1991) 143–60 at 147–8.

Despite the evident desire to associate key values with the EU, the intention was to *facilitate* the individual states 'to make their *own* contribution to the preservation of peace'. It was not for the EU to *assume* the responsibility. Any coherent sense of peace as a conditioning value rather than simply a hoped-for condition in the world was left to individual states' interpretation. Article 30(1) SEA indirectly reinforced this by placing the obligation to 'formulate and implement a European foreign policy' firmly on the Member States. Similarly, Article 30(6) made clear that the Member States were to 'maintain the technological and industrial conditions necessary for their security', a statement that obliquely ensured the nuclear capability of France and the UK could not be threatened by a collective desire to reduce international tension through disarmament. Beyond this superficial commitment to peace lay an ambiguity inherent in the continuing acceptance of Member State autonomy in foreign affairs. And again law was marginalised in both hard and soft terms. The former had no purchase whatsoever. The latter was so vague that the reality of any operative rule was doubtful.

Was this position radically altered after the end of the Cold War? Certainly the political environment changed dramatically. But from a constitutional perspective little changed with the Treaty of European Union in 1992. The Preamble resolved to implement the new Common Foreign and Security Policy (CFSP) so as to 'promote peace, security and progress in Europe and in the world'. Article 11(1) made an objective of this policy 'to preserve peace and strengthen international security, in accordance with the principles of the United Nations Charter as well as the principles of the Helsinki Final Act and the objectives of the Paris Charter'.[60] But, again, control of the principles' guiding action was left in the hands of the Member States. It was specifically for the European Council to 'define the principles and general guidelines for the common foreign and security policy, including matters for defence implications'.[61]

---

[60] The latter two documents were products of the Conference on Cooperation and Security in Europe in 1975. The Helsinki Act produced ten principles of inter-state relations in Europe that tried to establish a working and peaceful relationship between East and West. But the criticisms addressed against this notion of peace as restricted geographically and ignored globally remained valid. The Paris Charter updated Helsinki in 1991 reflecting the new order after the end of the Cold War. Its focus had become more specifically targeted at the Balkans where the threat of an escalating war in Europe was truly felt.

[61] Article 13(1) TEU, as was.

The limited appreciation of peace in the external sphere was further reflected in the amendments made at Maastricht to the development policy provisions of the EC Treaty. The EU's general objective in this field was expressed to be 'developing and consolidating democracy and the rule of law, and to that of respecting human rights and fundamental freedoms'.[62] Peace as an independent construct was not mentioned. This reticence could be explained partially by the almost complete concentration on economic ties with developing states prior to the end of the Cold War.[63] Political issues were very much peripheral to the Yaoundé and early Lomé Conventions to the extent that values, as understood by the Union, were only marginally reflected in the formal relationships with the African, Caribbean and Pacific States. It was with Lomé III of 1984 and Lomé IV of 1989 that human rights were able to inveigle their way into the predominantly economic nature of the EU's dealings.[64] Other values, such as democracy and the rule of law, had to wait until the supposed unleashing of ethics after the Cold War's end.

Taking the story up to date, the constitutional picture remained largely unchanged until the proposed Constitutional Treaty and the Lisbon Treaty. The rhetoric in the Preamble acknowledged that the parties wished 'to strive for peace, justice and solidarity throughout the world' thus at least connecting peace with other values rather than maintaining a basic distinction between them. But as we have already seen, the attainment of peace as a general value is not identified in Article 2 TEU as amended. It is left first to Article 3(5) TEU to articulate some kind of commitment, declaring that,

[i]n its relations with the wider world, the Union shall uphold and promote its values and interests. It shall contribute to peace, security, the sustainable development of the Earth ... as well as to the strict observance and the development of international law, including respect for the principles of the United Nations Charter.

More specifically as regards relations with its hinterland the EU was to 'develop a special relationship with neighbouring countries, aiming to

---

[62] Article 177(2) EC Treaty.
[63] James Mayall, 'The Shadow of Empire: the EU and the Former Colonial World', in Christopher Hill and Michael Smith (eds.), *International Relations and the European Union* (Oxford: Oxford University Press, 2005) 292–316.
[64] For a review of human rights in development policy see Andrew Williams, *EU Human Rights Policies: a Study in Irony* (Oxford: Oxford University Press, 2004) chapter 2.

establish an area of prosperity and good neighbourliness, founded on the values of the Union and characterised by close and peaceful relations based on cooperation'.[65]

The distinction between values and the pursuit of peace is further established in Article 49 TEU. The condition of eligibility for acceding Member States was framed by the acceptance that the 'Union shall be open to all European States which respect the values referred to in Article 2, and are committed to promoting them together'. There is no mention of Article 3 and the requirement to promote peace, which is surprising given the history of accession procedures. At the beginning of the enlargement process into Eastern and Central Europe the Luxembourg European Council of 1997 made clear that only those states which 'shared a common commitment to peace, security and good neighbourliness, respect for other countries' sovereignty ... and a commitment to the settlement of territorial disputes by peaceful means'[66] would be invited to take part. It would be hard to suggest that any state that was not so persistent in its commitment to peace would be entertained as a potential Member of the Union. But why the constitutional reticence? Was this poor drafting or a continuing failure to engage in the construction of a meaning of peace that would govern EU decision-making?

Interestingly, the matter has been clouded by the provisions proposed for the possible suspension of rights for existing Member States under Article 7 TEU. The procedure will not be engaged unless there had been, or there is a clear risk of, a serious breach of the 'values' in Article 2.[67] One could argue that any state which did not take the maintenance of peace seriously would also be breaching one or more of these values, particularly the rule of law and respect for human rights. But, equally, it is not impossible to imagine a scenario whereby attestations of self-defence, even of the anticipatory kind, were argued to be compatible with the search for peace.

When we look beyond the constituting texts and towards institutional practice over the past fifteen years the underlying and unresolved ambiguity seems to be sustained. First, the EU resurrected the relevance of the internal peace precepts but with a slightly more sophisticated approach in its response to the transition of Central and

---

[65] Article 8(1) TEU as revised by the Lisbon Treaty.
[66] Presidency Conclusions, Luxembourg European Council 1997.
[67] This partially mirrored the original Article 7 TEU although the scheme of values in the Lisbon Treaty is a little more expansive.

Eastern European States in the 1990s. The policy progressed from economic support for the new nations to offer the prospect of future membership of the Union in fairly rapid time. The role of law was vital here. By introducing specific criteria at the Copenhagen Council of 1993, by linking these to economic assistance through the PHARE and TACIS aid programmes, contracts constructed through EU agreements, and by promising membership as a reward for adherence to the plan, the EU was in effect applying its own formula for lasting peace on the 'other half' of Europe. Here at least peace appeared as a *value* to govern external affairs. Agenda 2000 stated that

[t]he Union must increase its influence in world affairs, promote values such as peace and security, democracy and human rights, provide aid for the least developed countries, defend its social model, and establish its presence on the world markets.[68]

I have traced the development of this policy elsewhere, particularly with regards to its implications for human rights.[69] But peace through integration was also central to the policy of enlargement. Unlike the accessions of the UK, Spain, Portugal, etc., which had less to do with preserving peace than enhancing individual states' economic and political prospects, the enlargement eastwards was of a different order. It embedded peace through the same processes of integration that inspired the Schuman Declaration and the formation of the European Economic Community. Economic benefits had a significant role to play but of equal importance was the creation of an enduring peace. In the light of the Balkans conflicts such a policy was viewed as a necessary condition for stability in that region and Europe more generally. And indeed, following the cessation of hostilities and later the overthrow of the Milosevic regime, even the combatant Balkan States have been encouraged to seek membership.[70]

The policy was labelled one of 'stabilisation and association'. But the pacific intent was clear as Romano Prodi, then President of the Commission, announced in 2000.

Having extended and ensured peace and security throughout the nations of Western Europe in the space of two generations, the European Union is now

---

[68] Communication of the Commission DOC 97/6 Agenda 2000, Vol. 1 Part One IV at 1.
[69] Andrew Williams, *EU Human Rights Policies* chapter 3.
[70] Croatia, Bosnia and Herzegovina, Macedonia, Kosovo and even Serbia are now identified as at least potential candidates for accession.

facing the historical, political and moral challenge of guaranteeing the same peace and the same security in and between the nations of the other half of Europe.[71]

This has been described as the export of the EU's 'legacy of reconciliation'.[72] Since the reduction in hostilities, the Commission has interpreted the EU's aim stating, in 2002, that 'EU leaders decided that a policy of emergency reconstruction, containment and stabilisation was not, in itself, enough to bring lasting peace and stability to the Balkans: only the real prospect of integration into European structures would achieve that'.[73] By adopting a flexible approach based on economic incentive and sanction (if only through the removal of that incentive) it was hoped the prospects for peace in the EU's 'neighbourhood' would be enhanced. The process required patience and adaptability. Faced with the 'resurgence of violence in the former Yugoslav Republic of Macedonia', the Commission acknowledged, also in 2002, 'the fragility of the region, and how easily parts of it can slip back into crisis'.[74] It noted crucial 'weaknesses in the rule of law and democratic institutions, endemic corruption, the threat of resurgence of extreme forms of nationalism, as well as poverty and social exclusion' as all posing a threat. But ultimately the challenge was for the EU 'to cope with this political volatility and institutional fragility while holding a steady course towards the strategic goal of integration of the countries of the region into the EU'.

Whether that will, or can ever be, achieved remains to be seen but the incentive to adhere to the attainment of a European Pacific Order, as we might call it, through economic and political integration is a real prospect.[75] It suggests that for this region, at least, decision-making is guided by a collective principled position, one where the commitment to the achievement of peace is fundamental. As the Commission noted in 2008 for the Western Balkans as a whole, 'Good neighbourly

---

[71] Message of European Commission President Romano Prodi to the International Forum on the Holocaust in Stockholm on 27 January 2000, http://ec.europa.eu/comm/external_relations/news/2000/01_00/ip_00_84.htm.

[72] L. Gardner-Feldman, 'Reconciliation and Legitimacy: Foreign Relations and Enlargement of the European Union', in T. Banchoff and M. Smith (eds.), *Legitimacy and the European Union: the Contested Polity* (London: Routledge, 1999) 66–90 at 67.

[73] Report from the Commission – The Stabilisation and Association Process for South East Europe – First Annual Report, COM/2002/0163 final.

[74] *Ibid.*

[75] We can see the economic aspects of reconciliation also reflected internally with the Commission's approach to the peace process in Northern Ireland. There the

relations and regional cooperation remain key in advancing towards EU membership'.[76] The strategy remained strongly in favour of the 'EU's commitment to the European perspective of the Western Balkans, and to point the way forward for an enhanced progress of the region towards the EU'.[77] Building up civil society and encouraging good governance was all within the aim 'to maintain the peace and stability of the region'. This could 'best be achieved by further enhancing the EU perspective and by making it as visible and tangible as possible for all the peoples of the region'.[78]

All this might indicate that a tendency to interpret the EU's activities as representing the creation of an identity based primarily on respect for human rights and democracy should be revised.[79] Although these elements are crucial, as I demonstrate later in this book, would the Balkans have attracted the same degree of commitment and intervention by the EU if there had been no inter-state conflict? If autocratic regimes had emerged from the former Yugoslavia with poor human rights records but were living in relative harmony with their neighbours would the response have been as forceful and persistent? After all, the EU had been happy to live with the regimes of the Warsaw Pact for years and even establish working relationships with them. Certainly the Balkans provoked a fear of spillover to the EU that demanded action but there is a case to be made that such fear was grounded in the total internal commitment to the peaceful organisation of inter-state relations. It was not a matter of economic interests prevailing. Here we might argue that peace is core to the institutional ethos.

Community Initiative Programme under regional policy is 'aimed at reinforcing the peace and reconciliation process in Northern Ireland and the six border counties of the Irish Republic'. The 'aid is targeted in particular at local economic and social players and has a double strategic objective: to favour those in the margins of local economic and social life; to take advantage of the peace process to stimulate socio-economic revival and growth' (see http://europa.eu.int/comm/regional_policy/reg_prog/po/prog_246.htm). Peace through economic regeneration is one of the key aspects of the original peace now adopted externally with regard to the Balkans.

[76] Communication from the Commission to the European Parliament and the Council – Western Balkans: Enhancing the European Perspective SEC (2008) 288, COM/2008/0127 final.

[77] Ibid.   [78] Ibid.

[79] See, for instance, Karen Smith, 'The EU, Human Rights and Relations with Third Countries: Foreign Policy with an Ethical Dimension', in Karen Smith and Margot Light (eds.), Ethics and Foreign Policy (Cambridge: Cambridge University Press, 2001) and Richard Youngs, 'Normative Dynamics and Strategic Interests in the EU's External Identity', Journal of Common Market Studies 42:2 (2004) 415–35.

It would be more difficult to sustain this interpretation when we move further away from the EU's borders. On the face of it, there *is* growing evidence that the value and principle of peace is establishing itself as an influential ethos component here as well. The development of the European Defence and Security Policy (EDSP), conceived at the Nice IGC, has purportedly ushered in an approach that mainstreams conflict prevention into the EU's relationship with the world. Article 43 TEU (after Lisbon) now provides that the Union can address 'humanitarian and rescue tasks, military advice and assistance tasks, conflict prevention and peacekeeping tasks, tasks of combat forces in crisis management, including peacemaking and post-conflict stabilisation'. The Council has instigated a programme for the prevention of violent conflicts which reiterates the 'political and moral responsibility to act to avoid human suffering'.[80] It contends that the EU 'is a successful example of conflict prevention' and suggests that the 'process of enlargement will extend this community of peace and progress to a wider circle of European states'.[81] The EDSP also offers the means by which such peace strategies can be adopted well beyond Europe. Relying on 'long-term instruments' that include 'development co-operation, trade, arms control, human rights and environment policies' the EU is now held out as a global purveyor of peace with a range of capabilities at its disposal. That these remain ultimately in the hands of the Member States does not necessarily detract from the collective embrace of this peace-focused mission. Law operates here less as a constraining and framing force and more as a tool. Its purpose as a means of contracting parties to adhere to certain norms may be based on international law principles.

The Commission has been swift to adopt similar rhetoric. Its 2001 communication on conflict prevention is seminal in this regard. Not only does it identify the EU as a 'peace project, and a supremely successful one' but it also maintains that '[t]hrough the process of enlargement, through the Common Foreign and Security Policy, through its development co-operation and its external assistance programmes the EU now seeks to project stability also beyond its own borders'.[82] Globally, the Commission contends, the EU 'has a duty to try to address the many cross-cutting issues that generate or contribute to conflict'.[83]

[80] European Council Goteborg, 11–12 June 2001, at www.eu2001.se/static/eng/pdf/violent.PDF.
[81] *Ibid.*
[82] Commission, Communication from the Commission on Conflict Prevention, COM/2001/0211 final at 5.
[83] *Ibid.*

This is stated as a 'moral and political imperative' although acknowledged as also making 'economic sense'.[84] There are no geographical limits in theory to the EU's activities in this area.

Indeed, the EU has been involved in a number of conflict resolution processes (through development and trade policies and specific projects of post-conflict assistance) since the policy was adopted. The Council adopted a Common Position regarding the Democratic Republic of the Congo, in 2003, which set the legal ambit of its peace initiatives.[85] It undertook a joint military mission in response to the UN Security Council Resolution 1484 ('Operation Artemis') that was limited in scope but represented the beginnings of military deployment in the name of the EU in the interests of peace. A succession of other operations in Macedonia, Bosnia and Herzogovina, Georgia (the first rule-of-law mission undertaken) and others followed. Substantial resources have been devoted to work in the field of conflict prevention.[86]

But can we be so certain that the evident developing peace component of the institutional ethos possesses strength in times of tension?

We need to cast our minds back to two conflicts to shed light on this question: the original conflagration in the Balkans during the 1990s and the invasion of Iraq in 2003.

The EU's response to the war in the former Yugoslavia has, of course, attracted significant analysis and attention over the years. Largely typified as providing the 'ultimate humiliation' for the CFSP, little more needs to be said on the details of these events.[87] It is common ground that the EU's interventions were hapless to say the least. Conflicting approaches to the conflict by individual Member States and the failure to agree a decent common policy was humiliating for those who claimed the EU was an important actor here.[88] The unilateral recognition by Germany of an independent Croatia was largely credited for

---

[84] *Ibid*.

[85] Council Common Position 2003/319/CFSP concerning European Union support for the implementation of the Lusaka Ceasefire Agreement and the peace process in the Democratic Republic of Congo (DRC) and repealing Common Position 2002/203/CFSP OJ L115/87.

[86] See, for instance, the Regulation (EC) No 1717/2006 of the Parliament and of the Council of 12 November 2006 establishing an Instrument for Stability which provides for 2.06 billion euros from 2007–13 to be expended on projects related to threats caused by armed conflict and other crises.

[87] John Peterson and Elizabeth Blomberg, *Decision-Making in the European Union* (Basingstoke: Macmillan, 1999) 242–3.

[88] See, for instance, Tony Judt, *Postwar: a History of Europe Since 1945* (London: Pimlico, 2007).

further fuelling the conflict.[89] Suffice to say, then, that if peace *had* been the commanding goal for the EU vis-à-vis the Balkans in 1993, the lack of cooperation between Member States ensured that it was super-seded by nationally perceived interests and general incompetence. It represented the relatively simple way in which the EU's external activ-ities were vulnerable to the whim of individual states' foreign policy decisions.

Even so, despite the tragic incompetence of the Member States in their initial approach to the Balkans, it would be hard not to accept that there was still an underlying resolve that peace was a necessary condition to be achieved. The fact that there was little consensus on how that could be done, particularly in the light of the ferocity of the hostilities, surely cannot detract from that basic commitment. It was perhaps more a point of failure of governance and effective coordin-ation. The lack of an EU coherent strategy, little systemic capacity to respond, little competence to act on decisions and an underdeveloped administrative order that could coordinate and implement planned activities, were all products of a failure of means rather than ends. Subsequent policy for the Balkans, as I have described, demonstrates how this may have been rectified. Ironically, the failings that were apparent in the face of those traumatic events in the 1990s may even have inspired a more effective and efficient policy predicated on peace as a fundamental principle.

But were the lessons really learned? The responses to the Iraq War of 2003 suggest not. John Peterson has told the story of the EU and the invasion pointing to the splits and intrigues that cast the EU into the political wilderness on the issue.[90] Although the individual Member States, as well as the then ten applicant states, managed to project their own political positions, the EU was rendered at best redundant. Then deep divisions between the UK, on the one hand, supported to one degree or another by Italy, Spain and certain candidates for accession, and France and Germany on the other, left the EU without a role to play. Such a rift could not be overridden by any stable administration or application of agreed principles given that foreign affairs effectively remained in the exclusive hands of the Member States. The animosity displayed between the two factions was apparently intense. Even so

[89] *Ibid.* at 674.
[90] John Peterson, 'Europe, America, Iraq: Worst Ever, Ever Worsening?', *Journal of Common Market Studies* 42 (2004) 9–26.

the Extraordinary European Council called in February 2003 still managed to produce a text that indicated a united position vis-à-vis Iraq. The declaration that emerged suggested that 'the primary responsibility for dealing with Iraqi disarmament lies with the Security Council', and that

[w]ar is not inevitable. Force should be used only as a last resort. It is for the Iraqi regime to end this crisis by complying with the demands of the Security Council ... [w]e are committed to working with all our partners, especially the United States, for the disarmament of Iraq, for peace and stability in the region and for a decent future for all its people.[91]

A sense of unity prevailed, on the surface, testament perhaps to the enduring power of the original institutional peace narrative. But the stories and comments that pervaded the press belied this impression. As David Allen and Michael Smith reported, 'Member States were pursuing fundamentally different and opposed policies at the UN'.[92] These evident political differences brought the EU's CFSP to a point of impotence.

Admittedly, once the invasion had begun and more particularly once the invasion had succeeded, the EU began to function again. The focus was on rebuilding and reconciliation. A communication from the Commission set the EU's revised agenda as the 'development of a secure, stable and democratic Iraq', the 'establishment of an open, stable, sustainable and diversified market economy' and the integration of Iraq into the international political and economic system.[93] Significant resources have been provided and we no longer hear much of the political outrage expressed against the United States and the UK for the invasion. Indeed, Peterson has pointed to the possibility that the Iraq experience, like the Balkans conflict before it, has opened the way for a strengthened and more effective European foreign policy.[94]

But nothing has materialised that would lead us to believe the EU is in any stronger a position now to influence external ventures of individual Member States that may threaten global peace in some

---

[91] Extraordinary European Council Presidency Conclusions, Brussels, 17 February 2003, online, available at: www.consilium.europa.eu/ueDocs/cms_Data/docs/pressData/en/ec/74554.pdf.

[92] David Allen and Michael Smith, 'External Developments', *Journal of Common Market Studies* 42 Annual Review (2004) 95–112 at 96.

[93] Commission Communication, 'The EU and Iraq: a Framework for Engagement', COM (2004) 417/1.

[94] Peterson, 'Europe, America, Iraq'.

way. More recent events provide contradictory evidence in relation to this issue. On the one hand, the 2006 invasion of Lebanon by Israel provoked the EU Commissioner to release condemnatory statements abhorring the military operations as disproportionate. This was in stark contrast to the ambivalent and prominent response given by the UK government.[95] On the other, the Russian incursion into South Ossetia in 2008 led to an EU response that was described as 'rapid and reasonably successful'.[96] A ceasefire was brokered thanks largely to a dynamic approach by 'a strong Presidency with whom the Russians were prepared to negotiate'.[97] The House of Lords European Committee believed that the 'EU was the obvious and perhaps only credible body to act as intermediary in the conflict, and acted with unaccustomed confidence and authority'.[98] How much this was down to Nicolas Sarkozy's efforts is, however, hard to judge. Taking peace seriously remains a hope rather than a fact.

If we stopped our deconstruction of the concept of peace here then we would be ignoring a third strand that might either support or unhinge this analysis. We need to examine the effect of 'security' and 'defence' on the institutional understanding of peace and how law has developed in this regard. Has the EU allowed a notion of peace that is contingent to become embedded in its institutional ethos? And has European law allowed that contingency to remain unchallenged? Or is the development of policies related to security and defence indicative of an acceptance that peace as a value, reflected in, and through law, might at last be gaining hold?

The new peace: security as a third dimension

It might seem perverse to speak of security in terms that suggested a conflict with the concept of peace. For, surely the two notions combine to make sense of each other; security being necessary to experience peace; peace being a condition that is the aim of security. But

---

[95] See, for instance, the remarks of Javier Solano, 'Press Statement of Javier Solana EU High Representative for the Common Foreign and Security Policy in Beirut 16 July 2006'. The UK did not call for an immediate ceasefire and there were reports that it had allowed flights of munitions to land in the UK from the United States for delivery to Israel. See 'UK Airport Flies US Bombs to Israel', *Daily Telegraph*, 26 July 2006.

[96] House of Lords European Committee, 'After Georgia – The EU and Russia Follow-up Report', 12 February 2009, online, available at: www.publications.parliament.uk/pa/ld200809/ldselect/ldeucom/26/2602.htm.

[97] *Ibid.*   [98] *Ibid.*

such an equation is fraught with problems. It presupposes a static definition of each concept. We have seen that peace cannot be so treated in the EU's hands. As the Union has progressed, as its influence and scope have deepened and widened, so the appreciation of what 'peace' for Europe might mean has evolved. Conceptions of security that have as their aim the achievement or preservation of peace must also have been adapted. The question for us now is whether a symbiosis between the concepts exists. If not, has the so-called 'security agenda' challenged the primacy of peace as an essential element of the European institutional ethos *or* become entwined with it, perhaps subverting and thereby undermining it? Does it indeed possess any purchase as an independent element of the ethos? If so, what effect might that have on the character of the Union? And how has law been engaged here?

A definition of security might be a useful starting point. We have no end of academic attempts to provide this. Some years ago Arnold Wolfers characterised security as 'the absence of threats to acquired values'.[99] More recently Ulrich Preuss has suggested that '[a]bsolute security demands nothing less than the control of all forces that could potentially endanger the territorial integrity or political independence of the nation'.[100] This implies that security is ultimately about state survival; the continued existence of a political formation, a culture, a people, a geographically determined territory, an economy, an identity even. The most readily acknowledged threat is of course military aggression. We can certainly see the direct relationship between security and peace formulated in international law terms. Under Article 1 of its Charter, the UN's principal purpose is,

[t]o maintain international peace and security, and to that end: to take effective collective measures for the prevention and removal of threats to the peace, and for the suppression of acts of aggression or other breaches of the peace, and to bring about by peaceful means, and in conformity with the principles of justice and international law, adjustment or settlement of international disputes or situations which might lead to a breach of the peace.

Although concentrated on inter-state conflict, the notion of 'collective security' has developed from this initial position so that we do not

[99] A. Wolfers, *Discord and Collaboration* (Baltimore: Johns Hopkins University Press, 1962).
[100] Ulrich K. Preuss, 'The Iraq War; Critical Reflections from "Old Europe"', in Amy Bartholomew (ed.), *Empire's Law* (London: Pluto Press, 2006) 52–67 at 53–4.

necessarily need to equate security purely with the singular state.[101] Rather, regional or international regimes can be and are equally concerned and affected by security issues.[102]

The concentration on the negative notion of 'threat' (rather than the positive notion of peace) has enabled the discourse of security to expand beyond purely military connotations. War no longer encompasses the totality of menace. So, the concept has lent itself more readily to Richard Ullman's claim that it cannot be understood 'until we are threatened with losing it'.[103] This provokes the possibility that anything perceived or promoted as a 'threat' to self interests in the short or long term can be included. The matter becomes one of political discretion, as we have seen most recently with the UN's attempts to develop the notion of 'human security' on a par with the national kind.[104] As the Commission on Human Security Report of 2003 indicates, human security 'complements state security by being people-centered and addressing insecurities that have not been considered as state security threats'.[105] Economic, environmental and societal interests have all been promoted under this rubric.

On one level, it surely does not matter whether or not an important interest is described in the language of security. Not if one rests in the domain of the rhetorical. It is a means by which an interest and call for action can acquire greater weight in political discourse. However, Buzan, Waever and de Wilde suggest that an open-ended appreciation of menace is counter-intuitive.[106] They argue that it must be restricted to threats against the survival of a referent object, whether that be state, international organisation or region, in an attempt to keep 'security studies' within reasonable bounds. But it is not just about academic convenience. This is a matter of the legitimacy of high politics. It is the survival aspect articulated by institutions of governance and authority that imbues 'security' with its symbolic power. Security,

---

[101] See Danesh Sarooshi, *The United Nations and the Development of Collective Security* (Oxford: Oxford University Press, 1999).

[102] Barry Buzan and Ole Waever, *Regions and Powers: the Structure of International Security* (Cambridge: Cambridge University Press, 2003).

[103] Richard H. Ullman, 'Redefining Security', *International Security* 8 (1983) 129–53 at 133.

[104] See Buzan and Waever, *Regions and Powers* at 9.

[105] UN Commission on Human Security Report 2003, online, available at: www.humansecurity-chs.org/finalreport/index.html.

[106] Barry Buzan, Ole Waever and Japp de Wilde, *Security: a New Framework for Analysis* (Boulder, CO: Lynne Rienner, 1998).

as metaphor for 'fundamental and urgent' challenges 'to the existing social and political fabric' provides the justification for immediate and decisive action.[107]

The identification of survival with security provides the latter with such political and legal importance that it can justify ascendancy over fundamental values and the countermanding of otherwise enforceable law. Human rights, democracy, justice, liberty can all be sacrificed to a lesser or greater degree.[108] 'The world of necessity is generated by a conflict between collective survival and human rights', Michael Walzer has argued.[109] But his concern was limited to the threat of war. Martti Koskenniemi suggests a wider consequence whereby, 'in the realm of vital interests, national security, peace and war, rules cannot constrain'.[110] Whether those interests include the variety of military, economic, environmental, social and cultural matters mentioned above is irrelevant. It is the scale of the threat and the political response necessary to counter it that is the issue. In this respect, the notion of 'human security' is separated, both in politics and law, from state or region security. The former is vulnerable in times of emergency. The latter takes precedence as an ongoing condition.

When we consider the EU in these terms we come up against a serious potential conflict of interest. On the one hand, the EU is a regional polity fundamentally organised on the existence of states. It incorporated this link between security and state survival through Article 297 EC Treaty now Article 347, Treaty on the Functioning of the EU (TFEU).

Member States shall consult each other with a view to taking together the steps needed to prevent the functioning of the common market being affected by measures which a Member State may be called upon to take in the event of serious internal disturbances affecting the maintenance of law and order, in the event of war, serious international tension constituting a threat of war, or

---

[107] Neil Walker, 'In Search of the Area of Freedom, Security and Justice: a Constitutional Odyssey', in Walker (ed.), *Europe's Area of Freedom, Security and Justice* (Oxford: Oxford University Press, 2004) 3–37 at 12–13.

[108] For instance, the European Convention on Human Rights allows for derogations from many of its provisions under Article 15 but only where the 'life of the nation' is threatened.

[109] Michael Walzer, *Just and Unjust Wars* at 325.

[110] Martti Koskenniemi, 'International Aspects of the Common Foreign and Security Policy', in Koskenniemi (ed.), *International Law Aspects of the European Union* (The Hague: Nijhoff, 1998) 27, at 27–8 as quoted by Maria-Gisella Garbagnati Ketvel, 'The Jurisdiction of the European Court of Justice in Respect of the Common Foreign and Security Policy', *International Comparative Law Quarterly* 55 (2006) 77–120 at fn9.

in order to carry out obligations it has accepted for the purpose of maintaining peace and international security.

Even the functioning of a common market (ironically the means by which the original peace was to be embedded in the Union) is subservient to the fundamental interests of state survival. On those few occasions when the European Court of Justice (ECJ) has been called upon to interpret Article 297, it has stressed the extraordinary circumstances implicit in the provision's terms. In *Johnston*, the ECJ stated that the article deals with 'exceptional and clearly defined cases' and does not lend itself 'to a wide interpretation'.[111] Security relates to threats of great magnitude. The aim of the Court may well have been to limit the exceptions to the primacy of Community law (noting as it did the need to prevent the impairment of its 'binding nature ... and its uniform application') but nonetheless it establishes the nature of security in this context as threats of a military or significantly violent kind rather than any other form of *insecurity*.[112]

But is this interpretation sustainable? If we look at academic analysis of the EU since its inception there is some indication that it is. Based on an examination of its structures, Karl Deutsch *et al.* described the nascent EU as a 'security community'. They were instrumental in relating the EEC in its original form as a means of attaining security through economic integration.[113] More recently, Buzan and Waever have called this process 'a meta-securitisation' based on 'a fear of Europe's future becoming like Europe's past'.[114] In this sense, we can perhaps equate security concerns with those of the original peace. The two were compatible because they shared the same ends and necessitated the same means.

In its early days, however, the term 'security' (in the sense of protecting the Member States from the external threat of war), was not associated constitutionally or institutionally with the EU's external

---

[111] Case C-222/84 *Johnston* [1986] ECR 1651 para. 26.

[112] The ECJ has confirmed this interpretation placing the onus on the Member State concerned to prove the necessity of any action under Article 297. See Case C-414/97 *Commission* v. *Spain* [1999] ECR I-5585 paras 21 and 22. For an in-depth review of the legal position regarding Article 297 see Martin Trybus, *European Union Law and Defence Integration* (Oxford: Hart, 2005).

[113] Karl Deutsch, Sidney A. Burrell, Robert A. Kann, Maurice Lee, Jr., Martin Lichterman, Raymond E. Lindgren, Francis L. Loewenheim and Richard W. Van Wagenen, *Political Community and the North Atlantic Area: International Organization in the Light of Historical Experience* (Princeton: Princeton University Press, 1957).

[114] Buzan and Waever, *Regions and Powers* at 353.

operations.[115] A significant rationale for the formation of the EU may have been the eradication of conflict between the participants but this did not extend beyond its borders. It was to NATO, the Western European Union, or individual states' own capabilities (or those of their allies) that security interests in this form were reserved. This was inevitable given the precedent set by the furious reaction of the French National Assembly in 1954 to the proposal for a European Defence Community.[116] Economic and social well-being was the political limit of the EU's early ambitions. Any deployment of the term 'security' was not intended to provoke the extraordinary responses that matters of defence normally demand.

Even when the possibility of encouraging an identity in the world was pursued at the end of the 1960s, security remained the preserve of the Member States and the various alliances to which they had become attached. Security issues beyond the EU's borders were conceived particularly with regard to the promotion of détente. Even then, the EU response was economically governed. So in the Paris Declaration of 1972, the promotion of peace through détente was focused on 'a common commercial policy towards the countries of Eastern Europe'.[117] 'Good neighbourliness', cooperation and reconciliation were the commanding terms at this time. Indeed, if we look again at the pivotal Copenhagen Declaration on European Identity of 1973, security was explicitly reserved *outside* the nascent European Political Co-operation. Paragraph 8 stated,

[t]he Nine, one of whose essential aims is to maintain peace, will never succeed in doing so if they neglect their own security. Those of them who are members of [NATO] consider that in present circumstances there is no alternative to the security provided by the nuclear weapons of the United States and by the presence of North American forces in Europe: and they agree that in the light of the relative military vulnerability of Europe, the Europeans should, if they wish to preserve their independence, hold to their commitments and make constant efforts to ensure that they have adequate means of defence at their disposal.[118]

---

[115] See, for instance, Frédéric Charillon, 'The EU as a Security Regime', *European Foreign Affairs Review* 10 (2005) 517–33 at 519–20.

[116] For the story of this early attempt to forge some form of European federation see J. Pinder, *The Building of the European Union*, 3rd edn (Oxford: Oxford University Press, 1998).

[117] Statement of the Conference of the Heads of State and Government of the Member States of the European Union, Paris, 21 October 1972, para. 13.

[118] Declaration on European Identity by the Nine Foreign Ministers, Copenhagen, 14 December 1973.

The importance then attested to the Final Act of the Conference on Security and Co-operation in Europe reinforced this position. Security was a matter that Leo Tindemans in his Report on European Union in 1975 *hoped* would be incorporated into the EU but even he recognised that this was a long-term objective.[119]

But as I have described, the understanding of peace experienced a transformation when the Cold War ended. Since then security has been ushered into the constitution of the EU in three main guises.

First, it has appeared as related to the 'existential threat', as posited by Buzan and Waever, of a fragmentation of Europe as a whole through internecine conflict.[120] Enlargement, or rather the promise of inclusion in the Union, and continuing internal integration, what used to be called the deepening process, are seen as legitimate security manoeuvres cast from the same understanding of original peace. The Tampere European Council made the link explicit:

> The European Union has already put in place for its citizens the major ingredients of a shared area of prosperity and peace: a single market, economic and monetary union, and the capacity to take on global political and economic challenges. The challenge of the Amsterdam Treaty is now to ensure that freedom, which includes the right to move freely throughout the Union, can be enjoyed in conditions of security and justice accessible to all.[121]

All those fundamental aspects of European integration, developed over the preceding decades, are intertwined with peace and security. The rhetoric used by heads of certain Member States at the beginning of the new millennium demonstrates how crucial the original peace-establishing purpose remains in justifying contemporary security policies.[122] 'We must not return to the ways of old', is the gist of the interpretation, although the recent acquisition of memory is used against an external threat rather than a way of reflecting upon Europe's capacity for 'evil' generally. Nevertheless, there is little doubt that the narrative of original peace and security remains symbiotic. The fear of European wickedness re-emerging to cause havoc and violence is a useful tool to justify maintaining the EU *and* expanding it. Given the anti-integration feelings that undoubtedly

---

[119] Report on European Union, 29 December 1975, Part II paragraph 3.

[120] Buzan and Waever, *Regions and Powers* at 356 et seq.

[121] Tampere European Council, Presidency Conclusions 15 and 16 October 1999, para. 2.

[122] See Buzan and Waever, *Regions and Powers* at 361–4.

operate within the EU, the memory of past self-destruction rather than simply prosperity remains a valid and vital means of legitimation. The fact that medium- and long-term approaches to the security threat posed by the Balkans conflict have been addressed through the promise of eventual incorporation into the Union reinforces the link between security at this level and the 'proven' constitutional means for achieving peace.

Second, security has also been linked to a *global* pursuit of peace as a unifying external face for the Union. The development of a Common Foreign and Security Policy was to 'strengthen the security of the Union in all ways' and to 'preserve peace and strengthen international security'.[123] As we have seen, this prompted the diplomatic response to peace and security that has increasing political relevance but is still affected by its incoherent and intergovernmental character. It has spawned the parallel European Defence and Security Policy (EDSP). The constitutional entrenchment of military independence for individual Member States has, however, been preserved explicitly. Under Article 17(1) TEU (now Article 42(2) after Lisbon), EDSP 'shall not prejudice the specific character of the security and defence policy of certain Member States and shall respect the obligations of certain Member States' regarding NATO. As if that were not plain enough the new Article 42(7) TEU (after Lisbon) provides that 'cooperation in this area shall be consistent with commitments under' NATO which, 'for those States which are members of it, remain the foundation of their collective defence'. The constitutional position of security issues associated with military defence against external threat rather than the resurgence of internal violence, continues to be outside the purview of the EU. French and UK approaches to nuclear disarmament reinforce that overall retention of sovereignty in this field. The French in particular have maintained their 'right' to possess and if necessary deploy an independent nuclear deterrent, even beyond the European sphere.[124] Whether that might change with the Presidency of Nicolas Sarkozy remains to be seen.[125]

---

[123] Article 11 TEU, slightly reformulated now in Article 21(2)(c) TEU since the Lisbon Treaty.

[124] See in particular, speech by Jacques Chirac to the Strategic Air and Maritime Forces at Landivisiau, January 19 2006, reported at www.elysee.fr/elysee/elysee.fr/francais/ interventions/discours_Et_declarations/2006/janvier/allocution_du_president_ de_la_republique_lors_de_sa_visite_aux_forces_aeriennes_Et_oceanique_strate- giques-landivisiau-l_ile_longue-finistere.38406.html.

[125] On 17 March 2009 the French National Assembly approved the President's plan to rejoin NATO.

Nevertheless, peacekeeping and peacemaking were incorporated into the external dimension for the first time in the Treaty of Nice, leading to several UN-related activities being adopted. Security began to take on a military and policing character as a move for *global* peace, as it might be called, rather than a peace focused on the defence and survival of the nation (or supra-nation of the EU). The narrative of 'world peace' player has acquired institutional purchase and is prompting the creation of institutions designed to give it effect. Once in place, there might be a tendency to deploy those structures whether or not the EU is best placed to act in the interests of international peace and security. So, for instance, was it really sensible for the EU to send a force to the Democratic Republic of the Congo in 2003? What kind of precedent did this establish? Did it merely give the newly created EDSP a concrete manifestation, indicating the political willingness to be engaged in peacemaking whether or not it was a good solution to local problems? Or was it an honest undertaking designed to begin the fulfilment of the EU's promise to assume greater responsibility for 'global security' and 'building a better world'?[126]

On the face of it, there is little to commend EU action in this region other than to demonstrate it has the resources and political motivation to operate as a significant global actor.[127] In doing so the EU presents itself as a complementary equal to the UN, capable indeed of fulfilling the UN Charter's mandate even though it is not a member of the UN itself. Certainly its involvement in Africa in this way raises the question of the ambit of actions in the name of security and peace. Direct intervention may well be predicated on the latter, at least when operating under the UN banner, but if it is determined by the former then do other considerations come into operation?

The history of the ESDP was carefully assessed by Mary Kaldor *et al.* in the 2007 Madrid Report.[128] Having scrutinised the activities of the EU a number of key problems were noted. In particular, it was suggested that a lack of clarity on the 'shared goals and principles' governing action

[126] 'A Secure Europe in a Better World: European Security Strategy', Brussels, 12 December 2003, online, available at: www.consilium.europa.eu/uedocs/cmsUpload/78367.pdf.
[127] If the decision is based on available resources then the EU might reasonably have a global role to play. Involvement will be decided by willingness to commit personnel. If the decision is based on other criteria, for instance political sensitivities or fields of influence, then the picture becomes confused and less focused on peace.
[128] See Human Security Study Group (convenor: Mary Kaldor), 'A European Way of Security: The Madrid Report of the Human Security Study Group Comprising a Proposal and Background Report', Madrid, 8 November 2007.

left initiatives 'confused and unfocused'.[129] The absence of principles greatly constrains the ability to adopt peace as a determining value. As the Report remarks, this is all 'bound up with political legitimacy'.[130] Given the continuing character of the policy, which prevents effective judicial scrutiny of operations, the separation of European law from strategies intimately concerned with peace abroad is reinforced. This takes us to the final narrative strand.

Third, security has changed shape in order to deal with an expanded notion of threat that takes us far beyond the desire to avoid inter or intra-state violence. There are good reasons to think that security has developed in such a way as to forge a separate identity from peace, to expand its remit towards those areas that stretch the link with survival. Two aspects attract attention, one internally focused, the other externally. The internal has become organised around the constitutional notion of a European Area of Freedom, Security and Justice (AFSJ). The external has acquired expression through the adoption of a supposedly coherent Community Security Strategy. The two are linked by policy identification rather than constitutional provision.

The AFSJ emerged in the Treaty of Maastricht, which introduced provisions of Justice and Home Affairs into a Treaty of European Union. Issues of immigration, police cooperation and criminal justice were drawn into the sphere of European competence for the first time. This eventually spawned the AFSJ, which was provided with defining characteristics, and milestones, at the Tampere European Council in 1999. These were intended to be the basis for assessing its successful imposition. So, matters of immigration, asylum, treatment of third country nationals, access to justice, and organised crime, were all brought under the umbrella of the 'Area'. The external dimension was not neglected, Tampere concluding that 'all competences and instruments at the disposal of the Union, and in particular, in external relations must be used in an integrated and consistent way to build the area of freedom, security and justice'.[131]

The implication of this policy was that the peace achieved within the Union required protection. By identifying these specific areas of concern, the Council expanded its public understanding of threats to peace. At least, it began to develop a sense of security that allowed

---

[129] *Ibid.* at 22.   [130] *Ibid.* at 23.
[131] Tampere European Council Presidency Conclusions, at para 59 ('Tampere Milestones').

for non-military threats to sit alongside traditional security issues. Thus, at Tampere, the AFSJ 'project' was expressed as responding to 'the frequently expressed concerns of citizens and has a direct bearing on their daily lives'.[132] Concerns over immigration, international crime, drugs and terrorism have therefore been encompassed within this domain following either specific events or more general public perceptions. None qualify under reasoned analysis, I would suggest, as matters of survival that equate with peace as otherwise promoted by the EU. That they might lead to internal conflict, even violence, does not necessarily mean that they exist at a level that warrants the association with peace as pre-condition. And yet, of course that is how these 'threats' are being promoted within the internal security realm.

This suggests that a constitutional environment is being created that sees peace as only one of many issues to consider in the name of security. If treated as merely one of a wide range of values, peace claims will not necessarily prevail over the political and legal initiatives that react to matters of immigration, asylum, terrorism or even economic recession. Indeed, if measures are enacted and policies structured around, say, eradicating international terrorism, which may contribute to, as well as prevent, conflict, there would appear to be a central countermanding of even a 'thin' conception of peace.[133]

Such a possibility is enhanced by the *external* narrative of security that has developed over the past few years, particularly but not exclusively in the shadow of the events of 9/11. The European Security Strategy, declared in 2003, demonstrates specifically the Council's appreciation of how security should be addressed in its external dealings.[134] Terrorism is the central and coalescing motif. It is included either as a component or consequence of each category of threat, be it the proliferation of weapons of mass destruction, trafficking in drugs, women, illegal migrants and weapons, regional conflict, or state failure. And it is pervasive as a justification for policy operation. Yet, in the Tampere milestones, constructed pre-9/11, terrorism warranted only one mention and that merely as an addition to the intent to

---

[132] Tampere Milestones para. 2.
[133] For a critique of the war on terror that demonstrates the fragility of the concept of peace in this context see Upendra Baxi, 'The "War *on* Terror" and the "War *of* Terror": Nomadic Multitudes, Aggressive Incumbents and the "New" International Law', *Osgoode Hall Law Journal* 43:1 (2005) 7–43.
[134] 'A Secure Europe in a Better World; European Security Strategy', Brussels, 12 December 2003, online, available at: www.consilium.europa.eu/uedocs/cmsupload/78367.pdf

tackle cross-border crime.[135] Thus from a subsidiary element of concern, terrorism has been identified as a central security issue within the EU. Indeed, the Lisbon Treaty's imposed new Article 43(1) TEU now identifies 'the fight against terrorism, including by supporting third countries in combating terrorism in their territories' to be a key focus for a common security and defence policy. The constitutionalisation of terrorism in this way embeds it as a component of war/peace rather than crime, a significant shift in attitude since 9/11. Although previously a clear worry for governments, accepted in the EU through various initiatives,[136] terrorism did not previously evoke such constitutional attention. Political memories may be short but the atrocities of Lockerbie, Omagh, Inniskillen, Bologna train station, Milan, the assassinations of Olof Palme, Aldo Moro and numerous others across Europe, the bombings and shootings in Northern Ireland, Spain, Italy, all provided a reason to produce a coordinated police response without provoking the kind of constitutional reaction that has now come to be associated with the word 'terrorism'. Nor was that terrorism equated with the discourse of security in such a central way. Does this suggest the threat is greater now, that the epithet 'international terrorism' has changed the threat to the public in any fundamental way? Or is this a political transformation grounded less in notions of value than political myopia? Or even perhaps in deep-seated racist prejudices? Is the fact that so-called 'Islamic terrorism' defines the threat redolent of a fear of the ethnic 'other' as much as fear of their actions?[137] Whatever the motivation, the pattern seems to have been set whereby the widening approach to security, notably in relation to terrorism, has had a significant impact on the value of peace within the EU.

---

[135] Tampere Milestones para. 43.

[136] The TREVI initiative in response to many incidents of terrorism in Europe was founded under the old EPC system. For a review of its workings see Malcolm Anderson, Monica Den Boer, Peter Cullen, William C. Gilmore, Charles D. Raab and Neil Walker, *Policing the European Union: Theory Law and Practice* (Oxford: Clarendon Press, 1995).

[137] It is a factor that the EU itself recognises, ironically, when dealing with issues of racial discrimination provoked by political association of Islam with terrorism. See, for instance, the European Monitoring Centre for Racism and Xenophobia report 'The Impact of 7 July 2005 London Bomb Attacks on Muslim Communities in the EU' (November 2005), online, available at: www.eumc.europa.eu/eumc/index.php?fuseaction=content.dsp_cat_content&catid=1.

Conclusion

The interweaving narrative represented above suggests that rather than peace occupying a straightforward place in the EU's institutional ethos it is a complex and ambiguous concept. The three strands presented do not rely on the same precepts. As far as the third strand is concerned there is a significant possibility that with the rhetoric and reality of a 'war against terrorism', peace in its Kantian sense (meaning the absence of war between states) is actively countermanded.

How then should we judge the value of peace in this context? Let us consider the strength of each strand in comparison with each other.

The original peace remains a persistent and significant value underlying the EU's practical as well as theoretical construction. It is entrenched constitutionally and legally. Through a legal system that binds states to each other economically and politically a pacific order has emerged that will not countenance military conflict between Member States. This has been an operating condition since the EU's conception, a brilliant if not original response to the age old rivalries of European history.

But how strong is this conceptualisation? The law may well act as a coalescing force and the constitution, predicated on non-military dispute resolution, may well manage issues of inter-state conflict peacefully, but this is dependent on a market-centred liberalism holding the political foreground and much of the hinterland as well. The theory underpinning the EU as a peace project is reliant on the notion of 'democratic peace' and the often stated belief that 'democracies do not go to war with each other'.[138] The argument proceeds, for as long as democracy is maintained within the Union's membership the legal structures will operate effectively to remove any questions of territorial or economic tension that was previously endemic in the European theatre. The theory has its detractors. The 'mythic' character of the democratic peace and the wisdom of constructing policy on such a flimsy premise have been questioned.[139] Indeed, one would have to ask whether in the EU, the theory has as much purchase in a Union of twenty-seven or more Member States as it appears

---

[138] Michael Doyle has been one of the chief advocates for such a contention. See Doyle, 'Kant, Legacies, and Foreign Affairs', *Philosophy and Public Affairs* 12:3 and 12:4 (1983) 205–35 and 323–53.

[139] See for instance, Christopher Layne, 'Kant or Cant: the Myth of the Democratic Peace', in Michael Brown, Sean Lynn-Jones and Steven Miller (eds.), *Debating the Democratic Peace* (Cambridge, MA: MIT Press, 1996) 157–201, and Errol Henderson, *Democracy and War: the End of an Illusion?* (Boulder, CO: Lynne Rienner, 2002).

to have had with the original six? The assumption is that it will hold good. Law in that sense is necessary to maintain the condition of peace as narrowly defined. This is the premise as more popularly articulated by commentators such as Mark Leonard. For him, law has been the means of instituting a 'surveillance society', one in which laws bind states together on the basis that as 'each member state wants its fellow members to obey the law, they are forced to obey it themselves'.[140] This has constructed the 'basis of their security'. Mutual interest reinforced through mutual interference. In this sense a just peace involving the recognition of others and renouncing claims so as to achieve consensus was an underlying precept for participation in the Union.

But law's implicit role here might also have allowed it to become non-cognisant of its relationship with peace as a value. It does not attempt, constitutionally or otherwise, to prohibit aggression. It does not look to influence Member States' action beyond its limited domain. No principle of peace operates to interpret exploits even within Community law. The only real (but limited) constraint exists through the discourse of fundamental rights and the rule of law.[141]

As with any theoretically constructed system, however, albeit one now grounded in more than fifty years of experience, it is only at times of crisis when its effectiveness is tested. Up until recent times the abundance of resources in Europe has ensured that there are massive incentives for maintaining, and joining, a pacific order based on respect for the law. But would that peace–law–market–economy nexus be strained to breaking point when energy resources, for instance, become scarce? Would economic disaster unlock those political passions that identify the nation as the limit of collective commitment and identity? Would peace embedded through law rather than moral precept involve 'the sacrifice of justice on the altar of stability and security' as Lauterpacht questioned many years ago?[142] Would it be strong enough to overcome the inflamed passions of popular historical consciousness?[143] Would

---

[140] Mark Leonard, *Why Europe will Run the 21st Century* (London: Fourth Estate, 2005) at 42.

[141] I examine this issue further in Chapters 3 and 4.

[142] Hersch Lauterpacht, *The Function of Law in the International Community* (Oxford: The Clarendon Press,) at 438.

[143] This might become a vital question, should new EU states be subject to old antagonisms? Balkan countries for instance must surely pose such a problem. Some evidence of continuing animosity despite selective enlargement appears from the case of Cyprus (which remains an unsettled conflict) and Greece's approach to Macedonia in attempting to veto that state's entry into NATO.

it, indeed, overcome those destructive forces of nationalism that have been reignited in the Balkans but also exist, perhaps hidden, in other EU countries?

The strength of commitment to a particular value is inevitably assessed by its application *in extremis*. But might this be challenged through the developing economic recession of 2009? We do not have enough evidence to question the EU's premise that peace will prevail internally provided it retains its liberal democratic, economically-focused, law-bound condition. We might still ask, however, if the Union provides the practical safeguards to ensure the theory is protected. The experience of the EU's response to the tragedy of 9/11 suggests that it is all too ready to discard the precepts of a just peace. Damian Chalmers has mapped out the significant dangers to political rights in this time of 'stress' but the threat is much broader than that.[144] It undermines the whole value of peace in the EU and suggests its influence is decidedly weak in the institutional ethos.

The counter position would look to the collective resolution of disputes and difficulties offered through the EU. By the selective and limited redistribution of wealth and by the 'prudent management' of the economy, the EU may represent an enduring and durable structural framework for maintaining the original internal peace.[145] But outside this main achievement there exist signs of impotence that perhaps talk against the EU's peace-maintaining capacity. The Northern Ireland 'troubles' demonstrated how the Union had little to offer in the *resolution* of an internal conflict that crossed internal borders. The conflict may never have threatened peace in Europe as a whole but the EU's determination to avoid political involvement over a protracted period, confirming the affair as outside its competence, suggests that the value of peace is treated as morally limited. Once peace had been brokered, the EU was able to demonstrate its peace–law–economy technique. By providing significant structural funds under its regional development policy it aimed 'to address the economic and social legacy of 30 years of conflict in the region and to take advantage of new

---

[144] See Damian Chalmers, 'Political Rights and Political Reason in European Law in Times of Stress', in Wojciech Sadurski (ed.), *Political Rights under Stress in 21st Century Europe* (Oxford: Oxford University Press, 2006) 55–83.

[145] European Monetary Union, the single currency, etc., have, however, questionable strength in themselves at times of economic stress. Member States still respond to the law in elective terms when it comes to securing national interests.

opportunities arising from the restoration of peace'.[146] Otherwise, the matter remained one of Member State internal security. Would the same arise in a significantly more complex regional dispute developing in say the Balkans? Something of a worrying indication that EU law will not equip itself to recognise the application of peace arose in Advocate General Kokott's recent opinion on matters relating to the Republic of Cyprus and the recognition and enforcement of judgments.[147] This suggested that the legal influence of the value of peace was peripheral at best. Recognising the sensitivity of land disputes amidst a land long divided by conflict Kokott nonetheless advised that the application of the regulation in issue could not be dependent on considerations of whether it would contribute or not to the resolution of the Cyprus problem. She declared that this 'would be contrary to the principle of legal certainty, respect for which is one of the objectives of the regulation'.[148] The danger of law focusing on an administrative principle regardless of the context of peace is perhaps reflective of the limits of EU law vis-à-vis this strand.

The second strand I explored was concerned with peace as an international and external value. Here the virtues displayed are different but perhaps of stronger consistency. Law in general no longer has a leading role to play. Action remains fundamentally intergovernmental and not subject to any strict legal regime. Member States retain control over decisions despite the constitutional attempt at coordination and 'a spirit of loyalty and mutual solidarity'.[149] A coherent approach to external peace or even adherence to the peaceful settlement of disputes will be difficult to guarantee. On the one hand, the rhetoric that emerges from the Council and the Commission, the policy statements and strategies that are reiterated from time to time, seem to suggest a degree of institutional consistency that identifies the EU as an organisation that 'will pursue its objectives with determination but above all using peaceful means'.[150] Resources are increasingly available and structures for effective decision-making, certainly for less obviously contentious

---

[146] EU Programme for Peace and Reconciliation in Northern Ireland and the Border Region of Ireland (2000–2004), which has made available approximately 740 million euros. See http://ec.europa.eu/regional_policy/themes/peace_En.htm.

[147] Case C-420/07 *Apostolides* v. *Orams*, Opinion of Advocate General Kokott, 18 December 2008.

[148] *Ibid.* at para. 48.   [149] Article 11(2) TEU, now Article 24(3) TEU after Lisbon.

[150] Martin Ortega, 'Military Intervention and the European Union', EU-ISS Chaillot Paper No. 45 (2001) at 118, online, available at: www.iss.europa.eu/uploads/media/cp045e.pdf.

matters of conflict (such as the Congo), are being put in place. However, the Madrid Report on the EDSP noted the lack of principle evident across the EU's initiatives, and spoke loudly about the emptiness of value-orientation in the name of peace. Failure to consider what peace might mean beyond the basic absence of military conflict and how it might incorporate notions of justice and respect for human rights, has demonstrated a dangerous vapidity that is worsened by the absence of law and its governing principles.

History, equally, tells us that the EU Member States are not always able, individually or collectively, to live up to this coordinated and principled commitment. The examples given of the response to the Balkans and more recently Iraq indicate the way in which the Union remains fettered when it comes to enacting its commitment to peace. The realist perspective frequently seems to be confirmed in times of crisis, allowing individual states to either pursue their own interests or block meaningful action by the EU as a whole.

This takes us to the last strand. It provokes the question whether the attachment of the EU's recent discourse of security to the inter-governmental character of external action ultimately privileges the national interest over putative communal values. Is the pursuit of peace forever subject to political qualification? The Union may *appear* to be moving towards a solid foundation for the peaceful settlement of disputes externally as well as internally. But if we see peace as necessitating achieving justice (howsoever that may be defined) on a global scale then we might refashion our judgement. For it seems peace as a grand idea, a project in its own right, will only be under-mined by associating it with a limitless spectrum of security issues. It suggests that peace is a state to be achieved, not a practice to be performed. And in the achievement of that state, all other salient values that I examine in this book, respect for human rights, the rule of law, freedom, and democracy, can be sacrificed. That again is the worrying possibility of the institutional response to terrorism post 9/11.

With such an analysis it is tempting to interpret the condition of peace in the EU not in terms of being disjointed, subject to three separ-ate strands, but as amounting to a '*pax europa*'. Johan Galtung suggested something similar in his rendition of a *pax bruxellana* some thirty or more years ago. He classified it as a system designed to re-impose Western Europe as a world power, to make the world Eurocentric again and to 'locate the center of Europe in the West, even with an explicit peace philosophy'.[151] He also referred to it as an imperialism that is built on by the EU rather than challenged. Thus his *pax bruxellana* was seen as 'a world order with its center in Brussels but also based on law and order according to well known European recipes'.[152] Contrary interpretations have been expressed. Robert Kagan suggested that Europe was 'moving beyond power into a self contained world of laws and rules and transnational negotiation and cooperation' as a 'realization of Immanuel Kant's "perpetual peace"'.[153] And Ulrich Beck has lauded the fact and potential of 'cosmopolitan Europe' based, in part, on peace founded on the removal of internal borders and a common currency and law.[154] But a *pax europa* with a legal regime that fails to clarify either the principles that underlie its external operations or to have any influence over the actions of its Members beyond the EU's borders might represent a *pax* more intent on preserving power and prosperity in Europe than any thicker notion of 'peace'. At best the underlying value is indeterminate and unlikely to operate so as to govern institutional decision-making where other, perhaps more catastrophic, threats than terrorism are concerned. Ken Booth has coined the phrase 'long hot century' to describe the scale of these threats ahead.[155] Environmental and financial crises are primary concerns here. The absence of an institutionally recognised notion of peace, which can both counter these threats and not disregard wider claims of justice, suggests a debilitating ethical condition for the Union.

It remains to be seen in this book, however, whether adherence to the other values and principles, which could form part of the EU's institutional ethos, are capable, and indeed successful, in countering this condition or whether they too fall victims to it. If the latter, peace might be condemned to perpetual gesture rather than an influential ethos element.

---

[151] Galtung, *The European Community: a Superpower in the Making* at 117.

[152] *Ibid.* 118.

[153] Robert Kagan, *Of Paradise and Power: America and Europe in the New World Order* (New York: Alfred A. Knopf, 2003) at 3.

[154] Ulrich Beck, *Cosmopolitan Vision* (Cambridge: Polity Press, 2006) at 174.

[155] Ken Booth, *Theory of World Security* (Cambridge: Cambridge University Press, 2007).

3   The rule of law

Introduction

On the 7 June 2006 Dick Marty produced a report for the Council of Europe that must have caused considerable political embarrassment within the EU.[1] That embarrassment would have related as much to the institutional response as to the report's content. Marty laid bare the extensive 'web' of intrigue that connected the CIA and its treatment of terrorist suspects with many European governments, including several from the EU. It involved practices of abduction, denial of legal safeguards and, most likely, torture. Marty believed that the rule of law was threatened by such disregard for those human rights norms and standards which have enshrined themselves within the European realm over the past half century.

Six months earlier, EU Justice Commissioner Franco Frattini had expressed the view that if any Member State of the Union were to be found to have colluded with US security and intelligence agencies in the transport and incarceration of 'terrorist suspects' without recourse to the due process of law, they should be subjected to a severe EU response.[2] 'I would be obliged to propose to the Council serious consequences, including the suspension of voting rights in the Council', Frattini was reported as declaring.[3] He was referring to the power under Article 7 TEU to apply sanctions to any Member State thought to

---

[1] Council of Europe, Parliamentary Assembly, Committee on Legal Affairs and Human Rights, 'Alleged Secret Detentions and Unlawful Inter-state Transfers Involving Council of Europe Member States', 7 June 2006 (Rapporteur, Mr Dick Marty).
[2] *Guardian*, 'EU Threat to Countries with Secret CIA Prisons', 29 November 2005.
[3] *Ibid.*

have been responsible for a serious breach of those original Article 6(1) TEU principles, which included respect for the rule of law.

When Marty's report appeared, however, the initial silence from Frattini was deafening. There was an ambivalent recognition that nefarious events had taken place but no recommendation for serious consequences was issued.[4] Frattini's language was now cautious, couched in terms that made institutional action extremely unlikely. The prospect of 'serious consequences' evaporated whether under Article 7 TEU or any other EU procedure. It was, indeed, probably a rush of blood to the head that caused Frattini to suggest such a thing in the first place. One can only imagine he was caught unawares. This is not to say that the matter did not *deserve* such a response as promised by Frattini or that it will not continue to elicit some rhetorical posturing by the EU Commission, Parliament, and human rights agencies generally. Rather, it is recognition of the political control that must make us pause when we think about the rule of law within the context of the EU. There is an irony here that should not be missed.

The whole sorry saga of extraordinary rendition represents something of a microcosm of the condition of the rule of law within the Union. It indicates the tensions between various potentially differing, albeit related, dimensions. Three in particular are relevant, all of which are engaged in the extraordinary rendition story at some level.

First, there is the *supranational* dimension. This represents a rule of law that is international in character and origin. Member States are subjected to laws and regulation through the Treaties as well as judicial decision. The principles of primacy and direct effect are central to this construction. But there are significant boundaries that criss-cross the EU's legal realm, dictating where and when Member States are to be subject to the rule of EU law and in particular to the legal review of their actions. Even though there may be outrage at a state's behaviour, as with extraordinary rendition, the law of the Union can be impotent. How can this be rationalised within any concept of the rule of law?

---

[4] Indeed Frattini was seen to backtrack from his initial (off-message?) comments as early as January 2006 when he stated more moderately that neither he nor the Commission 'will draw any conclusions or issue any judgements, or speculate on actions to be possibly taken at this point in time, as we are still in the process of establishing the facts'. See 'Statement by Vice-president Franco Frattini in Regard to the Information Memorandum Issued by Mr Marty on "Alleged Secret Detentions in Council of Europe Member States"', online, available at: ec.europa.eu/commission_barroso/frattini/doc/2006/speech_24_01_06_En.pdf.

Second, there is an *institutional* dimension. This relates to rule of law notions that might address the relationship between the EU's institutions and individuals affected by their actions. A 'government of laws' is a key notion in this respect, drawing on principles intended to protect individuals against the exercise of power in an arbitrary or discriminatory way. It provides a sense of law's ability impartially to control decisions that impact on people to ensure agreed rules are adhered to by those in authority. It is a concept inherently associated with law as a product and manifestation of state sovereignty, internally constructed in accordance with a state's system of governance. And it has been identified as an essential aspect of a democratic polity. But, of course, the EU is *not* a state. And its claims for democracy are poor. Even so, we have institutions that can and do act as though they have the power of state-sanctioned structures but operate beyond the state. The Commission's and the Parliament's powerlessness in the face of a blatant disregard for the rule of law in the rendition saga nonetheless highlights the variability of application of the concept. How then does this complex demarcation of power and practice affect the coherence of a rule of law applicable to the EU?

Third, there is the *extra-territorial* dimension. The EU purveys a notion of the rule of law in its external dealings, particularly in development, trade and accession policies. It is represented as a paragon of virtue when it comes to fulfilling aspects of the rule of law and promotes many projects associated with developing the ability of third states to adhere to the rule of law. But the apparent incapacity of the EU to exercise any value control over its Member States on rendition suggests an ironical distance between the external and internal adherence to this concept. Does the export of this idea, then, reflect something of the internal understanding? Or does it demonstrate the relative lack of application internally by comparison?

To understand the quality of the rule of law as a constituting value in the EU's institutional ethos, therefore, an exploration of these three dimensions is necessary. And indeed their analysis constitutes the bulk of this chapter. However, before considering each in turn it might be useful to have some idea of the possible parameters of the notion of the rule of law in the abstract. This is provided below. My intention is not to provide a complete theory here, nor to represent all the jurisprudential approaches that have been taken by analysts of the subject. Rather, it is simply to present a possible spectrum of interpretation against which the EU can be compared.

The conceptual spectrum

Any review of the concept of the rule of law will reveal a tension between the rule of law as a value in its own right and as a set of virtues that are designed to accomplish another value designation (respect for human rights or social or even global justice, for instance).[5] Frequently, this is represented as a distinction between a 'thin' and a 'thick' conception. Traditionally focused on the modern state, these perspectives contemplate a spectrum of possible interpretations. From a minimalist reading that associates the rule of law with legality, requiring clear and fixed rules governing people's lives, to one that broadly attempts to incorporate a 'fully elaborated theory of social justice', significant degrees of preference are offered.[6] There is considerable dispute between those adopting the two positions.

So, for instance, Joseph Raz in his seminal if brief essay on the subject, discounted 'legality', the slavish observance of the law by those in power, as the basis for the rule of law on the grounds that this was a self-evidently insufficient quality to acquire legitimacy for institutions of governance. Raz advocated for a conception that had a more substantive content, although relatively speaking it remained on the 'thinner' side. He suggested that three aspects should clarify it as a value.

First, it should present as a contrast with 'arbitrary power' in the sense that a 'government subjected to the rule of law is prevented from changing the law retroactively or abruptly or secretly whenever this would suit its purposes'.[7] Second, it should reflect the determination to maintain as a quality of law its 'fixed point of reference', which helps stabilise 'social relationships' and enables 'individual planning' in an environment of reasonable regularity and predictability.[8] Third, it should assist in ensuring respect for human dignity, in as much as it is based on a presupposition that people 'are rational, autonomous creatures' and are again able to plan within a system of law that encourages

---

[5] Although there are links between the Anglo-American rule of law notion and the German *Rechtsstaat* or the French *État de droit*, the terms are not synonymous. For a consideration of *Rechtsstaat* see Franz Neumann, 'Rechtsstaat, the Division of Powers and Socialism', in Otto Kirchheimer and Franz Neumann, *Social Democracy and the Rule of Law* (London: Allen & Unwin, 1987) 66–74.

[6] T.R.S. Allan, 'The Rule of Law as the Rule of Reason: Consent and Constitutionalism', *LQR* 115 (1999) 221–44 at 221.

[7] Joseph Raz, 'The Rule of Law and its Virtue', in Robert L. Cunningham (ed.), *Liberty and the Rule of Law* (College Station: Texas A&M University Press, 1979) 3–21 at 12.

[8] *Ibid.* at 13.

a sense of legitimate expectations. These are not exhaustive qualities but do provide the basis for Raz's conclusion that the rule of law 'is essentially a negative value ... designed to minimize the harm to freedom and dignity which the law may cause in pursuit of its goals, however laudable these may be'.[9] The sense here, therefore, is that it acts as a protection against a society of chaos and abuse.

This raises the possibility of the law being treated as morally neutral and the *rule* of law potentially justifying maltreatment and *unjust* practices and policies. As Raz acknowledges, it can suggest that certainty, clarity and the need for order are superior to other qualities, such as justice or human rights or freedom. This 'thinner' conception reflects a belief that people should not suffer or be punished without a breach of a prescribed law and that all people within a system should be subject to the same laws. Such bare procedural requirements emphasise the preference for states to be governed by prescribed law rather than arbitrary decision.

Of course, at this level of value, the rule of law appears blind to context. Raz may say that 'conformity to the rule of law is also a moral virtue, it is a moral requirement when necessary to enable the law to perform useful social functions' but it appears to have little to say about the overall morality of a state or supra-state order.[10] The virtues of certainty and order through law, for instance, and attendant administrative requirements, provide little basis to condemn the extremes of an 'evil' regime. Cruel, discriminatory practices may well be prescribed by law, may well be fixed and certain, may well be followed by state authorities, and may well allow individual planning to take place, without resulting in a morally acceptable society.

Nonetheless, the value of the rule of law as initially described by Raz, amongst others, has provided the base from which other appreciations have flowed. These vary enormously but all infuse the rule of law with some degree of moral content. Procedural safeguards may well be advocated but their purpose tends to possess some moral aim. Invariably, this aim is connected with a notion (not necessarily uniform but which can be recognised as such) of 'justice' or 'rights', 'peace' or 'democracy'.[11]

---

[9] *Ibid.* at 21.   [10] *Ibid.* at 19.

[11] Some distinction can be seen here in the context of international development discourse. The rule of law as a 'global public good' was adopted in connection with an understanding of 'peace', 'security' and 'justice' in David Hamburg and Jane Holl, 'Preventing Deadly Conflict: From Global Housekeeping to Neighbourhood Watch', in Inge Paul, Isabelle Grunberg and Marc Stern (eds.), *Global Public Goods: International*

So, the principles that make up the rule of law are open to individual delineation but are all designed to provide a means for distinguishing between 'good' law and 'bad' law and indeed 'good' rule or administration and 'bad' rule or administration.[12] This approach requires systems to choose an understanding of justice that is coherent and make this the basis for law's rule. Concepts of equality, rationality, proportionality and fairness can then be imported into the notion of the rule of law.

Undoubtedly, we can identify the Western liberal project, as it were, within these articulations. So much so that for some any law that does not enjoy the list of virtues cannot be considered to be law at all. It is rendered *illegal* by reason of its failure and thus antithetical to the notion of the rule of law.[13] In this case, there can then appear to be a confusion of the values which the law might be required to help realise (or at least not contradict) and the virtues that the rule of law should possess. For some authors such as Raz, who describes the rule of law as 'one of the virtues that a legal system may possess'[14] and proceeds to itemise various principles that characterise the concept,[15] it is more a case of *fusion* than *confusion*. The rule of law is to be presented as a value to be achieved *through* adherence to principles that are ethically sound. Certainty and order tempered by qualities of practice that need to be identified and selected.

T.R.S. Allan builds on this formulation by noting qualities that should inhabit the rule of law.[16] The significance of the separation of powers, the prohibition of acts of attainder, the application of judicial constraints on the executive when it exercises judicial functions,

---

Cooperation in the 21st Century (Oxford: United Nations Development Programme/ Oxford University Press, 1999) 366–81 at 375.

[12] Paul Craig and Carol Harlow have raised these perspectives in relation to public law in general and 'global administrative law' (in Harlow's case) in particular. See, for instance, Craig, 'Constitutional Foundations, the Rule of Law and Supremacy', *Public Law* (2003) 92–111 and Harlow, 'Global Administrative Law: the Quest for Principles and Values', *European Journal of International Law* 17 (2006) 187–214.

[13] Lon Fuller's account of the 'inner morality of the law' suggests such a conclusion. See Lon Fuller, *The Morality of Law* (New Haven: Yale University Press, 1964).

[14] Raz, 'The Rule of Law and its Virtue' at 4.

[15] These are that (a) laws should be prospective, open and clear; (b) law should be relatively stable; (c) making of laws should be guided by open, stable, clear and general rules; (d) independence of judiciary must be guaranteed; (e) principles of natural justice must be observed; (f) courts should have review powers over implementation of the other principles; (g) courts should be easily accessible; (h) discretion of crime preventing agencies should not be allowed to pervert the law. Raz, 'The Rule of Law and its Virtue' 7–12.

[16] Allan 'The Rule of Law as the Rule of Reason'.

the principle of no punishment without law, the availability of judicial review, administrative procedures to prevent the abuse of power, the restriction of delegated powers where they may lead to the abuse of liberties, and freedom of speech as a key aspect of constitutional government, are all used to delineate the rule of law as an independent concept.

Other more ambitious inferences from the concept have been drawn. The International Commission of Jurists in 1959 determined that the rule of law should encompass 'the establishment of social, economic and cultural conditions [which] would permit men to live in dignity and to fulfil their legitimate aspirations'.[17] This would imply a notion that fell foul of Raz's complaint that it amounted to a full social theory thus losing its specificity as an independent value in the process. Most interpretations, however, attempt to retain modest ambitions by comparison.

Nevertheless, we still have a value that lends itself to political and moral debate although within an environment that accepts the principle that the rule of law *in some form* should be universally respected. And as with any universal notion, this provokes potential conflict with the exercise of state sovereignty. It implies that there is an ideal construction of societies without necessarily stipulating the exact nature, emphasis or content of that ideal. Whether that can be remedied through projects such as those under the banner of 'global administrative law' seems unlikely unless it is presented as an anodyne concept that does not attract significant political objection. This would then suggest preference for a formal understanding that does not promote any other value too forcefully.

Naturally this environment makes our review of the rule of law as an element of the EU's institutional ethos difficult. But the truism that the rule of law is a necessary component of legitimate governance has been accepted both rhetorically and constitutionally within the EU. Walter Hallstein, as early President of the Commission, was fond of stressing that the EEC was a 'community of states which accepts the rule of law and therefore a community based on the rule of law'.[18] This was formally adopted finally through the inclusion of the rule of law as one of the EU's founding principles under Article 6(1) TEU. It was

[17] Lucian G. Weeramantry, *The International Commission of Jurists: the Pioneering Years* (The Hague: Kluwer Law International, 2000) at 53.
[18] Walter Hallstein, Speech to the European Parliament, 'Constitutional Problems before the EEC', EC Bull 11/62 at 6.

also revealed as a 'value' in the Constitutional Treaty and the Lisbon Treaty. But given the variable understanding of the concept in theory we have to question what it means for the EU in practice. Is it limited to a formal notion, which Craig notes 'addresses the manner in which the law was promulgated, its clarity and temporal dimension' but that 'does not however pass judgment upon the content of the law'?[19] Or does it have more of a 'substantive conception', one which fuses value with virtues?

As we have seen, there exists quite a spectrum of definition that at one end sees the rule of law as a means by which government can enforce its will and at the other as a scheme of protection for the individual against arbitrary government or even the development of an idea of the 'good' for whole communities. Power is still the theme here, either as regards its deployment or its restriction. But how can this translate beyond the state? Is it inevitable that we will expect the notion to attract more of a thin than thick conception? Such an assumption would be extremely dangerous to make. The EU may not possess all the qualities of statehood but it nonetheless exercises power. It is the locus for decision- and policy-making and implementation. Its legal framework ensures that it has the force of law, which in itself must suggest a 'rule of law' of some description. For this reason it is most appropriate that the rule of law in the three dimensions I mentioned at the beginning of this chapter should be examined to see where amidst the spectrum of meaning the concept is placed within the EU.

The supranational dimension

José Manuel Barroso made a speech in March 2006 that typifies the institutional rhetoric about European law. He declared that 'assuring the coherence of the [European] project is *only* possible through the rule of law'.[20] Although he recognised the political nature of the EU with political goals, he assured his audience that the Union was not to be 'based on the spirit of methodical voluntarism'. 'In a Union of many Member States', he went on, 'there will more often than not be a multiplicity of voluntarisms, on any given issue, at any given moment. For these voluntarisms to be brought to a fruitful synthesis, rather

[19] Craig, 'Constitutional Foundations, the Rule of Law and Supremacy' at 96.
[20] José Manuel Barroso, 'Uniting in Peace: the Role of Law in the European Union' Jean Monnet Lecture, EUI Florence, 31 March 2006, available at: www.iue.it/PUB/JeanMonnetLecturesPDF/JMLBarroso2006.pdf at 4.

than remaining in a thesis and antithesis stage, we need rules, i.e. the law'.[21]

Barroso's statement echoes a narrative that takes us back to the formation of the EU. It represents the belief that the effective development of the EU requires a degree of compulsion, not by the use of force but by the use of law.[22] Lord Mackenzie Stuart, an erstwhile member of the ECJ, summed up the proposition when he said, '[o]nly by uniform and simultaneous application of Community rules can the objects of the Community be achieved'.[23] He related this to the principle of the primacy of Community law as a necessary condition to fulfil the aims of the 1957 EEC Treaty. From his perspective, the whole project was dependent on the principle that 'the Community rule can only be preserved if as much of the regulatory power as possible is expressed in terms of right and not discretion'.[24]

Of course, there was precedent within the Treaty of Rome to make one believe that this was the founding intention. The creation of a European Court of Justice, with the duty to 'ensure that in the interpretation and application of [the] Treaty the law is observed' in Article 164 (later Article 220 TEC, now Article 19 TEU), established that law should provide an important route towards achieving the Treaty's goals. The necessity of this position was very much sustained and given legal direction by the ECJ.[25] In the judgments of *van Gend en Loos* and *Costa* v. *ENEL*[26] the Court was at pains to create a legal foundation that was unique yet familiar at the same time. Unique, because it could not be described as either purely international or municipal law. Familiar, because it would be recognisable as law with all that entails regarding observance and enforceability.

So, the argument was constructed that '[b]y contrast with ordinary international treaties, the EEC treaty has created its own legal system

---

[21] *Ibid.* at 5.
[22] We have to acknowledge that there might not be any distinction between the two concepts here. The use of law as the use of force might follow where we contemplate the exercise of power to achieve certain vested interests.
[23] Lord Mackenzie Stuart, *The European Communities and the Rule of Law* (London: Stevens & Sons, 1977) at 18.
[24] *Ibid.* at 124.
[25] See, for example, Renaud Dehousse, *The European Court of Justice: the Politics of Judicial Integration* (Basingstoke: Macmillan, 1998), and Karen Alter, *Establishing the Supremacy of European Law: the Making of an International Rule of Law in Europe* (Oxford: Oxford University Press, 2001).
[26] Case 26/62 *Van Gend en Loos* v. *Nederlandse Administratie der Belastingen* [1963] ECR 1, and Case 6/64 *Flaminio Costa* v. *ENEL* [1964] ECR 585.

which, on the entry into force of the treaty, became an integral part of the legal systems of the member states and which their courts are bound to apply'.[27] There was created 'a body of law which binds both [Member States'] nationals and themselves', justified on the grounds that the 'executive force of community law cannot vary from one state to another in deference to subsequent domestic laws, without jeopardizing the attainment of the objectives of the treaty'. The 'obligations undertaken under the treaty establishing the community would not be unconditional, but merely contingent, if they could be called in question by subsequent legislative acts of the signatories'. As if this were not sufficient, the ECJ continued, stating that it

follows from all these observations that the law stemming from the treaty, an independent source of law, could not, because of its special and original nature, be overridden by domestic legal provisions, however framed, without being deprived of its character as community law and without the legal basis of the community itself being called into question.[28]

The rationale was that if the project was to work, if it was to possess any efficacy, then states would have to respect Community law in the same way as they respected law domestically. Indeed, perhaps there would have to be greater respect given the power of governments in many legal systems to amend municipal law unilaterally.

Thus, even at a time when de Gaulle and France's attitude to the then EEC in the 1960s emphasised the contingency of the project, it was professed that the ideals of integration would *only* be achieved through a uniform application of the agreed law. The Luxembourg Accords of 1966, inspired by the French to ensure Member States retained a veto over decisions affecting 'issues of vital national importance', were not to be allowed to detract from the central understanding, namely any divergence in enforcement would undermine the EU, turning it into a project that might be tasted but not necessarily consumed. Such was the interpretation of the law as a tool for integration, one that was premised on the transfer of some sovereignty away from the Member States. It did not attest, in itself, to any concept of the rule of law containing a moral core. It was functional, dependent on the objects of the Treaties, which may or may not have been compatible with principles of justice or other values. As Karen Alter concluded simplistically but

[27] *Costa* v. *ENEL.*   [28] *Ibid.*

accurately in her study of the origins of the doctrine of supremacy, 'the rule of law means that governments follow the law'.[29]

At this primary level, then, the definition of an EU rule of law appears limited. Arguably, it may satisfy one of Joseph Raz's requirements by maintaining as a quality of law its 'fixed point of reference', so as to help stabilise 'social relationships' and enable 'individual planning' in a certain environment.[30] This relies upon a primarily judicial preference for certainty and order with a view to fulfilling the aim of the Treaty, the contract, whatever that aim might happen to be. In the beginning this was defined by Article 2 EEC and the stated purpose to create a 'common market'.

We can see the judiciary's acceptance of a 'Community rule of law' in the address of M. Robert Lecourt, President of the ECJ celebrating its tenth anniversary in 1968. He noted that 'there can be no unified market without a common law, no common law without uniform interpretation, no uniform interpretation unless the common law takes precedence'.[31] There is no direct and explicit moral appeal here, or at least there is no sophisticated moral content that necessarily underpins such a pragmatic approach. Adherence to the notion of judicial review, of the separation of powers, of checks and balances, and the independence of the judiciary that appear as important characteristics of the rule of law in theory may be present but the political, or intergovernmental, nature of much of the operation of the EU told against a rule of law concept, at least vis-à-vis its relationship with Member States, that adhered to more sophisticated principles. So in *Stork* the ECJ proclaimed it was 'only required to ensure that in the interpretation and application of the treaty, and of rules laid down for implementation thereof, the law is observed'.[32]

Although the Court has grown in sophistication since this early judgment, the message remains the same in rule of law terms. In *Commission* v. *Italy* the ECJ noted that 'a Member State cannot plead provisions, practices or situations prevailing in its domestic legal order to justify failure to observe obligations arising under Community law'.[33] It has also relied on Article 10 EC Treaty (now Article 4(3) TEU after Lisbon) to require Member States to 'take all appropriate measures,

---

[29] Karen Alter, *Establishing the Supremacy of European Law* at 220.
[30] Raz, 'The Rule of Law and its Virtue'.   [31]   EC Bull 12–1968 at 23.
[32] Case 1/58 *Stork* v. *High Authority* [1958–1959] ECR 17–40 at 27.
[33] Case C-212/99 *Commission* v. *Italy* [2001] ECR I4923, para. 34 and recently confirmed in Case C-119/04 *Commission* v. *Italy* at para. 25.

whether general or particular, to ensure the fulfilment of the obligations arising out of this Treaty'. The 'fidelity principle' or principle of
'loyal cooperation' has been applied by the Court not only to enforceable EU law but also to framework decisions under the TEU suggesting
that the rule of law as a value might have wider application than a
narrow interpretation might allow.[34]

Similarly, the line of decisions that determined that it was 'inherent in the system of the Treaty' that 'the principle of liability on the
part of a Member State for damage caused to individuals as a result of
breaches of Community law for which the State is responsible' was in
essence a re-emphasis of the rule of law principle in its basic form.[35]
National rule of law arguments made to protect the sanctity of decisions of national final courts of appeal were thus subject to the overriding rule of Community law.

This reading of the constitutional construction of a rule of law has
been given credence by the way in which the Commission reports on
the application of Community law. Its Annual Report on the subject is
expressed as 'vital in terms of the rule of law generally, but it also helps
to make the principle of a Community based on the rule of law a tangible reality for Europe's citizens and economic operators'.[36] It is not
explained what this reality means. The report seems to judge the matter merely on the number of complaints received by individuals about
Member States without providing any qualitative analysis. This leaves
one with the sense that the rule of law only means national adherence
to the legislation enacted through the EU.

Even this restricted definition has to be considered in the light of further limitations. The judgments of *van Gend en Loos* and *Costa* v. *ENEL*,
often interpreted as adopting a radical and even revolutionary position
for the ECJ, also contained an inherent strain of conservatism that
reflected political realities rather than idealistic desires. *Costa* v. *ENEL*
was central to the definition of the legal edifice as 'a community of
unlimited duration, having its own institutions, its own personality, its

---

[34] See Case 105/03, *Criminal proceedings against Maria Pupino* [2005] ECR I-5285 para. 42.
[35] See variously Joined Cases C-6/90 and C-9/90 *Francovich and Others* [1991] ECR I-5357,
para. 35; Case C-392/93 *British Telecommunications* [1996] ECR I-1631, para. 38; Case
C-5/94 *Hedley Lomas* [1996] ECR I-2553, para. 24; Joined Cases C-178/94, C-179/94,
C-188/94, C-189/94 and C-190/94 *Dillenkofer and Others* [1996] ECR I-4845, para. 20; Case
C-127/95 *Norbrook Laboratories* [1998] ECR I-1531, para. 106.
[36] 23rd Annual Report from the Commission on Monitoring the Application of
Community Law (2005) COM (2006) 416 final at 3.

own legal capacity and capacity of representation on the international plane and, more particularly, real powers'.[37] *Van Gend en Loos* continued the theme by determining that the 'Community constitutes a new legal order of international law for the benefit of which the states have limited their sovereign rights'.[38] All of which testified to the new legal environment that would enable, indeed *require*, a rule of law to function and have meaning.

But with the radical came the cautious. The Court acknowledged that the transfer of powers from Member States to the 'Community' occurred 'within limited fields'. The contract between states that was the Treaty of Rome, would not tolerate a wider appreciation. Any notion of the rule of law in the EU's institutional ethos had to reflect that realisation, constraining itself through regard for the primary source of law, the Treaties.

It is from this judicial acknowledgement of political reality, and the ongoing debate about the scope of competencies distributed between the Member States and the EU, that it is possible to see the rule of law notion developing along highly ambiguous and even ironical lines. Ambiguous, because the extent of the value appears forever in flux, subject to political and even judicial negotiation. Ironic, because even the basic understanding of the rule of law as a value, steeped in notions of certainty and order, has been subject to a discourse and practice of *indeterminacy*.

Clearly much of this condition results from the *sui generis* nature of the EU. As I will repeat, it was and is not a state nor simply an international agreement. It is a hybrid creation without adequate precedent. Any rule of law concept had, on the one hand, to reflect the inherent caution that accompanied the federalist pretensions associated with the EU and, on the other, to acknowledge the shift in power structures away from the Member States to give it practical effect. The legal path had to tread between these two appreciations. Perhaps this remains the genius of the EU as it materialised through the Treaties and their application, a successful negotiation between two extremes. In rule of law terms, however, it meant that it was difficult to develop a notion that was coherent. The municipal and international versions of the concept in the abstract did not individually fit the circumstances. Even Larry Siedentop's assessment that one has to examine the understanding of

---

[37] *Costa v. ENEL.*   [38] *Van Gend en Loos* at 12.

rule of law proposals in relation to their source (from Roman law or Common law jurisidctions) cannot cope with the specificity of the EU in legal terms.[39]

Whilst we can acknowledge this *sui generis* environment and its effect on any value of the rule of law, the question remains as to how the dual sense of ambivalence and irony has developed and whether it has undermined the institutional use of the term in the relationship with the Member States. The bland assertion in Article 6 TEU that 'respect for the rule of law' was a fundamental principle of the EU demands such analysis.

Let us then examine the charge of ambivalence towards the rule of law. How has this manifested itself in the EU? We only need to sketch the extent of this condition to establish the trends. Three particular aspects are noteworthy.

First, as the EU has evolved, a constitutional system has been devised that explicitly precludes judicial control in certain spheres of activity. This was undoubtedly a product of the evolving political determination of the fundamental question, how deep should the EU go? Originally, as the Treaties confined the application of the law, it was clear that any action made in concert by the Member States within the EU structure but outside the provisions of the Treaties, could not be reviewed by the ECJ. So, for example, when the European Political Cooperation system was constructed, action taken by the Member States in its name was not of European judicial interest. This approach was endorsed constitutionally with the Single European Act and subsequently Article 46 TEU as we saw in Chapter 2. The latter confirmed that activity under the Common Foreign and Security Policy was not to be subject to judicial review. Even if measures taken by the Member States within this policy framework breached fundamental rights, there was no recourse to direct legal remedy at a European level.[40] That position was reinforced by the Constitutional Treaty and now its replacement, the Lisbon Treaty. At a time when the EU through its Member States was advancing its activities in the world, with the deployment of peace missions of one sort or another (as we saw in the previous chapter), the determination to exclude judicial scrutiny suggests the rule of Community law is narrowly construed.

[39] Larry Siedentop, *Democracy in Europe* (London: Penguin, 2000) at 225–6.

[40] For a comprehensive review of this point see, generally, Maria-Gisella Garbagnati Ketvel, 'The Jurisdiction of the European Court of Justice in Respect of the Common Foreign and Security Policy', *International Comparative Law Quarterly* 55 (2006) 77–120.

Second, despite the clear statements in relation to the doctrines of direct effect and supremacy, which have underpinned the notion of the rule of law explored above, there remains a condition of ambivalence regarding their application in practice. The doctrines remain of uncertain character. Direct effect is limited in its application constitutionally not only with regard to foreign policy but also, by reason of Article 35(5) TEU, now Article 276 of the new Treaty on the Functioning of the EU (TFEU), to measures adopted in relation to police and judicial and cooperation matters. In particular, Article 35(5) states that,

[t]he Court of Justice shall have no jurisdiction to review the validity or proportionality of operations carried out by the police or other law enforcement services of a Member State or the exercise of the responsibilities incumbent upon Member States with regard to the maintenance of law and order and the safeguarding of internal security.

The political reasons for this restriction are obvious. National security has always been one of the areas that define the limits to the incursion on sovereignty by the EU. Areas of sensitivity, as regards Member States' attitudes to their preserved sovereignty, have also been subject to the exclusion of the direct effect doctrine. Criminal law and criminal procedure were, until the Lisbon Treaty, generally outside the Community's competence, although this principle was subject to limited challenge.[41] Nonetheless, *explicit* denial of direct effect was enshrined constitutionally with regard to 'framework decisions' adopted by the Council that related to all 'approximation of laws' that the Council decided, unanimously, to implement on police or judicial matters. The now updated Article 34(2)(b) TEU determined that,

Framework decisions shall be binding upon the Member States as to the result to be achieved but shall leave to the national authorities the choice of form and methods. They shall not entail direct effect.

Since the Lisbon Treaty has come into effect this is no longer the case. Any measures taken will be subject to the normal operation of direct effect under EU law. However, Protocol 36 TFEU states that the old regime will remain in place for the next five years as a transitional position. The Commission will still not be able to take action for failure

---

[41] Case C-176/03 *Commission v. Council* judgment 13 September 2005, at para. 47. The judgment both reiterates the general rule and considers the possibility of exceptions occurring under the auspices of the EC Treaty. In that case the concern was over the imposition of criminal sanctions in relation to a framework decision related to the protection of the environment.

to implement these existing decisions. In truth though, the boundaries of this limitation were already pushed, controversially, by the case of *Pupino*.[42] This decided that national courts called upon to interpret national law in the context of police and judicial cooperation 'must do so as far as possible in the light of the wording and purpose' of a relevant framework decision 'in order to attain the result which it pursues'.[43] Whether the ECJ can sustain such an obligation in old Third Pillar matters generally (and the European Arrest Warrant in particular) despite resistance by national Constitutional Courts remains to be seen.[44]

Similarly, with the sensitive issue of immigration and asylum previously encompassed by Title IV TEC, Article 68 provided for a restriction on the role of the ECJ to give preliminary rulings in this field, allowing references only from final courts of appeal in a Member State. This was repealed by the Lisbon Treaty allowing any national court to request a preliminary ruling. However, it remains the case that the Court 'shall not have jurisdiction to rule on any measure or decision taken' by any Member State 'relating to the maintenance of law and order and the safeguarding of internal security'. In practice this relates to rules covering controls on movement across the EU's internal borders. The Commission has complained that the implication 'is to exclude any possibility of judicial review' on such matters, a threat to any notion of access to justice that otherwise seems to characterise the EU's enforcement capabilities.[45] If we take the principle of access to justice as an essential element of the rule of law, a matter that appears in most rule of law accounts, we can see that the continual resistance to scrutiny and judicial review is constraining development of the rule of law beyond its most basic definition.

Indeed, the 'difficult' areas of justice and home affairs, and foreign policy, demonstrate how the EU legal system has had to accept ambivalence towards a rule of European law as an inherent condition. This is not simply a product of a split between EU and EC law. As we have seen with the justice and home affairs matters, key aspects of a sophisticated understanding of the rule of law remain absent. The House of Lords has noted this tendency. In its 2006 Report on the European Union, it heavily

---

[42] C-105/03, *Criminal Proceedings against Maria Pupino* [2005] ECR I-5285.
[43] *Pupino* at para. 43.
[44] See *Bundesverfassungsgericht* (German Constitutional Court), Decision of 18 July 2005 (2 BvR 2236/04) on the German European Arrest Warrant Law.
[45] Commission, 'Adaptation of the Provisions of Title IV of the Treaty Establishing the European Community Relating to the Jurisdiction of the Court of Justice with a View to Ensuring more Effective Judicial Protection', COM (2006) 346 final at 6.

criticised the lack of transparency and accountability in the development of what can be termed a *cabal* of six Member States (including the UK) meeting to determine policy towards terrorism, illegal immigration and organised crime.[46] The trend to avoid scrutiny and judicial review in such matters remains a persistent and troubling critique against the EU's commitment to the rule of law.[47]

Third, we need to consider those approaches of policy that have also given credence to the charge of ambivalence. This arises from institutional rhetoric, as well as policy, that makes a virtue of uncertainty. Over the last three decades we have been treated to a plethora of value-like statements that attempt to allow for a non-uniform Union. With the successive enlargements of the 1970s and 1980s and the great political contests that have since marked the debates about *how* the EU is to develop, a discourse of flexibility or differentiation has become ever-present. Indeed, it often seems that the institutions have been at excessive pains to find new terms for the same principle. Namely, how is a union to function within a professed rule of Community law when the political scene appears to accept that Member States should be able to deviate from that law? The terminology has embraced 'opt-outs,' flexibility clauses, differentiation, specific derogations, closer-cooperation clauses, 'variable geometry', multi-speed processes. If one was to try to construct a legal order less inclined to uniformity and certainty then such rhetoric would be the hallmark. As it is, many of these processes have found favour politically, judicially and even philosophically as they seem to reflect a willingness to recognise the need for pluralism in a post-modern world. They also accept the premise that diversity implies a creative and innovative influence. But, as Neil Walker has noted, flexibility has a Janus-like quality, being

a contest between, on the one hand, those states and other political actors who favour flexibility as a way of maintaining the momentum of integration against the caution of nationalist sceptics and, on the other, those same

---

[46] House of Lords Select Committee on European Union 40th Report, 11 July 2006, online, available at: www.publications.parliament.uk/pa/ld200506/ldselect/ldeucom/221/22102.htm.

[47] See, for instance, Sionaidh Douglas-Scott, 'The Rule of Law in the European Union – Putting the Security into the Area of Freedom, Security and Justice', *European Law Review* 29:2 (2004) 219–42, and Damian Chalmers, 'Political Rights and Political Reason in European Law in Times of Stress in Wojciech Sadurski (ed.), *Political Rights under Stress in 21st Century Europe* (Oxford: Oxford University Press, 2006) 55–83.

sceptics who favour flexibility as a way of endorsing a less monolithic – and so ultimately less powerful – EU.[48]

The question for us, however, is whether the ambiguity attached to notions of flexibility or differentiation, is compatible with a coherent value of the rule of law.

If the concept is viewed as imposing unity through a uniform application of the law against Member States, then any processes that subvert that basic maxim have to be destabilising. It starts to lose what little purchase it may already have possessed. So, differentiated obligations written into the constitutional text must suggest an entrenchment of contingency. The need for a legal environment that is certain in individual states might not be damaged here, as one could argue comfortably that any national citizen is still able to discern reasonable certainty within any particular state's system. However, if certainty *across* the Union is required to give the rule of law meaning at the EU level, then variable approaches *in relation to the same root policies* must be more confusing than comforting. Planning one's affairs within such an order of regulatory distinction might still be possible but probably only for those with access to sophisticated advice and sources of information.

Looking at areas of environment, where flexibility in implementation characterises the enforcement of pollution control, social policy, which allowed the UK to opt-out of the Social Chapter, treatment of third country nationals, where the Schengen agreement allowed exemption for the UK, Ireland and Denmark, and economic and monetary union, again allowing the UK and Denmark the right not to opt in, a constitutional acceptance of pragmatism rather than law seems to operate as a governing rule.[49] Similarly, the negotiations that saw the Lisbon Treaty enable the UK not to be bound by the EU Charter of Fundamental Rights has produced a classic demarcation that might well cause confusion and tension for those whose affairs cross borders.

---

[48] Neil Walker, 'Flexibility within a Metaconstitutional Frame: Reflections on the Future of Legal Authority in Europe', in Gráinne de Búrca and Joanne Scott (eds.), *Constitutional Change in the EU: From Uniformity to Flexibility* (Oxford: Hart, 2000) 9–30 at 10.

[49] For a review of some of this history see Maria Fletcher, 'Schengen, the European Court of Justice and Flexibility Under the Lisbon Treaty: Balancing the United Kingdom's "Ins" and "Outs"', *European Constitutional Law Review* 5 (2009) 71–98.

But perhaps the most significant indication of contingency with regard to the Member States has occurred with the adoption of the principle of subsidiarity. We need not interrogate this principle too deeply here, mainly because that would warrant a work of its own.[50] For the present, the notion that action should be taken by the Community 'only if and insofar as the objectives of the proposed action cannot be sufficiently achieved by the Member States' and that any action by the Community 'should not go beyond what is necessary to achieve the objectives' of the Treaties, is political recognition that a centralised interference in the affairs of Member States should be limited.[51] Taking decisions as close as possible to the people underpins the philosophy. Whether or not this is a product of pragmatic politics, in other words one based on the assumption that without such an approach the EU might find increasing public disaffection with its ability to intercede in people's lives, the fact remains that the concept of the rule of law from a point of view of certainty has been constitutionally limited. It is *uncertainty* on an inter-state level that imbues the adoption of subsidiarity as a necessary characteristic of governance.

Here, we find a theoretical tension with other values. The desire to enhance democratic processes by bringing decisions closer to the people whom they affect (a significant justification for subsidiarity) may not improve issues of legal certainty, particularly in a globalised economy where notions of 'local' are becoming more difficult to contain. Admittedly, as we have seen, Walter Hallstein noted in 1962 the constitutional dilemma of creating a 'community based on the law' whilst recognising the importance of the problem of 'dividing and properly apportioning its powers'.[52] But whether or not subsidiarity has been conceived as an exercise in efficiency or democracy, or pragmatic politics (or, of course, a combination of all three) there is an undoubted effect upon the nature of the rule of law as a result. It suggests that Community law has to be subject to variable application in order to make it acceptable across the EU landscape.

The Commission identified the parameters of this approach in its White Paper on European Governance in 2001. In relation to the linked principles of proportionality and subsidiarity it declared that:

---

[50] Indeed, such works have already been undertaken. See, for instance, Antonio Estella, *The EU Principle of Subsidiarity and its Critique* (Oxford: Oxford University Press, 2002).
[51] See Article 5 TEU (formerly Article 5 TEC).
[52] Walter Hallstein, Speech on 'Constitutional Problems before the EEC', EC Bull 11/62 at 67.

[f]rom the conception of policy to its implementation, the choice of the level at which action is taken (from EU to local) and the selection of the instruments used must be in proportion to the objectives pursued. This means that before launching an initiative, it is essential to check systematically (a) if public action is really necessary, (b) if the European level is the most appropriate one, and (c) if the measures chosen are proportionate to those objectives.[53]

Does this suggest ambiguity? One caveat provided by the Commission to this new environment of flexibility would suggest not. The White Paper made clear that there 'should be more flexibility in the means provided for implementing legislation and programmes with a strong territorial impact, *provided the level playing field at the heart of the internal market can be maintained*' (emphasis added).[54] The original conception of the rule of law as an instrument for constructing a common market seems to have been retained. The remainder of the White Paper also appears to support this interpretation. Its advocacy for transparency and participation is declared as 'not about institutionalising protest' but rather about 'more effective policy shaping'.[55] I will consider the impact of this further below but as regards the relationship with the Member States we can see that the EU's focus is to ensure that the law (however that is created) is actually implemented. This means a recognition that in order to achieve a working internal market some sense must prevail; sense that is of the need to accept local sensitivities and interests. Consequently, an approach to harmonisation has been seen to develop that, according to Catherine Barnard, combines 'the benefits of centralization together with local autonomy' relying upon 'a mix of centralized and decentralized regulation together with the involvement of a wide range of actors, both public and private'.[56]

None of this would suggest an ambivalence concerning the rule of law. Rather, it might be interpreted as a way of ensuring that the rule of law, in its highly limited conception as a mechanism of achieving integration, was not subverted. By embracing diversity and 'voice' the chance of achieving acceptance of regulation would be enhanced. But of course, if the discourse of the EU attempts to develop a more sophisticated notion of the rule of law the charge of ambivalence becomes more forceful. Multi-level governance becomes the alternative name

---

[53] Commission White Paper on European Governance COM (2001) 428 final at 10–11.
[54] *Ibid.* at 13.   [55] *Ibid.* at 15.
[56] Catherine Barnard, *The Substantive Law of the EU* (Oxford: Oxford University Press, 2004) at 535.

for a rule of law that bows institutionally to a rule of politics.[57] It certainly bows to state interest at times of tension, as was evident from the BSE crisis, when despite EU decisions France was able to ignore relevant regulations in 2002 in order to maintain illegal bans on British beef imports.[58] The economic meltdown of 2008/9 also promises to produce unilateral actions regardless of well-entrenched regulations of monetary union.

These three forms of ambivalence with regard to the basic force of the rule of law in the EU vis-à-vis the Member States, might well imply that the concept is developing along creative paths, enabling it to evolve in a more effective and politically satisfying way. But equally it might testify to the inherent suspicion some might have for EU protestations that the rule of law is a founding principle of the Union.

But before I develop this further let us consider the second problem of 'irony'. How does this manifest itself?

I want to take one significant example; the issue of *enforcing* the value of the rule of law through Articles 6(1) and 7 TEU. To appreciate the story we have to return to the late 1990s when the EU was faced with the prospect of enlargement and the need to establish the principles upon which membership should be determined. The rule of law had been a consistent requirement in this respect, as we have already seen. The Treaty of Amsterdam in 1997 provided it with constitutional weight through the introduction of Article 6(1) TEU which declared that the 'Union is founded on the principles of liberty, democracy, respect for human rights and fundamental freedoms, and the rule of law, principles which are common to the Member States'. A new Article 7 was also included to provide the authority for action in the event of a 'serious and persistent breach' of Article 6(1). Member States could have their rights under the TEU suspended.

The provision was almost immediately found wanting. The story has been told on numerous occasions.[59] Following national elections in

---

[57] For an account of multi-level governance see Liesbet Hooghe and Gary Marks, *Multi-Level Governance and European Integration* (Lanham, MD: Rowman & Littlefield, 2001).

[58] For a critical reflection on the impotence of the EU in this respect see, for instance, Jill Wakefield, 'BSE: a Lesson in Containment? Avoiding Responsibility and Accountability in the Compensation Action', *European Law Review* 27 (2002) 426–44.

[59] For good accounts of the Austrian affair see, Gráinne de Búrca, 'Beyond the Charter: how Enlargement has Enlarged the Human Rights Policy of the European Union', *Fordham International Law Journal* 27 (2004) 679–714 and Heather Berit Freeman, 'Austria: the 1999 Parliamentary Elections and the European Union Members' Sanctions', *Boston College International and Comparative Law Review* (2002) 109–24.

Austria, the Freedom Party (FPO), a self-consciously nationalist right wing 'populist' party, polled just over 25 per cent of the votes. This made them the second largest party. They then entered into negotiation with the third placed party (the Austrian People's Party or OVP) to form a working coalition government. This set in train a massive European-wide diplomatic reaction. Why? The leader of the FPO, Jorg Haider, and others in his party, had a certain reputation for making unpalatable public statements about immigration (Haider's Vienna campaign slogan was 'stop foreignization') and ambiguous comments about the Nazi regime (Haider had referred to concentration camps as 'punitive camps' suggesting, however obliquely, that they were somehow legitimate institutions of state-sanctioned criminal punishment).[60] Such inflammatory statements all seemed to echo xenophobic and intolerant messages from the Nazi era.

The other Member States reacted fairly quickly. But it was soon apparent that the EU, even with the new Articles 6 and 7 in place, could not be deployed. After all, there had been no serious or persistent breach of any of the now governing principles. Indeed, it would have been difficult to contend that any breach, serious or otherwise, had taken place. The only real complaint was against the views expressed and therefore the *possibility* of state-sanctioned discrimination and racism arising.

Faced with no valid avenue of protest through the EU, the fourteen other Member States committed themselves to diplomatic sanctions. They agreed to suspend official contact with an Austrian government that included the FPO, not to support Austrian candidates seeking placement at international organisations and only to receive Austrian ambassadors at a technical level.[61] No economic sanctions were introduced. No other direct measures seemed available.

The EU Presidency instituted an independent inquiry, which eventually produced a report that confirmed that the new Austrian government had *not* embarked on widespread racist practices or committed serious human rights abuses of any kind. However, the Report recommended changes to the Article 7 TEU procedures to enable the EU to respond more effectively to *potential* as well as actual significant breaches of principle.[62]

---

[60] See Freeman 'Austria'.

[61] Report by Martti Ahtisaari, Jochen Frowein and Marcelino Oreja, 8 September 2000, online, available at: www.eumc.at/general/report-A/report-en.pdf.

[62] *Ibid.*

Amendments were duly made in the Treaty of Nice 2000. Article 7(1) TEU now provided that

On a reasoned proposal by one third of the Member States, by the European Parliament or by the Commission, the Council, acting by a majority of four fifths of its members after obtaining the assent of the European Parliament, may determine that there is a *clear risk of a serious breach* by a Member State of principles mentioned in Article 6(1), and address appropriate recommendations to that State [emphasis added].

Article 7(2) retained the existing provision enabling the heavier imposition of sanctions in the event of an actual serious and persistent breach.

How do these laudable attempts to provide a system of enforcement for breaches of the rule of law, as one of the constitutional principles, provoke a charge of irony? The answer lies in the *method* of enforcement adopted, an issue central to the notion of the very principle purportedly being protected. The Commission explored the theme in its Communication on Article 7 in 2003 in an attempt to 'examine the conditions for activating the procedures' of that article.[63] By noting that Article 7 determinations of a breach are wholly within the discretion of the Council, regardless of the proposals that may be put to it, the Commission emphasised the 'political nature' of the provision. It referred to the possibility of a 'diplomatic solution to the situation' whatever that might be.[64] Dialogue was identified as the key. In full understanding of the sensitivity of the situation, the Commission committed itself, prior to making any proposal instituting Article 7(1) or (2) procedures, to contact the Member State concerned to 'present the facts' and seek its opinion.[65] This informal contact was not to preclude further action but it clearly showed intent to keep the matter under close diplomatic reins before having to go 'public'. The temptation for any issue thoroughly damaging to the Union to be kept from outside scrutiny remains a valid option for the Commission.

The Parliament's Committee on Constitutional Affairs did not appreciate this possibility from a rule of law perspective. It maintained that

all decisions taken under Article 7 ... [needed] to be as credible as possible to European citizens. Diplomatic consultations and other political talks

[63] Communication from the Commission to the Council and the European Parliament on Article 7 of the Treaty on European Union: Respect for and Promotion of the Values on which the Union is Based; COM (2003) 606 final at 3.
[64] *Ibid.* para. 1.2 at 6.   [65] *Ibid.* para. 2.2 at 10.

notwithstanding, the procedures must therefore be transparent, understandable and open to the public.[66]

Whether such a view would in practice sway the Commission is difficult to judge. But certainly the Commission's preference for treating these sensitive matters 'behind closed doors' runs counter to any rule of law conception that saw transparency as a key ingredient.

But perhaps of greater concern in this context, and where the sense of irony appears strengthened, is the constitutional provision of Article 46(e) TEU (now Article 269 TFEU) which limits judicial scrutiny to the 'purely procedural stipulations' of Article 7. The regime of enforcement of the rule of law has all the hallmarks of a system anathema to that very principle. As things stand, we might never learn what system has been instituted, if indeed any system has been structured at all. To date neither the Commission nor the Parliament has been inclined to incite Article 7 proceedings whether in relation to the actions of the UK in Iraq, for instance – a matter that could have provoked significant attention in relation to possible breaches of the rule of law as well as human rights[67] – or various Member States regarding the case of extraordinary rendition, to which I referred at the beginning of this chapter.

Will anything change now the Lisbon Treaty is in force? Certainly there will be greater clarity about the connection between the Union's declared 'values' including the rule of law and its objectives. The stated aim to promote its values suggests a stronger commitment might arise. But, in essence, little will be altered. The Article 7 procedure and substantive jurisdiction has been kept away from the ECJ and is likely to remain in the shadowy, non-judicially supervised form it currently possesses.

But will this illustration of the charge of irony be tempered by our assessment of the role of the rule of law in its *institutional* and *international* spheres? This will be discussed in the succeeding sections. Suffice to note that the rule of law does not operate in terms of a classic model regarding the relationship with the Member States. That is perhaps necessary given the unique nature of that relationship. We might be witnessing the evolution of a rule of law notion that is broad

---

[66] European Parliament Committee on Constitutional Affairs, Report on the Commission's communication on Article 7 TEU A5–0227/2004, para. 11(d) at 8.

[67] I explored this possibility in detail in, 'The Indifferent Gesture: Article 7 TEU, the Fundamental Rights Agency and the UK's Invasion of Iraq', *European Law Review* 31 (2006) 4–28.

but constrained, ambitious but pragmatic, spoken in idealistic terms but suffused with political sensitivity.

The institutional dimension

The question for this section is how the rule of law manifests itself in the relationship between the EU institutions and individuals? Traditionally, the qualities of judicial review and of access to justice have been crucial in assessing the scope of the rule of law for the EU. They partially reflect, indeed, the EU's own identification of those virtues considered capable of transforming European governance into 'good' European governance. The Commission's 2001 White Paper on Governance notes five crucial attributes: openness, participation, accountability, effectiveness and coherence.[68]

But whichever particular virtues one chooses, the objective point of departure would always be the principle confirmed by the ECJ in 1983 in *Les Verts* where the ECJ determined that the EU was

a community based on the rule of law, inasmuch as neither its member states nor its institutions can avoid a review of the question whether the measures adopted by them are in conformity with the basic constitutional charter, the treaty.[69]

The decision reflects one of the persistent attributes ascribed to a system that respects the rule of law. It is a general tenet of constitutional and administrative law throughout Europe that decisions of government should be subject to review by an independent judiciary. Although the EU clearly prides itself as operating in accordance with this virtue, we have already seen how such a statement is subject to much qualification obtaining any review within the Third Pillar. Until the Lisbon Treaty came into force, obtaining any review within the Third Pillar was subject to fundamental restriction if not denial. The actions and decisions taken by the Council under the Common Foreign and Security Policy, and in certain matters relating to justice and home affairs, still reveal a significant constraint on the possibility of judicial scrutiny.

The Commission has been conscious of such limitations and endeavoured to redress the matter with respect, at least, to the old EC Treaty parts dealing with 'visas, asylum, immigration and other policies related to the free movement of persons'. Its self-professed aim was to ensure consistency which, it claimed, required '[u]niform interpretation

---

[68] Commission, White Paper on European Governance COM (2001) 428 final at 10.
[69] Case 294/83 *"Les Verts"* v. *Parliament* para. 23.

of the body of legislation that has now been accumulated',[70] an aim very much in accordance with the attitude of the ECJ. Such consistency remains absent in this policy field. Similarly, 'effective judicial protection', noted by the Commission as 'one of the fundamental rights that help to define the very concept of the rule of law' was notoriously prejudiced here in relation to the limited jurisdiction offered by Article 68(1) EC Treaty. This provision only enabled reference to the ECJ for a preliminary ruling under Article 234 EC Treaty if national remedies, in effect, were exhausted. As the Commission pointed out, this might be impossible for people without the necessary resources. Again the exclusion of review for measures that relate to the 'safeguarding of internal security under Article 62(1)' was condemned. For the Commission, this in practice encompassed all 'Community rules for the abolition of controls on persons at the Union's internal borders'.[71]As we have seen, however, the restriction in Article 68(1) has been repealed, although 68(2) remains in place through Article 276 TFEU.

When *Les Verts* held that the EC Treaty 'established a complete system of legal remedies and procedures designed to permit the court of justice to review the legality of measures adopted by the institutions' it had not envisaged the restrictions that would be implemented in the sphere of justice and home affairs.[72] It might well be true that there have been a range of procedures available for reviewing the acts of the institutions. But in this crucial area, one that has been growing in importance in the advent of heightened fears of terrorist acts, judicial review has had limited purchase. Was this an aberration in relation to an otherwise consistent acceptance of this aspect of the rule of law? The amendments introduced by the Lisbon Treaty, which extended judicial review provisions to all previously Third Pillar issues, would suggest so.

But there is still little doubt that there has been unwillingness for EU institutions to interfere, judicially or otherwise, in matters of national security. I noted this above in relation to the supranational dimension of the rule of law. Articles 296–298 EC Treaty (now Articles 346–348 TFEU), in effect, allow states to take measures in the interests of national security, although this may be subject to review by the Court in camera at the request of the Commission or another Member

---

[70] Communication from the Commission on Adaptation of the Provisions of Title IV of the Treaty Establishing the European Community Relating to the Jurisdiction of the Court of Justice with a View to Ensuring more Effective Judicial Protection, Brussels, 28.6.2006 COM (2006) 346 final at 4.

[71] *Ibid.* at 6.   [72] *Les Verts* para. 23.

State. That is hardly surprising. It is an example of where the rule of law has been limited by reason of the partial transfer only of sovereignty to the EU.

But is there detectable a tendency for the Council, as an institution rather than a conglomeration of individual states, to enshrine this national interest at the Union level? Is the rule of law also restricted in terms of the possibility of review?

Recent cases have suggested that this might be a state of affairs arising in the wake of the various terrorist atrocities since 2001. Following the attacks in New York and Washington on 9/11, there was an understandable reaction by both Member States individually and collectively through the EU to do everything in their power to combat the perceived terrorist threat. A strategy was devised at Union level, however, that demonstrated the ability of the institutions to avoid the implications of an *effective* rule of law by directing its activities through those avenues of foreign and security policy, on the one hand, and police cooperation policy, on the other. Both areas have had limited opportunities for individuals to seek judicial review on actions taken. The then operative Network of Independent Experts on Fundamental Rights highlighted, in 2003, the fact that 'judicial controls are still very inadequate in the current institutional balance'.[73]

This has been most evident with regard to certain measures applied against people suspected of terrorist links. The method of action by the EU has been Common Positions under Article 15 (now Article 29) TEU. However, as action was deemed necessary within the legal parameters of the European Community to achieve enforcement across the Union Council regulations had to be instituted. This enabled legal challenges to be taken on the basis of the invalidity of these acts and their breach of various human rights. These all failed before the Court of First Instance.[74] But when the case of *Kadi* came before the ECJ, the Court was most willing to reinforce the necessity for judicial review even if this meant contravening a demand made by UN Security Council Resolution.[75] The Court repeated that review 'of the validity of any Community measure in the light of fundamental rights must

---

[73] EU Network of Independent Experts on Fundamental Rights, 'The Balance between Freedom and Security in the Response by the European Union and its Member States to the Terrorist Threat' 2003 at 9.

[74] See, for instance, Case C-266/05 *Jose Maria Sison* v. *Council*.

[75] Conjoined cases C-402/05 P and C-415/05 P *Yassin Abdullah Kadi and Al Barakaat International Foundation* v. *Council*, Judgment of the Court (Grand Chamber), 3 September 2008.

be considered to be the expression, in a community based on the rule of law, of a constitutional guarantee stemming from the EC Treaty as an autonomous legal system which is not to be prejudiced by an international agreement'.[76]

Nonetheless, we need to read this rhetoric in the light of actual sanctions that can be taken against the Council in particular for breaches of general principles of law. From preliminary rulings to actions for annulment, from references to the Ombudsman to encouraging the Commission to take action against particular Member States, the EU certainly *appears* to provide processes of review that are far reaching. But historically these are exceptions. The institutional structure, traditionally, has accepted that Member States acting in the Council should be subject to scrutiny only on very restricted occasions. The Union has possessed that character from its inception. However unpalatable, though, it was considered necessary that the workings of the Council should not be open to scrutiny. Although legislation could be challenged, the rule exercised through the Council was not to be open to public examination.

It must also be acknowledged that there are practical limitations in relation to judicial review in general. Access to justice issues stretch further than ensuring access to courts. Those rules that limit the rights of individuals to bring actions challenging the legality of institutional acts under Article 230 EC Treaty (now Article 263 TFEU) have been historically subject to criticism as being too restrictive.[77] So too have been the cost implications of litigation. And to this we would have to add the complexity of legislation and the differing methods by which it is implemented. The whole structure has been a lawyer's paradise. That some successes have been achieved for certain causes of social justice (notably sex equality in employment relationships) masks the generally restricted possibilities that Europe offers.

But perhaps this is not the most significant area of tension vis-à-vis the rule of law. Has the EU developed a system of decision-making in general that through its very structure obviates the role if not rule of law? The evolution of soft law methods may well represent an innovative means by which politically different positions can be accommodated without derailing movement towards deeper integration but

---

[76] *Ibid.* at para. 316.
[77] See, for instance, Laurence W. Gormley, 'Judicial Review in EC and EU Law – Some Architectural Malfunctions and Design Improvements?' European Law Lecture 2000, Durham European Law Institute.

they also attract criticism that they deny accountability and justicability.[78] By attempting to avoid political sensitivities highlighted in hard law processes (legislation) such approaches as the Open Method of Coordination (OMC) provide a new strain of governance that in effect sees any rule of law largely impacting at national, not EU, level.[79] The OMC was devised at the Lisbon European Council in March 2000.[80] The aim was to move towards convergence not harmonisation of laws by national implementation following agreed guidelines. Timetables for implementation would be set, benchmarks constructed, targets agreed and monitoring instituted to establish 'mutual learning processes'.[81] Governments are persuaded to coordinate policies. But the underlying lack of democratic participation at European level and the absence of any possible intervention by EU law ensure that any notion of the rule of law fails to take hold in this arena.

That may well be both legitimate and efficient. National systems are then left to provide the necessary rule of law safeguards. Arbitrary decisions, or ones which violate 'human dignity', need only be addressed through national processes. In that sense there is no challenge to the rule of law as a fundamental value. But the whole system inspires the thought that the lack of democratic credentials and the absence of possible judicial scrutiny can lead to unjust policies applied to individuals becoming so entrenched *before* they reach national legislatures that the opportunity for the rule of law to operate has to be highly constrained.

The above assessment has, of course, been focused on the internal dimension. But if we are to learn what the concept *might* mean in the EU's hands we now have to examine its application externally.

The international dimension

The history of the approach to the promotion of the rule of law in the EU's external affairs is variable. For much of its early years reference to the concept was rare. But the end of the Cold War seemed to unearth

[78] See David M. Trubek, Patrick Cottrell and Mark Nance, '"Soft Law," "Hard Law," and European Integration: Toward a Theory of Hybridity', *Jean Monnet Working Paper* (2005) 02/05.

[79] For one review of this method see Claudio Radielli, 'The Open Method of Coordination: a New Governance Architecture for the European Union?', *Swedish Institute for European Policy Studies Reports* (2003) 1, online, available at: www.sieps.su.se/_pdf/Publikationer/CR20031.pdf.

[80] Lisbon European Council Presidency Conclusions March 2000.

[81] *Ibid.* point 37.

an extraordinarily rich ethical appreciation. As seen in Chapter 2, the EU's external policies had the straightjacket of power politics loosened and a moral dimension quickly inserted. The rhetoric of 'good governance' was adopted that encompassed respect for the rule of law as a key element. This was in stark contrast to the vapid rhetoric that had preceded it. As with human rights and democracy, the rule of law appeared within the language of defining Europe's distinctive character but did not seem to possess much purpose when it came to international affairs.

Even after the Berlin Wall was dismantled, it still took some time for the mantra-like adherence to good governance to acquire some substance. The term may have been employed in cooperation agreements, in accession procedures, and in development operations but it was only in 1998 that a substantive outline of what the rule of law actually consisted became available. In that year, the Commission issued a communication that identified the components of the concept. They included the means of recourse enabling individual citizens to defend their rights; a legislature respecting and giving full effect to human rights; an independent judiciary; a legal system guaranteeing equality before the law; and an effective executive enforcing the law.[82]

There has since been a deluge of documents that have purported to clarify, expand upon and generally give substance to the notion. With each text, the inextricable link between human rights, democracy and the rule of law has become increasingly solidified. So, for instance, Council Regulations 975/1999 and 976/1999, which determined the legitimate scope of activity by the EU in its relations with Central and Eastern Europe and developing countries, fashioned an understanding of the rule of law as an element of 'democratisation' processes. Specifically included were

(a) upholding the independence of the judiciary and strengthening it, and support for a humane prison system; support for constitutional and legislative reform; support for initiatives to abolish the death penalty;

(b) promoting the separation of powers, particularly the independence of the judiciary and the legislature from the executive, and support for institutional reforms;

---

[82] Commission, Communication to the Council and Parliament 1998 COM (98) 146.

(c)   promoting good governance, particularly by supporting administrative accountability and the prevention and combating of corruption;

(d)   supporting national efforts to separate civilian and military functions, training civilian and military personnel and raising their awareness of human rights.[83]

Tautological in some respects (promoting good governance would naturally have encompassed democracy and the rule of law), general in others (promoting the separation of powers) and very specific in yet others (support for initiatives to abolish the death penalty) reflected the amorphous nature of the rule of law in this context.

The Commission also declared that 'primacy of the law is a fundamental principle of any democratic system seeking to foster and promote rights, whether civil and political or economic, social and cultural'.[84] This had, therefore, to 'shape the structure of the State and the prerogatives of the various powers'.[85]

On the basis of these institutional statements, various arms of the EU have drawn on the concept to direct policy and practice. So for instance, EuropeAid has now produced a handbook on promoting good governance that attempts to provide greater definition to the rule of law.[86] It is worth quoting in full, although one must acknowledge the informal, bureaucratic formulation that separates it from a document of governance in itself. Nonetheless, it contributes to the sense of institutional narrative that has been developed on the subject of the rule of law in the external.

A country operates under the 'rule of law' when it has: a legislature that enacts laws which respect the constitution and human rights; an independent judiciary; effective, independent and accessible legal services; a legal system guaranteeing equality before the law; a prison system respecting the human person; a police force at the service of the law; an effective executive which is capable of enforcing the law and establishing the social and economic conditions necessary for life in society, and which is itself subject to the law; a military that operates under civilian control within the limits of the constitution.[87]

---

[83] See Council Regulation (EC) Nos. 975 and 976/1999. Updated, but without any substantive or relevant change, by Regulations (EC) Nos. 2240/2004.

[84] Commission, Communication to the Council and Parliament 'Democratisation, the Rule of Law, Respect for Human Rights and Good Governance: the Challenges of the Partnership between the European Union and the ACP States' (COM) 98/146 at 5.

[85] *Ibid.*

[86] Commission, EU Handbook on Promoting Good Governance in EC and Development Cooperation 2006, online, available at: ec.europa.eu/comm/europeaid/projects/eidhr/pdf/themes-gg-handbook_En.pdf.

[87] *Ibid.* at 57.

There are clear parallels here with the United Nations discourse.[88] For the EU, the development context seems to have provoked a widening of the rule of law concept into all forms of governance and government. Reference to an 'executive ... capable of ... establishing the social and economic conditions necessary for life in society' in this particular rhetorical version seems to abandon any *thin* notion of rule of law and exchange it for one that is transformatory in nature. Any scheme or programme could be incorporated into such a vision. The only restriction would be the ideology of the observer/donor. What is 'necessary' would have to be subjective, something the rule of law discourse, particularly that purveyed as a 'global good' by international agencies almost without restriction or even critique, suggests is not the case. As with human rights, the suggestion is that the rule of law is *known* and accepted as a universally applicable value.

The questions that the handbook then considers, and indeed the range of projects instituted under the Commission's development portfolio, however, suggest a more constrained although still wide-ranging approach. Flights of fancy, into the means by which certain forms of social organisation through government might be provided, are kept outside the rule of law sphere. But questions concerning the level of physical safety, crime and its detection rates, accessibility to civil and criminal justice, efficiency of the justice system, fight against corruption, observation of due process, alternative mediation and dispute resolution availability, the penal regime, and mechanisms for review of law and legal services, are all posed to help direct project construction. Although these speak to *a* quality of life, or important aspects of it that might be affected by law or the legal process, it would be hard to equate them with *all* those social *and* economic conditions one might

---

[88] Kofi Anan, when Secretary General, was keen to universalise a concept of the rule of law, albeit within the context of conflict or post-conflict societies. The definition produced in his 2004 report provided that the rule of law, 'refers to a principle of governance in which all persons, institutions and entities, public and private, including the State itself, are accountable to laws that are publicly promulgated, equally enforced and independently adjudicated, and which are consistent with international human rights norms and standards. It requires, as well, measures to ensure adherence to the principles of supremacy of law, equality before the law, accountability to the law, fairness in the application of the law, separation of powers, participation in decision-making, legal certainty, avoidance of arbitrariness and procedural and legal transparency'. United Nations Secretary General, 'The Rule of Law and Transitional Justice in Conflict and Post-conflict Societies; Report of the Secretary-General 2004' at para. 6.

deem 'necessary'. For instance, issues of healthcare and education are not highlighted as priorities for consideration within a legal framework. The protection of 'vulnerable groups' is raised but not in the context of government-led social arrangement.

Projects actually delivered under the rule of law rubric are also fairly conservative in their content. The self-styled 'rule of law mission' in Georgia, for instance, sets familiar parameters for activity. The Council identified it as a creature of the European Defence and Security Policy and noted that it

will support the authorities in addressing urgent challenges in the judicial system, in particular the criminal justice system. Furthermore, the mission will assist in developing a co-ordinated overall Georgian approach to the legal reform process in full complementarity with current EU assistance.[89]

'Good law making seminars' for Baltic States, the administration of justice in Armenia, promoting understanding of the rule of law in Russia, and justice for all in Rwanda, were just some of the relevant projects that plied a specifically law-oriented approach to governance issues.[90] Training, reform, and management of the judicial system were significant objects deemed acceptable under the rule of law heading.

The sense of such project definition is that the rule of law discourse possesses a much more restricted application in practice than some of the rhetoric might suggest. The danger of this type of discourse that tries to act as an all-encompassing concept is that it reduces the intelligibility of the rule of law. It might include anything that observers, in this case the EU institutions, wished to promote from time to time. And indeed, something of the variable nature applied by the Commission to the ill-defined rule of law, would suggest that this danger is realised. In EuropeAid's 2006 annual work programme the objectives advanced included the 'progressively restrictive use of the death penalty and its eventual universal abolition'.[91] Undoubtedly a worthy aim but naturally

---

[89] Council, Press Release on 2591st Council Meeting, External Relations, 14 June 2004 at 14, online, available at: ue.eu.int/ueDocs/cms_Data/docs/pressData/en/gena/80952.pdf.

[90] These projects are samples from a multitude of financially supported programmes under the European Initiative for Democracy and Human Rights in 2000. See Compendium at: ec.europa.eu/comm/europeaid/projects/eidhr/pdf/compendium2000macro.pdf.

[91] Commission, European Initiative for Democracy and Human Rights Annual Work Programme 2006.

linking abolition of the death penalty directly with the rule of law suggests a 'value-judgment' on the concept rather than a reflection of its natural meaning. Similarly in the same programme the objective of supporting an effective functioning of the International Criminal Court seems to redirect the rule of law, most commonly associated with national governmental administration and brings into play the much more amorphous idea of an 'international' rule of law.

None of this is to suggest that the work undertaken by the EU in this field should be subject to criticism. It is to question the uncertainty of the concept in the external dimension. But perhaps the most significant test for its relevance as a part of the EU's institutional ethos would be at the cusp of admission. How has the rule of law been treated as a component of the enlargement process and the scrutiny applied to applicant states?

The Copenhagen Criteria of 1993 included rule of law as a necessary condition for applicant states to gain admission to the Union. This was phrased in the context of 'stable institutions' that could guarantee the rule of law as well as democracy and human rights. Each state accepted as a potential candidate would be subject to examination to determine how these criteria were or were not fulfilled. However, if we look at some of the matters that have been inspected we can perhaps understand how the rule of law manifests itself in the institutional understanding of the concept both externally in this case and indeed internally.

A recent example appears in the progress report of Croatia in 2005, which follows the familiar format adopted for all other applicants by addressing the rule of law in the context of the 'political criteria'.[92] It scrutinises the rule of law with democracy so it is difficult to identify where the boundaries lie. Nevertheless, if we ignore issues of parliament and elections, we are left with 'public administration', the civilian control of the armed forces, police reform, the operation of ombudsmen, the role and structure of the judicial system, the functioning of the judiciary (noted as particularly inefficient), and anti-corruption policy, as the accentuated issues.[93] The sense is that the parameters of investigation, and therefore definition, are determined by association with the processes of law rather than some clear classification.

[92] Commission, Croatia Progress Report 2005 COM (2005) 561 final.
[93] *Ibid.* 12–17.

This last point is supported by the approach adopted in the Commission's handbook for assessing the rule of law in a development context. By noting the 'strong linkages to the other good governance components' it proceeds to remark that for human rights the concern is with 'the treatment of human beings during a legal process (from detention, trial and penalties)', for democracy it is that 'governments are subject to the rule of law' and that for public administration 'it is important for a well functioning legal system that all citizens, including the public service, are subject to the rule of law'.[94] That this should then draw in notions of transparency and public participation is hardly surprising now that the EU has itself identified these issues as worthy of implementation within its own system of governance, an innovation, it has to be said, of fairly recent vintage.

The external promotion of the rule of law has not therefore developed along a readily understood line. An international rule of law may have appeared of interest (in terms of adherence to the UN Charter) but the focus has been upon purveying a model that is municipal in scope, reflects a Western European approach to the organisation of society based on a centralised legal system, and that sees law as the method by which a system can be judged for its worthiness. Worthy that is for admission to Europe or Europe's support.

Conclusion

Where does this review lead us? Is the approach in the EU indicative of what Timothy Endicott has described as the 'impossibility' of the rule of law?[95] Does it suggest a valorisation of vagueness and variable application so as to enhance the EU institutions' ability to act without undue constraint in a highly volatile and complex political and legal environment? Is the institutional ethos conditioned to advocate for the concept internationally yet recognise its debilitating tendencies when political solutions are required? Does the rule of law only extend to enforcing the European project rather than reflect a more expansive and idealistic vision for social change in Europe? These questions are central to an appreciation of the value of the rule of law in the EU.

---

[94] Commission, 'EU Handbook on Promoting Good Governance in EC and Development Cooperation'.

[95] Timothy Endicott, 'The Impossibility of the Rule of Law', *Oxford Journal of Legal Studies* 19 (1999) 1–18.

If they are answered in the affirmative then an ironic and indeterminate condition has been embraced. But can we be so definite in our analysis?

The key problem is, as we have seen, that European law possesses different purposes depending upon context. It moves from the international setting to the domestic, altering the depth of its appreciation of law as it travels. A coherent conception of the rule of law is continually under pressure despite its constitutional identification as an unqualified principle. T.R.S. Allan proposed that the rule of law should be interpreted as constituting a 'bulwark against the deprivation of liberty through the exercise of arbitrary power' and 'encompassing principles of procedural fairness and legality, equality and proportionality'.[96] It does not require a pre-ordained theory of justice to be applied but does require that 'government should adhere faithfully and consistently to some coherent conception of justice'.[97] This should be open to 'rational public debate and scrutiny'.[98] There must be significant concern that Allan's central requirements remain largely unfulfilled in the EU.

Indeed, in terms of the relationship with the Member States there is a strong sense of the rule of law operating as a means of ensuring the Project of European governance, integration in other words, is not undermined. Uniformity of application of agreed decisions is necessary if the Project is to be sustainable. This has not been with a view to fulfil the rights of the individual. It is pragmatic and functional and deemed necessary to ensure objectives are achieved. The concept in this dimension is thus very limited, consigned to the end of the spectrum that focuses on legality and governmental enforcement. It is positivist in nature, ascribing little value to law other than as a tool to assist the construction of a single market. Even in those terms, we can see that there remain significant patches where the rule of law has limited purchase.

When we visit the institutional dimension and the relationship with people as individuals and members of a community, the broader conception becomes more visible. The need to constrict arbitrary government is more keenly articulated and many of the features of a rule of law, as envisaged by the likes of Raz, Allan, and Fuller, have been promoted with the fairly recent rhetorical adherence to notions of internal

---

[96] Allan, 'The Rule of Law as the Rule of Reason' at 223.
[97] *Ibid.* at 231.   [98] *Ibid.* at 237.

good governance. There appears to be a commitment to pursue these 'rule of law' criteria. Whether or not this is based on a 'coherent conception of justice' as Allan required is not so clear. The identification of a social model preferable for the EU as a community may suggest a vision of justice applicable in part through law but this is hardly a coherent agenda with clear value goals. Whatever our conclusions in this context, there remain problematic areas (particularly with the role of the Council) that question the practical realisation of the rhetorical adherence to the rule of law in the institutional dimension. The possibility of arbitrary decisions remains 'normal' without being subject to meaningful judicial review or public scrutiny. The Lisbon Treaty may have improved the matter somewhat, but there remain gaps when it comes to issues of national security and law and order.

If we then look at the EU's external promotion of the rule of law, we also see a different conception being constructed. This appears to fall towards the end of the spectrum at which the danger occurs of subsuming the rule of law within a 'complete social philosophy', which Raz warns against. Indeed we begin to lose sense of any independent meaning for the rule of law in this context. It appears too frequently to be integrally associated with democracy and human rights to the extent that it becomes extremely difficult to extract where the rule of law operates. It might relate to judicial procedure or legal structures but at its margins there is a persistent lack of clarity. The valid critique that ensues, particularly as the EU consistently fails to operate with such criteria applicable to its own institutions, is that the rule of law represents an exercise in neo-colonialism. The promotion of good governance rhetoric partially in the guise of a value of the rule of law, which looks to support free market institutions and procedures through law suggests the imposition of capitalist ideology that takes little note of context or other political worldviews. It contravenes a basic sense of toleration for non-liberal (indeed non-free market) peoples which John Rawls promoted in his 'Law of Peoples'.[99]

Some commentators do not necessarily see this as a problem. There is a tendency to equate the rule of law concept with 'a culture of law' under construction that 'has been of crucial importance to European development and integration'.[100] It has been interpreted from the

---

[99] John Rawls, *The Law of Peoples* (Cambridge, MA: Harvard University Press, 1999).
[100] Armin von Bogdandy, 'Constitutional Principles', in A. von Bogdandy and Jürgen Bast (eds.), *Principles of European Constitutional Law* (Oxford: Hart, 2006) 3–52 at 15.

narrow perspective of a 'Community of Law' rather than by examining the full institutional narrative on the subject that has been outlined in this chapter. Analysis has concentrated on the evolution of European law through the ECJ, its application and its qualification, and has avoided the difficult task of assessing what the rule of law *can* mean for the EU both in theory and practice. In particular, there has been little consideration of the concept's place in relation to other values, particularly justice, and thus little assessment or indeed judgment of the role the rule of law might play not only in integration but also the future moral direction of the Union.[101] This may well be a product of a failure to examine what European 'justice' might mean, or indeed what the other values and principles mean in the Union's hands. Hence the variable nature of the concept of the rule of law has hardly been addressed at any level, whether political, bureaucratic or academic.

In sum, therefore, the value of the rule of law in the EU's institutional ethos clearly suffers from an ambivalence regarding the strength of its virtues. It is difficult to gauge what is included and what is excluded. The triple framed dimensions reviewed do not necessarily contradict each other but they do speak about the ordering of society, whether across Europe, within the Member States or outside the Union altogether, in subtly different ways. There appears to be a constant battle between viewing law as a functional system of control, on the one hand, and as a force for achieving a transformation of society (whether internally or externally) on the other. The former vision is more prevalent in the supranational realm, where the dominant theme, albeit one that is breached with great regularity, is the creation of a legal order, one imposed on states with a view to realigning matters of sovereignty. The latter flickers more brightly in the international rhetoric, where transformative elements are allowed significantly greater presence. Here, there is a sense that law's rule *can* and *should* play a vital role in the EU

---

[101] See, for instance, Maria Luisa Fernandez Esteban, *The Rule of Law in the European Constitution* (The Hague: Kluwer Law International, 1999); Paul Lasok QC, 'The Rule of Law in the Legal Order of the European Community', in Kim Economides, Lammy Betten, John Bridge, Vivian Shrubsall and Andrew Tettenborn (eds.), *Fundamental Values: a Volume of Essays to Commemorate the Seventy-Fifth Anniversary of the Founding of the Law School in Exeter 1923–1998* (Oxford: Hart, 2000) 85–114 and Anthony Arnull, 'The Rule of Law in the European Union', in A. Arnull and Daniel Wincott (eds.), *Accountability and Legitimacy in the European Union* (Oxford: Oxford University Press, 2002) 239–55, none of which come to grips with the complexity of the rule of law and its association with the other values and principles purportedly operating within the EU.

as it is portrayed outside the domain of Europe. It suggests that the rule of law can and should represent an ideal ethical commitment to a peaceful and just Union, if not world, that others (particularly those states wishing to join) should accept. Between these dimensions appears the institutional relationship with the individual. Here law operates almost apologetically, engaging in limited fields and often with significant deference to national authorities. Sometimes capable of intervention for the benefit of people by restricting state behaviour whilst also appearing impotent when confronted by action that clearly contravenes the EU's ethical commitments. The story of extraordinary rendition demonstrates both the desire for, but lack of, power in EU law.

The difficulty then appears in a conflict between the two visions of order and transformation. It represents a central value contradiction that lies at the core of many critiques raised against the EU as a whole. For how is it sustainable to sponsor a concept of the rule of law that purportedly governs individual Member State societies, European institutions, and supported third country governments, and yet is unable to apply itself to the fundamental relationship between the EU and its Member States? If these states are able to operate, even partially, either individually or through the Council *without* the control of due process, legal remedy and judicial review, then what value can be ascribed to the rule of law as a coherent component of the EU's institutional ethos? For all the certainty induced by consistency of interpretation by the ECJ and adherence to project design for rule of law issues externally, the faultline will continue to raise questions about the true scope of the concept. It may be no more than a rhetorical device that valorises vagueness to the point of indeterminacy leaving the rule of law less a contested concept and more an empty one.

We might reasonably predict that one of the most important milestones for assessing the future development of the rule of law as a significant rather than incoherent component of the institutional ethos will be in matters of justice and home affairs. We have seen how the Lisbon Treaty has brought these within the realm of judicial review but the test will come at the margins of fear. Where terrorism and ethnic unrest, migration flows, and economic recession have their greatest impact, we will either see the rule of law become reinforced or rendered subject to political manipulation. If the latter, questions of responsibility for establishing an effective community of law, as envisaged by Walter Hallstein and others early in the life of the Union, become extremely difficult to answer. Fundamentally this is a matter of clarifying the relationships of power that subsist in Europe. At present, the Union has steadfastly been unable to address that basic issue. The rule of law concept as continually promoted by the Union does little to help. Its lack of conception and its confused relationship with notions of diversity, respect for cultural difference, and hospitality, contributes to an environment of indeterminacy *in principle*. It is incapable of contesting its own inherent assumption; namely that the rule of law as espoused is inextricably interwoven with liberal capitalism. The concept in the EU's hands provides little opportunity *in itself* to address the private power that is accepted and deemed acceptable within a capitalist system. Influence through the market is not a concern in the European discourse of the rule of law. Indeed, it can be seen as legitimating the control corporate or private power can, and does, exercise over society as a whole. Through the EU its will is not only endorsed but expanded, providing yet another tier of practical and biased governance. It is taking on the form whereby a 'coalescence of power into a central depository' is becoming a possibility.[102] This is not to say that interest groups of all forms are not engaged in similar activities designed to influence decision-making. But the resources that are available to capital, and the covert methods of threat that can accompany 'lobbying', set it apart from citizen's groups.

Similarly, power that is exercised by states can find greater means of expression through the ambiguous rule of law concept. The sorry saga of Article 7 TEU's impotence in the face of both extraordinary rendition and involvement by certain Member States in the Iraq and Afghanistan wars provides some evidence of this. A failure to condemn in rule of law terms is equivalent to endorsement.

These are issues that I will address later in this book. But to determine whether there is a possible moral content to the rule of law we now need to look at the most embedded value in the EU's institutional ethos – respect for human rights.

---

[102] For a warning of this potential relating to the rule of law concept see Louis Althusser, *Montesquieu, Rousseau, Marx: Politics and History* (London: Verso, 1982).

4   Human rights

Introduction

When the European Economic Community was established in 1957, human rights did not figure in the political or legal landscape constructed by the Treaty of Rome. Their presence was at best subliminal.[1] The subsequent claim by the European Court of Justice, the Commission, the Council, and now all institutions of the EU that human rights were fundamental in the EU's *creation* is a myth.

The institutional practice and constitutional framework that has developed over the past thirty or more years has, nonetheless, placed respect for human rights at the core of the EU's stated values. Not only is respect for human rights a prominent and explicit feature of the *values* now identified by the Lisbon Treaty of 2007 but it has also helped frame an array of other implicit constitutional themes. From constructing an identity for the EU, legitimising its operations, providing a bulwark against extremism and the abuse of power, to acting as a spur to 'closer union' between the peoples of Europe, human rights provide an iconic concept without respect for which the EU would lack moral and enduring substance. This remains true even with the adoption of the Lisbon Treaty.

My aim in this chapter is to consider the nature of the EU's commitment to human rights. This does not require a comprehensive review of the EU's record in relation to adherence to human rights standards.

---

[1] Armin von Bogdandy reminds us that the creation of the EU was 'legitimated by goals that were to a large extent neutral with regard to constitutional issues'. These include respect for fundamental or human rights. See Bogdandy, 'Doctrine of Principles' Jean Monnet Working Paper 9/03 at 9, online, available at: www.jeanmonnetprogram.org/papers/03/030901–01.html.

Rather, it requires consideration of the scope of the principle of respect for human rights as it has been conceptualised and then applied in practice. A sufficient flavour of the EU's approach can then be gleaned to determine where human rights figure within the institutional ethos.

First, then, the chapter examines the nature of the operative principle. The meaning ascribed institutionally to 'respect' will be crucial. So will the range of human rights that are the subject of that respect. Both possess a fluidity of meaning that needs to be explored if we are to assess the extent to which the EU is committed to human rights.

The second part of the chapter then reviews the EU's practice. It will examine the approach of law emanating from the decisions of the European Court of Justice as well as policy implementation by the other institutions. The depth of commitment can be assessed, I suggest, by focusing on three different aspects: the conceptions of human rights that have been adopted; the measures of scrutiny applied; and the methods of enforcement available. Taken together, these provide plausible indicators of the extent to which human rights have been embraced in any international human rights system.[2] They are certainly significant for determining the value placed on human rights within the EU's institutional ethos. As with any polity a distinction must also be made between the external and internal record. One would expect to find differing approaches in these two arenas which would reflect the different levels of responsibility adopted. More sophisticated structures for determining and enforcing human rights are likely to be present *within* a system than those that are applied to non-constituents, whether these are states or individuals. The complication for the EU, however, revolves around the degree to which its institutions assume responsibility akin to that possessed by a state, with all the constitutional implications attached, or to that of an international organisation. Reviewing how one perspective or another is assumed, or indeed how the two are straddled, will be of great importance in assessing the coherence and determinacy of this particular value for the EU.

---

[2] This scheme is promoted reasonably in Gráinne de Búrca, 'Beyond the Charter: how Enlargement has Enlarged the Human Rights Policy of the European Union', *Fordham International Law Journal* 27 (2004) 679–714 at 681.

Establishing the principle

As we have seen already in this book, prior to Lisbon Article 6 TEU provided a fairly late constitutional moment of solidifying the principles that had purportedly already attained legal or political recognition in the EU. It revealed that the EU 'is founded on the principles of ... respect for human rights and fundamental freedoms'. Article 6(2) also assured that 'the Union shall respect fundamental rights' as guaranteed by the European Convention on Human Rights (ECHR) and the common constitutional traditions of the Member States. But these combined statements of principle are not wholly harmonious. Certainly, the former as a pre-conditional and almost historical assertion is complemented by the latter, which dictates immediate and future action. Tension is, nevertheless, apparent between the 'human' and 'fundamental' labels that are used. Why the distinction? Does it suggest a difference in substance? On a superficial level the term 'fundamental' appears reserved for internal consumption. The 'human' epithet attaches more readily to the external.[3]

Most commentators have found it easier, however, to suggest that the two terms are interchangeable, providing us with no residual legal or philosophical problems. It is probably best to accede to this line of reasoning. The difference may only be a reflection of loose drafting based on equally vague jurisprudence. But the suspicion remains that there is intended to be a distinction. It is just not clear what that might be.

Instead of focusing on the difference we can perhaps focus on the connection. Clearly, the underlying requirement is 'respect'. Whatever conception we have of the subject matter, the principle is to 'respect' it or them. The common usage of the verb 'to respect' surely encompasses: to consider, to take into account, to refer to, to treat with

---

[3] As if to emphasise this interpretation, the Commission transformed the Council's proposal for a 'Human Rights Agency', which had the potential to review external human rights policy, into a 'Fundamental Rights Agency' with limited internal monitoring powers. See Council Regulation (EC) No. 168/2007 of 15 February 2007 establishing a European Union Agency for Fundamental Rights. We can see the same dichotomy played out by the Charter for *Fundamental* Rights on the one hand (primarily a document for internal consumption although some attempt to apply it to the external has been made, albeit unsuccessfully), and the European Initiative for Democracy and *Human Rights* on the other, a project designed by the Commission for 'third countries' (see europa.eu.int/comm/europeaid/projects/eidhr/index_En.htm for details of the latter).

consideration, to refrain from violating, to show deference to, to honour. It has less resonance with those other terms traditionally deployed in contemporary human rights rhetoric, to 'realise', 'fulfil', 'promote' or 'enforce'. The range of ordinary definitions of 'respect', therefore, gives rise to a number of possible active and passive options. 'To honour', for instance, might well place the principle in the realm of the purely rhetorical, engaging no greater demands upon the institution than an obligation to reiterate the importance of human rights as a general concept. But such a restrictive interpretation would surely be disingenuous given the preponderance of and importance ascribed to the declaration and active protection of human rights in international law as well as the EU and its Member States.

But it is interesting nonetheless to see that in some human rights discourse 'respect' has acquired a fairly restrictive meaning. The Maastricht Guidelines on economic, social and cultural rights, for instance, make a virtue of distinguishing between 'respect', 'protect' and 'fulfil'. The Guidelines state that

to respect requires States to refrain from interfering with the enjoyment of economic, social and cultural rights ... to protect requires States to prevent violations of such rights by third parties ... to fulfil requires States to take appropriate legislative, administrative, budgetary, judicial and other measures towards the full realisation of such rights.[4]

The implication is that 'respect' is a negative process, a constraint placed on public authorities whereas 'protection' and 'fulfilment' suggest additional positive duties. But of course, there is nothing to suggest that the constitutional provisions of the EU mentioned above follow this pattern or indeed that this demarcation is generally accepted.[5]

What then are the realistic implications of identifying 'respect' as the operative institutional command? Does it imply a responsibility to act as a moral agent in relation to human rights, dictating an active or positive obligation?[6] Or does the principle merely possess a passive or negative nature, one that forbids the EU institutions from violating

[4] Maastricht Guidelines on Violations of Economic, Social and Cultural Rights 1997.
[5] The European Court of Human Rights does not feel so restricted in its judgments. In *Marckx v. Belgium* 13 June 1979 (No. 31), 2 E.H.R.R. 330 at para. 31 the Court said 'there may be positive obligations inherent in an effective "respect" for family life'.
[6] The possibility of institutions generally adopting a sense of collective moral agency is explored in some detail, although not as regards the EU specifically, in Toni Erskine (ed.), *Can Institutions Have Responsibilities? Collective Moral Agency and International Relations* (Basingstoke: Palgrave, 2003).

human rights but does not impose upon them a greater duty to promote and enforce human rights? The jurisprudence of the ECJ would seem to support a more restrictive interpretation. In *Opinion 2/94* on Accession by the EU to the ECHR the Court famously, if ambiguously, noted that '[n]o Treaty provision confers on the EU institutions any general power to enact rules on human rights'.[7] At the same time it acknowledged the declaratory importance of respect for human rights in the EU, noted that 'fundamental rights form an integral part of the general principles of law'[8] and maintained that 'respect for human rights is … a condition of the lawfulness of EU acts'.[9]

Beyond the ECJ, the development of a wide spectrum of fundamental rights texts, legislative rules, institutional practices, supported agencies, and applied resources testify to a broader and deeper conception of the commitment to 'respect' than a purely negative connotation would allow. Perhaps here we find the basis for an ethical struggle, a central tension lying at the heart of human rights in the EU's institutional ethos.

On the one hand the EU, howsoever it may have been created, has developed into a polity that possesses independent legal personality and institutions which are capable of making and implementing decisions and establishing a *praxis* without slavish reference to its founding text. On the other, constraints on what is possible are imposed by the Treaties. The reality must lie somewhere between these positions, leaving significant scope for political and legal debate. Thus, the institutions may be seen to have assumed responsibility that combines elements of a duty to act to respect human rights wherever possible whilst casting an eye towards its legally established parameters.

A prime example of this tension can be found in the approach taken to Article 7 TEU. Establishing a mechanism for enforcement (arguably an essential requirement for a 'functioning international human rights system')[10] that enables the EU to respond to a 'serious and persistent breach' of Article 6(1) principles or even a 'clear risk of serious breach', Article 7 as instituted through the Treaty of Nice suggested recognition of political responsibility. Thanks to Article 46(e) TEU (now Article 269 of the Treaty on the Functioning of the EU) the measure is

---

[7] *Opinion 2/94 on Accession by the EU to the ECHR* [1996] ECR I-1759 para. 27. The statement was ambiguous because it did not articulate what the EU *could* do with regard to human rights. It did not preclude the adoption of *specific* rather than general legislative measures.

[8] *Ibid.* para. 33.   [9] *Ibid.* para. 34.

[10] de Búrca, 'Beyond the Charter'.

explicitly non-justiciable save for its procedural provisions. And yet the Commission has declared that Article 7 helped 'equip the Union institutions with the means of ensuring that all Member states respect' the principles set out in Article 6(1).[11] On the strength of this it acceded to the European Parliament's suggestion that some form of monitoring of Member States' human rights records, irrespective of whether in relation to the implementation of Union law or not, was a precondition for Article 7. It also established an Independent Network of Experts on Fundamental Rights (now disbanded) to produce the necessary regular reports. But these actions did not resolve the friction. There remains the institutional acknowledgement that Article 7 is a purely political measure and as such does not represent an expansion of the EU's competence in human rights. The restricted mandate of the Fundamental Rights Agency (FRA), which avoids scrutiny of Member States in Article 7 terms, would seem to confirm this.[12] The Impact Assessment that preceded the FRA's creation claimed that there was no requirement for constant monitoring under Article 7 given that sufficient extra-Union systems already existed to carry out this function.[13] Consequently, the possibility for Article 7 to be the basis for an enhanced interpretation of human rights responsibilities was effectively curtailed.

It is clear, therefore, that the parameters of the principle to respect human rights remain highly contested. Paradoxically, this can both undermine and support the maturation of the EU's human rights policy. Whilst suggesting a failure to establish a clear approach to how the Union is to go about fulfilling its requirement to respect human rights it also provides important room for political, if not legal, manoeuvre.

We might find here an echo of the struggle that has appeared generally in Western notions of human rights. Theories of natural and positive rights also display conflict on how obligations might flow from human rights articulations. Is the EU playing out similar theoretical debates on the nature of its principle? Perhaps in practice it is adjusting itself to what Sen calls an 'ethical understanding of human rights' that

[11] Communication from the Commission to the Council and the European Parliament on Article 7 of the Treaty on European Union: Respect for and Promotion of the Values on which the Union is Based; COM (2003) 606 final at 3.

[12] Commission Communication on Fundamental Rights Agency, COM (2004) 693, Brussels, 25 October 2004.

[13] Preparatory Study for Impact Assessment and Ex-ante Evaluation of Fundamental Rights Agency Final Report (2005).

moves away from a 'law-centred approach' to seeing human rights as 'if they are basically grounds for law, almost "laws in waiting"'.[14] The practical effect may be to enable an environment that both restricts the application of human rights (by ensuring they only apply in specific contexts) and allows for their wider promotion through incremental, perhaps even ad hoc, institutional measures that emerge after considered debate.

I will return to the conceptual aspects later in this chapter. In the meantime, it is worth asking whether the Lisbon Treaty promises a change in direction with regard to the 'respect' principle, perhaps providing a solution to the tensions that evidently subsist. The revision to Article 2 TEU modifies slightly the Article 6(1) formula by providing that the 'Union is founded on the values of respect for human dignity, freedom, democracy, equality, the rule of law and respect for human rights, including the rights of persons belonging to minorities'. The crux of the principle of respect thus remains intact.[15] However, a small change in attitude might be inferred from the new Article 3, which states that the 'Union's aim is to promote peace, its values and the well-being of its peoples'. This suggests that 'promotion' of human rights would provide the Union with the authority to develop its human rights commitment further. The additional provisions for the EU to 'recognise' the EU Charter on Fundamental Rights, and giving power for it to accede to the ECHR, lend further credence to the argument. But the central tension between deepening its human rights work and keeping it within the parameters of EU law remains.

With these general comments in mind we now need to examine the practical application of the principle. Three aspects in particular demand attention.

First, we need to establish what is meant by human rights in the EU. There is a broad range of human rights norms incorporating both individual civil, political, social, economic and cultural rights, and collective rights. Understanding which of these are acknowledged and addressed will provide an important indicator of the accepted responsibility.

---

[14] Amartya Sen, 'Elements of a Theory of Human Rights', *Philosophy and Public Affairs* 32:4 (2004) 315–56 at 326.

[15] The addition of minority rights would seem to be only a point of political emphasis that serves little purpose other than to counter possible alternative views that human rights did not incorporate such rights. However, if this were the case then it begs the question: which other rights are not incorporated in 'human rights'?

Second, we need to determine the level of scrutiny the EU has adopted in order to assess adherence to these norms. We need to understand *who* is scrutinised and to what degree. The depth of commitment displayed institutionally may be reflected in the seriousness with which the EU monitors human rights conditions within its policy areas.

Third, we need to determine the consequences of scrutiny, those enforcement powers available within the institutional framework. This will indicate the extent to which the EU institutions are both capable and willing to act for human rights, again important for establishing the level of adherence to the value.

Within each of the above aspects we will need to consider the internal and external dimensions. We know already that these differ considerably. That is perhaps to be expected when confronting a system that looks both inward and outward, recognising that responsibilities for the two realms may develop along separate lines.[16] But the nature of that difference will have much to tell us about the quality of human rights as a consistent and clear value in the EU's institutional ethos as a whole. We may not expect complete coherence but any significant deviation from core principles in the conception, scrutiny and enforcement of human rights internally and externally could reveal the strength ascribed to human rights across the EU's activities. Some conclusions as to what is meant by respecting 'human rights' in the EU's hands might then be possible.

The conception of human rights in the EU

To talk of 'human rights' as a recognised and established body of norms and concepts would be fallacious. The subject has been and remains contentious. Despite numerous conventions, declarations and judgments, the scope of human rights that might be recognised formally or constitutionally continues to attract widespread debate. Different rights are approached in different ways, some acquiring greater acceptance in law than others. Some appear as mere aspirations, failing to acquire significant recognition that would allow protection through legal processes. Such is the character of the international discourse on

---

[16] I have written extensively elsewhere on the fundamental condition of 'bifurcation' that besets the EU's human rights activities. See Andrew Williams, *EU Human Rights Policies: a Study in Irony* (Oxford: Oxford University Press, 2004).

the subject. It is hardly surprising then that when 'human rights' are stated as the basis of policy and action in the EU, externally and internally, there may be confusion as to what exactly is being pursued.

Some continuity may, however, be evident in the institutional rhetoric. Over the last two decades, the promotion of the principles of universality, indivisibility and interdependence by the EU strongly infers that human rights are assumed to have a discernible and uniform content that will guide action in all spheres of activity.[17] The inference is that civil and political rights, as well as economic, social and cultural rights, should be treated as all of one body and respected by states wherever they may be situated.[18] The Council's Annual Reports on Human Rights have consistently stressed adherence to universality and indivisibility and the integration of human rights with 'peace and security, economic development and social equity'.[19] The Reports have said that the EU 'recognises the diversity of the world' but that 'regardless of different cultures, social background, state of development, or geographical region, human rights are inalienable rights of every person'.[20] The Commission has also referred to the EU Charter of Fundamental Rights as evidence of the EU's overall commitment to the principles of universality and indivisibility.[21] The Charter itself lauds the EU as 'founded on the indivisible, universal values of human dignity, freedom, equality and solidarity'.[22] No distinction in conception between the external and internal affairs is therefore immediately apparent. One might reasonably surmise that the human rights promoted externally would be of the same order and definition as those acted upon within the EU. But is this the case? Some comparison of the sources and practical promotion of rights in the two dimensions will help answer the question.

---

[17] This has been evident for some time. See Commission, 'The European Union and the External Dimension of Human Rights Policy: from Rome to Maastricht and Beyond', EC Bull Supp. 3–1995 at 29.

[18] The international bill of rights appears in the guise of the UN International Covenants on Civil and Political Rights and Economic, Social and Cultural Rights of 1966 respectively. These have been supplemented by a raft of other conventions that most commentators would assume to be incorporated in the corpus of international human rights to be recognised as universally applicable and indivisible.

[19] Council, EU Annual Report on Human Rights 1999. The wording has been repeated with minor variations ever since.

[20] Council, EU Annual Report on Human Rights 2000 at 8.

[21] Communication from the Commission on the Legal Nature of the Charter of Fundamental Rights of the EU 20 November 2000 COM/2000/0644 final.

[22] EU Charter of Fundamental Rights (2000) OJC 364/08.

The external experience

Externally, we can see that the sources relied upon to define the meaning of human rights are extremely wide. In foreign and development policies they have been vast. The Universal Declaration of Human Rights and the UN Charter have provided the basic inspiration. In 1994 the Commission stated that 'EU action to defend and promote human rights is taken in accordance with the United Nations Charter and the universal principles and priorities adopted by the international community at various world conferences'.[23] In Council Regulation 975/1999,[24] which authorised the EU's human rights activities in development, a more complete picture was supplied. This suggested action to promote human rights and democratic principles was 'rooted in the general principles established by the Universal Declaration of Human Rights, the International Covenant on Civil and Political Rights and the International Covenant on Economic, Social and Cultural Rights'.[25] The Regulation went on to be specific about other applicable instruments drawing in international humanitarian law (the laws of war) with particular reference to 'the 1949 Geneva Conventions and the 1977 Additional Protocol thereto, the 1951 Geneva Convention relating to the Status of Refugees, the 1948 Convention on the Prevention and Punishment of the Crime of Genocide and other acts of international treaty or customary law'.[26]

Further conceptions and expressions of rights have also been accepted. Notions of collective rights, through the protection of minority rights and of 'indigenous peoples, their rights and cultures', have been identified as worthy of active support by the EU.[27] In 2001 the Commission pointed to the need 'to protect minorities and indigenous peoples' in its programming of projects.[28] This remains a priority

---

[23] Commission, Report on the Implementation of Measures Intended to Promote Observance of Human Rights and Democratic Principles [1994] COM (95) 191 final, at 2.

[24] Council Regulation (EC) No 975/1999 [1999] OJL 120/1 amended by Regulation (EC) No 2240/2004 of the European Parliament and of the Council of 15 December 2004.

[25] *Ibid.* at Preamble para. 6

[26] *Ibid.* at Preamble para. 8.

[27] Commission proposal for a Council Regulation on the development and consolidation of democracy and the rule of law and respect for human rights and fundamental freedoms [1997] OJC 282/16.

[28] Commission, Priorities and Guidelines for the Implementation of the 2001 European Initiative for Democracy and Human Rights SEC (2001) 891 at 2.

theme in external relations.[29] The rights of the child have also been emphasised through the adoption of guidelines for intervention.[30]

The breadth of definition of rights is also apparent in the institutional recognition of a right to development as expressed in the UN Declaration on the Right to Development in 1986.[31] This declares that the right is 'an inalienable human right by virtue of which every human person and all peoples are entitled to participate in, contribute to and enjoy economic, social, cultural and political development, in which all human rights and fundamental freedoms can be fully realised'.[32] The substantial collective as well as individual rights connotations have been tentatively yet positively embraced in rhetoric from the EU.[33] The Council has recognised that it should support fulfilment of the right by helping to meet 'equitably the developmental and environmental needs of the present and future generations'.[34] In 2005 the so-called 'European Consensus on Development' was adopted. This was a free-flowing general commitment to the objectives of development as set out particularly in the UN Millennium Development Goals.[35] Although the right to development was not mentioned by the EU Council, the language was of development being a 'central goal by itself' within which human rights were considered of primary concern.[36] Whilst the EU institutions may still like to stress the individual human being as the beneficiary of the process, there is an implicit acceptance that collective rights are to be promoted as well. Whether this will ever translate into an acceptance of a duty to provide development assistance must remain doubtful although the Consensus document comes very close.[37] Nevertheless, the result has been a policy influenced by

[29] Regulation (EC) No 1889/2006 of the European Parliament and of the Council of 20 December 2006 on establishing a financing instrument for the promotion of democracy and human rights worldwide, at article 2(1)(b)(iv).

[30] See EU guidelines on children and armed conflict adopted at the General Affairs Council meeting on 8 December 2003 and Commission communication of 4 July 2006 – 'Towards an EU Strategy on the Rights of the Child' COM (2006) 367.

[31] UNGA Resolution 41/128 (1986) Annexing the Declaration on the Right to Development.

[32] *Ibid.* article 1.

[33] See European Political Co-operation Bulletin 29 March 1990 155–160.

[34] Council, EU Annual Report on Human Rights [2006] at 48 para. 4.12.

[35] Joint Statement by the Council and the Representatives of the Governments of the Member States meeting within the Council, the European Parliament and the Commission: 'The European Consensus on Development' [2005].

[36] *Ibid.* para. 7.

[37] *Ibid.* The Consensus document talked of responsibilities rather than duties. Para. 2 said, 'Developing countries have the prime responsibility for their own development.

a wide interpretation of human rights meanings. The EU institutions have recognised general rights claims and assumed the authority to intervene accordingly.

In accession policy, another key area of external affairs for human rights, a slightly more restricted approach to sources and definition can be seen. The European Convention on Human Rights (ECHR) has largely formed the basis for discussion although other instruments such as the Framework Convention for the Protection of National Minorities 1995 have been given prominence. Civil and political rights, and economic, social and cultural rights as well as specifically minority rights have also been the subject of scrutiny. No one complete statement of principle has been produced, however, that has satisfactorily established the full extent of the EU's human rights concerns in the enlargement negotiations. Rather, the directive texts and the implementation of policy need to be examined to determine what is recognised as a concern for the Union. The Copenhagen Criteria, produced in 1993 in order to set out the basic conditions required of all potential Member States, provides the starting point.[38]

In this respect, as a primary concern, applicant states had to guarantee 'respect for and protection of minorities'. For some this appeared as a wholly arbitrary requirement in the EU context. There was little evidence prior to the end of the Cold War that the EU was the focus for articulating let alone realising rights in this regard.[39] Agenda 2000, which represented the Commission's response to the Council's call for a detailed process of scrutiny of candidates, nonetheless looked towards a 'number of texts governing the protection of national minorities' (including those adopted by the Council of Europe) for assessing the standards expected.[40] In particular, the Framework Convention for the Protection of National Minorities 1995 was identified as safeguarding

---

But developed countries have a responsibility too. The EU, both at its Member States and Community levels, is committed to meeting its responsibilities'.

[38] Conclusions of the Presidency at the Copenhagen Council 1993, EC Bull 6-1993 at 13.

[39] Barbara Brandtner and Allan Rosas have pointed out that the reference to minority rights is not based in any tradition established through EU law. See Brandtner and Rosas, 'Human Rights and the External Relations of the European EU: an Analysis of Doctrine and Practice', *European Journal of International Law* 9:3 (1998) 468–90. See also M.A.M. Estébanez, 'The Protection of National, or Ethnic, Religious and Linguistic Minorities', in N. Neuwahl and A. Rosas (eds.), *The European Union and Human Rights* (The Hague: Kluwer Law International, 1995) at 135.

[40] Commission, 'Agenda 2000: For a Stronger and Wider Union' COM (97) 2000.

'the individual rights of persons belonging to minority groups'.[41] Although a number of Member States themselves have yet to sign and/or ratify the Convention this has not prevented the Convention from being recommended for applicant states.[42] This, of course, sends contradictory messages concerning the true value ascribed by the EU and its Members to both minority rights in general and the specific international agreements in particular.

Even so, the enthusiastic application of Agenda 2000 has indicated an extensive commitment by the EU to protect minority rights. In the case of most applicant states, problems associated with the recognition and protection of minority rights have been identified and demands made for their resolution.[43] A key target has been the situation of the Roma across Central and Eastern Europe. Being a people possessing a presence across the region, the plight of the Roma has become something of a litmus test for the seriousness accorded to minority rights. And the attention paid to their condition has indicated the extent to which the EU has been willing to intervene in this rights issue. A concerted attempt to recognise their problems and address them at every level, imposing standards and procedures on the applicants, has been made. This has rendered minority rights highly visible within the accession process, reinforcing a collective understanding of the rights involved. The fact that, since the accession of numerous states has been completed, analysts have begun to question the effectiveness of the approach to minority rights, does not deflect from the observation that minority rights has acquired significant presence in the EU's institutional thinking about human rights.[44] It remains of primary concern in this external dimension. The current review of Turkey's progress towards accession continues to emphasise the need to '[e]nsure cultural diversity and promote respect for and protection of

---

[41] See Briefing No.20 on Democracy and respect for Human Rights in the Enlargement Process of the European Union, 1 April 1998 PE 167.582 at 10.

[42] For details of signatories see http://conventions.coe.int/Treaty/Commun/ChercheSig. asp?NT=157&CM=&DF=&CL=ENG. Belgium only signed on 31 July 2001. France, Belgium and Greece, had yet to ratify by 2009. Turkey has been admonished for its failure to sign and ratify by the EU in its Progress Report of 2008 SEC (2008) 2699.

[43] See Williams, *EU Human Rights Policies* chapter 3.

[44] For critiques of the EU's policy vis-à-vis minority rights see Bernd Rechel, 'What has Limited the EU's Impact on Minority Rights in Accession Countries?', *East European Politics and Societies* 22 (2008) 171–91, and James Hughes, Gwendolyn Sasse and Claire Gordon, *Europeanization and Regionalization in the EU's Enlargement to Central and Eastern Europe: the Myth of Conditionality* (Houndmills: Palgrave Macmillan, 2004).

minorities in accordance with the ECHR and the principles laid down in the Framework Convention for the Protection of National Minorities and in line with best practice in Member States'.[45] Despite this injunction the 2008 Progress Report noted that '[o]verall, Turkey has made no progress on ensuring cultural diversity and promoting respect for and protection of minorities in accordance with European standards'.[46] Minority issues are similarly noted as demanding attention for Croatia and Macedonia as the other frontline candidates awaiting admission. Potential candidates are all being assessed strictly in relation to their adherence to minority rights.[47] Whether this will preclude entry is perhaps irrelevant. The fact is, minority rights notions are being recognised, their abuse is noted as worthy of condemnation, and the expectations are high that applicant states will address them.

The issue of civil and political rights is less problematic. These are understood in accession as focused on the ECHR and have underpinned condemnatory assessment throughout the enlargement process. Police misconduct, the fight against corruption, trafficking in women, the engagement of civil society, bias in state media, and a variety of other matters, have been the subject of comment and scrutiny.[48] It would not be too bold to suggest that there are few areas where the EU has feared to tread in this field of rights.

Economic, social and cultural rights have, on the other hand, received less prominence. Nonetheless, they still register a significant presence in the assessment of the political criteria for each applicant. They appear in their own right and as elements of the *acquis communautaire* supposed to be adopted wholesale by the applicants. Health and safety, employment rights, and consumer protection issues have surfaced as matters to be addressed where necessary. So, too, cultural rights attached to language, rights of equal opportunities, rights of

[45] Council, Decision of 18 February 2008 on the Principles, Priorities and Conditions Contained in the Accession Partnership with the Republic of Turkey and Repealing Decision 2006/35/EC [2008/157/EC].

[46] Turkey Progress Report 5 November 2008 SEC (2008) 2699, online, available at: http://ec.europa.eu/enlargement/pdf/press_corner/key-documents/reports_nov_2008/turkey_progress_report_En.pdf.

[47] See 2008 Progress Reports for Albania, Serbia, Bosnia Herzegovina, Kosovo and Montenegro, online, available at: http://ec.europa.eu/enlargement/press_corner/key-documents/reports_nov_2008_En.htm.

[48] See, for instance, the range of the review in the Commission's 2008 Progress Report for the Former Yugoslav Republic of Macedonia COM (2008) 674 at 17, where even bias in public television news broadcasts was noted as contrary to the freedom of expression.

trade unions, and rights of disabled people. The detail is less significant than the fact that these matters have been subject to regular assessment and comment. The EU through the Commission's examination has assumed responsibility for vetting a broad range of issues explicitly within rights terms.

All the above suggests that the concept of human rights adopted by and through EU institutions has been broad indeed. There is clear evidence of the application of a wide spectrum of human rights in a variety of contexts. Most importantly, the so-called three generations of rights (the civil and political; the economic, social and cultural; and group rights) are recognised in both rhetoric and operation. This is not to say that there is consistency of application or even seriousness in commitment to respect this broad corpus of rights in all the EU's external relations. Undoubtedly the EU institutions have failed to promote them effectively or even actively tolerated their violation by third-party states on countless occasions. But that would probably be the same for most if not all states and international organisations. Such is the condition of international politics and does not negate the observation that conceptually there are few constraints on the institutional recognition of a truly broad human rights spectrum.

Has this general external approach been reflected in the internal experience?

The internal experience

The sources of law that define rights within the EU are somewhat different. The EU Charter of Fundamental Rights purportedly provides the current expression of the EU's internal understanding. It claims to represent 'for the first time in the European Union's history, the whole range of civil, political, economic and social rights of European citizens and all persons resident in the EU'.[49] The preface states that 'the rights as they result, in particular, from the constitutional traditions and international obligations common to the Member States' are reaffirmed.[50] It then includes as precedents 'the European Convention for the Protection of Human Rights and Fundamental Freedoms, the Social Charters adopted by the EU and by the Council of Europe and the case law of the Court of Justice of the European Communities and of the European Court of Human Rights'.

---

[49] Preface to the Charter of Fundamental Rights of the European Union (2000) OJC 364/01.

[50] *Ibid.* at 8.

The reference to 'international obligations' does not directly relate to the corpus of human rights texts applied in the EU's external affairs. Rather, the obligations are only those 'common' to the Member States. This was reconfirmed by the ECJ in *Kadi* when it stated that

the Court draws inspiration from the constitutional traditions common to the Member States and from the guidelines supplied by international instruments for the protection of human rights on which the Member States have collaborated or to which they are signatories. In that regard, the ECHR has special significance.[51]

Thus, although international instruments may be considered relevant the main criteria for judgment of potential breaches of human rights rest with the ECHR or the constitutional traditions of the individual Member State. Since *Nold* the Court may have held that '[i]nternational treaties for the protection of human rights on which the Member States have collaborated or of which they are signatories, can supply guidelines that should be followed within the framework of EU law'.[52] But the *Nold* criterion was established with the ECHR very much in mind and that remains the focal point.[53] That was the international instrument that held the attention of the ECJ at the time. The intention was not obviously to open the gates to the burgeoning library of human rights texts. It is unsurprising, therefore, that the ECJ's reference to other international instruments has been limited.[54]

The ECHR remains the key instrument of reference. AG Maduro recently reiterated why. He suggested that

the commitment which each Member State has expressed to the Convention demonstrates the status of those rights as corresponding to values common to

---

[51] Conjoined cases C-402/05 P and C-415/05 P *Yassin Abdullah Kadi and Al Barakaat International Foundation* v. *Council* Judgment of the Court (Grand Chamber) 3 September 2008 para 283.

[52] *Nold* v. *Commission* Case 4/73 [1974] ECR 491. See also *Opinion 2/94 on Accession by the EU to the ECHR* [1996] ECR I-1759 para. 33.

[53] Case C-540/03 *European Parliament* v. *Council of the European Union* [2006] ECR I-5769 reiterates the commitment to universal human rights standards but that does not mean the focus of attention is not still European.

[54] *Ibid.* The UN International Covenant on Civil and Political Rights was mentioned in Case 374/87 *Orkem* v. *Commission* [1989] ECR 3283 and other international instruments have been referred to occasionally. But one could not extrapolate from such references any judicial recognition of the application of international human rights norms *tout court*.

the Member States, which therefore necessarily wish to safeguard them and reproduce them in the context of the European Union.[55]

He went on to suggest that through the ECHR in conjunction with the EU's Charter on Fundamental Rights 'a process of informal construction of a European area of protection of fundamental rights' had begun.[56] There is a real sense here then of a European understanding of rights that does not necessarily operate under a principle of universality. Nor does it necessarily encompass the range of rights recognised in the EU's external dealings. The Preamble of the EU Charter refers to 'common values' and the EU's 'spiritual and moral heritage' as inspiring the Charter's construction. When talking of the 'preservation and development of these common values' respect is paid to 'the diversity of cultures and traditions of the peoples of Europe as well as the national identities of the Member States'. Although articles of the Charter relate to equality and the right not to be discriminated against[57] (which undoubtedly seek to protect peoples not of Europe), its preambular language indicates a preference for promoting cultures and traditions that emanate from Europe not elsewhere. Europe's 'others' are effectively excluded within the very core of the EU's human rights creative and promotional rhetoric. Exceptions may be evident (for instance the explicit reference to the UN Convention on the Rights of the Child through the Charter's identification of child rights)[58] but they do not represent the rule. The selectivity of the Charter and its failure to be all embracing from the outset suggests an interior interpretation of human rights that is 'located', not 'universal'. Maduro's opinion reflects this preference. It identifies as an institutional objective the creation of a specific European area of protection of fundamental rights.

The original Article 6 TEU might confirm this interpretation. This determines that the EU shall respect fundamental rights as guaranteed by the ECHR 'and as they result from the constitutional traditions common to the Member States' and 'the national identities of its Member States'. As I have said this includes international instruments. But the parameters for interpretation are set. European texts are to govern European behaviour. There is no extension of the principle to the identities and principles that might have developed outside Europe even

---

[55] Opinion of Advocate General Poiares Maduro delivered on 9 September 2008, Case C465/07 M. Elgafaji, N. Elgafaji v. Staatssecretaris van Justitie at para. 22.

[56] Ibid.

[57] See for instance Article 21 EU Charter of Fundamental Rights.

[58] See Communication from the Commission, Towards an EU Strategy on the Rights of the Child, COM/2006/0367 final.

though a substantial proportion of Europe's inhabitants originated from other regions. What place, then, can Islamic cultures and traditions, legal or otherwise, have within the rhetorical landscape that the EU's constitutional texts inscribe?[59] The political debate over Turkey's accession might well indicate the underlying prejudice, questioning the ability of the EU to entertain the membership of a state with a predominantly non-Christian population.[60]

The distinction with the external approach is also manifest in the realm of collective rights. As we have seen, little has occurred in the EU's history prior to the Yugoslavian conflict to suggest a willingness to promote minority rights per se. Bruno de Witte has argued that the EU's concern in this field is for export only.[61] Armin von Bogdandy also notes that even in the Constitutional Treaty (followed by the Lisbon Treaty) 'there is only a feeble reference to minorities and diversity within the states (Art. I-2 TCE); it does not provide for competences'.[62] This is not to say that real attempts have not been made to address issues of racism and xenophobia. Article 13 EC Treaty (now Article 19 TFEU) introduced by the Treaty of Amsterdam has been touted as providing the impetus for action at EU level. Even so, significant questions remain over the provision's efficacy in countering racism in the ways that are possible externally. In particular, the methods chosen to apply Article 13 demonstrate an institutional hesitancy about interfering directly on this matter in the affairs of Member States. Two directives, one to combat discrimination in the labour market on all grounds referred to in Article 13 (except for sex) and one to combat discrimination on grounds of racial and ethnic origin in areas beyond employment, and an Action Plan setting out a programme 'in particular by enabling exchanges of experience and good practice between the Member States' provided the framework.[63]

---

[59] Silvio Berlusconi gave an indication of the type of rhetoric that might surface after the attacks on the World Trade Centre in New York on 11 September 2001. He reportedly spoke of the 'supremacy' and 'superiority' of Western civilisation and called on Europe to recognise its 'common Christian roots'. See *Guardian*, 27 September 2001.

[60] See, for instance, Wolfgang Shäuble and David L. Phillips, 'Talking Turkey: is Europe Ready for a Muslim Member?', *Foreign Affairs* 83:6 (2004) 134–7.

[61] Bruno de Witte, 'Politics Versus Law in the EU's Approach to Ethnic Minorities', EUI Working Paper (2000) RSC No. 2000/4.

[62] Armin von Bogdandy, 'The European Union as Situation, Executive, and Promoter of the International Law of Cultural Diversity: Elements of a Beautiful Friendship', *European Journal of International Law* 19:2 (2008) 241–75 at fn140.

[63] See, Council Directive 2000/78/EC establishing a general framework for equal treatment in employment and occupation, Council Directive 2000/43/EC implementing

But the very choice of form for these measures is problematic. By adopting directives rather than regulations the Commission again fell foul of treating the Member States with deference in a matter that is supposed to be core to the EU's human rights policies. In the Ninth Report of the UK parliament's Select Committee on European Union a Commission spokesperson is quoted as admitting that 'in respect of both the principle of subsidiarity and proportionality it is better to address the issue on a very broad, objective basis while leaving for Member States a lot of margin of manoeuvre to adapt their legislation in response to their specific cultural diversity'.[64]

Such sensitivity may be welcomed by the Member States but it is hard to square with the statements of fundamental principle that are otherwise presented. The fact that by mid 2003 the Commission was compelled to issue a press release condemning the failure of 'most Member States' to transpose the Racial Equality Directive into their national laws serves to reinforce the point.[65] That problem remains acute with half of the Member States still failing to meet the Directive's requirements in 2008 according to the Commission.[66]

The scope of the directives, in any event, indicates the limited institutional ambition to confront the Member States constitutionally on the issue. The failure to address the matter in direct terms suggests the EU's internal determination to tackle racism and its commitment to minority rights in general should be treated with some circumspection.

But what of the EU's practical initiatives, the secondary legislation, soft law and the work conducted by the institutions? On one level, the changes to the EC Treaty with regard to racism and discrimination suggest that such matters are no longer considered to be the sole preserve of the Member States. Some of the EU's practices over the past decade or so would even suggest that the divide between EU and Member State on the issue is being slowly eroded.

the principle of equal treatment between persons irrespective of racial or ethnic origin, and Council Decision 2000/750/EC establishing an EU action programme to combat discrimination (2001 to 2006).

[64] Select Committee on European Union, Ninth Report 1999 Part 5 para. 30.

[65] Press release IP/03/1047 'Commission Concerned at Member States' Failure to Implement New Racial Equality Rules'.

[66] See Communication from the Commission to the European Parliament, the Council, the European Economic and Social Committee and the Committee of the Regions, 'Non-discrimination and Equal Opportunities: A Renewed Commitment', Brussels, 2 July 2008 COM (2008) 420 final.

We might return to the example of the Roma in this respect. As we have already seen the predicament of the Roma throughout Eastern and Central Europe has occupied considerable attention in the accession process. A difficult example of institutional discrimination that transcends national boundaries was recognised by the EU and serious attempts were made to encourage, if not enforce, change. It remains an issue for all the potential candidates for accession.

The treatment of the Roma within the EU is no less a cause for concern. The Roma possess a significant presence in many Member States. The European Parliament's Committee on Civil Liberties and Internal Affairs have long acknowledged both the size of the Roma minority in the EU and the extent of the racism and discrimination that they suffer. It has continued to draw attention to the problem.[67] Organisations such as the European Roma Rights Centre (ERRC) have highlighted significant discrimination within Member States. So too has the UN Committee on the Elimination of Racial Discrimination (CERD). The EU's Fundamental Rights Agency has undertaken a major survey in recent times that demonstrates the endemic nature of discrimination and racism suffered.[68] The sheer scale of ill treatment by national authorities and the perceived complete lack of governmental concern or willingness to address the position are striking findings.

Despite such revelations, recognition, and the implementation of Article 13 EC Treaty, no legally binding framework for direct institutional intervention in the affairs of the Member States on minority rights has been constructed in the name of the EU. Some early support for Roma was provided through initiatives in education and culture,[69] but it is only recently that the matter has been taken a little more seriously. The Brussels Council in December 2007 stated that it was 'conscious of the very specific situation faced by the Roma across the Union' and invited 'Member States and the Union to use all means to improve their inclusion'.[70] The Commission was asked to look at the matter and provide a report. It responded by issuing a detailed communication outlining

---

[67] Report on Countering Racism and Xenophobia in the European Union A5–0049/2000 Preamble para. T 9.

[68] Fundamental Rights Agency, 'European Union Minorities and Discrimination Survey: Data Focus Point: the Roma' 2009, online, available at: http://fra.europa.eu/fraWebsite/attachments/EU-MIDIS_ROMA_EN.pdf.

[69] See, for example, Resolution of the Council and the Ministers of Education, meeting within the Council, of 22 May 1989 on school provision for gypsy and travellers' children [1989] OJC 153/3.

[70] The Brussels European Council 14 December 2007 at paragraph 50.

what was already being done and identifying 'lessons learned'.[71] The Brussels European Council similarly called on Member States 'to make better use of the Structural Funds, the Pre-Accession Instrument and the European Neighbourhood and Partnership Instrument to promote the inclusion of the Roma, particularly in the fields of education, housing, health, employment and access to justice and to culture'.[72] This was all in the context of an acknowledgement of a continuing problem of discrimination and exclusion of minorities.[73] The riots and events in France in 2008 and the general and widespread discrimination and ethnic hatred emerging against Muslim communities since the 9/11 attacks have only reinforced concerns from a human rights perspective. The apparent unwillingness within the EU to grasp the nettle of racism and the discourses of hate that accompany it represents a possible lack of institutional commitment to do something meaningful to address the position. Instead the approach is 'persuasive', revolves around the promotion of 'best practice' and is generally diplomatic. Sanctions for any systemic violation are absent.

The legal position of minority rights has not helped matters. Indeed, the notion of group rights does not figure within the ECJ's reasoning to any appreciable extent, if at all. When deciding its understanding of those rights that must be respected as 'an integral part of the general principles of law',[74] the ECJ confined itself almost entirely to those individual rights protected by the ECHR. Even when faced with a possible group right in the shape of a people's language in *Groener* v. *Minister for Education* it avoided the discourse of rights altogether. Instead it concluded that the 'EEC Treaty does not prohibit the adoption of a policy for the protection and promotion of a language of a Member State' whilst adding the proviso that 'the implementation of such a policy must not encroach upon a fundamental freedom such as that of the free movement of workers'.[75] It did not frame the issue in terms of rights at all. This is in direct contrast to the position adopted externally.[76]

---

[71] Commission Staff Working Document accompanying the Communication from the Commission on Community Instruments and Policies for Roma Inclusion COM (2008) 420 final.

[72] Council Draft Conclusions Brussels 26 November 2008 para. 11.

[73] See Communication from the Commission COM (2008) 420 final.

[74] Case 11/70 *Internationale Handelsgesellschaft* v. *Einfuhr- und Vorratstelle fur Getreide und Futtermittel* [1970] ECR II 1125–1155.

[75] Case 379/87 *Groener* v. *Minister for Education* [1989] ECR 3967.

[76] Council Regulation 975/1999 OJL 120/1 states that support for minorities and promoting and protecting 'the right to use one's own language' are two items worthy of receiving development aid.

Niamh Shuibhne may suggest that there is scope for the EU, and thus the Court, to develop its 'visibility' in the language rights field but acknowledges that attaining influence over 'minority language rights protection within its Member States is a more problematic concept'.[77] The ambition may be present but the competence and will are less evident, something that has been given credence by the most blatant failure to address the question in the EU Charter of Fundamental Rights. No mention was made of minorities in that text, a fact that may be tempered by anti-discrimination rhetoric but which nevertheless misses the very point assumed by the EU in its relations with third countries in general and applicant states in particular. Group rights require *recognition* as well as promotion to ensure that institutionalised and widespread discrimination and racism is countered. Internally, the Charter indicates a total absence of minority rights as a separate rights construct.[78] It, therefore, directly countermands the Commission's own suggestion in 2001 that the Charter should 'promote coherence between the EU's internal and external approaches' on minority rights.[79] It is indicative of an approach that externally is keen to promote collective rights but internally is reluctant to even discuss them in such a fashion. The very concept of rights in this context is therefore subject to a fundamental distinction. There may be some hope that the changes introduced by the Lisbon Treaty could amend this tendency by the specific reference to minority rights in its lists of values. But without the competences attaching to the EU institutions and without any fundamental shift in jurisprudential thinking about collective rather than individual rights it is difficult to imagine a complete reorientation taking place.

Can the concept of universalism appear as anything other than an ambiguous construct in the EU's hands given this condition? It certainly seems to be constantly subject to a basic distinction. For whatever reason, internal rights are not affected by the same considerations and approaches as the external. The choices as to which human rights are promoted, scrutinised and enforced by the EU in each sphere are

---

[77] Niamh Nic Shuibhne, 'The European Union and Minority Language Rights', *MOST Journal on Multicultural Societies* 3:2 (2001) para. 4.2.

[78] It was criticised by the Assembly of the Council of Europe for that reason. See Report of the Parliamentary Assembly of the Council of Europe Resolution 1128(2000) at 3.

[79] Communication from the Commission to the Council and the European Parliament, 'The European Union's Role in Promoting Human Rights and Democratisation in Third Countries' COM (2001) 252 final at 3.

subject to different understandings and criteria. Dissimilar boundaries for action and interference are drawn that belie the very meaning of the universal. In particular, there is a willingness externally to embrace a collective conception of rights that finds little expression internally. Individuals are the holders of rights within the EU legal order, not groups or peoples.

Has this condition of conceptual confusion at least been resolved in the case law of the ECJ? Sionaidh Douglass-Scott notes that fundamental rights in the Union possess a floating concept that encompass so many possibilities that any and every claim could potentially qualify.[80] Of course, such an approach, if true, can hardly help construct a value that has a clear content. The indeterminacy makes assessing the relative importance of human rights in the EU's institutional ethos most difficult. Nonetheless, the adoption of respect for fundamental rights as a general principle of EU law would suggest that some clarity has been achieved. AG Maduro has gone so far as to give the protection of fundamental rights a constitutional status that gives meaning to the EU enterprise as a whole. He suggested,

it cannot be denied that [Articles 6 and 7 TEU] give expression to the profound conviction that respect for fundamental rights is intrinsic in the EU legal order and that, without it, common action by and for the peoples of Europe would be unworthy and unfeasible. In that sense, the very existence of the European Union is predicated on respect for fundamental rights. Protection of the common code of fundamental rights accordingly constitutes an existential requirement for the EU legal order.[81]

But in deciding which rights would be recognised and protected in this 'existential' way, the Court has focused on the constitutional traditions of the Member States as well as the ECHR. This has provided a fluid and restricted environment for establishing the corpus of human rights to be accepted. So, although we might find various individual rights recognised by the ECJ, and the catalogue produced has become quite extensive over the years, the approach has been piecemeal and by no means all-inclusive. This has been achieved without any certainty over what *should* be accepted as a human right in EU law. As pointed

---

[80] Sionaidh Douglas-Scott, *Constitutional Law of the European Union* (London: Longman, 2002) at 435.

[81] Case C-380/05 *Centro Europa 7 Srl* v. *Ministero delle Comunicazioni e Autorità per le garanzie nelle comunicazioni and Direzione generale per le concessioni e le autorizzazioni del Ministero delle Comunicazioni* Opinion of Mr Advocate General Poiares Maduro delivered on 12 September 2007 at para. 19.

out above, for instance, linguistic rights have not achieved the same status as other rights.[82] The rights of those suffering from disabilities, the rights of the elderly, child rights, and environmental rights, have not attained the same form of adherence as civil and political rights or economic rights arising in the context of the market. Nor, as we have seen, have minority rights acquired the kind of legal status that might be implied from the Union's external promotions.

The general condition of indeterminacy might be further emphasised if there is in place a general proviso that respect for fundamental rights will be subject to fulfilling the Treaty aims of the EU. In other words, the interests of the single internal market may overcome individual rights. This certainly has been the overall approach of the ECJ over the years. In terms of language rights, Anneleen Van Bossuyt has noted that

the ECJ always balances the (minority) language arrangements of the Member States against the interests of Community law, namely the well-functioning of the internal market. Only if they do not hinder this goal, may they be retained, under certain conditions. In other words, linguistic diversity is merely seen as a tool to realise the well-functioning of the internal market rather than as an individual goal.[83]

For some commentators, however, the cases of *Omega*[84] and *Schmidberger*[85] have suggested an alteration to the proviso, a shift in balance in favour of fundamental rights as opposed to market freedoms. But in truth they hardly represent a fundamental reappraisal. For instance, the claims that the case of *Omega*, which pronounced on the lawfulness of the Bonn police authority banning a laser simulated-killing game, solidified a right to human dignity in EU law are extremely dubious. No such right has been established by this decision that could logically attract any application beyond the circumstances of that case. The deference paid to a national authority's interpretation of human dignity may suggest a willingness to give greater expression to human rights, or greater autonomy to Member States to interpret rights as they see appropriate, but in the absence of any particular rights definition evaluated

---

[82] See Takis Tridimas, *General Principles of EU Law*, 2nd edn (Oxford: Oxford University Press, 2006) at 309 and Case C-85/94 *Piageme and Others* v. *Peeters* [1995] ECR I-2955.

[83] Anneleen Van Bossuyt, 'Is there an Effective European Legal Framework for the Protection of Minority Languages? The European Union and the Council of Europe Screened' *European Law Review* 32:6 (2007) 860–77 at 875.

[84] Case C-36/02 *Omega* v. *Bonn* [2004] ECR I-9609.

[85] Case C-112/00 *Schmidberger* v. *Austria* [2003] ECR I-5659.

by the Court it is extremely difficult, if not impossible, to understand how this might give rise to a more substantive approach to respect for human rights both specifically and in general. The only principle that this case advanced was that of proportionality. Whether the national authority decision in *Omega* went 'beyond what is necessary in order to attain the objective pursued' was the critical question. It was not that human dignity had a meaning recognisable across the constitutional traditions of the Member States and thus deserved a place at the heart of sensibilities apparent in EU law. No substantive enquiry into what this right might mean was undertaken or acknowledged.

One can hardly claim, therefore, that this case was illustrative of a new approach to human rights, one that had begun to temper respect for the internal market with an ethical perspective. Indeed, the ECJ still made clear that it would interpret any derogation from the free movement principles (which the Bonn ban allegedly accomplished) strictly 'so that its scope cannot be determined unilaterally by each Member State without any control by the Community institutions'.[86] If the authorities in *Omega* had banned all video games that depicted killing on the same grounds one wonders whether the decision of the ECJ would have remained the same.

Similarly, *Schmidberger* has the appearance of a victory for human rights over the interests of the market. But in looking at the temporary restrictions placed on travel through the Brenner Pass by the Austrian government in order to allow a demonstration against heavy road transport to take place, the Court's key concern was again the principle of proportionality. There was no real attempt to understand or apply a particular human right. The Court referred to both the rights to freedom of expression and association on the one hand and the free movement of goods as equal 'interests' on the other. Thus 'the interests involved must be weighed having regard to all the circumstances of the case in order to determine whether a fair balance was struck between those interests'.[87] Although national authorities were accorded a 'wide margin of discretion' ultimately it was for the ECJ to decide whether their actions were 'proportionate in the light of the legitimate objective pursued, namely, in the present case, the protection of fundamental rights'.[88] As with *Omega* it would be hard

---

[86] See *Omega* at para. 30. See also Case 41/74 *Van Duyn* v. *Home Office* [1974] ECR 1337 at para. 18 and Case 30/77 *Bouchereau* [1977] ECR 1999 at para. 33.

[87] *Schmidberger* at para. 81.   [88] *Ibid.* at para. 82.

to imagine any appreciable interference with the free movement of goods being forgiven under this approach unless the human rights matters related to the occurrence of tangible and significant (and probably physical) suffering.

In all, therefore, although concern for the cause of human rights has been evident within the ECJ's judgments, and generally in the EU's internal policy areas, and despite the creation of the EU Charter, a miasma of indeterminacy as regards both the nature and priority of human rights remains an enduring condition for the Union. Their scope and conception have not been fixed.

Of course we might say that this is to be expected of any polity and adjudicative practice. It might indeed hold true in those states where the common law has developed over time to produce legal rights that are forever in a state of evolution. The philosopher James Griffin even claims that indeterminacy is the condition of modern human rights as a whole.[89] Be that as it may, when a *sui generis* polity that operates in internal and external affairs in increasingly intrusive ways falls between the common law and constitutional bill of rights approach, the impact is likely to be persistent ambiguity. For all the statements of principle, the proof will be in the application. It is to this element that I turn now.

Scrutiny and surveillance

The mere establishment of a normative framework of human rights would suggest that the conditions and behaviour desired will require some sort of enforcement. In other words, the reference to *right* pre-supposes, at the very least, the possibility that the object of such rights is or may be prevented in some way. Whether this is by individual members of a community or the institutions which govern it, some form of protection and realisation of those rights will be necessary. If that proposition is accepted, then it follows that other institutions will be needed to monitor both the condition of the rights-bearers and the behaviour of potential wrong-doers. The quality of the scrutiny that would follow will tell us a great deal about the seriousness with which any human rights mandate is taken. In the case of the EU, we again need to examine both the external and internal approaches.

[89] James Griffin, *On Human Rights* (Oxford: Oxford University Press, 2008).

The external dimension

The scale of monitoring of human rights in countries outside the Union by the various EU institutions has become vast. Processes have evolved that are intrusive and extensive. If they were not, the very procedure for determining whether applicant states fulfil the criteria for entry or developing states are worthy of receiving aid would become suspect. Even though Philip Alston and Joseph Weiler suggested that there has been an 'absence of any systematic approach to monitoring and reporting'[90] in the EU's external relations, the evidence from accession, development, and foreign policy is that the practices adopted have been sweeping in nature. The Commission, the Parliament and the Council have all been engaged in this enterprise. It might be worth highlighting the major contributions of each.

Unsurprisingly, it is the Commission which has been at the forefront of extensive monitoring abroad. The practice reached a zenith with the accession policy prior to the various enlargements after the end of the Cold War. The 1997 'Agenda 2000' document provided the basis for scrutiny here as we have seen. It created three thematic fields of enquiry: (1) democracy and the rule of law; (2) human rights; and (3) respect for minorities. It then confirmed the grounds upon which that investigation would proceed. Following this template, the Commission has approached each applicant state with a view to conducting a 'systematic examination of the main ways in which public authorities are organised and operate, and the steps they have taken to protect fundamental rights'.[91] This is a regular process. Annual reports are compiled about each applicant state and published.[92] And candidate countries 'are expected to address the issues'[93] presented in the reports even though a general statement might be made that the political criteria is already satisfied. The scheme of examination has, therefore, represented more than an exercise in data-gathering. It also applies public pressure through a classic naming-and-shaming process.

---

[90] Philip Alston and J.H.H. Weiler, 'An "Ever Closer Union" in Need of a Human Rights Policy: the European Union and Human Rights', in Philip Alston, Mara Bustelo and James Heenan (eds.), *The EU and Human Rights* (Oxford: Oxford University Press, 1999) 3–97 at 13.

[91] This formula was repeated for all initial accession states in the late 1990s. See, for instance, the Commission Opinion on Bulgaria's Application for Membership of the European Union, EU Bull Suppl. 13–1997 at 15.

[92] The European Luxembourg Council 1997 para. 29 established the regime for the delivery of 'regular reports'.

[93] Council, EU Annual Report on Human Rights 1999 Doc. 11380/99 at 5.

The scheme of scrutiny has been applied to all applicants. It has now been complemented by a more general European Neighbourhood Policy which attempts to apply an accession type scrutiny for geographically proximate states even if they have no prospect of joining the Union. Through the application of Association agreements and accompanying periodic Action Plans, the Commission has set human rights priorities for each state concerned. In theory, these enable the Commission to respond to information that human rights obligations have been violated or have not been realised in line with agreed recommendations. Such information can be taken seriously in the context of implementing financial support through the agreements suggesting that the monitoring that does take place can have a significant impact. States have to be aware that they are under surveillance. Whether or not they choose to ignore that (and we have seen various examples where the actual response of the Union to noted violations has been muted)[94] the fact remains that monitoring has a role to play in determining appropriate action for human rights through the EU.

The same applies in the context of development and foreign policies. There again structures are in place for the Commission to take note of information concerning human rights conditions outside the EU. It possesses its own evaluative mechanisms, relying upon EU personnel to provide collated information about topics of concern. A system of EU delegations, fact-finding missions, and research is in place that enables the Commission to enhance other sources of information. This clearly gives weight to possible monitoring processes that might be extremely useful in assessing human rights conditions on an emergency or systemic basis.

The Parliament also becomes involved in the structure of monitoring, although with less coordination and with less capacity. It does institute the compilation of human rights reports and has appointed *rapporteurs* and ad hoc MEP delegations on numerous occasions to investigate and analyse particular human rights issues and situations.[95]

The Council is the weakest of the three institutions in monitoring. This is hardly surprising given its lack of resources and its political

[94] See for instance the limited response to Israel's condemned interventions in Lebanon in 2006 and Gaza in 2008/9.

[95] For a recent example see the ad hoc delegation to Moldova, which reported violations of human rights following a visit in April 2009. See Report by Mrs Marianne MIKKO, online, available at: www.europarl.europa.eu/meetdocs/2004_2009/documents/dv/200/200905/20090504_repmoldovarev_en.pdf.

role. Nonetheless, it does engage in monitoring processes of sorts either through the collation and dissemination of information accumulated from the other institutions and through Member States, or the consideration of such material in making political decisions. Its Annual Reports on Human Rights have become increasingly detailed over the years although the content is largely anodyne and self-congratulatory. It certainly does not possess a self-critical dimension to any appreciable extent. The report of 2008 gives a flavour of this lack of modesty:

> The unique place which the European Union holds in the world leads it to commit itself particularly strongly to the protection and promotion of human rights. Victims of violations expect the EU to help put an end to the injustices which they experience on a day-to-day basis. Human rights defenders look at the EU to support them in their relentless efforts to promote human rights. This report shows that the European Union is endeavouring to fulfil these expectations through constantly renewed efforts and making use of the large number of instruments available to it.[96]

Despite this, it would be hard to deny that the institutional structures for monitoring are in place. Whether they amount to more than responding to the work of serious human rights organisations and NGOs is another matter. But there is strong evidence that scrutiny of human rights in the world is at least acknowledged as an important aspect of policy and action.

The internal dimension

If we first look at scrutiny of the EU institutions and their actions in human rights terms, it is apparent that there is no formal external review. The EU is not a member of an international human rights regime. The ECJ's Opinion 2/94 ensured that from a legal standpoint accession to the ECHR could not be undertaken without Treaty amendment.[97] The Member States have to agree unanimously to such a step, something they steadfastly refused to countenance for decades. Only with the demand for a constitutional treaty has the issue become one for serious intergovernmental decision.[98] This is now a commitment in the Lisbon Treaty although it is uncertain how this will be achieved.

---

[96] Council, EU Annual Report on Human Rights 2008, COHOM 105 27 November 2008.
[97] *Opinion 2/94 on Accession by the EU to the ECHR* [1996] ECR I-1759.
[98] Article I-7(2) of the Draft Constitutional Treaty of 2003 proposed that the EU 'shall seek accession' but inserted no timetable or other requirement for the completion of the process. The Lisbon Treaty followed suit.

The absence of exterior review has been a source of concern for both commentators and national constitutional courts alike. The EU's development of the principle that 'fundamental rights form an integral part of the general principles' of EU law assuaged some of the criticisms as we have already seen. The ECJ has been empowered to review the acts of EU institutions to ensure they are compatible with fundamental rights. But of course this does not provide any kind of monitoring process.

The European Ombudsman, however, is specifically authorised to oversee EU acts under Article 195 EC Treaty (now Article 228 TFEU). Individuals who are citizens of the EU or legally resident within it are entitled to bring complaints. The Council has recognised that the Ombudsman's role should be 'to examine alleged cases of maladministration in the actions of the EU institutions or bodies [and] to undertake investigations on his own initiative' that might 'relate to questions of human rights, particularly freedom of expression and non-discrimination'.[99] In practice, the Ombudsman's investigative role is piecemeal and prompted by specific information and complaints received against the EU's institutions. In no sense can it claim to provide comprehensive or regular scrutiny.

The European Parliament has acknowledged the lacunae that exists and has attempted to rectify the position. The Committee on Citizens' Freedoms and Rights, Justice and Home Affairs noted that:

it is the particular responsibility of the European Parliament (by virtue of the role conferred on it under the new Article 7(1) of the Treaty of Nice) and of its appropriate committee to ensure (in cooperation with the national parliaments and the parliaments of the applicant countries) that both the EU institutions and the Member States uphold the rights set out in the various sections of the [EU Charter].[100]

Article 7(1) TEU as amended by the Treaty of Nice gave the Parliament the discretion to determine 'that there is a clear risk of a serious breach by a Member State' of respect for human rights as contained in Article 6(1) TEU. The institutions are not mentioned in this provision. It is questionable authority for examining the institutions' human rights record, as I explored in Chapter 3. Nevertheless, the Parliament took it upon itself to undertake a process of monitoring the EU using the EU

---

[99] Council, EU Annual Report on Human Rights 2000 at 8.
[100] Committee on Citizens' Freedoms and Rights, Justice and Home Affairs Report on the Situation as Regards Fundamental Rights in the EU (2000) [2001] A5–0223/2001.

Charter as its guide. Although this was an innovative move it fails to match the processes available in external policies in two ways.

First, by focusing on the provisions of the Charter it does not provide the means for examining the EU's work in rights outside that instrument. Group rights as we have seen are largely excluded.

Second, the Parliament is almost entirely reliant upon other sources for its information. Individual communications, reports from NGOs and publicly available data from international organisations such as the Council of Europe provide the material for assessment. It does not have the facilities to undertake a continuous assessment of human rights issues.[101]

The position has been no better in relation to scrutiny of the Member States regarding their observance of human rights. The institutional approach has been that 'the protection and promotion of human rights is primarily a matter for the Member States of the Union, in accordance with their own judicial systems'.[102] We know that 'no Treaty provision confers on the EU institutions any general power to enact rules on human rights'.[103] And Member States have given no indication that they would appreciate a change in this approach. Rather, the EU has generally relied upon the argument that, being signatories to the ECHR and numerous international human rights instruments and procedures, Member States are already subject to a rigorous system of scrutiny by outside agencies.

Despite these arguments and restrictions, the general critique that internal powers should be commensurate with those exercised externally has been recognised by the EU institutions up to a point. The European Parliament said explicitly

if the promotion of human rights outside the Union is to be credible, we must begin by examining the human rights situation at home. Numerous reports remind us that there is not always complete congruence between the ideals as they are printed in international Conventions and national Constitutions vis-à-vis the situation experienced by citizens and residents in Member States.[104]

---

[101] The Rapporteur for the year 2000, Thierry Cornillet, was pained to admit 'the lack of resources available'. *Ibid.* at 24.

[102] Council, EU Annual Report on Human Rights 2000 at 11.

[103] *Opinion 2/94* at para. 27.

[104] Committee on Citizens' Freedoms and Rights, Justice and Home Affairs Annual Report on respect for Human Rights in the European Union (1998–1999) [2000] A5–0050/2000 at 20.

The Parliament has indeed attempted to provide some of this much needed scrutiny but again it does not have the resources or infrastructure to do justice to the need. Any reports issued have been general reviews on the situation within the Member States as well as the EU institutions. Concerns in Member States are invariably covered sketchily if specified in any detail at all. The vagueness continues to undermine the Parliament's intentions.

Similarly, the fact that the Parliament operates independently of the Commission and Council weakens the effects of its actions. Externally, the whole weight of the EU is behind its practice. Politically and economically it is imbued with a severe authority whatever cynical view of the EU's presence in the world one may have. Scrutiny by the Parliament simply does not possess that capacity.

The Council achieves less. Originally, its Annual Reports on Human Rights were to 'enhance the transparency of the Union's human rights policies'.[105] But, almost perversely, these have focused increasingly on external matters. The only concession to the charge of inconsistency has been to acknowledge that 'the picture would be incomplete without at least making a reference to EU action related to developments in the EU area'.[106] But the latest report, for 2008, makes no pretence that it is attempting to provide scrutiny of Member States vis-à-vis *their* human rights record. This accords with the general acceptance that human rights are the preserve of national jurisdiction.

Such a position may be readily understandable from a political perspective. The fear of governmental embarrassment resulting from abuses noted by the EU may be real. But how does that accord with all the institutional rhetoric applied to the notion of the universality of human rights and their place at the core of the Union's ethical framework? The sensitivity evident with the lack of critique offered against the UK in its actions in Iraq, the policies adopted by various Member States regarding the treatment of suspected terrorists, the story of extraordinary rendition told in Chapter 3, all failed to provoke any meaningful attention within the EU system. The clear indication from all these examples (and the many that have accrued over the years) is that internal scrutiny is simply outside the EU's jurisdiction. This can only be detrimental to claims that respect for human rights is a central

---

[105] EU Annual Report on Human Rights 1999 at 1.
[106] *Ibid.*

plank of the EU's institutional ethos, particularly given the importance of monitoring for the effectiveness of any such commitment.

Some possible remedy for this condition has appeared in the formation of the EU Fundamental Rights Agency (FRA). Emerging out of the
Monitoring Centre for Racism and Xenophobia, this agency has a mandate to review the human rights records of both the EU institutions and
the Member States in relation to the articles of the EU Charter. But it is
still constrained in what it can do. This is most evident in the failure to
incorporate within its remit any ongoing review of Member States for
the purposes of Article 7 TEU monitoring. Although the Preparatory
Study for the Impact Assessment on the FRA noted the argument that
'given the seriousness of implications of evoking Article 7 procedures,
the basis for [identifying events attracting concern] should be a regular, systematic and independent monitoring of respect for common
values in all Member States'[107] and suggested that 'an Agency capable
of providing the Council with reliable, systematic and independent
information relating to common values and fundamental rights would
be useful',[108] the final Impact Assessment made clear that a limited
remit for the FRA was preferred.[109] It suggested that the cost would
be excessive to police Article 7 conditions. Instead, it preferred to rely
upon an understanding that any Article 7 'crisis would be identified
without any specific mechanisms at the EU level'.[110]

The hope that consistent institutional monitoring of Member States'
human rights records would be embraced by the EU through the FRA
has thus been severely undermined. In turn, this has made the possible
link between the revealing of human rights violations (by Member
States or the EU institutions) and any enforcement action fairly strained.
Rather than be a precursor to action the FRA's limited remit, like the
EUMC's before it, will place the issue of human rights fully within the
diplomatic realm allowing national government sensitivities to be protected. Although there must be value in the compilation of data and
its publication there is bound to be a largely non-judgmental approach

---

[107] *Preparatory Study for Impact Assessment and Ex-ante Evaluation of Fundamental Rights
Agency*, February 2005 at 42.

[108] *Ibid.* at 43.

[109] Commission Staff Working Paper Impact Assessment Report 30 June 2005 COM
(2005) 280 final.

[110] See http://europa.eu.int/comm/justice_home/fsj/rights/fsj_rights_agency_en.htm for
details of the public consultation undertaken. Details of the Impact Assessment
are available at http://europa.eu.int/comm/justice_home/doc_centre/rights/doc/
sec_2005_849_En.pdf

taken. The FRA will rely on the reports it commissions to speak for themselves. The FRA's position will be officially non-judgmental. Does that serve the cause of human rights? Up to a very restricted point only. The power of the external approach lies in the capacity for the EU to act upon human rights related information. The link between monitoring and enforcement is central. Internally the disjuncture between the two is reinforced by the FRA's restricted mandate. This is a serious faultline in the institutional commitment to human rights. But is this remedied in other enforcement practices available?

Enforcement

The argument against the involvement of the EU in the internal human rights affairs of its Member States has always focused on questions of competence and jurisdiction. Direct involvement in such internal matters might be 'an invitation to a wholesale destruction of the jurisdictional boundaries between the EU and its Member States'.[111] However, the Council itself has not been shy in recognising the 'relativity of the principle of non-interference'.[112] At Luxembourg, in 1991, it maintained that externally 'different ways of expressing concern about violations of rights, as well as requests designed to secure those rights, cannot be considered as interference in the internal affairs of a State'.[113] The imposition of various forms of human rights conditionality, including that applied in the pre-accession strategy, has received formal and legal approval. An apparent contradiction between the arguments raised at the internal level and the practices at the external could not be clearer. From our consideration of conceptualisation and monitoring of human rights we can predict that enforcement is bound to be restricted accordingly. Nonetheless, we still need to chart briefly the approaches adopted in the two dimensions.

The external dimension

The EU appears to have become committed to a wide range of meaningful enforcement measures in its external affairs over the years.

---

[111] Alston and Weiler, 'An "Ever Closer Union" in Need of a Human Rights Policy' at 23.

[112] Commission Communication to the Council and the European Parliament, *The European Union and the External Dimension of Human Rights Policy: From Rome to Maastricht and Beyond*, COM (95) 567, at 10.

[113] Declaration on Human Rights, Luxembourg European Council 1991, quoted in *ibid.* at 10.

It has constructed a number of procedures putting into effect those extensive normative commitments I noted above. The approach to states seeking accession to the Union has demonstrated specifically the extent to which human rights could be the subject of serious intervention. The EU institutions have been able to apply considerable pressure on applicant states on human rights issues. This is something I have considered in detail elsewhere.[114] It remains the case for those states still seeking admission, particularly Turkey and certain Balkan States. The combination of encouragement through the prospect of membership and financial support together with the withdrawal of these incentives should there be significant slippage in human rights matters by the state concerned, suggest a robust and potentially highly effective procedure of enforcement. Serbia in particular has felt the force of this conditionality. The official requirement that all states from the region seeking admission as well as interim support should comply with the Copenhagen Criteria and those matters specifically identified in the relevant Partnership Agreement has been used as a means for enforcing change.[115] In particular, the breach of the requirement that Serbia cooperate fully with the International Criminal Tribunal for the Former Yugoslavia led to the suspension of the admission process in May 2006. They resumed only upon Serbia's commitment to undertake such cooperation in 2007. Practical adherence to that obligation was noted with enthusiasm in the Commission's 2008 Progress Report following the arrest of Radovan Karadžić in July of that year.[116] Of course, Serbia still falls short in numerous other human rights related factors, something the Progress Report is at pains to note. Consequently the pressure of conditionality, although relieved, remains in place.[117]

---

[114] For full details of the measures employed see Williams, *EU Human Rights Policies*, chapter 3.

[115] The relevant text for Serbia is currently Council Decision of 18 February 2008 2008/213/EC: on the principles, priorities and conditions contained in the European Partnership with Serbia including Kosovo as defined by United Nations Security Council Resolution 1244 of 10 June 1999 and repealing Decision 2006/56/EC.

[116] Serbia Progress Report 2008, Communication from the Commission to the European Parliament and the Council Enlargement Strategy and Main Challenges 2008–2009 COM (2008)674.

[117] The problem of sustaining this pressure post-accession is something that I note below. It is also considered in many other analyses. See for instance Catherine Dupre, 'After Reforms: Human Rights Protection in Post-communist States', *European Human Rights Law Review* 5 (2008) 621–32.

In development policy, significant possibilities for addressing human rights concerns have also been developed.[118] Through political and economic pressure and through an active engagement in international human rights fora, the EU has demonstrated a broad appreciation of human rights and the circumstances in which they should be considered, promoted and/or enforced. Many criticisms of consistency and political interference can and have been directed at the EU's role in these matters but generally the willingness to adopt a working policy applicable by and through the institutions has been notable. From positive measures to sanctions a wide range of action may be taken. Of particular note is the Commission's acknowledgement that a state's human rights performance 'including economic, social and cultural rights' will be taken into account when deciding the quantity of funds to be made available under the development cooperation programmes.[119]

Similarly, in general foreign policy the positive and negative measures both made available to the EU and actually applied are reasonably intensive.[120] Diplomatic, economic and political tools are readily available. The powers are broad indeed and remain the proud boast of the Council.[121] They might be criticised for being inadequate, partial, and subject to political interference, as well as inconsistent, but they probably represent a good range of institutional measures that exceed most if not all other global or regional human rights organisations or agencies. The very fact that the EU can bring to bear economic pressure in particular, through sanction and incentive, separates it from the UN and the Council of Europe. Its centralised system of decision-making also enables action to be taken swiftly if desired. Again this is not a quality that other international organisations possess with any abundance. Whether or not the EU institutions choose to deploy the enforcement measures it owns is of course an issue. But the fact that they are within their power and have been utilised with some regularity testifies to the depth of commitment here.

---

[118] See Williams, *EU Human Rights Policies* chapter 2. See also Lorand Bartels, *Human Rights Conditionality in the EU's International Agreements* (Oxford: Oxford University Press, 2005).

[119] Communication from the Commission to the Council and the European Parliament, 'The EU's Role in Promoting Human Rights and Democratisation in Third Countries' COM (2001)252 final at 12.

[120] See Urfan Khaliq, *Ethical Dimensions of the Foreign Policy of the European Union: a Legal Appraisal* (Cambridge: Cambridge University Press, 2008).

[121] The Council's Annual Reports on Human Rights chart the use of its available measures in much detail.

Can the same be said internally? What comparable internal power does the EU possess?

The internal dimension

The possibility for actual enforcement of human rights norms within the EU by its institutions has always been extremely restricted. The overarching internal condition is that human rights *tout court* lie outside the competence of the EU.

That this extended principle has been subject to some amplification by the ECJ has not seriously undermined the expressed restriction, reiterated, it has to be recalled, by the EU Charter of Fundamental Rights. Article 51 ensures that the provisions of the Charter are addressed to Member States 'only when they are implementing Union law'. A fundamental restriction on enforcement action is thus inherent within the EU's legal structure. The fact that there 'are many, many areas where [Member States] face EU generated negative constraints or must respect positive prescriptions'[122] does not change the fact that the ECJ and the EU as a whole remains constrained in human rights cases. Even when EU law might be engaged, Armin von Bogandy notes that 'there seems to be a mismatch between the range and depth of the EU activities and the tiny number of human rights cases involving EU intrusion brought'.[123] Judicial enforcement and institutional practice is highly restricted in practice notwithstanding various attempts to extend the EU's influence in this area through persuasive measures such as mainstreaming, human rights impact assessments, and the Open Method of Cooperation.

Even when addressing a subject that many might think would not be constrained by any political sensitivity, this is still the case. Witness for instance the approach to child rights. The Commission declared in 2006 that in addressing the rights and needs of children 'the situation in the Union is still not satisfactory'.[124] It noted the European Council's demand that Member States should 'take necessary measures to rapidly and significantly reduce child poverty' and that child rights

---

[122] Giorgio Sacerdoti, 'The European Charter of Fundamental Rights: from a Nation-State Europe to a Citizens' Europe', *Columbia Journal of European Law* (2002) 37–52 at 48.

[123] Armin von Bogandy, 'The European Union as a Human Rights Organization? Human Rights and the Core of the European Union', *Common Market Law Review* 37 (2000) 1307–38 at 1321.

[124] Commission, Communication from the Commission, 'Towards an EU Strategy on the Rights of the Child'.

'form part of the human rights that the EU and Member States are bound to respect'. But nonetheless it had to accept that the 'EU does not have general competence in the area of fundamental rights, including children's rights' and had to fall back upon a 'general duty' for the EU to 'abstain from acts violating these rights, but also to take them into account wherever relevant in the conduct of its own policies'. Even then, the principles of subsidiarity and proportionality had to be respected, leaving the EU with limited opportunities of 'legislative action, soft-law, financial assistance or political dialogue'. This sums up the restrictions on enforcement measures available internally. It is only when an issue touches upon the political vision of the institutions or falls within the ambit of matters relating to the single market that intervention can really be effected.

The introduction of Article 7 TEU may have suggested a willingness to consider an enforcement mechanism that could have corresponded in theory to that employed externally. But, as Manfred Nowak has observed, the requirements for suspension set out, 'are, of course, even more stringent' than the accession criteria we have already encountered.[125] Koen Lenaerts further suggested that it is 'not very probable that the sanction mechanism as it now stands will easily be applied'.[126] This has since been confirmed, as I considered in Chapter 3. No action has been taken against any Member State and it is hardly prescient to suggest that Article 7 will never be deployed unless dictatorship of some kind takes hold.

The range of political and economic sanctions available to the EU to enforce human rights internally therefore scarcely matches the external measures. The European Parliament's attempts to fill the void do not compare favourably with the external approach. They are neutered by the fact that they are not supported by the powers of enforcement or persuasion available to the Commission. Institutional dialogue, economic assistance (or its withdrawal) and ultimately the threat of exclusion are reserved for external states, producing a highly persuasive package that can operate to change human rights conditions. The comparison with the accession procedures in particular demonstrates the disparity. States that have obtained entry to the Union are simply

[125] Manfred Nowak, 'Human Rights Conditionality in the EU', in Philip Alston, Mara Bustelo and James Heenan (eds.), *The EU and Human Rights* (Oxford: Oxford University Press, 1999) 687–98, at 694.
[126] Koen Lenaerts, 'Fundamental Rights in the European Union', *European Law Review* 25:6 (2000) 575–600 at 587–8.

not subject to the same level of potential enforcement. The stories of human rights slippage, of work begun under the accession procedures but effectively abandoned once admission was effected, are growing.[127] A.G. Toth warned of this danger a decade ago, noting 'if the status quo continues the Court of Justice will not be in a position … to ensure compliance with … a whole range of vitally important human rights issues (e.g. oppression of ethnic and other minorities) simply because they fall outside the scope of EU/Union competence'.[128] That has come to pass. The conjunction of strategies open to the EU externally is simply unparalleled internally.

Having said this, we do have in the ECJ an institution that has legal authority to enforce those fundamental rights recognised as applicable in EU law. Clearly, this sets the internal condition apart from the external. Or does it?

The Court has, over time, been able to extend its limited remit. Although only those actions by Member States undertaken within the scope of EU law can prompt ECJ jurisdiction, *Wachauf* enabled the ECJ to examine acts taken implementing an EU provision.[129] *ERT* extended this to include circumstances when Member States derogated from an EU measure.[130] But the fundamental principle is that competence to enforce human rights is severely limited. Two restrictions operate specifically to constrain the judicial enforcement capability further.

First, there is the limitation on *locus standi*. Although the principle of effective judicial protection is a general principle of Community law, confirmed by the ECJ,[131] there remain structural barriers to effective access. The difficulty for an individual to bring an action for the review of the legality of acts of EU institutions directly to the ECJ is notorious. Article 230 EC Treaty (now Article 263 TFEU) has been interpreted by the Court as imposing a heavy burden on individuals to demonstrate that they have been affected by a measure 'by reason of certain attributes which are peculiar to them or by reason of circumstances in which they are differentiated from all other persons'.[132] Interested

---

[127] See, for instance, Gulara Guliyeva, 'Lost in Transition: Russian-speaking Non-citizens in Latvia and the Protection of Minority Rights in the European Union', *European Law Review* 33:6 (2008) 843–69.

[128] A.G. Toth, 'The European Union and Human Rights: the Way Forward', *Common Market Law Review* 34 (1997) 491–529 at 529.

[129] Case 5/88 *Wachauf* v. *Germany* [1989] ECR 2609.

[130] Case C-260/89 *ERT* [1991] ECR I-2925.

[131] See, for instance, Case C432/05 *Unibet* [2007] ECR I2271, at para. 37.

[132] Case 25/62 *Plaumann & Co.* v. *Commission* [1963] ECR 95, at 107.

parties who cannot fulfil this test are excluded. As AG Francis Jacob suggested this has the potential of leaving people without effective judicial protection.[133] Similarly, the only other route to ECJ review, a request by a national court to the ECJ for a preliminary ruling under Article 234 EC Treaty (now Article 267 TFEU), is not a 'remedy available to individual applicants as a matter of right'.[134] Although the ECHR requirement that domestic remedies be exhausted is not applicable the structural restraints lay further obstacles in the path of those who wish to assert their human rights. Whichever avenue for review is taken, long delays attach to these procedures and there are significant cost implications. It is hardly surprising therefore that the number of human rights challenges heard by the ECJ have been few in number and of those many have emanated from well-resourced corporations.

Second, there have been significant areas where the ECJ has had no, or restricted, jurisdiction over the actions of the Member States. As we saw in Chapter 3, the Court is still precluded from ruling on restrictions to free movement of persons based on 'the maintenance of law and order and the safeguarding of internal security'.[135] Similarly, judicial review for acts in the area of police and judicial cooperation in criminal matters have been subject to varying restrictions. In these fields, the EU system has interpreted its commitment to respect human rights through a sharp political lens. The dangers of this position were heightened with the increasing possibilities for human rights violations occurring as a result of EU institutional decisions. The European Parliament Civil Liberties, Justice and Home Affairs Committee has warned of the 'stakes' involved in the external dimension of the Area of Freedom Security and Justice.[136] Noting the migration control systems being put in place across the EU's borders under the rubric of FRONTEX, it has condemned the tendency towards a 'zone of indistinction and arbitrariness' regarding the application of human rights, which is 'contrary to the EU values'.[137] Overall, decision-making in this area is criticised for being 'fragmented' and leading to the blurring of 'accountability and responsibility'.[138] Issues of security and migration are inextricably linked so as to threaten individual human rights in a systematic rather than isolated fashion.

---

[133] See *UPA* [2002] ECR I-6677 AG Jacobs Opinion at para. 62.
[134] *Ibid.* at para. 42.   [135] Article 276 TFEU.
[136] European Parliament, 'External Dimension of the Area of Freedom, Security and Justice' March 2009 PE 410.688.
[137] *Ibid.* at 18.   [138] *Ibid.* at 23.

Despite these institutional restrictions there are some indicators that the ECJ could develop a more human rights conscious approach. The opinions of Advocate General Maduro might indicate this. It is worth quoting again his comments in *Centra Europa 7* that

respect for fundamental rights is intrinsic in the EU legal order and that, without it, common action by and for the peoples of Europe would be unworthy and unfeasible. In that sense, the very existence of the European Union is predicated on respect for fundamental rights. Protection of the common code of fundamental rights accordingly constitutes an existential requirement for the EU legal order.[139]

He went on to say that '[a]gainst this background, the Court fulfils its function of ensuring the observance, by the Member States, of fundamental rights as general principles of law'.[140] Helpfully, he then set out the limitations. In doing so he provided a fascinating insight into a potential radicalisation of EU law regarding human rights.

20 ... a distinction must be drawn between, on the one hand, jurisdiction to review any national measure in the light of fundamental rights and, on the other hand, jurisdiction to examine whether Member States provide the necessary level of protection in relation to fundamental rights in order to be able adequately to fulfil their other obligations as members of the Union. The first type of review does not yet exist and is not within the Union's current competences. However, the second type of review flows logically from the nature of the process of European integration. It serves to guarantee that the basic conditions are in place for the proper functioning of the EU legal order and for the effective exercise of many of the rights granted to European citizens. Though the degree of protection of fundamental rights at national level does not have to be exactly the same as the degree of protection of fundamental rights at the level of the European Union, there must be some measure of equivalence in order to ensure that the law of the Union can operate effectively within the national legal order.

21. The scenario may seem unlikely at first sight, but I do not discount, offhand, the idea that a serious and persistent breach of fundamental rights might occur in a Member State, making it impossible for that State to comply with many of its EU obligations and effectively limiting the possibility for individuals to benefit fully from the rights granted to them by EU law. For instance, it would be difficult to envisage citizens of the Union exercising their rights of

---

[139] Case C-380/05 *Centro Europa 7 Srl* v. *Ministero delle Comunicazioni e Autorità per le garanzie nelle comunicazioni* and *Direzione generale per le concessioni e le autorizzazioni del Ministero delle Comunicazioni*, Opinion of Mr Advocate General Poiares Maduro delivered on 12 September 2007 para. 19.

[140] *Ibid.* para. 20.

free movement in a Member State where there are systemic shortcomings in the protection of fundamental rights. Such systemic shortcomings would, in effect, amount to a violation of the rules on free movement.

22. My suggestion is not that any violation of fundamental rights within the meaning of Article 6(2) EU constitutes, of itself, an infringement of the rules on free movement. Only serious and persistent violations which highlight a problem of systemic nature in the protection of fundamental rights in the Member State at issue, would, in my view, qualify as violations of the rules on free movement, by virtue of the direct threat they would pose to the transnational dimension of European citizenship and to the integrity of the EU legal order. However, so long as the protection of fundamental rights in a Member State is not gravely inadequate in that sense, I believe the Court should review national measures for their conformity with fundamental rights only when these measures come within the scope of application of the Court's jurisdiction as defined in its caselaw to date.

This, possibly, is a declaration of intent, an invitation even. It acknowledges the existing highly restricted potential for judicial scrutiny and judgment on the actions of Member States. But it also alludes to the prospect of an individual bringing to the Court a 'systemic' failure of human rights in any particular Member State that would, in effect, mean those economic rights enshrined in the internal market freedoms could not be uniformly relied upon. The invitation for an aggrieved individual to present to the Court evidence of a systemic failure of human rights is manifest.

But surely such 'serious and persistent violations' amounting to a systemic problem would be the territory of Article 7 TEU, a provision that the ECJ is explicitly prevented from reviewing? Is this mere bravura by AG Maduro? Or is there something more subtle being claimed here? If all that Maduro is saying is that the current regime of restricted interpretation by the ECJ on fundamental rights grounds is to be respected, this still serves to emphasise the relative impotence of the ECJ to fulfil its mandate of 'ensuring the observance, by the Member States, of fundamental rights'. Alternatively, if he is suggesting that the current political settlement, reflected in the legal framework, could be subverted through adjudicative processes, then he is attempting to forge a deep and direct connection between fundamental values and the role of law in the Union.

It is doubtful that there is support for such a radical change within the legal realm, let alone the political. Although human rights have been generously interpreted in recent years the enduring position is that their enforcement through EU law remains severely constrained.

When coupled with a relative lack of coherence between the monitoring available and what is heard legally, this restricted regime of legal action, with its limited access for judicial review and its limited ability to review measures by Member States, we have an internal system that cannot pretend to privilege human rights. Their value is contingent upon the exigencies of the market and the power structures enshrined in law.

Conclusion

What then is the quality of respect for human rights in the institutional ethos? The evidence to date is that the EU as an independent entity simply will not identify this value as a priority for action. All those potential mechanisms for conceptualisation, scrutiny and enforcement, which I have examined and upon which human rights litigation and practice ultimately depend, have largely been eschewed in favour of the main purpose of the EU; the construction of an internal market. The economic interpretation of 'well-being' is still predominant. It is this that has underpinned the EU, has provided its *raison d'être*, and established the parameters for judgment in EU law. AG Maduro's opinion in *Centra*, for all its radical implications, still recognises this key fact.

So we have seen that the difficulty faced by the ECJ in applying human rights norms other than in the context of the operation of European law, the restricted mandate of the Fundamental Rights Agency, the politicised context for the development of human rights (for example in relation to the saga of extraordinary rendition, which demonstrated the impotence of the EU in crucial human rights problems), the incoherence between external and internal approaches in the construction, scrutiny and enforcement of human rights, and the specific irony of subjecting accession states to considerable scrutiny before entry and little afterwards, provoke a persistent critique. They all speak of a human rights model that is pre-conditionally focused on the preservation of the *institution* rather than the attainment of any other form of justice.

What has been revealed, therefore, is that despite the consistent pronouncements in favour of human rights we have yet to experience coherence in the EU's institutional activities that could place human rights at the head of any list of value priorities. The lack of clarity in the nature of its ethical commitment, the confusion of what human rights might mean, the ambiguous nature of its adherence to qualities associated with the realisation of human rights standards, all point to a tepid devotion. Human rights are important to the Union. It has overseen an institutional reinvention of their place in the EU dominion. And human rights initiatives appear to guide a significant number of policy decisions. But overall, would anyone seriously believe that the EU as presently structured and governed could be trusted to administer a human rights regime that maintained a principled approach to relevant standards? At every turn we can see enthusiasm and rhetorical flourish but in practice human rights are undermined by an institutional incapability to make them truly fundamental. The relative failure to even recognise the qualities that should be associated with this element reflects upon an institutional ethos that is characterised by enthusiasm but also lack of competence. I am not suggesting here that the EU's personnel are in anyway unable to meet the demands posed by human rights. And it is evident in the level of interest of human rights organisations to establish bases in Brussels that the EU is seen as wielding substantial influence of one kind or another. But I *am* claiming that the institution as a whole has been incapable of, first, sufficiently identifying the needs of a human rights policy and, second, putting those that are recognised into meaningful practice. That is the condition of this value that I claim has evolved in the institutional ethos.

5   Democracy

Introduction

It is a simple irony that if we compared those international organisations that had a significant impact on people's lives around the world, we might conclude that the EU was the most democratic of them all. Of all those regional trading and regulatory regimes that have sprouted around the globe over the last twenty years or more, none can truly match the EU in its democratic credentials. Aspects of transparency and accountability may be replicated in some corners of supra-state governance but there is little to compete with the institutional development of democratic-type structures and practices of the Union. For some the EU even compares well with the realities of 'political representation, deliberation and output' experienced in 'advanced industrial democracies', although this might not be a commendation.[1]

And yet, 'European Union' and 'democratic government' are two phrases rarely uttered together positively in the same sentence. Indeed, whenever 'democracy' is raised in the context of the EU it struggles to avoid the immediate association of 'deficit'. One might be forgiven, indeed, for assuming that 'democratic deficit' was *the* condition of Europe forever condemning the Union to illegitimacy. No doubt such a view could be justified by highlighting the lack of institutional commitment to state-like democratic processes evident since the construction of an 'economic' rather than political 'Community'. Alternatively, one could argue that none of the other international regimes one could mention have had such an impact on people's lives as the EU (although no doubt those in the developing world might well argue that the

[1] Andrew Moravcsik, 'In Defence of the "Democratic Deficit": Reassessing Legitimacy in the European Union', *Journal of Common Market Studies* 40:4 (2002) 603–24.

World Bank and the IMF have exercised immense influence over them). We might, therefore, perhaps expect a great deal more from the EU. We might expect an institutional commitment to practices of democracy familiar to modern Western states. We might even expect *greater* adherence to democratic processes as well as an imaginative approach to their delivery.

Whatever the strength of these two contrasting perspectives, there is no doubt that democracy *is* a value or principle that has been announced as fundamental for the EU. This was confirmed by Article 6 TEU and the Lisbon Treaty. Nonetheless, we still need to establish the depth and scope of this value. We have to consider its practical influence amidst the evident rhetorical institutional attachment to its term.

As a prelude to specific consideration of the EU record vis-à-vis democracy this chapter first examines some general conceptions of this value that might be applicable in theory. All I intend here is to provide a brief overview of the concept so as to enable us to assess where in a spectrum of possible understandings of democracy the EU sits. Inevitably, these understandings are associated with discourses about democracy beyond the state. For, as we keep hearing, whatever the EU may become, it is presently *not* a state. It might be invidious, therefore, to superimpose a range of visions of ideal democracy associated with nation-states upon the Union at this stage. That is not to say that this will not be a necessary future endeavour. Indeed, it might well form an important element of a political settlement before too long. Even so, the level of democracy still needs to reflect the extent to which the EU as institution is given power and to which it has an impact on the lives of individuals and communities. That is if we are to stand by the principle that people should have a say in the governance of their lives and the construction of their political environment. Then the question of what kind of democratic apparatus may be possible has to be addressed. So, although we might have to have an eye on the potential future political arrangement of the EU we need nonetheless to assess the current state of this value of democracy.

The chapter will then look at the way in which elements of democratisation have been realised in the EU, and what role law has played in their construction and development. These historical and jurisprudential perspectives are intended to provide the platform for an evaluation of the depth of attachment to democracy in the EU's institutional ethos and its relative weight vis-à-vis other values considered in this book.

The concept of democracy beyond the state

'Government of the people, by the people, for the people' is an aphorism so often repeated that it has begun to take on the appearance of cliché rather than principled template. But if we look a little more closely, we might find that Abraham Lincoln's words provide key constituent elements for any modern understanding of democracy. At the very least they might establish a useful basis for considering the relevance of modern democratic discourses for a supra-state polity such as the EU. This would certainly be the case if we followed Jürgen Habermas' dictum that a 'democratic order does not inherently need to be mentally rooted in "the nation" as a pre-political community of shared destiny'.[2] Whether we go so far as to adopt a cosmopolitan perspective, which looks to the creation of a form of world citizenship, is perhaps irrelevant at this stage.[3] It is enough to imagine democratic formations falling outside political state structures. So, we should be concerned about the notions of 'government', 'people', and the various manifestations of relationship between the two, envisaged by the prepositions 'of', 'by' and 'for'.

First then, let us consider the term 'government'. A simple interpretation would suggest the word merely means any system of ruling and managing. In that sense, government has no natural correlation with democracy. Nor is it inevitably associated with states. It can apply to any system of control, whether authoritarian, egalitarian or otherwise, exercised over individuals who together are treated as some form of collectivity or community. However, for our purposes it is generally associated with the public rather than private sphere. In other words, the connection is with forms of societal control rather than say corporate or familial arrangements. So Jürgen Habermas is able to refer to government as 'an apparatus of public administration ... specializing in the administrative employment of political power for collective goals'.[4] The basis for the imposition of that system of social rule or its construction through agreement, as well as the form that it takes, is of course the very stuff of modern political philosophy and practical politics.

---

[2] Jürgen Habermas, *The Postnational Constellation* (Cambridge: Polity Press, 2001) at 76.

[3] See, in particular, David Held, *Democracy and the Global Order* (Cambridge: Polity Press, 1995) for a key text on the possible forms of cosmopolitan democracy.

[4] Jürgen Habermas, 'Three Normative Models of Democracy', in Seyla Benhabib (ed.), *Democracy and Difference: Contesting the Boundaries of the Political* (Princeton: Princeton University Press, 1996) 21–30 at 21.

It would be as well to make reference here to the connection between 'government' and 'governance'. Although clearly we are dealing with fairly fluid terms we can probably assume that the latter transcends the public/private divide and relates to the ways in which 'individuals and institutions ... manage their common affairs'.[5] James Rosenau, for instance, defines it as 'rule systems that serve as steering mechanisms through which leaders and collectivities frame and move toward their goals'.[6] It is often equated with the administrative processes that are applied in those varied contexts and relates to formal and informal arrangements of exercising control over the relevant sphere of influence. It can be macro or micro in character, finding application at multiple levels of rule systems. These might be economic, political, social and cultural in nature. Some have seen this as of particular concern for the EU because of the absence of 'political rule through responsible institutions', in other words *government*, which allows for political problems outside forms of deliberative democratic processes.[7]

Of course, my overall concern is with the general public sphere where political theory again is relevant. Even though some might 'contend that the term "governance" is a bureaucratic, apolitical construct meant to convey the notion that all problems can be resolved through technical fixes without the need for addressing fundamental political conflicts and choices',[8] many would impute that notions of justice must have as much a role to play here as with the interpretation of 'government'. Indeed, in the public sphere the relationship between the basis of government formation and the way in which that government conducts its operations are often difficult to separate. Similarly, we are obliged to encompass the legal dimension, given the inevitable issues of law that relate to these operations. As we will see in a moment, concepts of democracy and law have as much to say about the systems of governance as they do about the form of governments.

---

[5] Commission for Global Governance, *Our Global Neighbourhood* (Oxford: Oxford University Press, 1995) at 2.

[6] James Rosenau, *Distant Proximities: Dynamics Beyond Globalization* (Princeton: Princeton University Press, 2003) at 393.

[7] See E.O. Eriksen and J.E. Fossum, 'Europe at a Crossroads: Government or Transnational Governance?', in Christian Joerges, Inge-Johanne Sand and Günther Teubner (eds.), *Transnational Governance and Constitutionalism* (Oxford: Hart, 2004) 115–46 at 120.

[8] Kalypso Nicolaidis and Justine Lacroix, 'Europe's Competing Paradigms', in Rosemary Foot, John Lewis Gaddis and Andrew Hurrell (eds.), *Order and Justice in International Relations* (Oxford: Oxford University Press, 2003) 125–54 at 150.

By relating governance to government in this way we can ensure that questions of democracy are not excluded from discussion of the EU simply by suggesting that there is no European Government. Even if it was a valid view that only states are able to produce a 'government', it would not be difficult to show the EU is nonetheless engaged in acts and whole systems of governance. Consequently, issues of democracy must still be confronted.

If we then turn to the notion of 'people' in our very broad concerns with democracy we are perhaps doing no more than construct a partial tautology. For of course the word democracy emerges from the Greek 'demos' meaning 'people'. Democracy as a whole relates then to a particular form of government 'of' the people. Some might think that Lincoln's phrase can therefore be paraphrased by the one word 'democracy'. But this would obscure some significant qualifications (to which Lincoln, perhaps unwittingly, alluded) in using the prepositions 'of', 'by' and 'for'.

The very definition of 'people' is not a simple matter in this respect. Immediately it conjures up problems of territory or borders, in the sense that it does not necessarily relate to all people in all locations except perhaps in utopian narratives. Rather, the term 'people' arouses a plethora of boundary issues: who is to be treated as part of the people? Who is to be excluded? Who are included as subjects, participants, or beneficiaries of government? Is there to be a distinction between these three categories? We might also need to consider whether 'people' implies connectivity that transcends politic borders. Is it implied in the term that there exist fundamental identifications that bind individuals together? And is the resultant identity a necessary precondition for self-government? In other words, without a feeling of attachment and togetherness (or practical interdependence through social and economic activity) so-called democracy becomes essentially an imposed system of rule however it is packaged. That is certainly the logical implication of the 'no *demos* thesis' that has so frequently been expressed regarding the EU. Even if the same argument could no doubt be applied to all states and the Member States in particular, this has not prevented the critique from underscoring arguments suggesting the EU cannot hope for democratic legitimacy.

These then are crucial political and legal questions. And of course they speak to all the major issues of modern politics and inform the range of positions and interpretations with regard to the application of democracy in whatever location. So, when government 'of the people' is considered some care has to be taken as to the scope of control or rule that is exercised. Usually we would be talking about a people within a defined geographical territory. That would be the correlation expected of an adherence to state and sub-state forms of democratic process. But what is the position when the acts or effects of government or governance are felt by those outside any defined borders? Given the fact that authorities often operate consciously or unconsciously so as to impact the lives of those beyond their jurisdiction it would be very difficult to assume that the 'people' governed are naturally one and the same as the people for whom some benefit accrues through that government. Even within a defined territory, such 'people' may be subject to qualification through the applicable law. This might be based on citizenship, capacity determined by age, health (mental or physical), or other attributes (those individuals deemed to have forfeited any right to be considered full members of the people for one reason or another). Even when we discount the effects of direct discrimination that deliberately exclude certain categories of 'people' from government, there is still a range of individuals who are left outside the definition by indirect discrimination.

Similarly, when it comes to considering government 'by the people' democratic theory generally accepts that a distinction *can* be made between those governed and those governing. Governance even makes a virtue of this dislocation by assuming that rules are applied and systems constructed without encompassing the whole class of people considered to be subject to its rule.

It is here that democratic theories have nevertheless struggled to establish schemes and regimes that would address the seemingly inequitable nature of government or governance by one set of a people over another. Indeed the application of 'democracy' to 'government' (or governance) is a way in which rule of, by, and for the people is justified. It is the philosophical foundations of such justification that determine the form of democracy preferred. It would do no harm to sketch out the range of responses that this has provoked, although the subject has been of unceasing debate over the centuries. However, we might be able to identify some basic landmarks.

First, then, the issue of government by the people has led to the development of various degrees of direct or indirect democracy. The former could conceivably countenance the opportunity for all the 'people' subject to government to take part in decision-making on an equal basis. This would encompass notions of participation that, depending on the scale, could range from continual involvement to ad hoc engagement on specific issues and at specific times. So the plebiscite, referendum, the technology driven calls for opinion, the adoption of deliberative processes, all speak to the means by which collective will-formation is established and acted upon. At the indirect end of the spectrum there is a ready acceptance that such perpetual participation is just not practical in societies where the territory controlled and the people concerned and the issues under consideration are simply too extensive, too numerous and too complex. Some form of mediation is then required to translate the will of individuals into the will of the collective. Even if schemes whereby the people, howsoever designated, are still called upon to give their opinion from time to time, the general nature of government is by way of representatives speaking and acting on behalf of the people. The process adopted is one of authorisation for certain individuals to 'exercise public power'.[9]

As soon as such indirect arrangements are forged, critiques emerge that focus on the inherent difficulties of consensus formation, majoritarian rule, and the likelihood of abuse of the system by private power. Safeguards are then mooted to make up for the obvious defects when such representative processes are matched against direct democratic ideals. Hence we see the law and *its* rule appear as crucial to confirm certain principles in the processes of government and governance. Notions of political equality, individual rights, judicial protection against arbitrary decisions, accountability and transparency all have been given significant roles to play. Public law in particular is often seen as promoting these values or virtues to one degree or another as we have seen in my discussion on the rule of law and on human rights. And theories of constitutional and administrative law relevant to operation, and legal control of government and governance all have something to say about the relationship between democratic formations and law.

Whether we label any particular democratic discourses as 'liberal', 'capitalist', 'republican', 'socialist' or otherwise, all of these elements are the subject matter of systemic choice. How the conundrums are addressed are political matters and are the product of 'a normative theory that justifies' the definition of democracy preferred.[10] They range

---

[9] Joshua Cohen and Charles Sabel, 'Directly-Deliberative Polyarchy', *European Law Journal* 3:4 (1997) 313–42 at 317.

[10] This point is made by Seyla Benhabib, 'Toward a Deliberative Model of Democratic Legitimacy', in Seyla Benhabib (ed.), *Democracy and Difference: Contesting the Boundaries of the Political* (Princeton: Princeton University Press, 1996) 67–94 at 68.

from an idea that the lives of individuals should be affected as little as possible, leaving them to make choices unfettered by any kind of collective interference, democratic or otherwise, to those who accept some limited control is required to protect the freedom of the individual, and on to those who wish to see extensive control framed by a vision of what constitutes the collective good. Similarly they presuppose methods for enacting democracy that are bound up with the normative position favoured. In the modern age the geographical focus for determining which solution is to be preferred has been the state and its constituent territories. The people *for* whom government is conducted can therefore be easily identified and restricted to those citizens of the state and to a greater or lesser extent those living in the state.

All these presuppositions, however, have been increasingly challenged following a growing awareness of the processes of governance, even government, that operate *beyond* the state. Whether this is a product of globalisation or not is perhaps beside the point. The fact is few would argue against the proposition that the impact on sovereignty (state, community, individual) of actors and forces that are not domestically produced has reached a point of real significance in people's lives. From the rather amorphous influence of global capital to the planned interventions of international organisations and states acting beyond their borders, there are clear patterns of control being exercised from locations that are not determined within the state. These may reflect at one end of the spectrum, the influence of a wealthy elite, or at the other, a broader grassroots civil society.[11] The question, then, is what roles do the theories and practices of democracy, which I have very roughly spoken about above, play in these circumstances? Can they be brought to bear to legitimise the interference resulting from these supra-state sources? And if not, does this render *any* institution created to exercise control across state borders necessarily *illegitimate*?

All of which brings me back to the EU. Some might argue, in immediate response, that any enterprise that operates beyond the state is not a suitable entity to be assessed in accordance with any state-centric notions of democracy. If legitimacy is the issue then different standards might and should apply. In particular, if we are speaking of an arrangement between 'Governments', then any assessment of legitimacy might

---

[11] Strong arguments for global democracy through civil society have been made by, for instance, Richard Falk, *On Human Governance: Towards a New Global Politics* (Cambridge: Polity Press, 1995) and Ronnie Lipschutz, 'Reconstructing World Politics: the Emergence of Global Civil Society', *Millennium* 21:3 (1992) 389–420.

require a threefold test. First, are the constituents of such an arrangement themselves democratic? Second, if they are, is the aim of their col-
lusion acceptable under a set of norms that can be agreed between them?
And third, are the means by which the aim is carried out also acceptable
according to another but interdependent set of agreed norms?

The answers to the second and third questions might not necessarily
have anything to do with any democratic tradition or position. It might
suffice that all the parties should be democratic in name, if not practice
to fulfil the basic injunction of rule for, by, and of the people for any
inter-state arrangement. The claim here would be that the preservation of democratic government was a necessary condition of relations
between peoples. If each state joining an international cooperative
venture possesses democratic pedigree then this would ensure that
the institutional product of that cooperation should also enjoy virtue.
That this relates to the concept of 'democratic peace' as postulated by
John Rawls and others is no coincidence, as I discussed in Chapter 2. It
may be that the focus for examination is not then on the *structures* of
an international regime such as the EU (and whether they adhere to
direct or indirect democratic methods) but rather on the assessment
of democratic credentials of its constituent states. As Rawls maintains
with regard to democratic peace, all depends on 'how far the conditions
of a family of constitutional regimes attain the ideal of such regimes
with their supporting elements'.[12] Whatever that ideal is and whatever
supporting elements are preferred, the point of assessment would be
more the constituent states and less the institution they help form.

Rawls' analysis no doubt stretches the notion of a condition of
democratic peace. But when we re-examine Immanuel Kant's vision
of perpetual peace and the requirement of some kind of system of
cosmopolitan 'governance', we can see that again it is the structures
and institutions of the states that are of primary concern. If these are
in place, the thesis goes, then any supranational structure will most
likely be acceptable. An element of 'good faith' would accompany its
construction. Whether or not specific institutional actions would be
considered appropriate would be another matter.

The Kantian-inspired vision has, of course, come under extreme
strain in recent times with the realisation that 'government' is increasingly affected by non-state actors. The inviolable sovereignty of each

---

[12] John Rawls, *The Law of Peoples* (Cambridge, MA: Harvard University Press, 2003) at
54.

state might still be an articulated principle but the globalising impact of technology, risks, commerce, media and communication, suggests that this has become increasingly rhetorical rather than reflective of reality. In this environment, well documented and discussed over the past thirty years or more, it is perhaps unsurprising that we have moved to a discourse of 'governance' rather than 'government' as I have already discussed. However, the first question posed above (concerning the constitution of any cooperative institution) suggests that the focus for democratic assessment should not, in the first instance pass to the supra-state institution but should remain at the level of the state.

None of the above is to say that the EU institutions should not be assessed according to some democratic criteria. Rather, this might be reserved for an examination of its methods of operation as contained within strict power limitations.[13] Even then, the second essential enquiry (determining a 'right' aim for the arrangement between states) would have to be considered. If the objective of the EU was believed to be 'just' in accordance with standards rightfully agreed between democratically legitimate parties then there would be little justification in looking further. Indeed, that might be a necessary consequence of the form of representative democracy actually assumed in any particular Member State.

But let me turn to the third query, namely, the assessment of the operation of powers invested in an institution acting beyond the state. If the two previous elements had been satisfied, if the constituents were themselves adequate democracies and if the aim of their cooperation were considered just, then one would still need to enquire as to *how* those powers were exercised. Unjust means used in attaining a just aim may well lead to unintended injustice that might contravene other fundamental values. Again we would need to agree a set of norms and practices to apply here. Human rights would seem to be crucial in this respect. But we might also see as part of this evaluation the need to adopt virtues of democracy that valued such qualities as transparency, accountability and procedural fairness.[14]

---

[13] Giandomenico Majone notes the limited ability of the EU to tax and spend, a fact that should be reflected when assessing the depth of democratic qualities that the EU should be expected to possess. See Majone, 'Europe's "Democratic Deficit": The Question of Standards', *European Law Journal* 4 (1998) 5–28.

[14] Majone recognises these are necessary for an EU that does not replicate democratic structures of nation states but rather operates as a regulatory regime designed to increase efficiency particularly with regard to the 'market'. See Majone, 'Europe's "Democratic Deficit": The Question of Standards' at 37–8.

Undoubtedly, some commentators would see in this scheme a representation of what has happened over time with the EU and its relationship to government and governance. Equally, there will be some commentators who will argue that the above reasoning to construct a system of evaluation is crucially flawed. This might be on the grounds that democracy, as with many of the other values considered in this book, is not something to *choose*. It is a precondition for the legitimacy of any institution that has more than a trivial impact on the lives of people.

Without attempting to reach a conclusion on such matters we can at least note that approaches to the question of democracy and the EU are numerous. Many perspectives seem possible. So, some might prefer to judge the Union according to whether the 'market' can function without interference. Some might set great store in the formation of a public will that aims to achieve 'mutual understanding or communicatively achieved consensus' in relation to the achievement of a 'common good'.[15] Some might be intent on improving or even revolutionising the influence of civil society. Some might look to a post-national order that bypassed the dominance of state-based democracy. Some might simply wish to see legal controls placed on the disproportionate influence of specific interests that could result from particular forms of democracy. And some might suggest that we should not be using one model of democracy to judge the EU, rather various models should be applied depending on the particular nature of its varied operations.[16]

Such ideological positions are bound to suffer from lack of precision unless they have a clear definition of terms and a clear vision of the way in which they may be applied in practice. The point here, however, is not at this stage to attempt to prefer an ideal position of any kind. It is first to assess whether any of these notions of democracy has gained a hold in the EU's institutional ethos. If so, how has it manifested itself and what weight does it own? Only then can we judge its relative value and indeed its quality vis-à-vis any vision for democracy one might advocate. The remainder of this chapter undertakes this task.

---

[15] See Habermas, 'Three Normative Models of Democracy' at 21.
[16] See, Joseph Weiler, Ulrich R. Haltern and Franz C. Mayer, 'European Democracy and Its Critique', *West European Politics* 18:3 (1995) 4–39.

Democracy in the EU

Let us start with a provocation: the EU was always established with democracy as an underlying value. The rhetoric that preceded the EEC Treaty and the statements made by significant actors associated with the enterprise never dismissed the concept as irrelevant. Indeed, there were many occasions when the principle of democracy was reiterated and embraced. Along with the discourse of the rule of law, it was assumed that the notions of representative democracy reflected the 'common traditions' of the states engaged in creating the EU and thus could not be overridden *by* the EU. The institution of a European Parliament was a product of this assumption. Whether or not the scheme applied lived up to the standards at national level was another matter. At that time there were no practical models of democracy in action beyond the state available to replicate. It was not, then, a question of ignoring democratic demands. Rather the inventors of what was the EEC simply had insufficient resources to construct something that could pass as akin to a state-democracy.

Perhaps in hindsight we can dismiss these moves by any democratic tradition as rhetoric without real substance. Which suggests we could make another provocative observation: the EU has never been constructed as a democratic institution in any meaningful way. What structures that have been put in place do not in reality possess any convincing democratic characteristics. But let us look at the institutional narrative that has been constructed. We might do this by examining two inter-related aspects. First, the constitutional and policy positions: those key texts and initiatives which provide statements of intent if nothing else and their practical expression through institutional action. Second, the legal position: how has EU law supported the constitutional commitment to democracy for the Union as a founding principle?

The constitution of democracy in the EU

As with human rights, democracy in whatever form, did not appear as a direct commitment in the EEC Treaty of 1957. But one would be blind not to read an acknowledgement that the principle possessed fundamental relevance to the enterprise. Reference in the Treaty's preamble to 'ever closer union among the peoples of Europe' recognised that this was an endeavour that transcended an agreement between states. Or at least it had pretensions towards a project *of* the people rather than just *for* the people. Similarly, the institution of a European Parliament, consisting of 'representatives of the peoples' of the Member States, under the original Article 137 EEC Treaty, more than suggested a desire to engage democratic sensibilities. Of course the reality of the commitment was another matter. It took nearly another twenty years before the principle of direct universal suffrage was properly embraced.[17] But the fact that the term 'democracy' was not used in either the EEC Treaty or the Suffrage act is perhaps not as 'telling' as von Bogdandy for one has made out.[18] It might have suggested the unwillingness to make democracy a 'legal principle' but the underlying constitutional intent to rely on the concept as a *fundamental* proposition for the Union nevertheless held some weight. Even if we took the view that 'representation' at this new European institutional level may have been considered by relevant actors only to amount to a process whereby members of various elites were brought together for their expertise rather than as the product of election, the association of the project with national democratic institutions was still present.

A number of constitutional-like statements issued from the end of the 1960s onwards help to reinforce this interpretation. At the Paris Conference in 1972, for instance, the then Member States reaffirmed their 'resolve to base the Community's development on democracy' as well as other values.[19] The Declaration on European Identity in 1973 noted the will 'to defend the principles of representative democracy' and the 1975 Report on European Union stressed the foundation of union upon principles foremost among which was 'democracy'.[20] There could be little dispute that democracy was fully embraced as a concept binding the Union to its Member States and the people of Europe generally. Democracy was taken as a 'given condition', a necessary characteristic of government even if its particular elements were not seen as applicable to the structures of the EU itself.

Of course, the constitutional presence of the European Parliament has always highlighted the ambivalent position the Union has held to democracy through its constitutional structure. For the UN and other international organisations there has never been any effective call for

---

[17] Act concerning the election of the representatives of the Parliament by direct universal suffrage, OJ L 278, 8 October 1976, 1.

[18] See Armin von Bogdandy, 'Constitutional Principles', in A. von Bogdandy and Jürgen Bast (eds.), *Principles of European Constitutional Law* (Oxford: Hart, 2006) 3–52 at 21.

[19] EC Bull 10–1972 at 15.

[20] See EC Bull 12–1973 118–22 and EC Bull Suppl. 5–1975 para. 4 at 9 respectively.

democratisation of their general assemblies. It is assumed that states provide representation. That is the consequence of an adherence to the legal and political principle of state sovereignty so ingrained in the Westphalian system of international law. The problem with this, however, is that the Westphalian attempt to sanctify states as the sole depositories of power was always a myth, a myth constructed *through* international law, and a myth *upon which* international law was constructed. Power was never so centralised and so neatly encapsulated whatever seemed apparent in the times of empire, dictatorship and tyranny. The non-territorial sources of power exercised considerable influence in Europe particularly, albeit to varying degrees. Through commerce, through international society, through kinship (royal and aristocratic most obviously but also spiritually, culturally, and politically), any pretension that states possess a monopoly of sovereignty has always been challenged.

The reality of this lack of state control, therefore, informed the movement towards a European union in the mid twentieth century as much, if not more than, the premise that states should give up degrees of sovereignty for a cooperative venture. Jean Monnet interpreted the initiative as involving the 'abnegation of sovereignty in a limited but decisive field'.[21] In other words, the idea of European union was a product of recognising that 'people' (in the form of inter-European commerce, politics, culture, religion, etc.) were already operating beyond nations, influencing economies and societies regardless of state origins.[22] This possibility was recognised by some of the early analysts of the European community, although only within limited parameters.[23] 'Democracy', loosely defined, represented both the way in which government by the people (or at least a restricted cohort) was already a fact

---

[21] As quoted in Neill Nugent, *The Government and Politics of the European Union*, 3rd edn (London: Macmillan, 1994) at 39.

[22] See, for instance, David W. Ellwood, *Rebuilding Europe: Western Europe, America and Postwar Reconstruction* (Harlow: Longman, 1992) who noted the role of the Christian democratic movement across Western Europe in seeking to establish 'democracy' that included a 'spiritual and intellectual development of the individual in a context of a social solidarity' based on a 'catholic version of the welfare state in an atmosphere of national reconciliation', at 9.

[23] Karl Deutsch and his colleagues, for instance, acknowledged the importance of the sudden leap in frequency of contact between elites in Europe as an impetus for integration. See Karl Deutsch, Sidney A. Burrell, Robert A. Kann, Maurice Lee, Jr., Martin Lichterman, Raymond E. Lindgren, Francis L. Loewenheim and Richard W. Van Wagenen, *Political Community and the North Atlantic Area: International Organization in the Light of Historical Experience* (Princeton: Princeton University Press, 1957).

of political and economic life *and* a term that could be used to legitimise the EU by suggesting integration was contained within democratic
not autocratic processes. The power of democracy, as security against
extremism and the arbitrary interference with people's lives, was therefore a constituting premise and even a constitutional inevitability.

The problem that has arisen constitutionally in the EU, however,
has been the *degree* to which democracy could be legally incorporated
rather than *assumed* as part of its institutional ethos. The history of
the constitution of Europe reflects this tension. It confirms a central
ambivalence but only in so far as the means by which democracy
should be incorporated. So we have the institutional statements of
the late 1960s and early 1970s, maintaining a line that democracy
was an essential value that merely required some form of agreeable
implementation.

This brings us back to the position of the Parliament. The original
construction of an Assembly was to provide very limited supervisory
and advisory functions. Representatives from the national parliaments
of the six Member States were appointed but only in the recognition that the body would become an elected chamber in due course.
Although all accounts demonstrate that the Assembly had little if any
influence on governance in the EU early on, it did not simply accept its
apparently neutered role. Throughout the 1960s it pressed for greater
powers, its strongest argument being the democratic legitimacy this
would bring to the whole Union. All this can be seen from sporadic
references in the institutionally produced texts.

So, in 1961, the Commission argued that the value of elections by universal suffrage to the European Parliament would be to 'reinforce [the
Communities] popular basis and, indeed, the entire European edifice'.[24]
A little later Walter Hallstein claimed that the new European order had
to be based on 'a democratically constituted Europe'.[25] At the same time,
in 1963, the European Parliament passed a resolution that considered
its powers had to be 'broadened to strengthen the Community's democratic structure and the Community spirit'.[26] In 1964 the Commission
pressed for universal suffrage to counter the disappointment and
'impatience' perceived to be experienced by the populace of the then

[24] Introduction to the Fourth General Report on the Activities of the Community, 5
June 1961, EEC Bull 5/61 at 15.
[25] EC Bull 2/63 at 17.
[26] European Parliament, Resolution on the Competence and Powers of the European
Parliament, EC Bull 8/63 at 59.

six Member States in partial response to the constitutional crisis that resulted from the French veto of UK membership.[27]

These statements hardly reduced over succeeding years. A report to the European Parliament in 1966 concluded in frustration that 'no progress had been made towards making the Community more democratic'.[28] The Parliament passed another resolution noting how essential the 'strengthening of the principles recognised in the six countries of a constitutional democracy based on the rule of law' was.[29] And, with the grand gesture very much in mind, it declared, through its President of 1969, Alain Poher, the need for direct elections as 'part of a vast political rebirth' of Europe.[30]

Such arguments failed for many years to tempt the Member States to make the efforts required to bring some form of democratic elections into place. Perhaps M. Piccioni, President of the Councils in 1963, summed up the states' attitude when he said that he did not consider that 'the question of the election of the Parliament by universal suffrage was of immediate urgency'.[31] Gradually, this political position lost its validity as the Member States looked first to enlarge the EU to incorporate other states *and* adopted the kind of rhetoric of identity, which included a strong dimension of democracy as we have seen, in the early 1970s. It still took until 1976 for the Act Concerning the Election of the Representatives of the Assembly by Direct Universal Suffrage to be passed and two more years before elections actually took place.[32] Even then the powers of the Parliament were barely increased.

Nonetheless, all this demonstrates that the commitment to democracy as a constitutional condition always occupied *some* space in the institutional ethos, albeit an ambivalent and indeterminate one. The fact that in practice only limited attention was paid to the principle does not undermine that observation. Indeed, we can see that even once the Parliament had obtained greater legitimacy as an institution, through the election process, the realisation of democratic practices remained to be addressed. So from 1978 onwards the search for *deepening*

[27] Commission, Communication to the Council and the Governments of the Member States, EC Bull 11/64 at 5.

[28] EC Bull 12/66 at 15.

[29] European Parliament, 'Resolution on the Position of the Parliament with Respect to Institutional Developments in the European Communities', EC Bull 12/66 at 80.

[30] Alain Pher, 'Tradition and Future of the European Parliament', EC Bull 1–1969 at 28.

[31] EC Bull 1/63 at 21.

[32] See OJ L 278, 8 October 1976, at 1.

democracy continued. Over time, this was recognised through various means in the Treaties themselves, partially through the inclusion of a commitment to democracy, partially through the extension of powers of the Parliament, and partially through the adoption of practices that could be said to possess democratic credentials.

Article 6 TEU established the first of these. It noted democracy as one of the foundational principles of the Union. This did little more than reflect the existing discourse *and* the myth that the EU was always infused with democracy. As with respect for human rights, democracy was assumed to have been a conditioning principle all along despite all the overwhelming evidence to the contrary. The myth has been frequently affirmed by pointing to the condition (constitutionally demanded by Article 49 TEU) that states applying to join the Union should prove that democracy was guaranteed in their constitutional systems.[33] Nonetheless, succeeding Treaties, including the Constitutional Treaty and the Lisbon Treaty, have introduced more democratic-like provisions. The latter now promotes a four-fold approach to democracy based on democratic equality, representation, participation, and the importance of national parliaments.[34] These have related, first, to improving the influence of the Parliament in the law-making process of governance, second, to increasing the power of review of the actions of the Council and the Commission, and, third, to establishing the presence of democratic virtues such as participation and transparency in the institutional business of the EU.

We do not have to trace the full extent of the legislative powers of the Parliament here, however. That has been undertaken by many quality European textbooks already. Suffice to say that the scope for legislative initiative and influence through the supposed democratic auspices of the Parliament has been subject to much critique. Without reaching any judgment about deficit in democracy, we can say safely that the degree to which directly elected *European* representatives exercise influence has increased but remains limited. The Council retains much of the power in these respects. That is the chief criticism levelled against the EU in democratic terms. Whether or not the current restriction is acceptable, necessary, undesirable, or simply dangerous, is irrelevant for my purposes. Even with increased powers for both the

---

[33] See also the Copenhagen Criteria contained within the Conclusions of the Presidency at the Copenhagen Council 1993 EC Bull 6–1993 at 13.
[34] See new articles 9–12 TEU introduced by the Lisbon Treaty.

European Parliament and National Parliaments (as introduced by the Lisbon Treaty),[35] the criticism will not disappear.

The same could be said about the powers of scrutiny and review available to the European Parliament. Other than a few notable examples of interference in the decisions made by and operations of the other institutions (the threatened dismissal of the Santer Commission, in the late 1990s, is a story that has often been used to demonstrate the possible control that can be exercised)[36] the Parliament has not interposed too drastically in the life of the Union. Certainly, its powers have not been commensurate with any democratic credentials established through its direct election by the people of Europe, or at least those who choose to vote. It might have the right to be consulted or to be involved in a decision to the extent of exercising or threatening a veto as regards certain legislation (in theory),[37] but it remains generally lacking significant power in the Union.[38] Whether this will change with the application of the Lisbon Treaty remains to be seen.

Certain democratic *virtues*, as opposed to powers, have also acquired constitutional presence in the EU. But what are these virtues? As we saw in the first part of this chapter, participation, transparency, and accountability have acquired considerable discursive purchase in Western societies, in particular, during the twentieth century, and in musings about a burgeoning global administrative law.[39] The rhetoric of good governance has been significant here, not least for the EU. Indeed, given the continual mutterings about democratic deficit, it is unsurprising that there should be an institutional attempt to incorporate some sense of these virtues into its constitutional make-up. This was given explicit expression in the Commission's White Paper on European Governance in 2001, which identified five areas where the

[35] The Protocol on the Application of the Principles of Subsidiarity and Proportionality will require, for instance, drafts of EU legislative acts to be sent to national parliaments for their scrutiny and possible objection within a tight time limit.

[36] See Committee of Independent Experts, 'First Report on Allegations of Fraud, Mismanagement and Nepotism in the European Commission', 15 March 1999. See, also, Adam Tomkins, 'Responsibility and Resignation in the European Commission', *Modern Law Review* 62:5 (1999) 744–65.

[37] The exercise of this veto was notoriously infrequent. Between 1999 and 2004 it was used twice in 403 possibilities. See European Parliament, *Activity Report for 5th Parliamentary Term*, PE 287.644, at 10.

[38] See Christopher Lord and Erika Harris, *Democracy in the New Europe* (Basingstoke: Palgrave, 2006).

[39] Carol Harlow, 'Global Administrative Law: the Quest for Principles and Values', *European Journal of International Law* 17:1 (2006) 187–214.

Union had to improve its performance.[40] Transparency and participation were particular targets. The question, however, is the extent to which these virtues have been realised? Has there been a release of government to the 'people' enshrined in text and systemic behaviour?

When we look at transparency, although there has been a publishing extravaganza regarding EU documents ever since 1957 (ballooning with the advent of the internet) this has been a 'blind' endeavour in terms of a constitutional commitment to democracy. No rights adhered to this practice until 1993, when the Council issued a Decision on public access to its documentation.[41] The Amsterdam Treaty then enshrined a right through Article 255 EC Treaty (now Article 15 of the Treaty on the Function of the EU (TFEU)), which stated that '[a]ny citizen of the Union, and any natural or legal person residing or having its registered office in a Member State, shall have the right of access to European Parliament, Council and Commission documents' subject to certain conditions of 'public or private interest'. This resulted from greater institutional acknowledgement that openness was essential if the EU were to convince its constituents of *any* democratic credibility. 'Open' government has become the key phrase, attaching an individual right to a practice of publication. Regulation No. 1049/2001 set the position regarding public access to documents, defining its principles and limits.[42]

This is now the subject of review following the Commission's decision in 2005 to launch a 'European Transparency Initiative', which included the publication of a Green Paper on the subject.[43] The Commission revealed that the majority of requests for information were placed by 'specialists in EU affairs: economic operators, law firms, NGOs and the academic world'.[44] This is hardly surprising. The form of transparency that places the initiative on the public to discover information by specific request is always going to be a closed world for most of the

---

[40] The five areas were: openness, participation, accountability, effectiveness, and coherence. See, Commission, 'European Governance, A White Paper', Brussels, 25 July 2001 COM (2001) 428 final.

[41] Council Decision 20 December 1993 on public access to Council documents, 1993, OJ L 340 at 43.

[42] European Parliament and Council, Regulation (EC) No 1049/2001 of 30 May 2001.

[43] Minutes of the Commission's meeting No 1721 of 9 November 2005, item 6; see also documents SEC (2005) 1300 and SEC (2005) 1301, and Commission, 'Public Access to Documents held by Institutions of the European Community: a Review', COM (2007) 185 final.

[44] Commission, 'Public Access to Documents' at para. 1.1.

populace. Specialists who know the system (what can be obtained and how) are more likely to use the avenues available. But this does set up a sense of paradox with regard to this particular virtue. Accompanying the realisation of a right of access to documents must be the fear that the institutions will become overwhelmed if the ability to make requests is too freely activated. Hence the paradox. Too much realisation and the system will not be able to cope. Too little and in practice it betrays the very principle that has been introduced.

Of course, we have to read this in conjunction with the process of publication that has increasingly accompanied the EU's activities over its history. Documenting its activities has been an essential aspect of forging an identity. The EU has long appeared to look to self-constituting means to project its existence, decisions, and policies. From its inception, it has been recorded and projected as a polity through an increasingly sophisticated and comprehensive documentary archive. This may now be the product of an expressed desire for transparency but the transmission or communication of the EU's project has always occurred largely through published text. Indeed, one could reasonably contend the EU has become primarily a textual enterprise, a 'print community' that has arisen as such in the absence of any mass movement or *demos*.[45] The existence of this 'print community' may be borne out by the preference that has been accorded to text in the life of the EU. Since 1957 a mass of literature concerned with its creation, its history, its development, and its practices has been produced. Largely the assumed responsibility of the Commission, although all of the EU organs contribute, the EU regularly generates remembrances of its progress and explanations of its purposes as well as simply recording the 'output' of the EU's institutions. Rather than through public displays that herald its presence in European life and seek to promote its ambitions, the EU's project and programmes have been officially *published*. The EU's political field and identity have been defined and promoted through its institutional texts, not by other concrete manifestations.

The textual explosion has, however, enabled the Commission to recognise the way in which greater 'dissemination' can obviate the need for public members to demand particular documents. If they are publicly available, the right of access does not require institutional *response*.

---

[45] There are intended echoes here of Benedict Anderson's consideration of 'print capitalism' that played a vital role, he claims, in creating nations as 'imagined political communities'. See, Benedict Anderson, *Imagined Communities: Reflections on the Origin and Spread of Nationalism* (London: Verso, 1991).

It will have already been realised. The current proposals are more concerned with developing 'a more systematic policy of making documents directly accessible to the public in the most user-friendly way'.[46]

All of these constitutional type advancements in transparency (which now include particular reference in the Lisbon Treaty following the provisions of the Constitutional Treaty)[47] are generally being embraced within the EU. Although there have been the inevitable criticisms of the institutions' collective and individual failings to live up to the constitutional requirements, overall there is at least an acknowledgement that the principle should be respected. Francesca Bignami goes so far as to suggest, 'the negotiations and political deals ... are coming under pressure, albeit still limited, from the European right to transparency'.[48] Whether the process of publication will stretch to counter any tendency to refuse requests on the grounds of security or public or private interest is a matter that will always be tested. Indeed, the European Ombudsman's existence is, in part, to carry out these tests. And he has shown some willingness to criticise the institutions where their approach to the release of information is poor.[49]

When we turn to participation (beyond electoral engagement) we become submerged in a significantly more direct form of democratic virtue. At least that is the case in theory. But do the EU institutions have a coherent understanding of participation to any degree of sophistication?

Clearly, we can point to a number of initiatives that might be considered to reflect a commitment to participation as an ideal. The emerging determination of the Commission to engage in 'dialogue' with civil society has been increasingly promoted over recent years.[50]

---

[46] See Commission, 'Public Access to Documents' at para. 5.2.

[47] For instance, the Lisbon Treaty has introduced the Treaty on the Functioning of the European Union in which article 15 (formerly Article 255 EC Treaty) now provides: 'In order to promote good governance and ensure the participation of civil society, the Union institutions, bodies offices and agencies shall conduct their work as openly as possible'.

[48] Francesca Bignami, 'Creating European Rights: National Values and Supranational Interests', 2005 Duke Law School Working Paper Series, online, available at: http://lsr.nellco.org/duke/fs/papers/2 at 64.

[49] See, for instance, Decision of the European Ombudsman on complaint 1875/2005/GG against the Council of the European Union where the Ombudsman heavily criticised the Council and suggested that its failure to treat a 'request for access to documents properly and carefully constituted maladministration'. See www.euro-ombudsman. eu.int/decision/en/051875.htm.

[50] For a comprehensive review of this tendency see Bignami, 'Creating European Rights'.

Article I-47 of the draft Constitutional Treaty suggested a basis for a constitutional principle of participatory democracy by giving 'citizens and representative associations the opportunity to make known and publicly exchange their views on all areas of Union action'. The Lisbon Treaty adopted this position *and* the innovation that '[n]ot less than one million citizens who are nationals of a significant number of Member States may take the initiative of inviting the Commission, within the framework of its powers, to submit any appropriate proposal on matters where citizens consider that a legal act of the Union is required for the purpose of implementing the Treaties'.[51] Whether this is really a gimmick, given the conditions placed on the call for action, remains to be seen. But we can also see a willingness to involve civil society in constitutional change through the convention and consultation processes that appeared so innovatively in the late 1990s.[52] The involvement of NGOs in decision-making and, more generally, public consultation are the hallmarks of this approach.

None of these initiatives really demonstrate how the EU institutions have interpreted the relationship between participation and the construction of a 'public sphere'. For that, some recent pronouncements by the Commission might be more instructive.

The Commission's communication relating to the grandly named 'Plan-D for Democracy, Dialogue and Debate' is particularly revealing in this respect.[53] The line taken by the Commission is based on a central conceit. It *assumes* that democracy has always been a significant feature of the European infrastructure. The EU's institutions are referred to, unquestioningly, as 'democratic'. The plan is intended to 'reinvigorate European democracy', 'restore public confidence' and engage in a 'democratic renewal process'.[54] The evident myth underpinning this rhetoric is that somehow democracy has been allowed to slip away from the EU. Consequently, the emphasis is placed on

---

[51] New Article 11 (4) TEU.

[52] See, in particular, the processes that gave rise to the EU Charter on Fundamental Rights and the Convention on the Future of Europe. For a critique of the latter, however, as regards the human rights dimension, see Andrew Williams, 'EU Human Rights Policy and the Convention on the Future of Europe: a Failure of Design?' *European Law Review* 28:6 (2003) 794–813.

[53] Commission Communication to the Council, the European Parliament, the European Economic and Social Committee and the Committee of the Regions, 'The Commission's Contribution to the Period of Reflection and Beyond: Plan-D for Democracy, Dialogue and Debate' COM (2005) 494 final 13 October 2005.

[54] *Ibid.* at 2–3.

communication as to the EU's added value and possibility for citizen participation in its decision-making rather than a practical enhancement of that engagement.

We can, of course, dismiss such material as pure institutional rhetoric. But that would be a mistake. For, the communication helps pinpoint the EU's central difficulty in assessing the problem of democracy in order to resolve it. By assuming that the structure of the Union is democratically sound there is less chance of a strategy being constructed that will address general democratic concerns that have been voiced. Instead, the accent has been placed on tactics or virtues of democracy, which do not necessarily improve the underlying democratic quality of the Union.

Nonetheless, there is an apparent determination to encourage 'the emergence of a European public sphere, where citizens are given the information and the tools to actively participate in the decision making process and gain ownership of the European project'.[55] The Commission seems to be echoing some pertinent academic works here. In particular, it matches the call for a 'constitutional patriotism' promoted by Jürgen Habermas and others. Justine Lacroix, for instance, suggests this 'should emerge from different national traditions'.[56] It would depend on 'an open deliberation and confrontation process among the various national cultures involved in the European Union'. Habermas suggests that 'a European constitutional patriotism would have to grow together from various nationally specific interpretations of the same universalist principles of law'.[57] In other words, consensus through deliberation might be achieved and a sense of allegiance to the project formed as a result. This in turn might produce a paradoxical post-national character for the form of democracy pursued in and through the EU in that it would still be bred from national routes.

The Commission appears to have accepted such a possibility by emphasising the key role of national Parliaments in communicating the value of the EU. The assumption is made explicitly that 'a greater voice for Parliaments is a greater voice for Europe's citizens'.[58] It is the national political sphere that can 'reinvigorate' the sense of connection between people and Union. The Lisbon Treaty has tried to give

---

[55] *Ibid.* at 2–3.
[56] Justine Lacroix, 'For a European Constitutional Patriotism', *Political Studies* 50 (2002) 944–58 at 954.
[57] Jürgen Habermas, *Between Facts and Norms* (Cambridge: Polity Press, 1997) at 507.
[58] Commission, 'Plan-D for Democracy' at 4.

some added prominence to this theme by establishing more ways in which national parliaments can scrutinise the output of the EU and enforce the principle of subsidiarity. How far this can be pushed without destabilising the Community method remains to be seen.

One must reserve a certain degree of scepticism, however, when attempting to relate theoretical propositions to actual practice. There is certainly a danger of conscious initiatives for a 'public sphere' appearing as a public relations exercise designed to give credence to the EU rather than truly govern its direction. The Commission's communication on Plan-D consistently reminds everyone that its strategy is about communicating to the people of Europe the EU's 'achievements' and 'concrete benefits'.[59] There is little question of allowing debate to lead to a *reduction* in the competences of the institutions or indeed the EU's right to be involved in key decisions relating to security, freedom, external relations, consumer protection and so forth. The message is that those wishing to participate can help the institutions 'to better define its priorities' building 'on achievements to date, and following the course set already'.[60] One has to wonder, therefore, whether this is really a contribution to a public sphere or one masquerading as such. There might even be the temptation to suggest this confirms the political theorist Chantal Mouffe's question concerning what the real meaning of 'dialogue' and 'deliberation' can be 'if no real choice is at hand and if the participants in the discussion are not able to decide between clearly differentiated alternatives'.[61] There is little sense of democracy in play where people have had, effectively, their decisions set for them.

Running parallel with this putative sense of a public sphere sustained at national level, has been the desire to enhance the role of 'civil society'. The Commission's discussion paper on 'the Commission and Non-Governmental Organisations: Building a Stronger Partnership'[62] in 2000 signalled the intention to enable NGOs to become more involved in EU work. This was for the stated purposes of strengthening participatory democracy, ensuring the representation of the views of specific groups of 'citizens', and allowing NGOs to contribute to policy making,

---

[59] Commission, 'Plan-D for Democracy' at 5.
[60] Communication from the Commission to the European Council, 'A Citizens' Agenda: Delivering Results for Europe' COM (2006) 211 final at 3.
[61] Chantal Mouffe, *On the Political* (London: Routledge, 2005) at 3.
[62] Commission, 'Discussion Paper on the Commission and Non-Governmental Organisations: Building a Stronger Partnership' COM (2000) 11.

project management and 'European integration'.[63] Such bold aims recognised the importance of acquiring some kind of public acceptance of the EU's actions generally. However, it is not open-ended. The Commission recognised that not all such organisations had the *right* to participate in its decision-making processes. Some kind of selection was necessary during which attention would be paid to each NGO's 'structure and membership', the 'transparency of their organisation and the way they work', any 'previous participation in committees and working groups', their 'track record as regards competence to advise in any specific field', and 'their capacity to work as a catalyst for exchange of information and opinions between the Commission and the citizens'.[64] As the Commission stated, '[i]t is important for NGOs and groupings of NGOs to be democratic and transparent as regards their membership and claims to representiveness'.[65] The Commission 'encourages organisations to work together in common associations and networks at the European level since such organisations considerably facilitate the efficiency of the consultation process'.[66]

Many would accept such limitations as necessary for the proper construction of dialogic processes. But one must question the degree to which it leads to the institutionalisation of public deliberation, allowing established and 'acceptable' NGOs into the decision-making fold, as it were, whilst casting doubt on those less formalised groupings that do not appear to have the resources to act as a 'catalyst' for the Commission. Clearly this cries out for in-depth research into the role of NGOs and *dis*-organised civil society and their impact on policy-making by the EU (a study that has begun, at least theoretically, in certain quarters).[67] In the meantime although we might applaud the intentions we have to wait and see how the commitment to civil society dialogue develops.

This is not to say that some form of engagement with non-state actors has been absent within the constitutional make-up of the Union since its inception. The Economic and Social Committee was premised on the basis of some civil society representation. Article 194 of the original EEC Treaty required the Committee to be composed of representatives

---

[63] *Ibid.*   [64] *Ibid.*   [65] *Ibid.* at 9.   [66] *Ibid.* at 9.

[67] See, for instance, contributions to the September 2003 issue of the *European Law Journal* including, Hans Lindahl, 'Acquiring a Community: the *Acquis* and the Institution of European Legal Order', *European Law Journal* 9:4 (2003) 433–50, and Michael A. Wilkinson, 'Civil Society and the Re-imagination of European Constitutionalism', *European Law Journal* 9:4 (2003) 451–72.

of agriculture, transport, industry, trade, and the professions, with a view to providing advice. Employers, employees and other interests are now appointed from the Member States. The Committee must be consulted on a broad range of policy areas prior to legislation. These include agriculture, internal market issues, social policy and regional policy. It can also be consulted by the Council and Commission whenever those institutions think appropriate under Article 304 TFEU. But there is very limited information to suggest that the Committee exercises any influence whatsoever on the legislative process. There is no obligation for its opinions to be adopted or for the Council or Commission to act in any way on its views. Nonetheless, over succeeding Treaty amendments the Committee has been identified, and indeed now identifies itself, as 'a bridge between Europe and organised civil society'.[68] Using a rapporteur system and developing a programme of structured policy consideration by civil society organisations, there is now an increased role for the Committee in gauging some sense of the 'public interest' and communicating this to the institutions.

On the face of it this would appear to be an increasingly important constitutional process for realising participatory democracy. But let us look a little more carefully. The following is a quote from the Committee's 2007 report on its activities:

The EESC is determined to continue with its initiatives, in close cooperation with the EU institutions and all other civil society players, with a view to contributing, on the one hand, to creating a real European public space of dialogue and debate and, on the other, to instilling new impetus into the European project built on a forward-looking vision of the future of Europe for its citizens.[69]

The remainder of the report is peppered with such asides. Of course, this accords well with the rhetoric of all the institutions. But it does not necessarily accord with the principle of *open* discussion. For if the understanding is to give 'new impetus to the European project' there is something of a closed quality to dialogue through the Committee's work. Indeed, a careful reading of the report, and those of previous years, demonstrates that the Committee is seen and sees itself as a creature of the Union. It might object to legislative proposals or policy

---

[68] See ESC website at www.eesc.europa.eu/documents/publications/pdf/booklets/EESC-2007–002-EN.pdf.

[69] Report on the Activities of the European Economic and Social Committee during the Portuguese Presidency of the Council of the EU DI CESE 50/2007.

directions. But the participatory element of democracy is inherently restricted. It belongs to the institutional system rather than a potential challenge to it. The project is sacrosanct as a precondition. The danger then is of a version of 'constitutional patriotism' that demands allegiance to the EU as a prerequisite of engagement with it. In that way it makes the same claims as a state – something that remains highly contentious given the constitutional debates that have always surrounded the EU. If there *is* a prospect of the disbandment of the EU (or a massive scaling-down of its competences), which might be considered a legitimate result of a series of national democratic decisions and movements, then some form of institutional process to allow for this possibility must be accepted. The threat this may pose might just have to be the price worth paying for acquiring a more democratic institution.

We encounter more concerns about the depth to which the virtue of participation is realised when we consider measures designed to promote public consultation. Undoubtedly there is now a commitment to imbed dialogue into the workings of the EU. The Commission's initiative 'Your Voice in Europe' may have the feeling of a public relations exercise only but it does at least record the way in which resources are being expended on consultation processes.[70] But how seriously is this taken?

Let us examine one example of the recently instituted consultation initiatives. In 2007 the Commission raised the question, 'Discrimination; does it matter?' as an issue for open consultation. This is an issue of pre-eminent concern to the EU, or at least so it could be supposed from the rhetoric and action over the past twenty or more years. Passing first over the dubious nature of the question raised, which given the EU's apparent historical commitment to countering discrimination regardless of popular opinion seems otiose, we can see that the process adopted was designed to highlight that various Member States have differing standards of anti-discrimination legislation in operation. It was also to query whether this 'situation causes a real problem, if that is acceptable, and if not, what would be the best way to tackle it'. But the means by which this was to be achieved was by way of questionnaire with extremely limited multiple-choice options. So, for instance, when considering the 'best way to tackle' the problem (if indeed the respondent saw any problem at all) the only options provided were (a) legislation banning discrimination; (b) non-binding codes of good

---

[70] See 'Your Voice in Europe' website at http://europa.eu.int/yourvoice/index_en.htm.

practice; (c) training; and (d) information campaigns, all of which had to be rated in order of preference for the form to be accepted.

Is this form of public consultation, producing a vox-pop type result, really worthy of including as a form of democratic participation? Does it suggest that with the development of internet questionnaires, restricted to the most banal of questions, consultation becomes more a product of technological possibility rather than a meaningful engagement of the constituents of Europe? Given the seriousness of the issue one wonders what is actually being achieved with the adoption of such practices. Is democracy really enhanced?

These are serious questions that drive to the heart of consultation as a practical element of participation. No doubt EU adherents will point to the significant work undertaken on discrimination by the EU Monitoring Centre for Racism and Xenophobia, for instance, and now the Fundamental Rights Agency, where debate and sharing of best-practice achieves a much more defined space. But if that is truly the case then why is it necessary to engage in these internet consultations? If it is purely window dressing then it has little value in any conception of 'deliberative democracy'. Such activities are surely better left to *Eurobarometer* or the private poll agencies to assess the views of 'Europeans'.

Any identification of participation as a virtue of democracy deserves more considered treatment. We may well look to a practical rationalisation for participation (as the best means of achieving acceptance of a policy or particular programme) but this might not suffice when faced with complex circumstances that require amendments to standard processes. For instance, a determination to engage with civil society does not alone take into account structures of inequality that might undermine the principle of participation. Gender distortions in certain dialogues with established social patriarchal structures are a case in point already recognised in development discourse and eventually adopted by the EU in project and policy construction.[71] Other differentiating factors, however, do not necessarily receive the same attention; language, race, class, caste, minority status, and access to resources (or poverty) all will be negative influences for any participatory process if not addressed, making it not only flawed but even a contributor to inequality. By adopting consultation processes that favour advanced

---

[71] Many critiques of participatory development practices appear in B. Cooke and U. Kothari (eds.), *Participation: the New Tyranny?* (London: Zed Books, 2001).

technologies, meetings of invited groups, and time limits that are extremely short (or worse, un-engaging and superficial questionnaires) it seems unlikely that the principle of democracy, howsoever defined, can be enhanced.

From this broad-based review, we cannot really say that participation in the form of consultation has any definite constitutional role yet. To suggest that it amounts to the institutionalisation of a European public sphere seems extremely optimistic. But then, if this is to be a means by which democracy becomes established beyond the state, so as to compensate for democratic inadequacies in the power distribution system, any move in this direction needs to be firmly embedded in practice. That is the crucial test.

Having examined some of the practice of various EU institutions we must now consider the way in which European law has sustained the value of democracy, if at all. Does law have a significant role to play in the formation of this element of the institutional ethos?

Law and democracy in the EU

What then has been the contribution of EU jurisprudence? And what can we deduce about the relationship between EU law and democracy?

In truth, very little. If EU law operated on the basis that democracy was a fundamental principle one would have to question, in theory at least, the whole legality of decision-making in the Union. It would be a nonsense for a legal system to construct itself without presuming its own legitimacy, unless the personalities engaged within the system felt governed by an ethical code that superseded the institutional powers vested in them. Certainly there might be space at the margins to question the *operation* of the system, to ensure it accords with some of the administrative virtues I identified above. But it would be constitutional suicide to countenance any deeper probing. That would, on the face of it, be against the role, if not rule, of law. For some it would turn the law into an individually autonomous political and moral animal without a constituting context rather than a representative institution seeking to preserve the interests of the 'people'.

I will return to this dilemma in the conclusion to this chapter. But for the moment we should still consider whether the strength of the value of democracy has been contemplated by the European Court of Justice, either directly or obliquely. The obvious technique for such a sleight of hand would have been to focus on the constitutional questions that emerged from time to time. In other words, a court might challenge the scope of its own (and its fellow institutions') democratic authority by debating the nature of institutional jurisdiction and power. The ECJ has indeed been forced to undertake such a display throughout its history. But in so doing has it given judgment so as to enhance democracy as a founding value? Or has it seen to its suppression?

We must raise a question here as to whether, in this respect, there has been a limited reading of crucial judgments. By focusing on constitutional arrangements and the Court's own position within them, sight has perhaps been lost of the impact of the framework of decisions on those values that form part of the institutional ethos. The common interpretation is that the ECJ was engaged in something of a heroic endeavour, outstripping the achievements of national constitutional courts as an innovative judicial actor, and successful in constructing a 'jurisprudential edifice' that provoked relatively little resistance.[72] In other words it became an actor in European integration and in the formation of its own legal foundations without significant opposition. The tendency has therefore been to see the development of certain values (in the form of general principles), at least prior to explicit mention in the Treaties, as the product of judicial activism. But my analysis throughout this book, and as regards democracy in this chapter, has been to demonstrate that these values have always possessed some presence, however flawed, regardless of their expression through the ECJ's decisions.

If this is accepted then the role of European law in the institutional narrative of democracy must be examined from a wider perspective. We must question not just what 'edifice' has been constructed and why but also what implications arise for the definition of democracy in the EU's hands. Has the ECJ taken democracy seriously?

Let us first return to some of those crucial constituting judgments. They relate to the standard territory of supremacy, direct effect, as well as fundamental rights.

The familiar case of *van Gend en Loos* remains the inspiration for EU law as *law*. Few would doubt its importance in establishing the jurisprudential dynamic necessary to provide the EU and the ECJ with authority to construct its project without the prospect of derailment through varied and uncertain application by national courts. In particular the judgment that articles of the Treaties produce 'direct

---

[72] See for instance Renaud Dehousse, *The European Court of Justice: the Politics of Judicial Integration* (Basingstoke: Macmillan, 1998) at 118.

effects' and create 'individual rights which national courts must protect' has been presented as a product of interpretation. In other words, the Treaties have been the source of law. This might well be true. But interestingly the key statements of the Court are based on a particular form of interpretation, one that is founded on a democratic fiction. So, the ECJ stated,

[t]he objective of the EEC Treaty, which is to establish a common market, the functioning of which is of direct concern to interested parties in the Community, implies that this Treaty is *more* than an agreement which merely creates mutual obligations between the contracting states [emphasis added].[73]

What 'more' could this be? Later we learn it is 'a new legal order of international law for the benefit of which the states have limited their sovereign rights, albeit within limited fields, and the subjects of which comprise not only Member States but also their nationals'. But is this the complete answer? When we turn to the basis of justification for reaching its judgment we find the Court's view confirmed

by the preamble to the Treaty which refers not only to governments but to peoples. It is also confirmed more specifically by the establishment of institutions endowed with sovereign rights, the exercise of which affects Member States and also their citizens.[74]

The first part clearly attempts to acquire popular endorsement by default. Whatever the actual involvement of the people or peoples of Europe, the original EEC Treaty was constructed in their name. Similarly, whether they like it or not, they are affected by what has been agreed to be imposed. The whole structure is a product of some ill-defined, even amorphous, democratic act of creation. That is the implication given further emphasis when the Court went on to state that

it must be noted that the nationals of the States brought together in the Community are called upon to cooperate in the functioning of this Community through the intermediary of the European Parliament and the Economic and Social Committee.[75]

Why should this possess *any* weight unless it is supposed to convey a participatory quality to the then EEC that transforms it from an ethereal and functional construction of text to one that possesses real democratic dimensions? Only then can the Court go on to declare

[73] *Van Gend en Loos* v. *Nederlandse Administratie der Berastingen* [1963] ECR 1.
[74] *Ibid.*   [75] *Ibid.*

that '[i]ndependently of the legislation of Member States, Community law therefore not only imposes obligations on individuals but is also intended to confer upon them rights which become part of their legal heritage'.[76]

The circularity of the argument only makes sense through a democratic prism. Otherwise we have the faintly ludicrous propositions flowing in this order. The Treaty imposes obligations and rights. These were imposed in the people's name. Therefore the EEC must be a product *of* the people. Therefore the Treaty is entitled to impose obligations and rights, which rights become part of *the* people's legal heritage because they have been produced *for* and by them.[77]

This can only be made sensible if the democratic underpinnings are assumed to exist. The reference to some rather pathetic forms of public participation in the forms of governance in the initial phase of the EU are only worthy if they reflect deeper democratic roots. It is of course possible that greater faith was placed in the institution of the Parliament and the ESC at this time then was subsequently justified. Perhaps it was wishful thinking. Or perhaps it was merely a gesture. Notwithstanding these possibilities they provided some clothing or, more appropriately, some skeletal substance that was based on the value of democracy to allow the ECJ to make the argument for supremacy of EU law.

Interestingly, the next great constituting case, *Costa* v. *ENEL*, did not adopt the same legitimating rhetoric. On the contrary, the ECJ moved to a much more functional rationale. It declared,

the EEC Treaty has created its own legal system which, on the entry into force of the Treaty, became an integral part of the legal systems of the Member States and which their courts are bound to apply. By creating a Community of unlimited duration, having its own institutions, its own personality, its own legal capacity and capacity of representation on the international plane and, more particularly, real powers stemming from a limitation of sovereignty or a transfer of powers from the States to the Community, the Member States have limited their sovereign rights, albeit within limited fields, and have thus created a body of law which binds both their nationals and themselves.[78]

---

[76] *Ibid.*

[77] Hans Lindahl has also, perhaps more elegantly, noted the circularity of this reasoning although in a more philosophical vein. See Lindahl, 'Acquiring a Community: the *Acquis* and the Institution of the European Legal Order' at 437.

[78] Case 6/64 *Costa* v. *ENEL* [1964] ECR 585

The tone is one of legitimisation by contract rather than public will (inferred or otherwise). The *law* becomes the functional framework for this contractual determination. It is the Treaty rather than any underlying force that provides the authority. The ECJ then went on to give further substance to this interpretation. It suggested that the

integration into the laws of each Member State of provisions which derive from the Community, and more generally the terms and the spirit of the Treaty, make it impossible for the States, as a corollary, to accord precedence to a unilateral and subsequent measure over a legal system accepted by them on a basis of reciprocity.[79]

We cannot just skip over the notion of reciprocity here. In the context of this statement it has little to do with any moral philosophical understanding that the Member States *should* act so as to recognise the rights of other states in 'the context of shared activity with others in pursuit of commonly agreed-upon ends'.[80] Rather reciprocity is minimal in character, a feature of contract law; states are *obliged* to follow those provisions in the Treaty because that is what they have contracted to do. That is the most persuasive interpretation one can place on the Treaty if it is to have sense as a Treaty. So, the ECJ goes on,

[t]he executive force of Community law cannot vary from one State to another in deference to subsequent domestic laws, without jeopardizing the attainment of the objectives of the Treaty set out in Article 5 (2) and giving rise to the discrimination prohibited by Article 7.[81]

The rationale is that the effectiveness of the Treaty qua Treaty (or contract) would be undermined by failure to adhere to the law agreed to be placed over national legal systems. This is an argument that does not require any kind of test of democratic legitimacy. It is a functional position and a reflection of the power of law. As the Court said,

[t]he obligations undertaken under the Treaty establishing the Community would not be unconditional, but merely contingent, if they could be called in question by subsequent legislative acts of the signatories.[82]

In short, the Treaty would be forever undermined, made ineffective.

---

[79] *Ibid.*
[80] See Carol Gould, *Globalizing Democracy and Human Rights* (Cambridge: Cambridge University Press, 2004) at 41.
[81] *Costa* v. *ENEL.*   [82] *Ibid.*

Of course, the contractual arrangements do not operate within a political vacuum. A political environment that is based on liberal democracy might be assumed.[83] But it is an environment that is implicit rather than explicit. It is certainly not a prerequisite of the agreement itself unless one apportions greater weight to the spirit of the Treaties as including a democratic content, as *van Gend en Loos* attempts.

The relevant question for the examination of the relationship between ECJ jurisprudence and the value of democracy then is whether the ECJ's turn in *Costa* shifted the institutional approach as a whole towards a legalistic rather than value-laden position, at least in terms of democracy. The judgment in *Internationale Handelsgesellschaft* would suggest this was indeed the response. There the ECJ deployed the same rationale as *Costa*, noting that

[t]he law stemming from the Treaty, an independent source of law, cannot because of its very nature be overridden by rules of national law, however framed, without being deprived of its character as Community law and without the legal basis of the Community itself being called into question.[84]

It did not seem to matter to the Court how or why any national provision might be constructed. Although it might have concluded that respect for fundamental rights was nonetheless guaranteed by EU law, this was a result of the imputation of such respect to be a general principle, not because the legal systems of Member States demanded it. Fundamental rights were inferred as, in essence, an implied condition of the contract *not* as the result of a democratic process determined to set the EU's ethical character.

Similarly, in *Simmenthal* the Court reiterated the predominance of efficacy rather than underlying popular authority by concluding,

any recognition that national legislative measures which encroach upon the field within which the Community exercises its legislative power or which are otherwise incompatible with the provisions of Community law had any legal effect would amount to a corresponding denial of the effectiveness of obligations undertaken unconditionally and irrevocably by Member States pursuant to the Treaty and would thus imperil the very foundations of the Community.[85]

---

[83] This might be the inference if we took the interpretation of law as a product of morality in the way that Lon Fuller does in *The Morality of Law* (New Haven: Yale University Press, 1964).

[84] Case 11/70 *Internationale Handelsgesellschaft* v. *Einfuhr- und Vorratstelle fur Getreide und Futtermittel* [1970] ECR II 1125–55.

[85] Case 106/77 *Amministrazione delle Finanze dello Stato* v. *Simmenthal* [1978] ECR 629 at para. 18.

Those foundations are clearly considered to be contractual and textual rather than spiritual. They are not premised on a system of governance by, for and of the people. The system is its only authority.

One can appreciate the preference for this brand of functionalism, or principle of interpretation so as to give effect to the Treaties, rather than rely on democratic foundations. If the latter course had been pursued, as *van Gend en Loos* might have suggested, it would be easy to predict the consequent battles over levels of democratic legitimacy. How could the ECJ sustain the democracy argument if faced by a incompatible piece of national legislation explicitly passed as the result of a parliamentary process? The danger of the Union's rationale imploding would have been severe. How could it sustain an argument based on democratic routes *without* any continuing expression of public deliberation and choice? So, when faced with the issue in *Factortame*, for instance, the ECJ adjudged

Community law must be interpreted as meaning that a national court which, in a case before it concerning Community law, considers that the sole obstacle which precludes it from granting interim relief is a rule of national law must set aside that rule.[86]

In short, the English court was authorised to ignore the principle of parliamentary sovereignty so as to ensure Community law was preserved. Effectiveness overrode any national interests determined through the democratic process of parliament. Arguments about democratic legitimacy did not therefore need to be entertained.

It is unsurprising that decisions based on this reasoning now provide the focus for the Court and the whole system of EU law. The attempts in *van Gend en Loos* to provide some kind of democratic basis were unconvincing and unsupportable particularly given the failure of the European Parliament to exercise any legislative function worthy of the name.

If the ECJ could not look to the value of democracy with any conviction vis-à-vis the constitutional framework this did not mean that it needed to ignore it in all respects. By looking towards democratic virtues, evident in relation to administrative law, the Court could at least refer delicately to the democratic underpinnings first noted in *van Gend en Loos*. Indeed, as the powers of Parliament have increased so

---

[86] Case C-213/89 R. v. *Secretary of State for Transport, ex parte: Factortame Ltd and others* [1990] ECR 2433 at para. 23.

too have the opportunities for the ECJ to bring this restricted democratic argument back into its judgments. So, for instance, in *SA Roquette Frères* v. *Council* in 1979 the Court was able to reflect on the nature of then Article 43(2) EC Treaty, which required the Council to receive the opinion of the European Parliament on the measure before adopting a regulation with regard to an aspect of the common agricultural policy. This rather ineffectual requirement nonetheless appeared to have been ignored by the Council, prompting a complaint by the applicant on the basis that an essential procedural requirement under then Article 173 had been infringed. The Court reached its judgment in favour of the applicant by determining that

[t]he consultation provided for in the third subparagraph of article 43(2) ... is the means which allows the Parliament to play an actual part in the legislative process of the community, such power represents an essential factor in the institutional balance intended by the Treaty. Although limited, it reflects at community level the fundamental democratic principle that the peoples should take part in the exercise of power through the intermediary of a representative assembly. Due consultation of the parliament in the cases provided for by the Treaty therefore constitutes an essential formality disregard of which means that the measure concerned is void.[87]

Of course, the democratic character of the Treaty provision is relatively unimportant. Whether or not it reflects any value, the Court would still be obliged to give effect to its term. But the statement does add a rhetorical flourish to the judgment that registers sensitivity towards the democratic nature of those provisions.

This has been reiterated more recently in the case of *IATA* v. *Department of Transport*.[88] A regulation designed to deal with common rules on compensation and assistance to airline passengers as a result of cancellations or flight delays was in issue. The claimants raised a point concerning the legislative history of this regulation, suggesting that because the Conciliation Committee proceedings, used to address differences between the Parliament and the Council in the drafting process, were not held in public, the 'principles of representative democracy' had been undermined. The Court again recognised that 'genuine participation of the Parliament in the legislative process

---

[87] Case 138/79 *SA Roquette Frères* v. *Council of the European Communities* [1980] ECR 3333 at para. 33.

[88] Case C-344/04 R., *on the application of International Air Transport Association and European Low Fares Airline Association* v. *Department for Transport* [2006] ECR I-00403.

of the Community, in accordance with the procedures lain down by the Treaty, represents an essential factor in the institutional balance intended by the Treaty'.[89] But it concluded that this was respected by the fact that eventually the Parliament would still have to review the Committee's joint text in open session. Thus 'genuine participation' would be achieved 'in compliance with the principles of representative democracy'. No guidance was offered about what would or would not constitute '*genuine* participation'. The assumption made was that adherence to the Parliament's 'normal' procedures would suffice. It is difficult to imagine that the Court had any notion of creating an abstract principle of democracy in EU law or to adopt a position that might critique the adequacy of Treaty provisions in democratic terms. Rather, it seems to have extracted a principle from the *fact* of representation established through the Treaties.

Similarly, when it comes to assessing the adequacy of respect for other democratic virtues, such as public access to documents, the tendency of the Court has been to accept the right of the institutions to develop procedures as it chooses. In the *Netherlands* v. *Council*,[90] for instance, although the ECJ noted that Declaration 17 annexed to the TEU reaffirmed the right to access, the institutions were not obliged to introduce specific procedures complying with such a right. Instead, they could follow the 'trend' of gradual exposure through measures of 'internal organisation'.[91] There was no question of constructing a legal right in the absence of a legislative provision. This has remained the position despite the introduction of Article 6(1) TEU. Indeed, cases involving particular issues of democratic representation have failed to provoke reference to this constitutional principle.[92] In *Spain* v. *UK* the Court's position was to flinch from giving democracy any substantive definition in terms of representation.[93] It left the question as to whom would be allowed to vote in EU elections to the Member State.

All of this would suggest we have to be circumspect about imputing as a general principle respect for democracy in any way similar to the approach to fundamental rights. The latter were included as an ethical obligation almost *regardless* of what the Treaties said. Democracy on the other hand is *only* respected in so far as it is expressed within

---

[89] *Ibid.*, para. 61.   [90] Case C-58/94 *The Netherlands* v. *Council* [1996] ECR I-02169.
[91] *Ibid.* paras. 35–37.
[92] See Case C-145/04 *Spain* v. *United Kingdom* [2006] ECR 2006, I-07917.
[93] *Ibid.*

the Treaties. Those provisions that require Parliamentary involvement may well be a product of a democratic urge but they are accepted by the Court because they are in the text *not* because they can be inferred. Does this make respect for democracy any less of a general principle for the purposes of EU law and the institutional ethos? Yes, for the reason that there seems to be no prospect of imposing democratic obligations on the EU without explicit agreement. Even the constitutional location of democracy as a founding principle in the TEU does not assist greatly given the complete absence of definition of the term and the unwillingness, wholly understandable, of the Court to use this as the basis for any radical jurisprudence.

Perhaps the most lucid examination of this condition was presented by AG Maduro in the case of *Sweden* v. *Commission*.[94] With exceptional skill, Maduro was able to chart the development of principles associated with a democratic system whilst also recognising their limited influence in the EU's history. He was also able to question the underlying tensions that appeared between these principles and the notion of democracy as an ideal value in itself. In reviewing its history in the EU, he pointed out that as regards openness,

[i]f one wished to be provocative, one could doubtless question the alleged relationship between transparency and democracy. Is it not the symptom of a general feeling of suspicion on the part of citizens towards those in power and of the representative democratic system? There is, moreover, a risk that transparency will not be used in the same manner by all citizens and that it will serve to promote privileged access to the political system for certain interest groups.[95]

He was keen then to outline an earlier lack of commitment by the Court to the principle of transparency.

Despite that progressive affirmation of the right of public access to documents of the institutions, despite the invitations from its Advocates General or some of its Members, despite being spurred by some of the stands taken by the Court of First Instance, and even though it itself recognised that the right of public access to documents held by public authorities is enshrined as a constitutional or legislative principle by the majority of the Member States, the Court of Justice has not formally established it as a general principle of Community law.[96]

---

[94] Case C-64/05 P *Kingdom of Sweden* v. *Commission and Others* [2007] ECR I-11389, Opinion of Mr Advocate General Poiares Maduro, delivered on 18 July 2007.
[95] *Ibid.* at para. 41.   [96] *Ibid.* at para. 38.

The Treaty of Amsterdam finally brought the principle into the constitutional mix. As Maduro went on to say, '[w]ith the advent of the right of access to documents held by public authorities, transparency has become aimed more at reinforcing the democratic legitimacy of Community action'.[97] But the key characteristic of this legitimising process rests not in the construction of the system but in the individual fundamental rights now engaged. Naturally, this is the least problematic way for the Court to approach any commitment to democracy. But it reinforces the view that technical virtues become the legal substitute for processes that possess more radical democratic credentials. Direct participation and direct deliberation remain distant from the European level. And EU law is not in a position to remedy that condition. Nor, as Maduro confirms, has it been predisposed to do so.

Conclusion

There is a school of thought at the moment that the EU does not need to have any meaningful democratic structures in a form commonly ascribed to modern Western states.[98] It is considered sufficient that there is in place layers of democratically inspired processes that infuse the workings of the Union. These suggest the construction of a kind of haphazard democratic circle.

We begin with the basic proposition that the EU is a product of democracy, being the creation of democratic states. The Lisbon Treaty recognises this by noting that

Member States are represented in the European Council by their Heads of State or Government and in the Council by their governments, themselves democratically accountable either to their national parliaments, or to their citizens.[99]

In other words, there is a democratic proxy in operation.

On this foundation we then have the direct representation that appears through the European Parliament. This provides the forum for the 'people' (the citizens of the EU). Like national Parliaments, such

---

[97] *Ibid.* at para. 39.
[98] See Majone, 'Europe's "Democratic Deficit"' and Moravcsik, 'In Defence of the "Democratic Deficit"'. For a challenge to this approach see Jukka Snell, '"European Constitutional Settlement", an Ever Closer Union, and the Treaty of Lisbon: Democracy or Relevance?', *European Law Review* 33:5 (2008) 619–42.
[99] New Article 10(2) TEU.

representation is limited. The boundaries have been extended over recent years to create greater powers for the Parliament to exercise some kind of influence over the Union's activities. But those powers remain suspiciously underdeveloped.

Parallel to the representative dimension, the EU has adopted a series of measures to increase the level of participation by citizens in its policy construction. Some of these have been associated with the discourse of fundamental rights. Access to documentation may have caused some difficulty, when refusals represent a significant proportion of requests, but it remains a path for engagement of a kind. When coupled with a general increase in transparency through the publication of documents we can see a ready willingness to emerge from a culture of *great* secrecy to one of *reasonable* openness. These terms I use reservedly for it remains the case that the sheer volume of material and the undoubted club-like atmosphere of the European machinery are not tailored for public accessibility. But what government is?

We also see a developing culture of consultation. There has always been a de facto engagement by the institutions with interest groups and private agencies through traditional committees or lobbying processes.[100] But this hardly amounts to respect for democracy. However, the recognised need to get the 'people' on the side of the EU, actively seeking their opinions if not necessarily responding to their elicited demands, suggests 'dialogue' might be possible. Whether this can really amount to a 'public space' for democratic deliberation seems fanciful at present but not altogether impossible.

And then beyond these constitutional processes and practical measures we have the national parliaments, whose complicity in the construction of certain legislation and whose role in the governance of the EU through perpetual review has begun to be emphasised as the completion of the democratic circle. We return to the Member States to establish democratic credentials.

It is not difficult to recognise within this model something of a Kantian influence.[101] A 'federalism of free states' where freedom is

---

[100] The key committees have been the Economic and Social Committee and the Committee of the Regions.

[101] See, in particular, Immanuel Kant, 'Toward Perpetual Peace: a Philosophical Project' in Mary J. Gregor (trans. and ed.), *Immanuel Kant: Practical Philosophy* (Cambridge: Cambridge University Press, 1996) 315–51. J.H.H. Weiler makes the connection more explicit in 'Federalism Without Constitutionalism', in Kalypso Nicolaïdis and Robert Howse (eds.), *The Federal Vision* (Oxford: Oxford University Press, 2001).

essentially located in the state and where right operates as the linking theme across the domestic, international and cosmopolitan planes. Democratic processes are placed emphatically in the national sphere. But of course the EU has gone some way beyond that vision. The very creation of a European Parliament has forced the EU to grapple with extending democracy beyond the state and not simply through the application of individual rights. It has provided initial justification for the primacy of European law (as with *van Gend en Loos*) *and* it has provoked internal critique that points to the necessity of matching democratic substance to form. If the institution of Europe bases its legitimacy on the presence of a democratic foundation it becomes obliged to fulfil the promise of that ethical substratum. It then becomes a matter of determining how far it can go without encountering destabilising political opposition.

From this perspective, the observations of Moravcsik, Majone and others really do not carry significant weight. However accurate they may be in pointing out the relative success of the EU in respecting certain aspects of democracy when compared to Member States (let alone other international organisations), the fact remains that those who advocate ever-greater democratic processes and procedures are likely to prevail. With the demise of the 'permissive consensus' that seemed to accompany the EU's early years and the emergence of both significant political or public opposition and apathy, the democratic route remains the only identified avenue for institutional development.[102] Other values may contribute (we have already visited the appeal of human rights and security) but when it comes to decision-making the emerging institutional ethos seems to favour greater attention towards democratic value *and* virtue.

Confusion has arisen, however, with the recent institutional emphasis on virtue rather than value through a discourse of 'democratic governance'. Paul Magnette interprets this as based on a 'double observation'.[103] First, there is no 'vocation' for the EU to become a

---

[102] The original thesis that the EU was the product of a 'permissive consensus' appeared in Leon N. Lindberg and Stuart A. Scheingold, *Europe's Would-be Polity: Patterns of Change in the European Community* (Englewood Cliffs, NJ: Prentice-Hall, 1970). The notion that the permissive consensus has disappeared as a result of electoral rebuffs for the Constitutional Treaty has been challenged by Achim Hurrelmann in 'European Democracy, the "Permissive Consensus" and the Collapse of the EU Constitution', *European Law Journal* 13:3 (2007) 343–59.

[103] Paul Magnette, *What is the European Union? Nature and Prospects* (Basingstoke: Palgrave, 2005) at 174 et seq.

state and therefore there is no need to embrace a notion of a European people for whom democratic *government* might otherwise be desirable. Second, as the EU's functions are generally regulatory, fulfilling the collective aims of the Member States, there is no need to establish any system that mimics parliamentary democracy. All that is required is a structure that ensures adherence to good principles of administration within which the voice of the people can be taken into account. Of course, this approach has not replaced those seeking democratic legitimacy through parliamentary processes. And the constitutional efforts of recent draft Treaties remain intent on retaining the commitment to parliamentary democracy. But Eric Hobsbawm's observation that there was little point in talking about democratic deficit because the EU 'wasn't supposed to be a democracy', indeed that if it had been 'it would never have reached its current degree of integration', remains particularly apposite.[104]

Should we then be considering democracy in the institutional ethos of Europe more from the perspective of global than national templates? If so, what might this mean for the future? Would it suggest a willingness to put up with the existing limited democratic aspects of the Union in the knowledge that this was a relatively progressive position to adopt given the lack of similar credentials held by other international organisations? In terms of the rhetoric and promise projected through the EU, such a conclusion would seem to be unwelcome. The institutions have for some time now been intent on establishing a legitimacy that entailed a closer relationship with the 'people'. These efforts may have been thwarted by the resistance of national interests engaged in maintaining political power at national level but they nonetheless represent an endeavour that promotes democracy to a much deeper degree than a purely cosmopolitan perspective would necessarily entail. But either way, the underlying character of this value in the EU remains indeterminate so long as political form cannot be settled. A general acceptance of a system of multi-level governance would even suggest that any democratic fixity would be counter-productive to current systems in place. Different policy areas and different tasks may require different democratic models to be adopted.[105]

---

[104] Eric Hobsbawm, *The New Century* (London: Abacus, 2000) at 91.
[105] See, for instance, Colin Scott, 'The Governance of the European Union: the Potential for Multi-Level Control', *European Law Journal* 8:1 (2002) 59–79.

How does European law sit within this environment? Can law provide some kind of determinacy so as to substantiate the value? Given the tendency of the ECJ to avoid democracy as an inspiration for judgment and scrutiny, responding rather to a philosophy based on a theory of interpretation that privileges the text by giving effect to its provisions rather than its underlying values, the current constitutional development of a European democracy might seem unlikely to acquire legal support. But will the ECJ alter its perspective with the Lisbon Treaty? Would the reaffirmation of the value of democracy release the ECJ from its virtuous constraints in any meaningful way? Or would the continuing emphasis on governance reinforce the tendency of European law to adopt a restricted approach? These have to remain open questions. But there is little evidence to suggest the Court has any desire to become embroiled in really addressing democracy, in any independent form, with conviction. It has certainly eschewed those few opportunities presented to it so far.

What then does this mean for the institutional ethos? It would suggest that there exists a strong tension between law and constitution that inevitably suppresses the impact of this particular value. Indeed, the current state of affairs has led some to note the existence of a debilitating paradox. Wojciech Sadurski points out the irony associated with the EU being perceived by new Member States 'both as a source for the promotion of democracy and as a threat to democracy (through a transfer of powers to European institutions, whose democratic legitimacy is put in doubt)'.[106] Can EU law really function effectively when affected by such tensions? And can the place of democracy as a fundamental value really be established for the EU with any determinacy whilst this paradox made apparent through legal challenge remains?

There seems little prospect of democracy attaining any greater degree of certainty in the near future. Constitutional initiatives simply do no more than alter the margins of activity rather than fulfil any substantive content for a particular democratic model. As a fundamental value, therefore, democracy remains inherently ambiguous across the EU landscape. Its indeterminacy far exceeds any reasonable degree of uncertainty.

---

[106] Wojciech Sadurski, '"Solange, Chapter 3": Constitutional Courts in Central Europe – Democracy – European Union', *European Law Journal* 14:1 (2008) 1–35 at 5.

6   Liberty

Introduction

An abundance of ambition attaches to the EU when it comes to values. We have already seen in the previous chapters the adoption of a constitutional language that claims the institution is integrally bound by some of the grandest principles of Western political philosophy. And modesty has never been a quality the EU institutions have evaded in this respect. They seem to embrace an almost messianic narrative when it comes to projecting 'values' to the EU's constituents and to the world. The Union is presented as not only the guardian of these values internally but also the beacon for all other societies, a model for other regional ventures to follow.

Liberty (or freedom, we need not distinguish between the two) is undoubtedly one of these fundamental values. The term has been ever present within its constituting texts. In the preamble to the EEC Treaty the signatories declared their resolve to 'preserve and strengthen' freedom. Much later, with the end of the Cold War, liberty was proclaimed as the first of the EU's 'founding principles'.[1] Now somewhat down the pecking order, relegated behind 'human dignity' in the Lisbon Treaty's list of values, liberty, nonetheless, has assumed an ever-present quality in institutional rhetoric. But, of course, the fact that constitutional-type statements have been adopted does not mean that there is clarity about the concept. What does it mean for the EU? And how is it reflected in practical action?

At the outset, we have something of a dual definitional problem here. Not only is the meaning of liberty generally 'so porous that there is little interpretation that it seems able to resist', as Isaiah Berlin

---

[1] Article 6(1) TEU.

197

remarked,[2] but when the complexities of the EU's specific position vis-à-vis its Member States, their citizens and all those individuals and legal persons over which some authority is exercised directly or indirectly, are added to the mix, the definitional difficulty is compounded. How then can we view this value in the EU's hands? It is clearly insufficient to rely upon the statement, now constitutionally enshrined, that the EU *is* an 'area of freedom, security and justice'. That is an assertion, a political claim rather than a fact.

Instead, we can start by asking a number of questions. What promises have been made, what actions have been taken, what policies have been constructed and what analysis has been undertaken institutionally that would provide some clue as to its nature and quality? This requires an examination of institutional rhetoric and practice. And, indeed, my aim for this chapter is to consider each with regard to the EU's relationship with its Member States on the one hand and its citizens and individuals, on the other. But before embarking on this exercise, we really need some idea of what liberty *might* mean in theory at such a supranational level. For we are not only asking, as J.S. Mill did in *On Liberty*, what the 'nature and limits of the power which can be legitimately exercised by society over the individual' might be, but also what power might be exercised legitimately by a supranational institution over states as well as peoples generally.[3] The EU not only crosses jurisdictional boundaries but operates in varying ways when it does so. The ensuing complexity means that we have to think about the possible meaning of liberty from a number of perspectives if we are to evaluate its quality as a value in the EU.

I also intend to consider, in this respect, the relationship between freedom and other values. Given the concept's slippery nature one can be forgiven for thinking that it has no independent normative meaning beyond that provided by other concepts. In particular, arguments have been made that liberty at this level only takes shape through the expression of equality. Armin von Bogdandy, for instance, asserts, in this vein, that '[t]rue liberty can only be conceived as the same liberty for all legal subjects' and that this understanding has entrenched an idea of 'equal liberty' into EU law.[4] Although highly contestable, and

---

[2] Isaiah Berlin, 'Two Concepts of Liberty', in Isaiah Berlin, *Four Essays on Liberty* (Oxford: Oxford University Press, 1969) at 121.

[3] J.S. Mill, *On Liberty* (Oxford: Blackwell, 1946) at 1.

[4] Armin von Bogdandy, 'Constitutional Principles', in Armin von Bogdandy and Jürgen Bast (eds.), *Principles of European Constitutional Law* (Oxford: Hart, 2006) 3–52 at 14.

indeed demonstrably *un*true when we look at the various dimensions of liberty that might be engaged, this thinking has to be taken seriously. For the idea of equality can and has arisen as an important value in relation to both states and peoples within the EU and in conjunction or perhaps juxtaposition with the value of freedom.

With the above in mind, the first part of this chapter considers the concept of liberty in the abstract. Its relationship with equality is also addressed as a potentially important element of its definition. The second part then examines the record of the EU in so far as it may be considered to enhance or restrict freedom collectively and for individuals. Here, I assess the prominent evidence of the EU's engagement with activities that affect liberty in one dimension or another and try to assess the depth to which freedom is understood institutionally.

The concept of liberty

It would be invidious to suggest that I can construct a single normative understanding of liberty against which we might then judge the EU. Given the malleable nature of the concept, attempting to fix a theory would likely as not be partial and ideologically biased. As with all the values addressed in this book, all I can hope to do as a preliminary task is to sketch out some of the parameters for investigation. By providing a spectrum of possible meanings we can then examine the history of the EU to see approximately what approach has been taken institutionally. The quality of liberty as part of the institutional ethos can then be judged.

It might help to distinguish at the outset between freedom and *freedoms*. The latter I take to relate to specific rights or privileges that often appear separable and an integral part of human rights discourse and practice. Although the collective realisation of these freedoms will be relevant, freedom is a notion that lends itself to a holistic rather than fragmentary perspective, echoing its identification by Kant as an 'inner value of the world'.[5] We need, therefore, to look beyond the limited sense of freedom as a collection of 'freedoms' if the full scope of liberty is to be understood in the EU context.

---

[5] Martti Koskenneimi reviews the relationship between freedom and international law in the Kantian mode in 'Constitutionalism as Mindset: Reflections on Kantian Themes about International Law and Globalization', *Theoretical Inquiries in Law* 8:1 (2007) 9–36.

Similarly, another distinction can be made between negative and positive connotations of liberty. The former indicates the desire for the least interference as possible in the lives of individuals by the state or any other authority or power. The latter suggests a societal project for the assumption of positive duties to enable people to acquire greater collective freedom. The distinction between these dimensions might not, at first blush, seem to be very acute. Ensuring the conditions are present to enable either a 'community' or individuals to develop freely according to their own wishes, for instance, might be little different from preventing interferences with such development. In political philosophy, indeed, there has been much debate about the legitimacy of any distinction between positive and negative versions.[6] However, when we are concerned with the relationship between freedom and an international institutional system of governance, as we are here with the EU, the distinction is merited. Positive connotations suggest a *proactive* approach towards creating the conditions for freedom. Specific policies and practices specifically designed to enhance freedom would be characteristic of such a method. Negative connotations suggest a *reactive* approach. They would relate to measures taken that (a) would operate to prevent interference with liberty by private or public power or (b) would have a detrimental impact on people's freedom.[7]

With these caveats in mind, two general dimensions of liberty appear particularly apposite to consider for the EU. These are *not* mutually exclusive but interact and impact upon each other. The first is collective in character, the second concerns the individual. Both incorporate a wide range of possible meanings and require some exploration. I will not attempt to construct or impose a complete theory of liberty here though. Rather, my intention is simply to consider the possible scope of the concept through a reasonable normative spectrum.

Collective liberty

The starting point for thinking about 'collective liberty' is the relations between 'peoples' or 'states' in community with one another. Its basis manifests itself in principles of modern international law. These assume

---

[6] See, for instance, Isaiah Berlin, 'Two Concepts of Liberty' and Gerald C. MacCallum Jr., 'Negative and Positive Freedom', *The Philosophical Review* (1967) 312–34.

[7] I use these terms 'private' and 'public' in recognition that a range of potential influences might be exercised on individuals or communities, emanating from states, corporations or other individuals. Psychological (both social and individual) forces might be relevant here.

both positive and negative aspects. Finding a fundamental influence in liberal internationalism and manifested in the UN Charter and other important texts since, they require that inter-state relations should be 'founded upon freedom, equality, justice and respect for fundamental human rights and of developing friendly relations among nations irrespective of their political, economic and social systems or the levels of their development'.[8] Non-use of force, non-intervention in the affairs of other states, equal rights and sovereign equality of nations, self-determination and independence, provide the key injunctive principles underpinning international law with the freedom of peoples as an overriding objective.[9] Positive contributions to enhancing liberty manifest themselves through discourses of the duty of states to cooperate with each other for the benefit of all. The right to development is one expression of this approach but it could also extend to the *lex mercatoria* and the private law sphere.[10]

These collective liberty aspects relate primarily to integrity of the 'nation' or state, which requires autonomy 'to act and not to be acted upon', in Isaiah Berlin's words.[11] This would include freedom from domination *and* freedom to 'prosper' and 'progress'. The absence of the imposition of rule by those from outside the state, in this sense, should be seen as both a factor of collective freedom and a precondition of individual liberty.[12] Of course, the 'rule' referred to might take various forms. Direct subjugation by conquest or war, gradual assumption of control through processes of colonialism, insidious means of oppression through economic or cultural avenues, could all entail a type of domination. They are forms of external interference which can affect a 'peoples' freedom. Such terms are, of course, loaded with immense

---

[8] Declaration on Principles of International Law concerning Friendly Relations and Co-operation among States in accordance with the Charter of the United Nations General Assembly Resolution A/RES/25/2625 [1970].

[9] *Ibid.*

[10] In drafting principles to determine core aims of a European private law, for instance, 'freedom' was identified as the second value worthy of protection, although little by way of definition was provided. See, 'The Draft Common Frame of Reference: Principles, Definitions and Model Rules of European Private Law', authored by C. von Bar, E. Clive and H. Schulte-Nölke and H. Beale, J. Herre, J. Huet, P. Schlechtriem, M. Storme, S. Swann, P. Varul, A. Veneziano and F. Zoll, Interim Outline Edition (Munich: Sellier, 2008) at 13.

[11] Berlin, *Four Essays on Liberty* 138.

[12] The strength of the analogous link between personal and state liberty in modern international law is charted by Charles Beitz in *Political Theory and International Relations* (Princeton: Princeton University Press, 1979).

political and ideological significance. They are open to continual debate and negotiation. But they encapsulate one important aspect of collective freedom that should not be ignored.

The EU's position as a polity in its own right, comprising its Member States and constituent peoples, may have two basic reference points for assessing collective freedom in its domain. The first is outward looking, where freedom might be called upon as a counterpoint to interference from outside its borders. The EU here would be representative of a 'community' of European states. We have already seen this adopted in the discourses of security in Chapter 2. Those forces, in the form of external or internal states or corporations or perhaps even criminal networks, which threaten collective autonomy, attacking the foundations of self-determination or state 'sovereignty', may be seen as affecting the collective liberty of 'Europe' as a whole. The development of policy responding to threats considered fundamentally against the interests of all the EU's constituents would entail the development of a 'European' view of what constituted a threat. The nature of the freedom assumed by the EU in this dimension will be reflected in the political choices it makes or develops which relate to collective security issues.

The second reference point is inward looking and relates to the relationship between the EU as an institution (acting independently or as an agent of party states) and its constituent peoples and Member States. The positive and negative impact on general liberty resulting from action taken by the EU is of course the concern here. The transfer of sovereignty to the EU provokes such an assessment. An understanding of freedom in this context emanates from the degree to which power is exercised to either enhance or restrict liberty. Here we encounter a difficult if not dangerous juxtaposition. Hannah Arendt noted the inherent contradiction between sovereignty and freedom, claiming that 'where men wish to be sovereign ... they must submit to the oppression of the will, be this individual will with which I force myself or the "general will" of an organized group'.[13] She suggested, 'if men wish to be free, it is precisely sovereignty they must renounce'.[14] It is in defence of 'sovereignty' indeed that *freedoms* so often become casualties, something I examined when considering the actions taken in the name of

---

[13] Hannah Arendt, 'Freedom and Politics', in David Miller (ed.), *The Liberty Reader* (Edinburgh: Edinburgh University Press, 2006) 58–79 at 73.
[14] *Ibid.*

perceived security interests. But it can have greater application where a state's freedom of choice is consciously restricted by allocating sovereignty to an international institution, in our case the EU. This does not necessarily mean that 'freedom' as a governing concept is undone. Instead it might mean the basic principle of non-interference is subject to agreed restrictions for a wider collective freedom. In the EU's case the danger of this developing from a basic wish to preserve the individual political character of its Member States into an assumption that 'Europe' as a cultural, perhaps even ethnic, entity can be represented and developed through the EU has to be considered.

Other characteristics of collective liberty should also come within assessment. Again these can take on a negative or positive hue. They are represented through discourses of development and social welfare and the well-being of a community's constituents as a whole. They are bonded by an approach that sees the progress of a community so that all its members have their freedom enhanced. In Amartya Sen's terms, for instance, development 'can be seen ... as a process of expanding the real freedoms that people enjoy'.[15] 'Development as freedom' relies upon determinants 'such as social and economic arrangements', civil and political rights and, more from a negative freedom perspective, the 'removal of major sources of unfreedom; poverty as well as tyranny, poor economic opportunities as well as systematic social deprivation, neglect of public facilities as well as intolerance or overactivity of repressive states'.[16]

This approach has acquired increasing salience in international development discourse.[17] Liberty here requires collective action by states domestically and internationally. It fixes itself to freedom *from* want and fear, and freedom *to* live in dignity. Much of this rhetoric repeats accounts of global justice. It, nonetheless, demonstrates the possible adherence to an understanding of freedom that is collective in nature for the benefit of the people of the world, not just one's own citizens.[18] At the peculiar level of the EU it could also have purchase in so far as the EU operates in the field of development both internally

---

[15] Amartya Sen, *Development as Freedom* (Oxford: Oxford University Press, 1999) at 3.

[16] *Ibid.*

[17] See, in particular, UN Secretary General, Report *In Larger Freedom: Towards Freedom, Security and Human Rights for All* (2005) A/59/2005.

[18] The many dimensions and aspects of freedom in this context are charted further by Amartya Sen in *Rationality and Freedom* (Cambridge, MA: Harvard University Press, 2002).

and externally. Thus, the redistribution of resources or providing what is thought to be more efficient means of attending to its constituents' well-being might be considered. Collective freedom in this respect is often viewed through the construction of conditions that allow for the flourishing of a community's members en masse. This underpins much of the group rights discourse for instance. But it is also redolent within socialist theory. Freedom here is only possible for individuals if the state or polity concerned directs the community over which it holds sovereignty so that inequalities which undermine freedom can be eradicated. These notions of freedom are often juxtaposed against capitalism as a political and economic environmental condition. When G.A. Cohen, for instance, described the 'collective unfreedom' of a capitalist society he was also intent on demonstrating that a socialist alternative attended to freedom in a different way by attempting to address obstacles for liberty constructed through the class system.[19] Whether successful in practice or not, the notion of collective emancipation lay at the heart of the argument.

Alternatively, understandings of development based on an adherence to a free market economy have also been presented in terms of collective freedom. The construction, management, promotion and protection of a capitalist-based society could have as much to do with particular notions of freedom as those of the socialist tradition.[20] It might be based on private property but that does not mean that the state (or collective) absents itself from the equation. Rather, market regulation or 'balancing' then can become a theme of positive liberty where it is undertaken to address inequalities that might arise.

A final aspect of collective liberty we might consider is inextricably interwoven with all the above. Based on a form of governance recognising the will of its citizens, this relates to the whole process of freedom as participation in politics. It does not have to be synonymous with representative democracy for, as F.A. Hayek pointed out, being able to select one's own government does not necessarily mean that freedom is thereby secured.[21] However, to then suggest, as Hayek does, that a collective form of liberty based on participation in the choice of government, in legislative process and in controlling the administration

[19] G.A. Cohen, 'Capitalism, Freedom and the Proletariat', in Miller, *The Liberty Reader* 163–82 at 180.

[20] *Ibid.* Cohen says it would be misguided and simplistic not to acknowledge that capitalism is also founded on a particular conception of liberty.

[21] Friedrich Hayek, *The Constitution of Liberty* (London: Routledge and Kegan Paul, 1963).

should be kept apart from individual liberty seems to be overstating the case. Freedom could be conjoined in these two forms by realising that any freedom of the individual means little if not enjoyed in common with others. This is reflected, as David Miller has pointed out, in part of Berlin's description of 'positive liberty'.[22] Miller identifies freedom in this sense as 'the condition where each person plays his part in controlling his social environment through democratic institutions'.[23] This is a matter of governmental structure that is premised on the participation in those decisions made that affect the lives of a community's constituents. Again, this is not to determine the precise nature of that democracy, but rather to suggest that democratic processes are a precursor to socially enacted freedom. Even so the dangers of the collective will in relation to that of the individual remains apparent. It is an issue that frequently besets discussions on liberty and again is a matter for the EU given its capacity to make and enforce law in relation to its Member States. I have already considered much of the issues relevant here in the previous chapter.

In sum, therefore, collective aspects of liberty clearly fall within the ambit of the EU's operations. From matters of security to matters of governance, it is the location for action or practice with the potential for affecting people's collective freedom. Notions of equality clearly re-surface here. The association of equality amongst peoples (or states) might well be thought essential to preserve the dimensions of collective freedom considered above. It might also reasonably be inferred as an aspect of justice that accompanies the discourses of development I have mentioned. Evaluating how the EU interacts with these collective issues in terms of liberty will be necessary for my assessment of this value.

Individual liberty

The second key perspective of liberty occupies more traditional political philosophical ground and is concerned with the relationship between the state and the individual. It can relate to the imposition of rule by *any* institution. It also describes the ability of the individual to make decisions free from imported or imposed desires.

The central question lying at the heart of enquiry here is how the individual can be 'free' within a society, invariably constructed on rules.

[22] David Miller, 'Introduction', in Miller, *The Liberty Reader* 1–20 at 10.
[23] *Ibid.*

This assumes that a 'society' is an inevitability of human existence, closely followed by the realisation in a modern Western context that the 'state' traditionally provides the overarching political framework for that society. From that flows the idea that individual autonomy, or 'negative liberty' in Berlin's understanding, partially concerns itself with 'the area within which a man can act unobstructed by others'.[24] Ronald Dworkin predictably terms this as 'freedom from legal constraint' although no doubt other forms of constraint than those produced through law might be included.[25] The potential constriction is frequently represented as emanating from structures of state government, law providing a significant focus for that concern, but corporate, cultural, religious and other institutions, as well as individuals in general, acting globally as well as nationally, are important influences.

The positive aspects of this form of liberty may incorporate the sense of individual freedom *to* attain self-fulfilment (howsoever that might be interpreted). It often relies upon an understanding of a society designed to facilitate, if not encourage, that attainment. Dworkin refers to this as its normative sense, which describes 'the ways in which we believe people ought to be free'.[26] Again, the state can be the primary focal point here, this time in relation to making claims against it to realise the facilitation deemed necessary. It might also incorporate the belief that the collective can and should act *in assumption* of what individuals need to attain. This particular approach has been predicated on a view (neatly paraphrased by Zygmunt Bauman) that 'freedom, if not monitored, always verges on licentiousness and so is, or may become, an enemy of good'.[27]

So much has been written on the nature of, and differences between, individual 'negative' and 'positive' liberty in this respect that it would be impossible to cover the ground sensibly here. However, it is sufficient for my purposes to map out two specific parameters against which the EU might possibly be seen to have a role to play given that, whatever else it might be, it is presently *not* a state.

First, the role of rights through law that are designed to reinforce individuals' autonomy by protecting them *from* interference in making their life choices. Jürgen Habermas notes the Kantian interpretation of

[24] Berlin, *Four Essays on Liberty* at 122.
[25] Ronald Dworkin, *Sovereign Virtue: the Theory and Practice of Equality* (Cambridge, MA: Harvard University Press, 2000) at 120.
[26] *Ibid.* at 125.
[27] Zygmunt Bauman, *Postmodern Ethics* (Oxford: Blackwell, 1993) at 6–7.

this aspect as 'the legal guarantee of individual liberties' that 'secures the space for an authentic and autonomous conduct of life'.[28] We should not become embroiled in trying to define the 'authentic' here. Suffice to say that the collective protection of freedom may well infer a world-view that is not necessarily shared by all.

Second, the role of those social conditions that also constrain individual freedom through their oppressive nature or consequences. These might be 'natural', through the influence of environment, the result of economic activity, culturally driven, institutionally constructed, or government inspired 'social engineering'. This strays into the aspects of liberty that revolve around the relationship between individual and state, or, in the case of the EU, individual and extra-state sources of authority. The sense of liberty here relates to the more unconscious or subconscious influences that are often the product of narratives of authority that rely upon individual and collective acquiescence. In that sense we could describe these conditions affecting individual freedom as 'cultural'. Perhaps this cannot be divorced from any or all of the above manifestations of liberty. Nonetheless, the intensely personal notion of liberty is an apt way of focusing upon the possibilities of 'freedom' for individuals who are of necessity a part of society and thus subject to its influence.

Issues of upbringing and education are of great moment in this respect but so too might be matters of communication, in the insidious aspects of language generally and the media in particular. Certainly, those who have advocated for equality and fought discrimination of various hues have frequently addressed the pernicious and under-appreciated effect of forms of communication on the freedom of individuals or groups. Those philosophies of liberty that inhere in identity politics, such as the feminist movement, are of relevance. We are then concerned with matters of culture and the 'particular constellation of personal and institutional social relationships that constitute our individual and collective histories'.[29] These shape the possibilities for freedom to be and to choose.

Both of these spheres are of interest for the EU. They do not capture the whole spectrum of possibility but they will provide a reasonable

---

[28] Jürgen Habermas, *Between Facts and Norms* (Cambridge: Polity Press, 1997) at 532 n42.

[29] Nancy Hirschmann, 'Toward a Feminist Theory of Freedom', *Political Theory* 24:1 (1996) 46–67 at 51.

starting point for analysis. Some of this must at least cast an eye towards the libertarian belief that the ability of the individual to make life choices without, in particular, state interference is the chief hallmark of freedom. Any imposition of control from the EU as a supranational polity would no doubt attract critique from this perspective.

The various aspects of the collective and individual dimensions referred to above provide a basic spectrum for assessing the value's meaning in the EU. There might be a tendency to concentrate on political freedom but given the EU's institutional rhetoric, as we will see, it would be premature to ignore the other aspects. The extent to which the EU enhances or restricts liberty is the general issue we need to address if we are to better assess the quality of this value in the institutional ethos.

We must also not forget the relevance, if not congruence, of the notion of equality at this juncture. For both the collective and individual dimensions, equality can be seen to have a role. In order to fulfil notions of freedom in either, we might have to consider the idea of equality of peoples or states *and* equality of individuals within any inter-state cooperative venture whose institutions exercise power over them. These may produce variable notions of equality as John Rawls suggested in his *Law of Peoples* when he claimed that 'equality holds between reasonable or decent, and rational, individuals or collectives of various kinds when the relation of equality between them is appropriate for the case at hand'.[30] Whether we are talking about 'equal liberty' or 'liberties' or formal or substantive equality, this co-value will require some consideration. It might best be represented by an enquiry into the extent to which the benefits and burdens that are the concern and perhaps product of the EU's operations are distributed between its people and Member States.

Collective liberty and the EU

My review of this dimension has to reflect the general distinction I made between the EU's role in maintaining or enhancing the quality of freedom against external interference and its relationship with its internal constituents. This will inevitably draw in some of the issues already discussed in previous chapters.

---

[30] Rawls, *The Law of Peoples* (Cambridge, MA: Harvard University Press, 2003) at 69.

The starting point for analysis is, however, to look at the approach the EU has taken to the survival of 'Europe' (as a poorly defined ideal construct). Although the avoidance of war is of course key, survival surely attests to more than simply the absence of military conflict. As we saw in Chapter 2, the facets of security acknowledged by the EU now incorporate a far wider range of threat than destruction caused by external attack. Indeed, there has always been a strong European discourse that has related freedom to the preservation of a 'way of life', a 'common heritage', a European civilisation. This has possessed both negative and positive aspects. The former has concerned itself with addressing external (or internal) forces that threaten the 'European' identity. Action has been required in order to protect the freedom associated with a perceived civilisation. The positive side has involved a form of collective liberty that is developmental in character. In this sense, freedom has attached itself to a condition of collective survival that is progressive rather than simply static. Europe requires positive action through a framework of governance enabling people and societies to 'develop' freely. The meaning of 'development' in this context is crucial for it determines the character of freedom that is to be pursued. In the EU, this has invariably brought to the fore the economic element.

These two aspects of the survival–freedom nexus have always intersected at the EU site. Liberty as a general term appeared in the preamble of the Treaty of Rome coupled with the resolution to strengthen and preserve peace. But the prevailing economic focus should not be seen as divorced from this ambition. The word 'free' rather than 'freedom' or *liberté* only appeared in relation to the creation and maintenance of a common market and although analysts have retrospectively applied the term the 'four freedoms',[31] the Treaty itself made no such reference. Indeed, the language was concentrated on the '*free* movement' of production factors, namely, persons, capital, goods and services. These were identified as the integral elements necessary to create a 'common' or 'single' market. By freeing these factors of production from governmental interference, 'obstacles' in the language of the

---

[31] The German term *vier freiheiten*, and the French *quatre libertés* are both inventions subsequent to the formation of the original text. Thorsten Kingreen remarks that the German term *Grundfreiheiten* only gained currency in the 1990s despite its use occasionally by German academics prior to that period. See T. Kingreen, 'Fundamental Freedoms', in Armin von Bogdandy and Jürgen Bast, *Principles of European Constitutional Law* (Oxford: Hart, 2006) 549–84.

Treaty, which prevented their movement from one state to another, economic integration could be enhanced. 'Free' competition would be encouraged or at least not constrained. This initial concentration on the free movement of production factors, with a clear view to creating a union through a regional free market between Member States, was and remains the EU's great conceit. But we must recall, as discussed in Chapter 2, that economic integration was seen as a necessary method for achieving a lasting peace in Europe. It would be naïve to suppose that economic integration was an end in itself.

Such a view is supported by the realisation that the economic–survival–freedom nexus was the intellectual and practical cornerstone for much pan-European discourse both during and after the Second World War.[32] Advocates for a union of European states were seeking long-term solutions to the problem of European inter-state conflict. David Mitrany in 1943, in particular, pursued the association between peace and active economic cooperation.[33] This 'functionalist' approach was adopted by Jean Monnet and the 'founding fathers' and under-wrote both the European Coal and Steel Community of 1950 and the EEC in 1957. The preamble of the former intended to 'establish, by creating an economic community, the foundation of a broad and *independent* community among peoples long divided by bloody conflicts' (my emphasis).

Here then we find the connection between the economic preference of the original scheme and the collective understanding of liberty. For in seeking peace *through* economic cooperation and prosperity, liberty in the sense of freedom from domination could legitimately be identified as an important purpose for the EU. Such liberty had two particular features. First, it related to the internal independence of Member States from invasion or domination by each other. Economic bonds would create disincentives for inter-state conflict that had historically threatened the survival of European nation-states. Second, externally, it represented independence from third states, in particular the two superpowers; the United States in relation to perceived economic domination through financial dependence, and the USSR in relation to ideological or military

---

[32] For one short story of this connection see Perry Anderson, 'Under the Sign of the Interim', in Peter Gowan and Perry Anderson (eds.), *The Question of Europe* (London: Verso, 1997) 51–71.

[33] David Mitrany, *A Working Peace System* (Chicago: Quadrangle Books, 1966).

conquest.[34] The principle of 'solidarity' could be cited as an expression of this aspect. From the institutional loyalty inspired by the original Article 10 EC Treaty (now Article 4(3) TEU after Lisbon), which bound Member States to 'take all appropriate measures, whether general or particular, to ensure fulfilment of the obligations arising out of [the Treaty] or resulting from action taken by the institutions of the Community', to the foreign policy stricture of Article 11(2) TEU (now Article 24(3) TEU), which requires Member States to 'refrain from any action which is contrary to the interests of the Union' and which requires them to 'work together to enhance and develop their mutual political solidarity', the rhetoric reflects the connection with collective survival.[35]

For both of these internal and external fronts, liberty (as a collective, nationally-inspired condition achieved crucially through economic solidity as well as diplomatic cohesion) may be interpreted as the desired outcome of cooperation. Prosperity and unity would reinforce independence. It is from this perspective that Alan Milward's famous thesis that the EU was the 'rescue' of the nation-state for its members, and by extension all of Europe, might be read.[36]

Of course, the above interpretation suggests a view of liberty that is relatively shallow even if it is also vital. It does not address deeper understandings of 'domination' and independence that might be inferred, let alone matters of distribution. It ignores issues of 'power'. It also suggests that the chosen method for achieving this limited conception, namely the creation of a free market between Member States, possessed the quality of a virtue rather than an inherent value for the EU. Economic 'freedom' provided an effective means of achieving a particular aim, the collective preservation of independence, and the survival of those states taking part in the venture. In other words, one could interpret the EU as fundamentally a technocratic enterprise

---

[34] For an early analysis of this aspect see, Stanley Hoffman, 'Europe's Identity Crisis: Between the Past and America', *Daedalus* 93:4 (1964) 1244–97. This debate has been resurrected in the light of the Iraq War of 2003. See, Daniel Levy, Max Pensky and John Torpey (eds.), *Old Europe, New Europe: Transatlantic Relations after the Iraq War* (London: Verso, 2005).

[35] The principle of solidarity might for some necessitate a chapter on its own. However, although it is identified as a central principle of the EU it lacks any value in the absence of a desired 'end'. The 'end' I ascribe to solidarity relates to freedom in this chapter but it could also relate to all of the other values considered in this book. For this reason, I would suggest it does not possess the quality of an independent value.

[36] Alan Milward, *The European Rescue of the Nation State* (London: Routledge, 1992).

intent upon creating structures led by 'experts' that would *enable* Member State economies to come together, flourish and thus enhance the prospects for those states to survive.[37] Functionalism, the prevalent theory of integration for the EU at the time, described this process.[38]

One can see more than an element of this identification from the EU institutions. The Commission pronounced as early as 1959 that the fulfilment of the 'four freedoms' was 'one of the essential objectives of the economic policy of the countries of the *free* world' (my emphasis).[39] The connection then between the 'free' market and the 'free' world was explicit. Such a position adhered to a liberal perspective where economic freedom was perceived as a prerequisite for a society that proclaims liberty as an operative collective condition.[40] It accords with the notion of freedom through a positive injunction to encourage 'development' of a particular capitalist character. On such a basis the 'four freedoms' might be seen as necessary elements of an overarching but limited value of market liberty. Indeed, Kingreen characterises the German academic understanding of the 'fundamental freedoms' as restricted to 'market access rights'.[41]

We should not ignore here the ambient post-war domestic political determination of the key states involved in the original construction of the EU. Their national re-constitutionalisation (as it might be more accurately called, although the term more often applied is 'reconstruction') all indicated the intention to put in place a politicised moral core around which society could be developed. The French Constitution of 1946, the German Basic Law and the Italian Constitution both of 1949, all sought to imbed human rights and freedoms within a liberal democratic system of one form or another. As a protection against internal totalitarianism, these constitutional moments possessed great significance. They laid out the basis upon which these individual states would respond to the trauma of the Second World War and the era of dictatorship that preceded it. The political solution for the excesses and failures of

---

[37] See Paul Magnette, *What is the European Union? Nature and Prospects* (Basingstoke: Palgrave Macmillan, 2005) 14–15.

[38] See, in particular, E. Haas, *Beyond the Nation State: Functionalism and International Organization* (Stanford: Stanford University Press, 1968).

[39] Commission communiqué on the establishment of the convertibility of pounds sterling and of currencies of the Community, EEC Bull 1/59 at 20.

[40] G.A. Cohen identifies the connection between libertarianism as an extreme form of liberal philosophy and capitalism more precisely in *History, Labour, and Freedom* (Oxford: Oxford University Press, 1988).

[41] Kingreen, 'Fundamental Freedoms' at 567.

nationalism may have been 'inspired' by the United States and its financial as well as military support but there was still some consensus as to
the constitutional response based on a free market economy, individual
rights and democratic institutions.[42] They also embraced the development of a social welfare component that addressed issues of inequality
invariably provoked by the vagaries of the free market. In Germany, for
instance, the Basic Law attempted to combine notions of the *Rechsstaat*
with that of a *Sozialstaat*. Whether condemned or supported, the combination nonetheless reflected a political intent to temper the processes
of capitalism with a state-inspired social welfare system. The same was
also evident in the other original Member States and was reflected in
many other West European countries. A collective notion of freedom,
therefore, had its political place enshrined in some form across the
Member States albeit subject to continual contestation. One might characterise this as a battle between neoliberalism and regulated capitalism
(although no doubt other descriptions could be employed).

To what extent has this been reflected in the EU? A social dimension
has always been evident from its founding Treaty and the subsequent
adoption of a 'European Social Model' rhetoric. But what has been promoted? A positive notion of liberty that emanates from an interven-
tionist approach aiming to achieve the deepest condition of freedom
for the greatest number? Or an unfettered attitude to capitalism, thus
giving greater preference to the liberty of individuals as individuals?

To map this political condition, we have to examine the way in which
discourse has developed. The starting point should be the presence of a
social dimension in the original Treaty of Rome. This was addressed in
Title III EEC Treaty. Article 117 established the aim 'to promote improvement of the living and working conditions of labour so as to permit
the equalisation of such conditions in an upward direction'. This was
planned to 'result not only from the functioning of the Common Market
which will favour the harmonisation of social systems, but also from
the procedures provided for under this Treaty and from the approximation of legislative and administrative provisions'. Collaboration between
Member States in the 'social field' would focus upon work-related matters,
including, under Article 118, employment, social security and collective bargaining. A European Social Fund was set up 'in order to improve

---

[42] For one account of this trend see Peter Brandt and Dimitris Tsatsos, 'From the
Constitutionalisation of Europe to a European Constitution', in Detlev Albers,
Stephen Haseler and Henning Meyer (eds.), *Social Europe: a Continent's Answer to Market
Fundamentalism* (London: Europe Research Forum, 2006) 9–31.

opportunities of employment of workers in the Common Market and thus contribute to raising the standard of living'.[43]

As the EU has widened and deepened, this social dimension has been subject to much hesitant negotiation. The Commission may have said in 1968 that 'economic growth does not of itself lead to balanced social progress'[44] and that social conditions had to be improved as a 'fundamental objective' under the Treaties but formal Community competence was only acquired in the field of social policy in the mid 1980s with the Single European Act. Even then it was limited in its effect. The institutions were to 'support and complement the activities of Member States' in defined areas.[45] Defining minimum standards, encouraging dialogue and closer cooperation, were the limit of the institutional ambition.[46]

The very inclusion of these social issues suggests an acceptance that governments needed to address the vagaries of the market. 'Freedom' could not be purely associated with unfettered capitalism. The market threatened liberty by sometimes, if not frequently, leading to economic conditions that removed people's ability to make choices as regards their future. By attempting to support welfare schemes that protected workers in particular, such unwanted consequences might be addressed to some degree. Equally, it spoke of an ideology that saw the development of social welfare as part of the underlying common heritage worth preserving. By extension, liberty would then be deepened. Indeed, the Commission called down the spirit of the Treaties in 1968 to conclude that its actions on Europe's social future would be based on 'the necessary convergence of social and economic exigencies, so as to contribute, by all the means in its power, to the welfare of the peoples of the Community'.[47]

But have social policy initiatives really been implemented with a view to enhancing a collective sense of freedom? Have they been

---

[43] Article 123 EEC Treaty.

[44] Commission report to the European Parliament on 'Development of the Social Situation in the Community in 1967' EEC Bull 3/68 at 27.

[45] Article 137 EC Treaty, now Article 153 of the Treaty on the Functioning of the European Union.

[46] As Sean van Raepenbusch and Domink Hanf have demonstrated, this reflects an adherence to a flexible approach to governance, one that embraces 'differentiated integration'. See Sean van Raepenbusch and Domink Hanf, 'Flexibility in Social Policy', in Bruno de Witte, Domink Hanf and Ellen Vos (eds.), *The Many Faces of Differentiation in EU Law* (Antwerp: Intersentia, 2001).

[47] *Ibid.* at 29.

focused on the 'unfreedom' created through poverty or repression? Or do we have a rhetoric of welfare that remains steadfastly designed to leave matters to the Member States' discretion *within* an unchallenged market economy? To answer this we need to look briefly at the discourse of a European Social Model (ESM).

Anthony Giddens has characterised ESM as

A general set of values: sharing both risk and opportunity widely across society, cultivating social solidarity or cohesion, protecting the most vulnerable members of society through active social intervention, encouraging consultation rather than confrontation in industry, and providing a rich framework of social and economic citizenship rights for the population as a whole.[48]

Giddens may be sensible enough to note that ESM is 'essentially a contested notion'[49] but his working definition does mirror recent rhetoric emanating from the EU. For instance, at the Nice European Council in 1997 ESM was 'characterised in particular by systems that offer a high level of social protection, by the importance of the social dialogue and by services of general interest covering activities vital for social cohesion, is today based, beyond the diversity of the Member States' social systems, on a common core of values'.[50] But are these related to freedom as I have described it or some other values?

Ironically, the attempt to identify a sense of commonality in social protection has been combined with an acknowledgement that 'Europe' should not stray too deeply into this preserve of national governments. The evident and accepted diversity of models within a model has suggested that any core values are difficult to identify. No doubt the rhetoric can therefore be viewed cynically. The argument could be made that the underlying concern was to establish a system of free competition. And differing social policy decisions taken nationally could have as much of a distorting effect on that goal as economic policies. Consequently, the only core value to be addressed in social policy has only ever been a negative one; to prevent barriers to the internal market.

There has also long been an acknowledgement that the EU has a limited role to play in this area. As Joaquin Almunia, European Commissioner for Economic and Monetary Affairs, admitted in 2005,

---

[48] Anthony Giddens, *Europe in the Global Age* (Cambridge: Polity Press, 2007) at 2.
[49] *Ibid.* at 1.
[50] European Council, 'Presidency Conclusions, European Social Agenda' EN SN 400/00, Annex 1 at para.11, 7–9 December 2000, Nice.

the Member States 'remain responsible for re-designing and implementing labour market and welfare state reforms'.[51] He confirmed that 'there is no economic case for centralising policy actions in these fields at EU level'. The sense that the EU is constrained in matters of social development to allow individual Member States to develop according to their own political determinations is very real. And as there is significant diversity in the extent to which states wish to deal with social 'security' issues, one might be tempted to see the EU as having little to contribute to collective freedom from this perspective other than maintaining the drive towards a single market. The very fact that an 'economic' case is required before action is taken suggests that the collective freedom potentially in issue is highly contingent and lacking in any power of its own.

Fritz Scharpf for one has suggested that the 'diversity of national welfare states, differing not only in levels of economic development ... but, even more significantly, in their normative aspirations and institutional structures' makes the EU's role here extremely limited.[52] The 'asymmetry' between economic integration and social-protection in practice, the former within the established legal compass of the EU, the latter only capable of influence through general persuasion, implies that the EU's role in promoting this aspect of collective liberty is weak and incoherent. It may have pretensions to create a uniform 'model' but in essence the matter is too political for serious institutional intervention. Hence the agreement on social policy, for instance, at Maastricht that saw the UK at liberty to avoid the application of measures nationally.[53] The agreement remains constrained by national difference and economic demands even though the UK has been subsequently brought into the fold. It requires Member States to take into account the 'diverse forms of national practice, in particular in the field of contractual relations, and the need to maintain the competitiveness of the European economy' when agreeing measures in this field.[54]

---

[51] Joaquin Almunia, 'The Future of the European Model', speech at Harvard, 26 September 2005.

[52] Fritz W. Scharpf, 'The European Social Model: Coping with Diversity', *Journal of Common Market Studies* 40 (2002) 645–70 at 666.

[53] For an account of this agreement see Jeff Kenner, 'The Paradox of the Social Dimension', in P. Lynch, N. Neuwahl and W. Rees (eds.), *Reforming the European Union: from Maastricht to Amsterdam* (London: Longman, 2000).

[54] Article 1 Agreement on Social Policy.

Nonetheless, there has been a growing tendency to believe that the EU does have, in, Gráinne de Búrca's words, 'a significant impact on the provision of welfare within and across its Member States'.[55] Through the discourse of solidarity, as I have mentioned, and through the effects of ECJ decisions relating to EU economic law, a growing influence on national welfare policy has developed. Equally, with the development of the 'Open Method of Coordination' there has been a willingness to believe that 'Europe might serve in a new way to enhance social protection in a period of increasing uncertainty by creating a forum for discussing and generalizing the results of the different national strategies of adjustment'.[56] Such a method is presumed to allow states to pursue the same goal of social protection but through encouragement of best practice rather than the imposition of (politically awkward) rules.

It would be very difficult to conclude from this that the EU's institutional ethos had really embraced a sense of collective freedom that was coherent. The term 'solidarity' in this sense seems to be misleading. To extrapolate from the rhetoric that it encompasses '*human* solidarity' through a form of Kantian moral obligation is stretching the point.[57] If anything, it attests to an inter-state desire to bind nations together economically in accordance with the original peace design of the EU. This does not really reach the depth of solidarity that has more relevance to people's perception of collective freedom, I would suggest. Rather, it is project-dependent.

It could be argued that the Union was preserving a tradition of social welfare by making this a theme of governance. And by extension one might suppose that this was intended to enhance a unified condition of people's freedom despite the economic pressures to reduce government responsibility in these areas (for instance in the provision for pensions). But there remains precious little in the way of concrete policy or regulation that would suggest that the EU has a coherent vision in this respect. Rather, national interest remains dominant. A 'welfare space'

[55] Gráinne de Búrca, 'Towards European Welfare?', in Gráinne de Búrca (ed.), *EU Law and the Welfare State: in Search of Solidarity* (Oxford: Oxford University Press, 2005) 1–9 at 4.

[56] Jonathan Zeitlin, 'Social Europe and Experimentalist Governance: Towards a New Constitutional Compromise?', in de Búrca, *EU Law and the Welfare State* 213–41 at 215.

[57] For one discussion on the scope and meaning of solidarity and the tensions that exist within philosophical interpretations of the term in the modern Western context see Richard Rorty, *Contingency, Irony and Solidarity* (Cambridge: Cambridge University Press, 1989).

might be developing within the Union through ad hoc measures and dialogue, and the OMC, but ultimately the lack of policy and attendant institutionalised virtues undermine any conclusion that freedom through welfare is manifest. Addressing 'unfreedom' in Sen's terms or supporting an environment of freedom are equally fragile.

However, if we can maintain that positive collective freedom associated with survival includes the attempt to provide a milieu that enhances people's development we must move beyond social policy. A concern for regional development might well be identified as relevant here. But the EU institutions do not adopt the language of liberty or freedom in this respect either. The rationale for regional policy has been couched in terms of 'cohesion' and, again, 'solidarity'. But in practice there is little vision beyond a limited economic interpretation. This can be seen in the 2006 guidelines for determining where structural funds were to be placed. The stated focus was 'on promoting sustainable growth, competitiveness and employment'.[58] In the light of the heavy demands for equalisation following enlargement, limited funds were to be directed to three priority areas: 'improving the attractiveness of Member States'; 'encouraging innovation, entrepreneurship and the growth of the knowledge economy'; and 'creating more and better jobs by attracting more people into employment or entrepreneurial activity'.[59] There is little in the way of redistribution beyond notions of 'trickle down' effects evident here.

Admittedly, certain underlying problems with 'cohesion' policy have been recognised institutionally as well as academically. A major review was completed by Fabrizio Barca in April 2009, which acknowledged that the policy had been largely dismissed historically as having only had 'trivial impact'.[60] But there has always been an apparent desire to see this policy as possessing more than simply a minimal contribution to 'correcting the effects of market integration'.[61] The application of 'equity' whereby different regions received support on the basis of

---

[58] Council Decision on Community Strategic Guidelines on Cohesion (2006/702/EC) Preamble para. 5, 6 October 2006.

[59] *Ibid.*

[60] Gian Paolo Manzella and Carlos Mendez, 'The Turning Points of EU Cohesion Policy', Working Paper Report, January 2009.

[61] Fabrizio Barca, 'An Agenda for a Reformed Cohesion Policy: A Place-based Approach to Meeting European Union Challenges and Expectations, Independent Report Prepared at the Request of Danuta Hübner, Commissioner for Regional Policy', April 2009 at 14, online, available at: http://ec.europa.eu/regional_policy/policy/future/pdf/report_barca_v2104.pdf.

need has been identified as a reasonable and necessary goal to pursue.[62] Barca indeed has recommended that Cohesion Policy should develop so as to enhance the value of 'social inclusion' which he defines as 'the extent to which, with reference to multidimensional outcomes, all individuals (and groups) can enjoy essential standards and the disparities between individuals (and groups) are socially acceptable, the process through which these results are achieved being participatory and fair'.[63] He suggests that such a perspective should govern a 'place-based' approach to improve the 'well-being of the least advantaged'.[64] Otherwise the dangers to the integrity of the EU project are manifest particularly at a time of financial crisis. The solution continues to be appreciated as 'an essential complement to the unification of markets, the creation of a single currency and the general erosion of national influence over economic developments'.[65] But that solution is constrained by the very limited budget that the EU possesses to pursue such equitable ideas. Freedom remains the preserve of the economic realm for the EU but it does not have the kind of financial capacity to undertake more than limited targeting for the benefit of its population. It certainly appears incapable of addressing matters of the distribution of benefits of integration with any notion of equality in mind. At best, it still seeks to provide limited responses to the perceived unequal distribution of economic burdens that cause social problems.

Overall, therefore, we might conclude that the sense of collective freedom in terms of 'survival' may not possess significant practical or intellectual force within the EU's institutional ethos. It is still heavily subject to national preferences regarding matters of defence *and* social welfare. Any negative freedom is largely restricted to the creation of a legal and policy framework that attempts to remove obstacles to economic related activity. Any positive dimension is limited to initiatives that are either rhetorical or highly constrained in their effects.

If the collective dimension is on the 'thin' and incoherent side what can we make of individual liberty?

Individual liberty and the EU

It seems to be a common perception, at least in some quarters of the popular press, that the EU is engaged in a constant interference with 'our' liberty. From stories of ridiculously pedantic, petty and intrusive

[62] *Ibid.*   [63] *Ibid.* at 30.   [64] *Ibid.*   [65] *Ibid.* at vii.

regulations to those of broad challenges to national identities, there has been a tendency to view the Union as a constant threat to individual freedom or at least an irritating presence in people's lives. Frequently these stories are coupled with representations of the Brussels bureaucrat making these infringements from an unsympathetic distance. The myth constructed is of an institutional force predisposed to undermining the freedom of individuals to live in accordance with their reasonable desires and traditions.

The task here is to unpick that myth as regards conceptions of individual freedom. What balance has been struck between the potential tendencies to intrude on or enhance individual freedom? In the interests of balance, we have to be careful in this assessment. If the state is seen as the fundamental guarantor of freedom for its citizens it might appear that the EU has a very limited role to play. The positive and negative aspects of an individual's relationship with the state on the surface seem to preclude the Union from having an active engagement here. But, as we know, the Union has gradually developed a method by which it *can* interfere in people's lives. We therefore need to consider the extent to which the EU has encouraged freedom (or not) in that operation.

We can review the levels of relationship to individual freedom in a number of ways. First, as regards the creation of an environment that affects freedom of choice. Given the original construction of the EU this is frequently presented as an economic issue, one in which the relationship between individual and state (with the EU sometimes operating in place of, sometimes as exterior to, the state) has to be examined. This encompasses two interrelated issues: the development in European law of the individual as a subject as well as object derived in particular from the understanding of the importance of individuals as actors within the original economic design of the European Project; and the notion of a European citizenship, whereby individuals are supposed to acquire increased benefits from identity with the Union. In both cases, the EU operates simultaneously as proxy for and addendum to the state, perhaps betraying the scope of adherence to freedom from an individual perspective.

Secondly, as regards protection *from* interference in the lives of individuals, the EU again operates in a strange position of surrogate state *and* panopticon institution. Here, the discourses of fundamental rights and equality (particularly with regard to non-discrimination) are crucial in assessing liberty as a condition within the Union. The discourse of 'security' also has implications for the EU's approach by question-ing to what extent individuals can be or are protected/abused by EU action.

These two dimensions are, of course, so heavily intermingled that they have become almost indistinguishable. My review of this aspect of individual liberty should, therefore, be something of an inter-related and free-flowing assessment. In this spirit, I will briefly review four particular aspects: the role of the market; the role of citizenship; the role of fundamental rights; and the role of security. No doubt others could be considered but these seem to me plausible areas where the quality of liberty in the institutional ethos can be gauged.

Individual freedom and the market

My starting point is the received wisdom that came to be epitomised by the ECJ in its early jurisprudential determination to establish the legal status of the individual in the EU. *Van Gend en Loos* proclaimed that the 'nationals' of the Member States as subjects and not just objects of Community law was a significant realisation of this premise. This we have already seen. The fact that it would be legal persons, in the shape of corporations, who would take the foremost advantage of this doctrine of direct effect, cannot lessen the sense of individual protec-tion of liberty that was nonetheless affected.[66] However, liberty in this context was still restricted to the economic realm. The focus was on the particular freedoms that were the components of the single mar-ket. Kingreen assessed these as 'to all intents and purposes the pub-lic law trampoline which gives to all participants in the economy the opportunity to vault over the normative barriers between the national markets'.[67]

The 'individual' under consideration has a peculiar connotation here. It is essentially an economic *actor*, a factor of production or related to someone who is. Although rights not necessarily associated with eco-nomic issues have seemingly inspired the ECJ in reaching some rulings on EU law, the context has invariably been based on an appreciation of free market economics. Miguel Poiares Maduro described the develop-ment of individual social rights in the EU as the 'prisoner of the values

---

[66] See, for instance, the account of the litigation strategy employed by corporations seeking to overturn national restrictions on Sunday trading by Richard Rawlings, 'The Eurolaw Game: Some Deductions From a Saga', *Journal of Law and Society* 20:3 (1993) 309–40.

[67] Kingreen, 'Fundamental Freedoms' at 561.

of market integration and not a consequence of a political conception of the social and economic protection deserved by any European citizen'.[68]

Indeed, it has become apparent that 'freedom' in this respect has been something of a double-edged sword. On the one hand, the logic of freedom of movement in an internal market dictated that EU law should establish if not enforce a harmonised system of social protection in order to ensure workers would not be discouraged from seeking work anywhere in the EU. Stefano Giubboni has suggested that '[e]quality of access to social rights recognised by the respective national welfare systems constituted an essential precondition for the very exercise of freedom of movement in the context of the common market'.[69] On the other hand, welfare systems are not premised on such market considerations. They are the reflection of a form of social justice that accepts some degree of redistribution of wealth. But such redistribution often assumes there is a bounded community, a limit to the beneficiaries of largesse. Thus, when it appears that the definition of 'workers' is extended in EU law to a wide range of people who are not directly in work it appears that some who wish to restrict generosity to citizens of the *State* rather than the *Community* have cause to argue that freedom is being abused. Hence, new Member States from Central and Eastern Europe have been subjected to controls on the migration of workers and their access to welfare systems in many 'old' Member States.[70] The spirit of solidarity has been contingent, if only temporarily, and individual freedom suffers as a result.

So one could conclude that freedom in this dimension remains firmly rooted in the association with a free market economy as condition precedent rather than some other more sophisticated conception of liberty. This might perhaps reflect a restricted sense of 'negative liberty' in Berlin's terms. The EU's legal structure could, indeed, be

---

[68] Miguel Poiares Maduro, 'Striking the Elusive Balance Between Economic Freedom and Social Rights in the EU', in Philip Alston, Mara Bustelo and James Heenan (eds.), *The EU and Human Rights* (Oxford: Oxford University Press, 1999) 449–72 at 455.

[69] Stefano Giubboni, 'Free Movement of Persons and European Solidarity', *European Law Journal* 13:3 (2007) 360–79 at 361.

[70] The Transitional Arrangements for 'old' Member States regarding 'new' Member States were allowed to be in place until 2011. However, by April 2009 Austria, Germany and the UK had measures restricting access to some degree in place. See, Commission Press Release Welcoming the Removal of Restrictions by Belgium and Denmark on 29 April 2009, online, available at: http://ec.europa.eu/commission_barroso/spidla/index.cfm?pid=whats_new&sub=news&langId=en&id=501.

represented as an attempt to enhance liberty through the removal of obstacles to economic freedom. Such a reading would have to be tempered by the realisation that the Treaty ensured that even this interpretation of freedom was never constituted as an absolute condition. For instance, the right of Member States to interfere with the operation of the four freedoms was enshrined in the Treaty provisions. So, for the free movement of goods, where the most extensive range of restrictions appears, Member States were entitled to impose limitations on 'the grounds of public morality, public policy or public security; the protection of health and life of humans, animals or plants; the protection of national treasures possessing artistic, historic or archaeological value; or the protection of industrial and commercial property'.[71] Naturally, this has led to an immense amount of litigation and academic and judicial interpretation.[72] Nonetheless, the tension is apparent within the very structure of the EU between the desire to attain a single market based on economic freedom and protect state assumed interests. The individual in that framework possesses a limited role; that of market actor with the possible right to challenge decisions at EU or national level either because they contravene the EU's aim to achieve a free market (thus acting as a surrogate enforcer of Community law) *or* they breach a fundamental right of that individual.

Whether or not the collective liberty aspects (including the social and cohesion policies in general) provide a counterpoint is hardly relevant. The pursuit of 'economic freedom' has as its goal a very limited conception of individual liberty. Of course, if one viewed the EU project as merely enhancing the ability of its Member States to forge ever-deepening conditions of freedom within their *own* borders then one would also have to accept that investing greater ambition for the EU, as a federal state for instance, would be problematic. Enhancing individual liberty *other than* through the narrow economic lens would suggest a political motivation towards a European superstate. That simply is not palatable at present.

Nonetheless, we should not underestimate the enhancement of liberty for individuals who have benefited from the free movement provisions of the single market. It is a connection made in classical economic theory with Adam Smith's *Wealth of Nations* looking to a 'system of natural

[71] Article 30 EC Treaty.
[72] The works on this subject are voluminous but for a good account of the issues and the law see Catherine Barnard, *The Substantive Law of the EU: the Four Freedoms*, 2nd edn (Oxford: Oxford University Press, 2007).

liberty' through market liberalism.[73] Being able to travel to, and work in, states across the EU must have increased many people's life choices from this point of view. But we do not have sufficient information to understand whether these beneficiaries are predominantly those who are already well-served in terms of wealth and opportunity. Have the economic freedoms really assisted those less advantaged? Or have we witnessed direct enhancement for a relative few and indirect for the remainder, who are supposed to benefit through general economic growth?

The EU Commission has attempted to keep track of these questions. Information has been presented through reports on social protection and social inclusion. These reveal considerable problems in the EU. For instance, it was shown in 2007 that, on average, 16 per cent of the overall population is classified as 'at risk of poverty'.[74] The figure is particularly worrying for children and those aged over 65. In 2006, the proportion of children living in jobless households was over 9 per cent. In 2008, the Social Protection Committee reported nineteen million children were living under the poverty threshold across the twenty-seven Member States.[75] This is not an insignificant number. Clearly the economic crisis of 2008 onwards will only exacerbate these conditions. They suggest that the correlation between market freedom and individual liberty is hardly self-evident. Perhaps we can say no more than this. But the assumption on the part of the EU institutions that liberty is naturally and automatically enhanced through market freedoms has to be questionable. Claiming that the Union is an 'area of freedom' because of free movement provisions is a little disingenuous given the numbers and sectors of the European population who are unlikely to benefit from them. By placing the emphasis on ameliorative measures designed to address 'exclusion' and poverty through coordination of policies across the EU Member States and providing some limited centralised support (through cohesion policy) we can see that there is little space for discussing individual liberty other than in the context of the single market. For all the talk of a social fund to help people the emphasis remains on growth and financial stability. Projects supported may be worthy but their impact is negligible given the scale of

---

[73] Adam Smith, *An Inquiry into the Nature and Causes of the Wealth of Nations* (London: Greenland and Norris, 1805).

[74] Commission, Joint Report on Social Protection and Social Inclusion, 6 March 2007 SEC (2007) 329.

[75] Commission, 'Child Poverty and Well-Being in the EU: Current Status and Way Forward' Report January 2008.

the problem. All this may merely mean that the EU is at best impotent in the face of addressing factors that contribute to *unfreedom*. But it also suggests a failure to take liberty seriously when it comes to overseeing an economic system that can and does have its casualties. *Their* freedom can be undone without any apparent institutional power to counter the effects of integration.

Individual freedom and citizenship

A second relevant dimension manifests itself in the notion of EU citizenship. Although this term has acquired considerable institutional rhetorical significance over the past thirty or more years it is still a struggle to obtain a comprehensible outline of what it means and how it is designed to develop. It could be characterised, indeed, as the ultimate gesture waiting for a political movement to give it substance and meaning. Again, we do not need to delve too deeply into the detail. Rather, we can rely on two sources to convey its institutional 'tone'. First, the Treaties' explicit reference to the dimensions of citizenship and second, the EU Charter on Fundamental Rights, which provides a section devoted to the matter.

First, then, even a cursory examination of the Treaties demonstrates that citizenship was only embraced explicitly with the advent of the Treaty of Maastricht. Articles 17–22 EC Treaty were inserted to provide a skeleton of 'rights' that might assist in the aim of 'bringing the Union closer to its people'. These included the right of free movement and residence throughout the Member States, the right to vote in municipal elections where the citizen resides (irrespective of nationality), and the right to petition the European Parliament and apply to the European Ombudsman. Article 255 also entitled the citizen to a right of access to European institutional documents. The key issue of identification is contained in Article 17(1) (now Article 20 of the Treaty on the Functioning of the European Union (TFEU)), which provides that citizenship of the Union, and therefore the accompanying rights, is only available to those who are nationals of Member States.[76]

These rights are still subject to possible interference and restriction. In particular, the right to free movement remains subject to those limits available to Member States incorporated in Article 39 (now Article

---

[76] The ECJ has also made clear that most citizenship rights only accrue when a national of a Member State is resident in another Member State. See, Joined Cases C-64/96 and C-65/96 *Land Nordrhein-Westfalen* v. *Uecker* and *Jacquet* v. *Land Nordrhein-Wesfalen* [1997] ECR I-3171.

45 TFEU), in relation to workers, and Article 46 (now Article 52 TFEU), in relation to the right to establishment. Issues of public policy, security or health will dictate the reality of these rights.

Second, the EU Charter on Fundamental Rights repeats the above list and adds the individual 'right to good administration', which is not restricted to nationals of Member States.[77] This addition potentially activates those virtues of governance the EU promoted in its White Paper on Governance. However, the Charter is very particular about the scope of this provision. It refers to every person having 'the right to have his or her affairs handled impartially, fairly and within a reasonable time by the institutions and bodies of the Unions'. In this specific regard it includes

the right of every person to be heard, before any individual measure which would affect him or her adversely is taken; the right of every person to have access to his or her file, while respecting the legitimate interests of confidentiality and of professional and business secrecy; the obligation of the administration to give reasons for its decisions.

The right to reparations is also mentioned as is the guarantee that everyone may write to the institutions in 'a language of the Treaties' and have a reply in the same language. Of course, this therefore excludes those minority languages not so recognised.

Have these Treaty provisions and specific rights made any appreciable difference to the quality of liberty recognised in the EU? Stefan Kadelbach comments that '[a]nalyses of the legal substance of Union citizenship as it was set forth in the founding Treaties usually show its limitations' and that the provisions in the Treaties 'have only resulted in an insignificant enhancement to the status of European individuals'.[78] Indeed, the notion of citizenship attached to Member State nationality might even suggest a negative impact on liberty if we were assessing the condition of all those living within the Union. Sionaidh Douglas-Scott goes so far as to suggest that Union citizenship in its current guise 'has a tendency to be exclusive and exclusionary'.[79]

Overall, therefore, the connection between Union citizenship and freedom fails to mirror that which is frequently associated with the

---

[77] Article 41 EU Charter on Fundamental Rights.
[78] Stefan Kadelbach, 'Union Citizenship', in Armin von Bogdandy and Jürgen Bast (eds.), *Principles of European Constitutional Law* (Oxford: Hart, 2006) 453–99 at 498.
[79] Sionaidh Douglas-Scott, *Constitutional Law of the European Union* (London: Longman, 2002) at 489.

role of the state. There is very little in the concept played out both legally and politically which really comes to terms with the possibilities. It would be difficult, therefore, to be optimistic that the discourse of citizenship reflects a more substantial understanding of liberty in the EU's institutional ethos. The experience of democracy considered in the previous chapter does not suggest that the limitations are compensated for by structures of participation or representation. As it stands, the discourse and policy of citizenship alone grants liberty an extremely limited meaning, building on the notion of economic freedoms but even then hardly encompassing their range. It represents a very partial acceptance of liberty in its individualistic sense.

One should not forget that Union citizenship might also have provided the opportunity to *exclude*, something that inevitably contradicts any sense of liberty that incorporates a principle of equality. In particular, non-economically active individuals and third country nationals have traditionally been either ignored or deliberately prevented from benefiting from the freedom associated with citizenship.[80] But perhaps this should not be surprising when we look at some of the theoretical works on liberty. A significant number treat the relationship between the concept and the citizen as axiomatic as well as necessary.[81] This is a product of the essential prerequisite of the existence of a 'state' to create an environment of what we might term 'organised' or 'normative' freedom. Such a correlation is founded on the understanding that any 'state' cannot have unlimited responsibility with regard to preserving and ensuring a condition of liberty. Legally, matters of jurisdiction materialize to regulate the extent to which a state might be obliged to act. With the notion of EU citizenship, the limits are further constricted. Responsibility is for the most part passed on to the Member States with only a few rights becoming the subject of EU citizenship. But what does this signify with regard to the meaning of freedom in the EU's domain?

---

[80] The lack of citizenship application to the economically non-active is highlighted by Michael Dougan, 'Free Movement: the Work Seeker as Citizen', in Alan Dashwood, Christophe Hillion, John Spencer and Angela Ward (eds.), *Cambridge Yearbook of European Legal Studies* Vol. 4 (Oxford: Hart, 2002) 93–133 at 131.

[81] This is the underlying position taken by Ronald Dworkin for instance throughout *Sovereign Virtue: the Theory and Practice of Equality*. See also Carol Gould, *Rethinking Democracy: Freedom and Social Cooperation in Politics, Economy, and Society* (Cambridge: Cambridge University Press, 1988) at 81 et seq.

It suggests, first, that those who see an essential connection between responsibility and freedom would not be able to identify the Union and its discourse of citizenship as providing much in the way of inspiration. Philip Pettit, for instance, makes a strong case for conceptualising freedom 'as fitness to be held responsible'.[82] This is based on an intuition that equates responsibility with freedom. If the former does not subsist then what kind of freedom can exist? The same would apply in the alternative. If there is no freedom then no responsibility can attach to the agent. Such a seemingly esoteric connection is, however, very instructive in relation to the EU. For the limitation of responsibility, passing as it does to the Member States in the case of rights, suggests that the EU only has a limited control over the development and persistence of freedom whether for its citizens or otherwise. So long as the Member States determine access to the rights of EU citizenship, the concept of liberty in the EU's practice must be restricted.

The distinction contrived between EU citizens and 'others' who otherwise reside in the Union but possess no Member State nationality, also tells us that freedom within its domain is conceived as both partial and contingent.[83] Individuals are required to pass 'tests' to be entitled to the liberties on offer. Of course, many liberties are removed from certain classes of people as a matter of regular governance. Children, those suffering from mental incapacities, and asylum seekers, have traditionally been considered subject to different constraints on their freedom than adults with deemed full capacity or status. Such restrictions have always attracted their critics and remain condemned in some respects by the EU itself through its professed commitment to equality and non-discrimination. Similarly, criminal offenders are subject to the deprivation of freedoms as a result of responses to their behaviour.

In truth, therefore, there is scant evidence within the discourse and practice of citizenship to enhance the understanding of freedom to any appreciable effect within the EU. This is the case despite the fact that the Union has attempted to link directly 'freedom' with citizenship through its discourse of overseeing an 'area of freedom, security and justice'. Freedom in this sense is heavily dependent on issues of

---

[82] Philip Pettit, *A Theory of Freedom: from the Psychology to the Politics of Agency* (Cambridge: Polity Press, 2001).

[83] This point is made strongly by Dora Kostakopoulou, 'On the Move: Ideas, Norms and European Citizenship: Explaining Institutional Change', *Modern Law Review* 68:2 (2005) 233–67.

free movement that have formed the bedrock of Union citizens' rights. The European Council at Tampere in 1999 noted that the 'challenge of the Amsterdam Treaty is now to ensure that freedom, which includes the right to move freely throughout the Union, can be enjoyed in conditions of security and justice accessible to all'.[84] Perhaps understandably definitions of 'freedom' were, and have remained, absent from the narrative, but the implication that free movement is fundamental continues to be strong. But through the deliberations and practical initiatives in this area, restrictions on movement for those of particular backgrounds have been a primary focus of concern.[85]

Overall then we see little in the way of concrete benefits from acquisition of citizenship and few would contend that it has been successful in assisting, other than peripherally, the development of a *demos* for the Union. This is not to say that in the future the EU cannot preside over a state of freedom through citizenship associated with itself rather than its Member States. But as we know, this would require a significant shift, favoured by many, towards a meaningful federal state. Until then, liberty through citizenship rights is likely to remain relatively unfurnished.

Individual freedom and fundamental rights

I have already addressed this subject in some detail in Chapter 4. But we still need to draw connections between human rights and the quality of freedom (as opposed to *freedoms*) in the EU's institutional ethos. Are fundamental rights deployed as an antidote to the EU's potential as an impediment to conditions of freedom? Or are they crucial for the positive realisation of individual liberty?

From a theoretical perspective, human rights have been touted as providing both elements. And as a result their exercise by individuals is seen as contributing to a broad understanding of freedom, one which 'carries with it a substantive view of equality'.[86] Sandra Fredman has

---

[84] Presidency Conclusions at www.consilium.europa.eu/ueDocs/cms_Data/docs/presData/en/ec/00200-r1.en9.htm.

[85] The restrictions might well become internal as well as external with further enlargement if the experience of other accessions, notably of Romania and Bulgaria, are anything to go by. The UK, supposedly learning from its experience following the enlargement eastwards, is not the only state to consider applying restrictions on those allowed to migrate from these countries to the UK looking for work. See http://news.bbc.co.uk/1/hi/uk_politics/5359688.stm

[86] Sandra Fredman, *Human Rights Transformed: Positive Rights and Positive Duties* (Oxford: Oxford University Press, 2008) at 9.

suggested that as 'human rights promote freedom by removing constraints, the promise of equality must require all to be in a position actually to enjoy that freedom'.[87] The connection between liberty, rights, and equality is significant in Western political philosophy. Carol Gould has charted much of this tradition and advanced the proposition accordingly that 'equal positive freedom' should entail acceptance of a principle of 'equal rights to the conditions of self-development'.[88] How this is achieved is of course the primary question.

James Griffin emphasises its importance by arguing that attaching human rights to liberty will never be enough. We will also need to 'know the contents of these rights. It is the formal and material constraints that determine their contents'.[89] This reflects the underlying dilemma that attaches to a notion of liberty that entails its enforcement through human rights. For, it is inevitable that by a claimant exercising any such rights so as to provoke the realisation of corresponding duties, the liberty of others may be affected. This might materialise indirectly through the deployment of limited collective resources or directly through the prevention of others from acting as they please where this is deemed an unacceptable interference on the claimant's freedom.

What then has been the approach of the EU? Historically we know it was not concerned with human rights. There is little to suggest, therefore, that the institutions were adopting consciously any understanding of liberty that was framed by human rights and their equal application. However, the development of an internal discourse, policy, and practice of human rights might now suggest an institutional recognition that liberty would be enhanced as a result of their respect. We saw this in Chapter 4. We also saw that those human rights acknowledged were interpreted and constrained through the prism of the internal market. But what is the practical character of the rights narrative regarding conceptions of liberty?

The first difficulty encountered relates to the confusion as to the concept of human rights in the EU. It is very unclear how far human rights notions stretch. The ECJ, as we have seen, may have demonstrated a willingness to invoke particular rights in its judgments. And, on the

---

[87] *Ibid.*
[88] Carol Gould, *Globalizing Democracy and Human Rights* (Cambridge: Cambridge University Press, 2004) at 34.
[89] James Griffin, *On Human Rights* (Oxford: Oxford University Press, 2008) at 174.

face of it, we might conclude that the EU has presided over the development of a rights discourse attached to the individual that actively
promotes a liberal interpretation of freedom protecting people from
the vagaries of acts of governance. But these judgments have seldom
suggested an institutional concern to establish any coherent regime of
liberty in the Union. The whole principle of respect for human rights
has been predicated on a restricted jurisdiction for the Court. The
parameters of EU law determine that individual challenge to the acts
of EU institutions is highly constrained. Article 230 EC Treaty (now
Article 263 TFEU) ensures that only those who are individually and
directly concerned by a measure may seek judicial review in the ECJ.
Clearly, issues of effective legal process require restrictions on access
to the Court and this is particularly so in the EU's case. But where there
is little in the way of institutional analysis of the 'public interest' and
how that might be protected through litigation, the underlying condition is one of highly limited access in practice.

The ECJ is further restricted by the principle that it can only intervene in actions of Member States in the application of EU law. As we
saw from Chapter 4, this was a pre-eminent condition of human rights
in the EU. The ECJ has little if any authority to interfere when Member
States operate outside EU law. Its ability to create through its judgments an environment of negative *or* positive liberty, in the sense of
promoting a condition of choice unimpeded by institutional *dictat*, or
superimposing a structure of rights that serve to enhance the general
condition of freedom, is highly suspect.

The question, however, is whether the application of human rights
as a fundamental value succeeds in expanding choice through the particular decisions of the Court. Certainly, the ECJ can occasionally trans-
mit a message about its willingness to recognise a particular right, and
thus encourage a degree of expectation in relation to the institutional
observance of that right. But there is little evidence that the ECJ's rulings provide any basis for an expansive reading of liberty. Frequently,
it has been incapable of understanding the dimensions of 'dignity' or
'freedom', invariably retreating into the 'free market' philosophy to
describe and analyse complex issues of society. The ECJ's approach in
SPUC v. *Grogan* has become emblematic in this regard.[90] Witness the way
in which the Court was totally unprepared and perhaps unqualified to

---

[90] Case C-159/90 *SPUC* v. *Grogan* [1991] ECR I-4685.

treat the issue of abortion services through any prism other than a market one.[91]

A similar ambivalent attitude to human dignity, and by extension freedom, arises in the approach taken to minority language rights. Will Kymlicka has made a strong argument that there is a vital bond between 'societal cultures', which would include language, and people's freedom.[92] Has the EU taken such an approach? Article 53 TEU (now Article 55) notes those languages that are considered to be 'equally authentic' for the purposes of the EU. These do not include the vast majority of minority languages that subsist in Member States. Revealingly, Article 55 TEU (as introduced by the Lisbon Treaty) adds that the 'Treaty may be translated into any other languages as determined by Member States among those which, in accordance with their constitutional order, enjoy official status in all or part of their territory'. New Article 3(3) TEU further claims that the EU shall respect its 'rich cultural and linguistic diversity'. The suggestion that the EU is moving forward in providing important space for minorities to exercise freedom in this vital matter of identity is strong. However, the ECJ has never embraced the subject of minority rights in any way other than as a factor in the free movement of workers. Judicial intervention only occurs when the matter of the market surfaces. In truth, this is often a forced connection that litigants attempt to create so as to bring an action through the ECJ. Such strategies are not designed to, nor capable of, providing a coherent sense of freedom *through* dignity within the EU.

Even so, there can be no doubt that the institutional desire to develop the social dimension that became increasingly evident from the end of the 1960s onwards, ensured that the social protection of individuals was an issue of concern for the Union. Crucially, this was played out both in terms of fundamental rights and collective responsibility. The former became evident through individual litigation that developed the depth of application of the non-discrimination and equal pay Treaty provisions.

Freedom may well be said to have been enhanced as a result of these rights based developments in two dimensions. First, the notion of 'negative liberty' presumes an approach to freedom that deepens the

---

[91] See Gráinne de Búrca, 'Fundamental Rights and the Reach of EC Law', *Oxford Journal of Legal Studies* 13 (1993) 283–319.

[92] Will Kymlicka, *Multicultural Citizenship: a Liberal Theory of Minority Rights* (Oxford: Oxford University Press, 1995).

individual's ability to make choices for themselves. It follows from this conception that the attempt at legal removal of restraints on choice through human rights inspired litigation, if successful, would by definition improve the condition of freedom in a society. And indeed, there is a general consensus of opinion that, for instance, the equal pay provision has been able to instigate significant improvements in the position of women in the workplace throughout Europe.[93] It might be that the area addressed is limited to the economic sphere but that alone would represent a vital and widespread field.

Second, if we conceive of freedom as incorporating a dimension of collective responsibility, based in part on a human rights discourse, in the sense that the EU has overseen the development of a deepening commitment of Member States to ensure individuals are not subjected to discrimination on specific grounds, then the story of equal treatment suggests a positive approach to liberty. In both cases, the language of human rights is either explicit or not too far distant from the topic. As the ECJ stated in *Deutsche Telekom AG* v. *Lilli Schröder* the economic purpose of Article 141 EC Treaty in addressing distortions of competition 'is secondary to the social aim pursued by the same provision, which constitutes the expression of a fundamental human right'.[94] We can therefore see something of an overlap between collective notions of liberty, whereby the EU has attempted to change the perceptions of society through law thus improving the freedom chances of whole cohorts of people (what we might call 'anti-discrimination principle'), and individual liberty, whereby there are certain avenues for individuals to pursue a justice of non-discrimination (a 'non-discrimination' principle).

Both principles are, nonetheless, affected by ambiguity. On the one hand there can be little doubt that the evolution of case law that encompassed indirect, as well as direct, discriminatory practices has placed the principle of anti-discrimination at the forefront of EU notions of liberty. On the other, we can see that this evolution has been

---

[93] Of course the story is not wholly positive. The Commission has reported on the continuing gap in rates of pay between women and men. See Commission, 'Report on Equality between Women and Men 2005' COM (05) 44 final. Twelve Member States have also been noted as slow to implement relevant legislation. In May 2009, the Commission referred Poland to the ECJ for 'non-transposition of EU rules prohibiting gender discrimination in access to and supply of goods and services' under Directive 2004/113/EC. See press release 14 May 2009, online, available at: http://ec.europa.eu/commission_barroso/spidla/index.cfm?pid=whats_new&sub=news&langId=en&id=511.

[94] Case C-50/96 *Deutsche Telekom AG* v. *Lilli Schröder* [2000] ECR I-743 at para 57.

extraordinarily partial. For much of the Union's history the only type of discrimination addressed related to sex. Even then, most case law was restricted to matters of employment or social security legislation. Other prevalent issues of discrimination, notably race, did not figure. It took a Treaty amendment as late as 1999 to even view racial discrimination as a matter that warranted specific Union response.[95] This reticence is difficult to justify particularly when placed in the context of a continent that had suffered the most extreme forms of racism, that had translated this into institutionalised atrocity, and that still laboured under popular prejudices that gave rise to both sporadic and chronic forms of violence.

So the story of individual rights in relation to liberty provides a confusing picture. It is difficult to extract any coherent sense of this value through the prism of human rights and their equal realisation. Inequality may even occur as a result of the partial application of rights in the EU. Whole cohorts of economic actors may benefit from the Union's actions but this still leaves large sectors of the population untouched by any actionable human rights.

Individual freedom and security

The final aspect of individual notions of freedom I will consider takes us back to the matter of security. As we saw in relation to the collective dimension, freedom and security have been inextricably linked in the EU with its geographical construction of an 'area of freedom, justice and security'. The assumption is that freedom becomes possible only when people have their security assured. Of course, security is never fully defined in this respect. Is it compatible or contrary to liberty? Some indication may now be provided by Article 6 T of the Treaty on the Functioning of the European Union introduced by the Lisbon Treaty.

The Union shall endeavour to ensure a high level of security through measures to prevent and combat crime, racism and xenophobia, and through measures for coordination and cooperation between police and judicial authorities and other competent authorities, as well as through the mutual recognition of judgments in criminal matters and, if necessary, through the approximation of criminal laws.

This seems to encompass a vast array of possible ills all of which are, by implication, threats to freedom. And we would have to add terrorism

---

[95] Article 13 EC Treaty was inserted with the Treaty of Amsterdam in 1999.

to this list as a further menace, although one specified elsewhere by the Lisbon Treaty.

The character of security issues here point to a strange understanding of freedom. On the one hand it is progressive or normative. Racism and xenophobia and crime are all identified as undermining people's freedom. And yet poverty and other forms of discrimination do not qualify for such a categorisation. This tells us a great deal about liberty for the EU's institutions. It points to a limited understanding of the concept that relies upon a partial definition of security. Of course, we have already seen that the connection between liberty and peace from the very beginning of the EU's narrative suggests that issues of security can never be far away from the subject. This was evident in Chapter 2. The question for us now, however, is whether liberty is the governing rationale of security policy or whether it is its fundamental critique. If actions taken in the name of liberty via the discourse of security can be de-legitimised by reason of the restriction of liberty then the collective notion that freedom might possess here comes into direct conflict with its individualistic turn. This sets up a conflict that must be resolved if the concept is not to be rendered ultimately self-destructive.

But what are the parameters of this dimension? Although I have already explored issues of security, the institutional emphasis was on the external threats faced. Even with terrorism, the expressed focus of EU concern was on the need to defend the Union against an invader, albeit one who might act covertly within 'our' midst.

The July 2005 bombings in London altered the terrain somewhat when it became clear that those responsible were UK nationals and therefore EU citizens. An external issue of defence became more a question of 'homeland security'. Keeping people out so that they could not even attempt atrocity was not a possibility. Matters of liberty then were brought to the fore on the basis that fighting such a threat might require strategies that extended beyond normal police practice. The UK presidency tabled a list of those particular practices deemed necessary to combat or prosecute terrorists in 2005. Four were mentioned, self-consciously striking a balance between liberty and security. The measures included retaining communication data, biometrics in identity cards and passports, gaining access to passenger name records within a border control system, and retention and access to CCTV recordings. In each case the UK government advocated for a European approach that saw to the coordination of efforts across the Union.

Of course, the EU has portrayed itself at the forefront of the move to protect the region in the face of the threat perceived since the 2001 New York and Washington atrocities. But in doing so, significant criticism has arisen about the impact on human rights and the whole edifice of 'freedom' that otherwise is boasted by the EU. In particular, Amnesty International has pointed to a raft of troubling issues that reflect a failure to coordinate approaches to counter-terrorism across the Union, as well as questionable practices within individual Member States.[96] Various areas of concern were expressed that directly affect the condition of 'freedom' otherwise a hallmark, supposedly, of the EU's area of Freedom, Security and Justice. A few are particularly noteworthy.

First, a failure to provide a clear definition of terrorism threatened the status, potentially, of legitimate forms of protest. If the definition could be widely interpreted then there was a real danger that the intended target of counter-terrorism activity, which provoked the need for unusual powers, could be deployed without discrimination.

Second, the process of terrorist blacklisting, which we encountered in Chapter 3, was a direct challenge to the notion that freedom required at the very least non-arbitrary interference in one's affairs by the state.

Third, the 'absolute principle' of *non-refoulement* was noted as under threat. Despite there being established precedent in the European Court of Human Rights,[97] the pressure from various EU states to change the position vis-à-vis suspected terrorists intensified.[98]

And of course the scandal of extraordinary rendition demands an EU response.[99] Amnesty's particular point being that this web of abuse simply did not register in the human rights framework of the EU, the Fundamental Rights Agency being effectively neutered in this respect. Thus, questions of freedom were set as contingent upon individual governments' policies and activities. Security in this sense appeared in the ascendancy.

---

[96] See for instance, Amnesty International 'Counter-Terrorism and Criminal Law in the EU', 31 May 2005, online, available at: http://web.amnesty.org/library/Index/ENGIOR610132005.

[97] See *Soering v. United Kingdom* (1989) 11 EHRR 439, Judgment of 7 July 1989 and *Chahal v. United Kingdom*, 70/1995/576/662, 15 November 1996

[98] See the interventions by the UK government and others in *Saadi v. Italy*, Application No. 37201/06, 28 February 2008 and Application No. 25424/05, *Ramzy v. Netherlands*, December 2005.

[99] See Amnesty International Press Release, 'EU Fundamental Rights; A Long Way to Go', 1 March 2007, online, available at: http://web.amnesty.org/library/Index/ENGIOR610092007.

Similarly, by repositioning matters of security at the forefront of policy, in the form of responses to the threat of terrorism, the dimensions of freedom in the EU was recast. Indeed, the whole edifice of the area of freedom, security and justice was transformed from a continual battleground of national perspectives into a European-wide coordination of measures that inevitably would restrict freedom. Suddenly, criminal law issues and matters of migration and movement of peoples were couched in contingent terms. That contingency was the interests of 'European' security. This then is not a matter of liberty from state interference. It is an attempt to define 'threat' as an 'other' matter. 'Threat' is a product of largely unknown actors, mythic figures almost, who are literally uncontrollable by any single state. Freedom *from* such threats, so as to achieve 'conditions of security', was only possible for individuals by coordinated European action. That is the implicit argument.

Before the 9/11 attacks, this perception of threat was very much associated with fears of global forces outside the control of any one state. The introduction of the notion of an area of freedom, security and justice was accompanied by a vision of the EU as guardian, providing the structures and conduits for achieving freedom by addressing anxieties of little understood risks. Immigration and crime were added, in effect, to the more EU traditional concern of obstacles to free movement, to provide focal points for action. But these have never been particularly coherent associations. And unsurprisingly, apart from the continuing project of harmonisation and legal action to reduce obstacles to free movement, little of significance was achieved to suggest that people's fears were addressed through European action. Immigration still continued apace and crime still affected individuals in local ways.

After 9/11 the response to terrorism has provided a European hub to the whole freedom–security nexus. In other words, crime, immigration, and free movement all could be re-envisioned through the prism of anti-terrorism. The initiatives that have been spawned within the Justice and Home Affairs division, the Framework Decisions and Directives, have all been assessed as potential contributions to the fight against terrorism.[100] Indeed, policy in this area is determined politically in this light. Terrorism is the defining concept even though

---

[100] See in particular the EU Counter-Terrorism Strategy, Brussels, 1 December 2005, online, available at: http://ue.eu.int/uedocs/cms_Data/docs/pressdata/en/jha/87257.pdf.

its incidence is relatively small. But of course terrorism is not about atrocities. It is the fear of atrocity that defines its political and public importance. Thus terrorism can be identified by all the EU institutions as a centralising matter for action.

The result of this repositioning is that prejudices and power can be interlocked to such a degree that any notion of freedom becomes dominated by fear rather than the 'joy of liberty'. Surveillance,[101] access to personal data and information,[102] and interruption of movement by those without EU citizenship, are all permissible in an ever deepening system of control. Individual freedom becomes contingent in order to take this environment into account. So the Commission can conflate protection within a common area of free movement to include threats 'caused by failure to comply with EC or national regulations; crime, terrorism, trafficking'.[103] As Damian Chalmers suggests, 'a political community concerned, above all, with its own security is necessarily concerned to place greater emphasis on the policing than on the management of individual self-governance'.[104]

The push towards a notion of collective freedom based around the concept of 'safety' is the result. Even the historical connection between liberty and market freedoms is eroded. They may still provide the basis of liberty in the EU but changing circumstances enable other matters to achieve precedence. If these give vent to deep-seated prejudices then liberty becomes a very restricted matter for the EU, one reserved for a class of citizens who ironically may also be suspect and subject to the restrictions on freedom in the presumed interests of their safety.

Conclusion

For some years now, the United States based organisation Freedom House, has been undertaking a survey of 'freedom in the world'.[105] Using a methodology that undoubtedly can be questioned with regards

---

[101] See http://www.i-cams.org/Surveillance_intro.html for an ongoing review of surveillance measures on a global level. The EU is a major coordinating player in this respect.

[102] See Regulation 871/2004/EC on the introduction of some new functions for the Schengen Information System OJ 2004 L 162/29.

[103] Commission, 'Towards Integrated Management of the External Borders of the Member States of the European Union', COM (2002) 233 Annex 1.

[104] Damian Chalmers, 'Constitutional Reason in the Age of Terror', Global Law Working Papers 06/04 Hauser Global Law Programme at xlv.

[105] See Freedom House at www.freedomhouse.org.

to its preference for freedom as a product of liberal democratic societies rather than any other conception, it aims to evaluate the adherence of states to standards of freedom 'as experienced by individuals'. Notwithstanding the flaws and limitations of the methodology it would be interesting to see how the EU faired if it were to be assessed using these means.

But of course, this would be something of a deceitful endeavour. Freedom House adopt a checklist split into two sections, the first concerned with political rights, the second with civil liberties. In each case, a series of questions are asked from which a rating is obtained. So, under political rights questions are posed on the electoral process, political pluralism and participation, and the functioning of government. Under civil liberties freedom of expression and belief, associational and organisational rights, the rule of law, and personal autonomy and individual rights are considered. Although some of the questions under these sections could be applied to the EU, the fact is the great majority have a very restricted meaning outside the confines of a state. Those pointed questions concerned with 'government' and the political process might well seem appropriate to ask (as indeed I have when talking about the democratic legitimacy of the Union) but in reality they are predicated on some form of state to give them meaning, to give a comprehensible context that makes sense of their application. The Union simply does not possess that character. Whether or not it can prove itself to have 'fair electoral laws' and allow for political pluralism, it is neither a creation of such processes nor ultimately bound by them.

Similarly, when it comes to apply the civil liberties checklist, there is again little to connect the Union to the freedoms expected for individuals. The EU does not in this sense 'govern' the media, religious institutions, academia, pubic expression, assembly, or the organisation of civil society groups. Its 'rule', such as it is, might affect any and every one of these. But it is difficult to establish a direct determination to do just that. A positive answer may be given to the question of possessing an independent judiciary but this is minor when compared to the raft of liberties that are clearly assumed to lie solely within the gift of states.

Naturally, the lack of appropriateness of this particular form of freedom indicators for the EU may be more a reflection of the limitations of the method designed. However, it does suggest that we cannot look to state models for our assessment of the value of liberty as a part of the institutional ethos of the Union. The only time it might have some application is when negative answers are to be given. In other words, when one can show the EU interferes with individual liberties through institutional action and legislation. It has much less to say about achieving a regime of freedom for the EU as a whole.

This might suggest, in turn, that all we need do is form some specifically designed questionnaire for the Union. But if we did this we would then be presuming a form of polity for the Union that has not necessarily been constructed. We might all agree, as Freedom House suggest, that liberal democracies are the best way of fulfilling liberty but this is a value judgment that does not necessarily have purchase in the EU. As I suggested when considering the value of democracy, it is by no means certain that democratic structures that operate in such liberal states are useful for the EU.

What then are we to make of freedom in the EU's institutional ethos? Its quality is certainly hard to identify despite the willingness to deploy the term with some ease. But we can perhaps recognise that liberty in this realm cannot be merely the accumulation of a list of individual rights and constitutional mechanisms of liberal democracy. The EU may well talk about these rights and may well enforce or promote them from time to time through the judicial and legislative system. But when it comes to governance, liberty is of a different order.

The fairly recent determination to identify freedom with security and justice clouds the issue. Indeed, it is probably a deflection given that it concentrates on the individual as an economic factor of production on the one hand and amorphous threats that need to be countered on the other. In each case there is little sense either in law or policy that suggests any coherence in institutional understanding about the quality of freedom to be promoted.

Perhaps, though, we can say the predominant characteristic of liberty in the EU is collective rather than individual. Individuals might well benefit from EU action, and we have seen some of this in relation to issues of anti-discrimination law and the provisions safeguarding free movement, but even these are consequential gains. They are only realisable through the cooperation and action of the Member States. Rather, freedom is something to be enhanced through a conditioning of the Union: an 'area' of liberty, indeed, not a regime. This is an important distinction and the rhetoric is revealing. The association between freedom and geography reflects the underlying thinking about what form of liberty is possible through the institution of the EU. It cannot, other than in a very limited and probably negative fashion by and large, act *for* the freedom of individuals. It can only provide an environment to that end. But as soon as we are concerned with environment, other factors and threats come into play. And given changing political concerns over time it is no surprise that the weight of freedom often seems lighter than the interests of 'security' and 'prosperity' and 'efficiency' and 'market harmony'. In other words, liberty is contingent. It means that the EU cannot ensure the freedoms of individuals when more pressing matters (or indeed interests of power, private or public) arise. It might even coordinate restrictions on those freedoms in the interests of the greater 'good'. Often these will appear pathetic, minor irritations that only vaguely affect people's abilities to live their lives as they choose. Lamentations as to bureaucratic and seemingly illogical interferences will give credence to those critics of the EU as a centralised and centralising monster with a tendency to make 'our' lives more difficult without any sensible benefit on view. At the more extreme level, however, it is possible to see that very real freedoms might be put in jeopardy in the name of these overriding interests. This is particularly so in relation to actions for 'security'. Damian Chalmers has suggested that the EU's concern with freedom is 'with the guardianship of a particular model of political economy, which does not protect itself through the consolidation of territorial sovereignty, but through dynamic and multiple forms of policing against risks to its functioning and macro-systemic stability'.[106] We are, therefore, just as likely to see restrictions on liberty arising through the actions of the EU as improvements in people's autonomy. Such is the condition of liberty, I argue, in the institutional ethos.

[106] Chalmers, 'Constitutional Reason in the Age of Terror' at vii.

7   The institutional ethos of the EU

Introduction

Phillip Allott, a renowned if idiosyncratic theorist of international law, once claimed that the EU lacked 'an *arche*', 'a coherent idea of its actuality, an ideal of its potentiality'.[1] In terms of its politics and its law, he seemed to suggest a philosophical void accompanied its development. But even whilst taking pains to itemise the failings that demonstrated this absence and the general inability to find a 'self-constituting ideal', Allott remained optimistic about the EU's future. What was needed was an awakening of '*l'âme et la personne de l'Europe* from its sad self-induced sleep'.[2] Then the promise of the EU might be fulfilled.

Allott's militant optimism, as his form of positive but severe critique might be called, typifies much of the ultimately friendly analyses of the EU. There are, however, two problems with his position. First, it assumes there is some form of 'soul' hidden in the popular consciousness of the 'people' of Europe that awaits rediscovery and which would define the point and nature of European unification. Second, it assumes that no operative philosophy other than one that is the product of a European society or general social movement is possible. Although I share Allott's optimism and much of his practical critique I do not accept either of these mistaken assumptions. Instead, this book provides an alternative vision that remedies Allott's double error. It claims that a form of constituting ideal *has* arisen but is manifest not through a popular consciousness but through an institutional ethos. To reiterate my claims in Chapter 1, this refers to an evolved way

---

[1] Philip Allott, 'The Crisis of European Constitutionalism: Reflections on the Revolution in Europe', *Common Market Law Review* 34:3 (1997) 439–90 at 488.
[2] *Ibid.* at 490.

of doing things within an institutional structure that is constrained by some ethical framework. This is not to say that the ethos is either coherent or palatable. It is merely an expression of the values observed politically and legally which defines the institutionalised parameters for action in the name of the EU. It is, therefore, demonstrably *not* a product of popular will or even demand. I also claim that EU law has provided the spine of this institutional ethos, the means by which it has been given particular definition. Contrary to Allott's supposition, this in turn infers that some philosophy of EU law *has* evolved.

With this basic vision in mind, the previous five chapters have attempted to chart the key points of the salient values that I suggest provide the trigonometric pattern of the institutional ethos. Although I accept other values play a role, the institutional reiteration of those upon which I have focused should give significant clues as to the nature of the ethos as it has arisen. Now my task is to bring this analysis together to provide an account of the institutional ethos as a whole.

I will do this in two ways. First, I will rehearse the dimensions of the values to reiterate what I take to be the main coordinates of the current institutional ethos. Second, I will strengthen this analysis by providing an interpretation of the philosophy of EU law, which is evident, I suggest, in the jurisprudence of the European Court of Justice. My argument, set out in Chapter 1, is that this philosophy both reflects and helps constitute the ethos. Consequently, a deeper assessment of the evolved philosophy will provide greater insight into the ethos as it stands. I intend to provide this evaluation through the medium of a series of supported propositions. Together I aim to show how both the philosophy and ethos as they have developed have been deficient. Fundamentally, they represent a failure to come to terms with justice as a cohering theme for the Union. And as a direct result, they undermine any claims that the EU is or can become a 'just institution'.

The value(s) of the institutional ethos

As I have said, a brief rehearsal of the key findings of the previous five chapters will be useful in plotting the main coordinates of the institutional ethos.

First, as Chapter 2 showed, the concept of peace has struggled to develop beyond a simple statement of fact; there is presumed to be no war in the EU, nor is there any prospect of military conflict between

Member States as things stand.[3] That fulfils the ambit of the term. Little in the way of value orientation is available here. The success of the Union in eradicating war between its Members has been reiterated accordingly. And prospective members have been induced, in part, to join in this success. Indeed, membership has been assumed to be the route to peace elsewhere in Europe. The method of resolution of the conflagrations of the first half of the twentieth century is assumed to be appropriate for those European conflicts since 1990. But, when we considered the approach to 'peace' *in* the EU we saw an unconvincing attempt to embrace a concept beyond the identification of this cessation of martial conflict between original, subsequent and potential Member States. The result has been that peace as a defining and guiding ethical precept has seen its influence lessen as threats of war between Member States have receded and the discourse of security gained precedence in its stead. Security has even been passed off as synonymous with peace as though a secure Union necessarily means a peace-filled and peace-governed Union.

Such reasoning is not completely without foundation. But it does not take into account with any conviction the ethical parameters that a more widely defined notion of peace might plausibly allow. We can probably determine that the concept adopted more closely resembles that which might find expression at nation-state level, being an internal state of affairs perhaps complemented by a non-aggressive external policy rather than a continuing commitment and philosophy to seek, maintain and reinforce a 'just' peace however that might be defined. The EU, and its law, does not engage so easily with supranational, cosmopolitan, or internationalist understandings of the concept.

The practical consequences are that peace fails to provide any significant ethical dimension beyond ideas of security and the restricted determination that internal conflicts between *Member* States will be resolved through political or legal channels. Given that we live in a globalised world, one which the Union is at the forefront of promoting rhetorically and practically, such a restricted approach is suffused with danger. The failures of the EU either to engage meaningfully and coherently in the interests of peace do not bode well in this respect. The evidence of the approach to the Balkans as well as Iraq indicates

---

[3] I say 'presumed' because this statement takes no account of any conflicts that have taken place across borders, most significantly the conflicts in Northern Ireland and the Basque region. Although these have been generally seen as internal terrorist activities there are some who will have seen them as 'wars'.

a fragility in any commitment to a unified external policy where the overriding interests of peace might mean more than the cessation of military hostilities. Similarly, the lack of any coherent policy towards the manufacture and sale of arms by EU states and enterprises that fuel the world's conflicts continues to suggest that peace is not a defining and pre-eminent value in the institutional ethos. Rather, a security that discriminates against the 'other' as a lasting precondition might well have the effect of fuelling resentment and aggressive reaction. Peace then becomes under perpetual strain, forever an excuse to discriminate in order to address some perceived threat or pursue some perceived interest.

As regards the rule of law, analysed in Chapter 3, we saw a different problem emerge. On the one hand, the notion embodies the simple vision to construct a 'community of law', a legal order that will ensure the EU is preserved. Of course, we might not be sure what the aim of this enterprise is, but from a legal perspective (as we will see later in this chapter) some basic structuring principles can be identified. In this sense the EU is conditioned by law. On the other hand, law's rule might be seen as transformational in intent, where a new *political* order becomes constructed through adherence to precepts embraced by a concept of the rule of law. Order versus transformation, control versus justice would perhaps sum up the choice. But instead of making that choice, a conceptual ambivalence is perceptible. There appears to be a fear that too little law and the EU might fail through lack of regard. Too much law, a condition of juridification for some, and the EU might provoke fierce resistance. By trying to follow a path between these two extremes, less and less attention has been paid to the meaning of the rule of law and its potential importance within the institutional ethos. So we have a basic indecision as to when the concept applies to the Member States. The failure to embrace a mechanism whereby their activities can be scrutinised on matters that offend the values expressed in the TEU, through the mechanism of Article 7, is symptomatic of this condition.

The same might be said for the processes associated with 'soft law', 'self-regulation' and 'co-regulation' developments in the EU. Given the political sensitivities that have been uppermost in the development of the Union, soft law type initiatives have been a diplomatic way in which the business of the EU can be conducted. They combine some sense of obligation without adhering inexorably to a strictly enforceable widespread legal regime. Instead, 'hard law', as traditionally conceived in EU law, has operated in restricted areas where consensus can be achieved or is deemed necessary in the interests of all Member States. For other areas where cooperation without compulsion is deemed politic, soft law methods, which tolerate varied adherence to 'rules', such as the Open Method of Coordination, flexibility, and differentiation, provide a semblance of progress in the face of localised opposition. This has been seen by some as creating a culture of law designed for diversity rather than uniformity.[4] It helps move integration forward where otherwise the search for unanimity or majority decisions would be unpalatable, perhaps even impossible. But although these processes and the language that accompanies them may have encouraged increased forms of participation for limited public and private actors and should still be subject to the 'fundamental principles of the EU legal order',[5] at least in so far as fundamental rights are concerned, there remains the danger that their preponderance and the vagueness they induce will sit uneasily with familiar, nationally-bound, rule of law conceptions. There is, indeed, a possibility that diversity will be *managed* so as to avoid opposition through law to political decision-making. The virtue of responding to difference could then transmute into the vice of division and rule. Transparency, certainty, equal application, and the potential for open review may well be sacrificed in the interests of this managed diversity, whose purpose may be to progress integration even in the face of public wariness or outright opposition. Similarly, the tendencies towards secrecy remain firmly in place. As the European Ombudsman had cause to note in June 2008, the resistance to the principle of access to information continues to appear in the small print of transparency proposals.[6] So, although many see the diversity processes as not necessarily threatening rule of law understandings, the capacity for abuse emerging through increased informality persists.

---

[4] See Linda Senden, 'Soft Law, Self-Regulation and Co-Regulation in European Law: where do they Meet?', *Electronic Journal of Comparative Law* 9:1 (2005) online, available at: www.ejcl.org.

[5] Deirdre Curtin makes this point in 'Emerging Institutional Parameters and Organised Difference in the European Union', in Bruno de Witte, Dominik Hanf and Ellen Vos (eds.), *The Many Faces of Differentiation in EU Law* (Antwerp: Intersentia, 2001) 347–77 at 377.

[6] See Contribution of the European Ombudsman, P. Nikiforos Diamandouros, to the public hearing on the Revision of Regulation 1049/2001 on public access to documents, European Parliament – Committee on Civil Liberties, Justice and Home Affairs, Brussels, 2 June 2008. The conclusion that access would be restricted through the changes proposed was indicative of the tendency for secrecy.

Are we on more solid ground when we turn to respect for fundamental rights, explored in Chapter 4? Superficially there is strong institutional support for this value. But we also found here ambiguity and indeterminacy. What rights are to be respected and promoted? Who is to have responsibility in ensuring their respect and promotion? And to what extent are they to be embraced? These are the questions that remain unresolved. We continue to witness a system that cannot decide how and when *human* rights should govern the EU's actions. In particular, incoherence between external and internal policies is steadfastly maintained. I have explored the dimensions of this incoherence elsewhere,[7] and little has changed despite firmer constitutional promises. Even though the Lisbon Treaty now makes the EU Charter of Fundamental Rights a legally binding instrument, and even though the EU is to be given the capacity to accede to the European Convention on Human Rights, neither of these initiatives will address the central ambiguity and irony as I have called it. A handicap is still placed on the application of EU law. Human rights will only appear relevant in restricted circumstances. As the new Article 6 TEU as amended by the Lisbon Treaty makes clear, neither the Charter provisions nor accession to the ECHR shall be allowed to 'affect the Union's competences as defined in the Treaties'.

All this means that fundamental rights remain too imbued with conflicting purposes and content to provide a solid ethical foundation. Armin Von Bogdandy proposed a solution to this problem through the adoption of a three-tiered system.[8] The first tier would promote the full range of human rights in the external dimension with reasonable vigour but without any formal regulatory framework. This would include ensuring that states seeking to join the Union would be subjected to intense scrutiny and demands for human rights reform where necessary, an intrusive and fairly robust enforcement of human rights across a broad spectrum. The second tier would see the Union promote *fundamental* rights internally within very restricted borders. Member States would only be scrutinised with regard to their application of EU law. Any human rights concerns that did not engage an EU law dimension

---

[7] See Andrew Williams, *EU Human Rights Policies: a Study in Irony* (Oxford: Oxford University Press, 2004).

[8] Armin von Bogdandy, 'The EU as a Human Rights Organization?', *Common Market Law Review* 37:6 (2000) 1307–38. See also his reiteration in 'Constitutional Principles' in Armin von Bogdandy and Jürgen Bast (eds.), *Principles of European Constitutional Law* (Oxford: Hart, 2006) 3–52 at 39.

would remain the preserve of national constitutional concern or international human rights bodies (including those creatures of the Council of Europe and UN). There would be limited regulation in this sphere. The third tier would be more heavily regulated and would apply to the EU institutions. These would be expected to act in accordance with the EU Charter.

In essence, Bogdandy's scheme does no more than reflect the status quo. And what it does is entrench two related ideas. First, that human rights *tout court* remain a matter of national sovereignty only occasionally interrupted by the EU. Second, that human rights never attain any sense of institutional certainty. The EU and its law will always be asking the question: what are we talking about when we talk about human rights? Indeterminacy again lies at the heart of this institutional ethos component.

Which brings us to democracy. Chapter 5 probably did no more than confirm the general perception that if democracy has a place within the EU's institutional ethos it has to be along new and untested lines. The post-national perspective has generally won out mainly for efficacious reasons rather than ones forged from political philosophy. This has not, however, prevented traditional visions of democracy focused on the state being used as cudgels against the Union. The rhetoric of democracy has acquired significant constitutional presence but the practicalities of its application at EU level remain uncertain. There has been a tendency to look towards democracy substitutes, less concerned with the value than the virtues of democracy. Initiatives for transparency and participation, which are often highly restricted and sometimes even laughable as democratic avenues, hardly represent a successful and radical reappraisal of the application of democracy beyond the state. The compromise adopted does little to address the question of the strength of democracy within the institutional ethos. Instead the argument is made that if the institutions preside over a regime that is governed by the rule of law and respects human rights then perhaps it does not matter if the citizens of Europe are ineffectually represented in EU decision-making. Andrew Moravscik and Giandomenico Majone have been at the vanguard of this commentary. They see EU democratic processes as reasonable in comparison to those operating at the national level. But whether or not the EU is no better or no worse than national polities, the value of democracy has failed to attain an overarching influence in the EU's development. Instead, the virtues of transparency and non-electoral participation have been deployed to generate a new interpretation of the concept, one useful, if not wholly convincing, for the working of the EU. Overall, however, the perceived and frequently restated problem of the democratic deficit acts as a constant barb that snags the Union. It is a charge that fuels opposition to further integration or even constitutionalisation through Treaty amendment.

What then of freedom? If peace, the rule of law, and fundamental rights pose difficulties of definition, liberty is the epitome of an enigma. Given that freedom in the EU has been built significantly upon these other values, values that are plagued by indeterminacy as I have argued, we have the almost clichéd construction of an enigma built upon a mystery. As Chapter 6 showed, probably the most we can say about the concept in the EU is that it dips into a multiplicity of meanings depending on context. So, although it might appear strong in terms of *freedoms* associated with the construction of the single market, it loses purchase when it looks to structures of democratic governance or the enhancement of civil liberties. The 'area of freedom' is highly contained and always subject to its constitutional bedfellows, security and justice. If we tried to envision freedom as a state-like concept we would probably be perturbed by the lack of institutional commitment to its possibilities. If we tried to see it from a post-national or meta-national perspective we would most likely be disappointed by the failure to demonstrate how it enhanced freedom rather than added another layer of bureaucratic restrictions upon it. All in all the absence of any suitable theory of freedom betrays the dilemma. Are we to see it in terms of collective or individual perspectives? How are the two to be reconciled outside national political dimensions? These questions not only remain unanswered in the EU, they are not even asked with any seriousness.

Given that all these values appear to be affected by indeterminacy of some significance it can be no surprise that the institutional ethos also has that quality. Although in some instances we can see how value aspects might be fulfilled there is no sense of when, where and how this should occur or when, where and how they should interact. Neither the Parliament nor the Commission serve as adequate institutional locations for debating the EU's ethical parameters. No effective alternative political sphere or public space has been created despite claims that this might be possible through the EU. The fundamental indeterminacy infects the role of all the values in their individual or collective capacity to determine policy and action. They are afflicted with a form that tends towards the weak end of any spectrum of possible meaning. The institutional ethos as a whole can, therefore, be plausibly described as chaotic, a patchwork of half-understood and contingent values which are forever in motion, altering in form and substance depending on the context of any actions. It is representative of a polity with an ethical framework that is, ironically, lacking in ethical guidance.

All this suggests that the values that could potentially define the quality of the EU's purpose are permeated by an immanent ambiguity. Their ability to attract loyalty and make sense of the EU, as well as to fulfil any plausible account for their own individual definition, is severely undermined. Even with the recent constitutional attempts to provide some expression of an ethical framework the confusion persists. These function as a form of political rhetoric concealing the depth of conflicts that might otherwise be lauded as a form of 'pluralism' or, in European discourse, 'diversity'. Alasdair MacIntyre appositely provided an indication of the consequent danger of such a condition.

In any society where government does not express or represent the moral community of the citizens, but is instead a set of institutional arrangements for imposing a bureaucratized unity on a society which lacks genuine moral consensus, the nature of political obligation becomes systematically unclear.[9]

It also becomes *systemically* unclear. For the EU systematic and systemic value indeterminacy suggests that it is a polity whose institutional ethos cannot plausibly operate as a substitute or even a counterweight to a vague or multiple political project. Instead, we have uncertainty of means accompanying an uncertainty of ends, a project that undermines itself like the mythical *ouroboros*, the self-consuming serpent.

This is, I suggest, the state of the institutional ethos revealed so far.

The philosophy of EU law and the EU's institutional ethos

Can my interpretation be further substantiated? My argument has been from the outset that EU 'law',[10] its application and expression,

---

[9] Alasdair MacIntyre, *After Virtue: a Study in Moral Theory*, 2nd edn (London: Duckworth, 1985) at 254.

[10] Although my emphasis is on jurisprudence of the ECJ I recognise that 'law' in this context can convey, in Deirdre Curtin's words, 'the propensity of the EU to adopt (legally) *binding* norms' and encompass a broad range of sources. It therefore should

has been fundamentally bound up in the development of those salient values that have given shape to the institutional ethos. The previous chapters demonstrate law's influence in this respect. Consequently, my understanding of the ethos as a whole should be enhanced by interpreting any apparent philosophy of EU law that has evolved. Specifically, the approach taken in the ECJ's jurisprudence to those values I have examined will be relevant.

But *how* can such a philosophy be revealed? Clearly this is a matter of interpretation and therefore argument. With that in mind, I wish to advance five propositions which will provide (a) a plausible explanation of the relationship and complicity of law in the institutional ethos, and (b) a description of the philosophy developed as a result.

I will set out the propositions briefly before considering each in greater depth.

First, the enduring condition of indeterminacy as reflected in the institutional ethos has meant EU law generally operates under a central paradox. On the one hand, one of its central precepts is that it provides a reasonable degree of certainty of rule and legal order. On the other, it has to operate in an uncertain environment that goes beyond any reasonable parameters of vagueness that might otherwise be valued in any judicial system as respect for difference or necessary for authoritative interpretation.

Second, the ECJ has coped with this environment not by relying on any understood *value* or set of values but by centring on *principles*, particularly the principle of effectiveness. These principles include, what I interpret to be, a weak notion of *virtue* that has been used as a substitute for any 'strong' ethical, or ideal, foundation.

Third, those salient values identified constitutionally, and deconstructed in this book, have been grafted onto the EU's institutional framework by the ECJ in an attempt to establish retrospectively, or reinforce some sense of, legitimacy or identity both for the EU *and* its law. Values have thus appeared at best ill-defined and at worst ancillary, contingent and incoherent. They are all interpreted with a view to ensuring the EU's continuation not the realisation of those values.

incorporate both formal ('hard') and informal ('soft') modes of governance. Together these rules or habits that govern practices are of particular importance in the constitution of my notion of institutional ethos, as I explained in Chapter 1. See, further, Deirdre M. Curtin, 'European Legal Integration: Paradise Lost?', in Deirdre M. Curtin, Jan M. Smits, André Klip and Joseph A. McCahery (eds.), *European Integration and Law* (Antwerpen: Intersentia, 2006) 1–54 at 10.

Fourth, the central condition of indeterminacy coupled with uncertain value definition and application suggests that the evolved philosophy of EU law rests upon a *theory of interpretation* at the expense of a *theory of justice*. Caught amidst a fundamental ambiguity, unsure whether international or some form of pseudo-national law provides the basic source of norms, EU law has been crafted jurisprudentially so as to abstain from defining salient values rather than making judgments about them. The varying political climate and structure of the Union is interpreted through a very narrow prism so as to give some effect to the perceived political will as expressed in the Treaties. Without any coherent or developed sense of justice underpinning its constitution or application (beyond an 'economistic justice' in Allott's phrase),[11] EU law has evolved so as to avoid conflict and preserve the law's primacy. What *telos* there is has become self-serving and self-referential rather than based on fundamental common values. In adhering to a philosophy so grounded in a theory of interpretation, the whole enterprise appears ethically vacuous if not duplicitous *despite* all those manifestations of respect for values that might be evidenced. Making a virtue of uncertainty through such notions as subsidiarity, respect for diversity, pluralism and multi-level governance, has done little to remedy or compensate for this fundamental defect.

Fifth, a regeneration of philosophy and institutional ethos is not achievable by relying on the ECJ *alone* to provide its own inspiration through the development of a doctrine of general principles. The recent saga of the case of *Kadi* illustrates how any optimism that legally enforced values (in this case, respect for human rights) might transcend politics is ultimately misplaced.[12] A sense of contingent justice in EU law remains too deeply ingrained despite any apparent judicial preference for human rights.

These propositions now require fuller discussion.

Proposition 1: the paradox of EU law

My *first* proposition is that EU law is conditioned by a central paradox. On the one hand, it has been imbued with a demand for certainty or

---

[11] Philip Allott, *The Health of Nations: Society and Law Beyond the State* (Cambridge: Cambridge University Press, 2002) at 250.

[12] Joined Cases C-402/05 P and C-415/05 P *Kadi* v. *Council* Judgment of the Court 8 September 2008 unreported.

order, expressed often and most forcefully by the ECJ as 'uniformity'.[13] That is a natural consequence of the adoption of law to give force to, and order, the EU, a strategy I charted in Chapter 3. The ECJ helped construct this approach through its formative decisions. The declaration in *van Gend en Loos* that the EEC Treaty imposed obligations and rights for individuals, Member States and the institutions 'in a clearly defined way' was an expression of this search for certainty through legal norms.[14] It was accepted explicitly by the Court that its task was 'to secure uniform interpretation of the Treaty', which in turn confirmed that Member States had 'acknowledged that Community law has an authority which can be invoked' by nationals in their domestic courts. The 'new legal order' constructed required certainty for the benefit of all concerned. Otherwise the whole project would be under threat.

In essence, this jurisprudential move did no more than play to some established understandings of modern Western law and its processes. The virtue of reasonable certainty for those constituents who are affected by its application, is a common attribute ascribed to law across a wide range of legal philosophy. Stability and order complemented by a capacity for change, as Roscoe Pound suggested, is a particular aspect of this appreciation.[15] One could draw a distinction here in relation to the application of *international* law, which may resonate stronger for the EU than it does at the domestic level. Even then, although uncertainty remains an inherent condition and political necessity, some certainty of application is at least an ambition, a means by which norms are enforced globally so as to create some kind of international order.[16]

EU law's *sui generis* location, crossing the national/international jurisdictional divide, has been built on these appreciations of domestic necessity *and* international ambition. It has been deployed to build a legal order that makes reasonably certain future relations between the EU institutions, the Member States, and their citizens. This goes beyond a functional general principle of legal certainty and

---

[13] European Court of Justice, 'The Future of the Judicial System of the European Union (Proposals and Reflections)' 1999, online, available at: http://curia.europa.eu/en/instit/txtdocfr/autrestxts/ave.pdf.

[14] *van Gend en Loos* v. *Nederlandse Administratie der Berastingen* [1963] ECR 1.

[15] See Roscoe Pound, *Interpretations of Legal History* (Gloucester, MA: P. Smith, 1967).

[16] Hersch Lauterpacht, for instance, charted the varying approaches to international law but insisted on the underlying acceptance that although weak there were rules to which states generally bound themselves. See Hersch Lauterpacht, *The Function of Law in the International Community* (Oxford: The Clarendon Press, 1933).

legitimate expectations. Although the development of such a principle by the ECJ, which Tridimas explains has been subject to varying application and interpretation,[17] is important, it does not reflect the overarching idea of certainty vis-à-vis the role of law in the EU's construction. Through legislation and judicial decision, law has been crucial in giving definition to what is permissible and what can be achieved through the EU.

The jurisprudential association of EU law with certainty has been mirrored in political assessment. Law here has been valorised for its ability to create certainty within a highly complex and contestable environment. Moravcsik, for instance, notes that the EU has developed a successful model of 'multi-level governance' with law at its core.[18] Even in the absence of any sense of social justice, as Ulrich Haltern has inferred, a certainty of action through law where we 'know' what the EU does (at least economically) even if we cannot be sure why it does it, has provided the EU with some enduring value.[19] Mark Leonard's polemical and no doubt intentionally provocative, *Why Europe Will Run the 21st Century* similarly sees law as crucial to the EU's 'success'.[20] It works 'not because there is a European police force state that will enforce [it], but because all European states want the system to succeed. Because each member state wants its fellow members to obey the law, they are forced to obey it themselves'.[21] Although there are some deep flaws in this analysis, Leonard's thesis registers an important view about law and its supposed value for the EU. In the absence of an engaging purpose beyond what Moravcsik aptly calls 'business', and Perry Anderson the 'last great achievement of the bourgeoisie', law provides a sense of self-contained legitimacy, one fundamentally based on a notion of certainty and order.[22]

Notwithstanding this clamour for order and certainty, EU law has had to evolve within a political and constitutional settlement that remains steadfastly conditioned by indeterminacy. This is a fundamentally disturbing paradox. As I have already outlined, the institutional ethos

---

[17] Takis Tridimas, *The General Principles of EU Law*, 2nd edn (Oxford: Oxford University Press, 2006) 242 et seq.
[18] Andrew Moravcsik, 'Europe Without Illusions', *Prospect*, July (2005) 25–6.
[19] Ulrich Haltern, 'Pathos and Patina: the Failure and Promise of Constitutionalism in the European Imagination', *European Law Journal* 9 (2003) 14–44.
[20] Mark Leonard, *Why Europe Will Run the 21st Century* (London: Fourth Estate, 2005).
[21] *Ibid.* at 42.
[22] See Moravcsik, 'Europe Without Illusions' and Perry Anderson, 'Depicting Europe', *London Review of Books*, 20 September 2007.

is composed of values that are at best ambiguous and at worst vapid, leaving EU law with few fixed ethical points. It has been restricted to an approach to legal certainty that is preconditioned by the reinforcement of 'the binding character of Community law and the obligations which ensue for Member States' and the 'integrity' of the Community legal order.[23] Although the ECJ has undoubtedly developed general principles that are reflected in the values analysed in this book, this has taken place without a plausible political or judicial determination of ideal meaning. As the EU has developed along increasingly, and for some despairingly, arcane and complex lines, the underlying condition of unreasonable uncertainty (of purpose, geography, demography, and philosophy) has ensured that no secure points of reference other than vague allusions to a mythic heritage have been available for law to embrace. Indeed, the ECJ acknowledged the lack of foundation in *van Gend en Loos*, perhaps unconsciously, when it referred to the rights conferred on individuals by the Treaty as *becoming* part of their legal heritage, rather than reflecting a heritage already in existence.[24]

Admittedly, since the early days of legal anxiety about the possible preservation of the EU (in particular when the threats posed by Member State constitutional courts had begun to decrease) a discourse of a common heritage has come more to the fore. This has alluded to a mutual *pre-existing* set of values, purportedly shared by all the peoples of Europe. The implication is that anyone who denies the appropriateness of these values is 'other' in European terms. But this has been more an exercise in myth-making than empirical research. The ECJ in particular has been party to such an enterprise. This has been partially a consequence of the lack of political resolution that would make clear the identity and substance of values deemed applicable to the EU. Even so, the Court has not been totally comfortable with imposing a myth of European values. The ECJ has struggled with the need to balance uniformity with difference throughout its history. It has assumed that law on the one hand should not be the surrogate method for imposing the EU on its constituents in some autocratic fashion. On the other, it has accepted that law as traditionally conceived can have little purpose or contribution to make if it does *not* act as a means of enforcing integration. This is the paradoxical environment that casts a

---

[23] See Tridimas, *The General Principles of EU Law* at 246.
[24] This is distinct from many texts of the Council of Europe, which treated the existence of a common heritage of values as self-evident.

blanket of uncertainty to the point of indeterminacy over the sense of certainty through order that is frequently invested in EU law.

Proposition 2: EU law: values, principles and virtues

This brings me to my *second* proposition. The ECJ has operated within the environment of indeterminacy not by relying on any understood value or set of values but by centring on *principles*. These have included, in particular, what I express as *virtues* of governance, which have less to do with fulfilling a clear ethical need and more with supporting the EU's continuing existence and development, maintaining its order and its processes and functions of ordering almost without regard to values common or otherwise.

Clearly I need to make a distinction between 'principle', 'value' and 'virtue' here. I accept that there may well be considerable philosophical overlap and confusion regarding these terms but I will try to make a general distinction that is at least plausible for the purposes of my argument.

So, by 'principles' I mean those 'legal norms laying down essential elements of a legal order'.[25] They refer to general propositions from which rules might derive.[26] They relate to standards that might be based in law or practice, which contribute to forming a framework for decision-making and action, and which 'form an essential building block of a legal system'.[27]

'Values' on the other hand engage a different understanding, one that acquires meaning when contrasted with principles. Jürgen Habermas' distinction between the two concepts is sensible and relevant here. Principles possess a deontological character 'whereas values are teleological'.[28] A sense of obligation attaches to principles whereas a sense of purpose is emitted by values, which 'are to be understood as intersubjectively shared preferences'.[29] Values are, therefore, those ends deemed worthy of pursuit. Politically, they describe those qualities and states of condition that are considered desirable for shaping

---

[25] See Armin von Bogdandy, 'Doctrine of Principles', Jean Monnet Working Paper Series 9/03.1 (2003) NYU School of Law, New York, 1–50 at 10.

[26] This is a slight paraphrase and reworking of the definition for 'principle' adopted by Tridimas in his assessment of general principles of EU law. See Tridimas, *The General Principles of EU Law* at 1.

[27] Carol Harlow, 'Global Administrative Law: the Quest for Principles and Values', *European Journal of International Law* 17:1 (2006) 187–214 at 190.

[28] Jürgen Habermas, *Between Facts and Norms* (Cambridge: Polity Press, 1997) 255.

[29] *Ibid.* at 255.

action or political programmes. Thus values and principles have different consequences. Principles *command* action and enable judgment, albeit within interpretative parameters. Values *recommend*. They are more aspirational in character, helping to provide a sense of 'ultimate ends' and filling those gaps which appear when principles fail to provide sufficient guidance or conflict with each other. Values can be further characterised as prudential or moral in character, the former indicating those conditions which can be identified as specifically best for oneself (or one's associates in community), the latter, what is best for all.[30]

By 'virtue' I mean 'a disposition or sentiment which will produce in us obedience to certain rules'.[31] This evokes a certain sense of mediation between principle and value. Virtues describe the way in which values can be enacted through the application of principles. They make the means palatable, or at least not unpalatable. Even so, they can often take on the appearance of value, by suggesting a shared preference, *and* of principle, by informing the construction of standards.

Of course, these concepts can and do overlap. For some they appear almost interchangeable. Indeed, my definitions would not find favour within the EU's constitutional texts or much of its academic analysis. Virtue as a term is largely ignored and there is considerable confusion between principle and value. As Von Bogdandy has pointed out, for instance, the 'values' mentioned in the new Article 2 TEU following the Lisbon Treaty, would have legal consequences. As the EU would be empowered to *promote* these values, they would become part of the normative framework, and therefore they would have been transformed into constitutional principles. Takis Tridimas suggests, conversely, that these newly identified values 'represent the EU legal order as it currently stands' and reflect 'the case law of the ECJ on general principles'.[32] Values and principles therefore suffer from a certain indistinction.

My definitions, however, provide a plausible alternative scheme for analysis. This returns me to my second proposition. Essentially, this is that ECJ jurisprudence, and EU law by extension, has relied upon

---

[30] Anthony Quinton reviews this general classification in 'The Varieties of Value', The Tanner Lectures on Human Rights, delivered at the University of Warsaw, 19 May 1988. See also C.I. Lewis, *The Ground and Nature of the Right* (New York: Columbia University Press, 1955).

[31] MacIntyre, *After Virtue* at 244.

[32] Tridimas, *The General Principles of EU Law* at 15.

certain principles (and virtues as a form of second order principles) rather than values in its evolution. This is a product of the political inability to adopt any coherent understanding of values, prudential *or* moral, emerging from any convincing collective consciousness underpinning the EU. Rather, the principles and virtues adopted in EU law have been arranged around the central goal of giving effect to the Treaties. A tendency to the technical rather than the ethical thus permeates the law.[33]

How might this reasoning be justified? It is fairly common ground that EU law was *not* provided with a scheme of general principles in its founding Treaties. Tridimas reflects received wisdom in referring to inherent (and deliberate) *lacunae* in EU law which were the product of the creation of a new legal order without the 'accumulated judicial experience, buttressed in case law, that national legal systems possess'.[34] The ECJ was left to construct a system of law without explicit guidance regarding principles that should govern that construction. It was given the authority to develop a 'new legal order' as it saw fit. Article 220 EC Treaty (now Article 19 TEU after Lisbon), which placed on the ECJ responsibility for ensuring 'that in the interpretation and application of this Treaty the law is observed', mandated 'the Court to work out a system of legal principles in accordance with which the legality of Community and Member State action must be determined'.[35] This provision has been interpreted as 'replete with values' although of course they are not explicit.[36] There may well have been certain values that all parties to the Treaties could have agreed upon, if they had been minded to do so, but the fact is they were not the subject of public or political discussion let alone agreement.

Here lies the root of the problem. The principles developed through ECJ case law have *not* been based on fundamental values that have any great coherence, even though the consistent use of rhetoric regarding specific values might suggest otherwise. Nor have they been considered in terms of how they interact with each other. Some principles may have been articulated and adopted with reasonable vigour. Proportionality, legitimate expectations, non-discrimination and transparency have all been embraced by the ECJ. Similarly, the discourse of good governance

---

[33] The critique levelled against the EU as a technocratic enterprise has been consistently deployed over the years. See, for instance, C.M. Radaelli, *Technology in the European Union* (London: Longman, 1999).

[34] Tridimas, *The General Principles of EU Law* at 18.

[35] *Ibid.* at 20.   [36] *Ibid.* at 19.

has encouraged the application of some administrative virtues.[37] But when we look at those *values* most often expressed as 'fundamental' or 'foundational' (and are now provided with some kind of constitutional veneer by the original Article 6(1) TEU and now the value provisions introduced by the Lisbon Treaty), they appear ambiguous. We cannot talk of a comprehensible 'rule of law' with any confidence. Nor can we look to 'peace' or respect for fundamental rights or liberty or democracy and recognise any clear expression of value that would adequately reflect some sense of shared preferences. Although we can interpret appreciations of value that are prudential (in the sense that some valuable end – perhaps a single market – is being pursued for the good of the constituents of the EU) and moral (in the sense, at least, that the good of others outside the Union is pursued through, for instance, EuropeAid and development policy) these are so marked by contingency that they lack any substantive grounding.

This is confirmed by the way in which the constitutionally unguided Court developed general principles. It constructed these without clear political direction, or apparent philosophical or cultural understanding or analysis, on the basis of a teleological interpretation of the Treaties.[38] As already noted, *van Gend en Loos* was instrumental in initiating the approach when the Court looked to the 'spirit' of the Treaties for interpretative inspiration but only in so far as that was commensurate with the 'objective of the EEC Treaty, which is to establish a common market'.[39] This led to the principles of primacy and direct effect. The creation of a common market was perceived to be only possible if enforced through law. State law had to be compliant. Otherwise the whole project, as narrowly defined by the Treaty of Rome's aims in the first instance, would collapse amidst a plethora of legal conflicts.

There is little to suppose that any fundamental shift has taken place since these early judgments. In 1999, the Court of Justice and Court of First Instance confirmed 'its role within the Community legal order' as 'to guarantee respect for the distribution of powers between the Community and its Member States and between the Community institutions, the uniformity and consistency of Community law and

---

[37] Commission, White Paper on European Governance COM (2001) 428 final. Transparency and participation were two key virtues promoted.

[38] The latter critique is fairly common ground. See Bruno de Witte, 'The Nature of the Legal Order', in Paul Craig and Gráinne de Búrca (eds.), *The Evolution of EU Law* (Oxford: Oxford University Press, 1999)

[39] *van Gend en Loos* [1963]

to contribute to the harmonious development of the law within the Union'.[40] It went on to quote from a previous report in 1995, when the Court of Justice said

[a]ny weakening, even if only potential, of the uniform application and interpretation of Community law throughout the Union would be liable to give rise to distortions of competition and discrimination between economic operators, thus jeopardising equality of opportunity as between those operators and consequently the proper functioning of the internal market.[41]

The establishment and functioning of the internal market thus provided and continues to provide the parameters for value definition. Von Bogdandy's assessment that EU law has been based on a 'principle of fulfilment of Treaty objectives and not of an absolute principle of integration *tout court*'[42] supports the argument here. His analysis points to the way in which the ECJ in particular has had to constrain itself. Although it might have acted radically in defining the principles of primacy and direct effect, it was nevertheless operating conservatively. It was attempting to *conserve* the EU in the least objectionable way.

Again, this appears as something of an irony, a response to the paradox of my first proposition. By looking to give effect to the basic aims of the Treaty of Rome, the ECJ had to act to a very great extent without undue deference to national systems. The whole 'community of law' idea could not survive sustained national legal opposition otherwise the spectre of an unenforceable system of law would crucially undermine the possibility of limiting sovereignty even in discrete areas. Greater ambitions of union could not occupy the forefront of the legal mind without explicit political direction. That would have been a step too far. Even though the ECJ's decisions were seen as radical legal interventions, they were no more than necessary to give effect to the fundamental aim.

A specific example of the ECJ's approach appears in its adoption of a principle of effectiveness. Tridimas recognises such a principle as deriving not from the laws of Member States but from 'the distinct characteristics of Community law, primacy and direct effect'.[43] The paradox is reinforced here. For the presumption is that general principles are

---

[40] European Court of Justice, 'The Future of the Judicial System of the European Union (Proposals and Reflections)' at 21.
[41] *Ibid.* at 22.
[42] Armin von Bogdandy, 'Constitutional Principles' at 38.
[43] Tridimas, *The General Principles of EU Law* at 418.

'superior to Community legislation' but themselves are purely a product of the EC Treaty. The general principle of effectiveness displays this condition. The principles are of a type that underpin the legal order rather than challenge it. Hence in decisions such as *Foto-Frost* the ECJ felt it necessary to deny the right of national courts to declare Community acts invalid on the basis that this would undermine the certainty required of a primary legal order emanating from the EU.[44]

We see a more recent expression of this in Advocate General Maduro's opinion in *Kadi*.[45] This involved the decision by the Council to place restrictions on the funds of named individuals, suspected of links with terrorist organisations, following various UN Security Council resolutions. Maduro made clear that 'although the Court takes great care to respect the obligations that are incumbent on the Community by virtue of international law, it seeks, first and foremost, to preserve the constitutional framework created by the Treaty'.[46] He went on to say,

[t]he EC Treaty, by contrast, has founded an autonomous legal order, within which States as well as individuals have immediate rights and obligations. The duty of the Court of Justice is to act as the constitutional court of the municipal legal order that is the Community.[47]

Maduro's opinion usefully illustrates the key legal assumption that the preservation of the constitutional framework is the cornerstone of legal evaluation. There may be conflicts of values (peace and security perhaps on the one hand, individual human rights on the other) but these have to be resolved in accordance with the overall aim of the legal order's existence. The preference still appears to be a restricted interpretation of fundamental principles (or virtues) rather than values.

It now becomes easier to understand why EU law has adopted a value-light approach. The relatively weak articulation of values, evident in the formation of the institutional ethos, has ensured that the ECJ has been extremely cautious in imputing values into its jurisprudence and therefore into EU law. Those values, perhaps expressed through the lesser media of virtues or principles, have been tempered by the central need to give effect to the Treaties. But of course as these

---

[44] Case 314/85 *Foto-Frost* v. *Hauptzollant Lübeck-Ost* [1987] ECR 4199 para. 15.
[45] Case C-402/05 P *Kadi* v. *Council and Commission* Opinion of AG Maduro delivered on 16 January 2008.
[46] *Ibid.* at para. 24. See, for instance, Opinion 2/94, [1996] ECR I1759 para. 30, 34 and 35.
[47] *Ibid.* at para. 37.

Treaties have established an uncertain, if not indeterminate, environment through their vague and varying designation of aims and purposes, a restrained interpretation of the texts has been evident. How, indeed, is it possible to give effect to values and principles which are plagued by indeterminacy other than by approaching them with hesitancy?

Proposition 3: the impact on values

My *third* proposition is that those salient values identified constitutionally, have been grafted onto the institutional framework of the EU by the ECJ in such a way that they are left at best ill-defined and at worst ancillary, contingent and incoherent. A very limited interpretation of principles masquerading as values has been applied so as not to unseat the perceived central purpose of the EU; the construction and maintenance of a common market.

Before attending to the specifics of this proposition we need to know why it is important in general. The contention requires us to appreciate the significance of values as providing a general mechanism for judging the legitimacy of a project and its specific programmes. By these last terms I mean, respectively, the fundamental aims which can define a collective enterprise and the methods by which those are to be realised. Cornelius Castoriadis' definition of programme as 'a provisional concretization of the objectives of the project ... in so far as their realization would lead to or would facilitate the realization of the project as a whole' is particularly appropriate.[48] Values can be used to order both project and programme to the extent that they offer some moral backdrop against which decisions and actions might be judged from time to time. If a project demonstrates adherence both rhetorically and through its programmes to particular values, which are assumed to be accepted by the mass of its constituents, then it can justify a claim for popular support in its operations. At worst, it can suggest it poses no threat to those values and avoid criticism concerning the value of its existence. Through this device, it can achieve a sense of positive legitimacy (where there is active consensus in support) or negative legitimacy (in the sense that there are no value-based fundamental critiques that can undermine its right to exist, what has been

---

[48] Cornelius Castoriadis, *The Imaginary Institution of Society* (Cambridge: Polity Press, 1987) at 78.

called 'permissive consensus').[49] Niklas Luhmann wrote aptly of the theoretical relationship between values and programmes:

If they are to perform their specific task in the best possible way, programs often must be formulated as highly complex, variable, and unstable with regard to details. Value consensus then alleviates communication about the program's contingency: about program development, adaptation to a situation, change in programs, or even their becoming obsolescent. In view of such problems, one can at least, in communication, use points of departure that are undisputed (or are very difficult to dispute because they are backed up by morality) and build on the expectation that everyone must agree on at least these values. Values serve in the communication process as a kind of probe with which one can test whether more concrete expectations are also at work, if not generally, then at least in the concrete situation one faces.[50]

Of course, the underlying assumption here is that values are identifiable and meaningful as general indicators of a system's ability to ascribe value to a particular goal. Let us, for the moment, just accept this to be possible. In which case the key recognition is that any system requires some moral foundations if internal judgments are to be made about the 'good' of any particular action or activity carried out in its name. The values identified provide the basis upon which principles can be constructed. These in turn can justify specific rules as well as practices. The notion of institutional ethos I have promulgated in this book builds on this understanding by indicating the overarching sense of the way in which these values interact, operate and influence institutional action and activity as a whole. It represents the way in which values can legitimate the EU and can be used to judge its ongoing worthiness.

But how do we recognise which values are being used in this fashion? Tridimas suggests that the principles developed and deployed by a court will 'tell us something about the values which the courts believe underlie the legal system'.[51] He is right that this is a matter of belief not fact. But this does indicate the importance of looking to jurisprudence when we try to assess the quality of those values. This requires a review of the way in which they were, as I say, grafted on to the EU.

[49] For an early identification of this notion see L.N. Lindberg and S.A. Scheingold, *Europe's Would-be Polity: Patterns of Change in the European Community* (Englewood Cliffs, NJ: Prentice-Hall, 1970).
[50] Niklas Luhmann, *Social Systems* (Stanford, CA: Stanford University Press, 1995) at 317.
[51] Tridimas, *The General Principles of EU Law* at 2.

In this respect, it would not be too much of a distortion to suggest that generally all of the values I have considered have struggled to become recognised in the EU even in abstract terms. Although undoubtedly the development of the Union, its institutions and its law has seen the gradual enhancement of value understanding, this has only taken place upon a suspect foundation. It is part of my argument that all of the values have suffered from the constitutional defect of value absence at the EU's inception. They have been developed, particularly through jurisprudence, with an inherent irony at work. By this I mean the irony that inhabits an institution that employs the rhetoric of values but knows that it does not possess the means of bringing about their realisation other than to a very limited (and probably unsatisfactory) extent.[52] This is exemplified by the reluctance to provide value definition to assist the construction and implementation of policy designed to fulfil the demands of that definition.

Is this visible in the jurisprudence of the ECJ? Much has already been considered in the preceding chapters but by reconsidering this particular aspect we might be able to see how the adopted philosophy of EU law contributes to the underlying value indeterminacy afflicting the institutional ethos.

So let us again first look at peace in this light. This has to be placed apart from the other values in legal terms because it has never been granted a meaningful presence by the ECJ within EU law. This is unsurprising given the weak constitutional reference to peace. Its preservation and strengthening was noted in the EEC Treaty Preamble but as a *consequence* of 'pooling resources', not as a governing precept. Apart from the notion that closer economic ties would reduce inter-state tension and thereby avoid war, there was no direct commitment to a system of justice that would address the demands of peace. Underlying antagonisms and causes of past conflicts were not assessed or tackled. It is hardly surprising therefore that peace as a value that might require the construction of principles of justice has not been recognised explicitly by the ECJ. There has been reference by the Court to 'social peace' but this has been extremely limited, as we saw in Chapter 2, and has been largely defined through the observance

---

[52] This derives partially from the description of an ironist by Richard Rorty as someone 'aware of the contingency and fragility of their final vocabularies' which he in turn terms 'a set of words' employed 'to justify their actions, their beliefs, and their lives'. I suggest that the same sense of irony can attach to institutions. See Richard Rorty, *Contingency, Irony, and Solidarity* (Cambridge: Cambridge University Press, 1989) 73–4.

of fundamental rights. 'Civil peace' has also been mentioned but in a recent opinion of Advocate General Kokott this concept is almost dismissed as only a 'noble cause' which cannot be regarded seriously as a 'rule of law'.[53] Whether the Lisbon Treaty's amendment to the TEU, making 'peace' an aim to promote, will alter the legal terrain remains to be seen. It might merely make more explicit Lauterpacht's notion that peace is a 'metaphor for the postulate of the unity of the legal system'.[54] 'Juridical logic', he claimed, 'inevitably leads to the condemnation, as a matter of law, of anarchy and private force'.[55] Such perspective still relies on an idea of peace as the absence of war in inter-state relations, a condition that now hardly seems sufficient. Obligatory arbitration may be a key element of the institutional ethos, but the mere confirmation of this through EU law will not satisfy deeper notions of peace that incorporated ideas of justice into their schema. It might just about suffice as one of those 'process values', promoted some years ago by Robert Summers, who saw 'process peacefulness' as indicating the need to avoid violence and disorder through the legal settlement of disputes as one of those standards for judging whether a legal system was 'good' or not.[56] But even then it would not tell us what substantive content 'peace' might otherwise possess in law. We can see that any putative development of the value is likely to remain conditioned by the system of law rather than underlying moral precepts beyond the superficial.

As regards the other significant values, we have a more obvious jurisprudential presence. But again all were fundamentally invisible early in the EU's history. Only later did they become appreciated as foundational. Perhaps the starkest example of this delayed endorsement was in relation to human rights. To say that the Court was slow to realise their importance would be an understatement, as Chapter 4 noted, a reflection, most probably, of their absence in the Treaties. Of course, as EU law developed in its scope and impact (in particular with the principles of supremacy and direct effect in the 1960s) the *possibility* of breaches of national rights through EU law became more apparent. How then could Constitutional Courts of Member States stand by and

[53] Case C-420/07 *Apostolides* v. *Orams* Opinion of Advocate General Kokott, 18 December 2008 at para. 110.

[54] Lauterpacht, *The Function of Law in the International Community* at 438.

[55] *Ibid.*

[56] Robert Summers, 'Evaluating and Improving Legal Processes – A Plea for Process Values', *Cornell Law Review* 60 (1974) 1–52 at 1.

accept such potential violations? The negative response to this question in France, Italy and most notably West Germany placed the whole
EU idea in jeopardy. Legally those national Courts were left with little
choice but to deny the foundations of the nascent EU law if it were possible that basic rights enshrined in national constitutions were to be
overturned through laws emanating from the European institutions.
Such potential breaches of hard-won constitutional rights would have
been impossible to countenance. It would undermine all those strides
made after the spectre of extremism had been suppressed post-1945.
Equally, how could the ECJ forfeit the principle of supremacy, which
it had only just formulated, at the first sign of legal conflict? The ECJ
recognised this impasse-in-the-making and solved it through the construction of a notion of 'unwritten Community law, derived from the
general principles of law in force in Member States'.[57] By reiterating the
primacy of EU law whilst incorporating the vague principle of respect
for Member States' fundamental rights provisions, the Court was able
to construct a powerful myth. The value of respect for human rights
was to be articulated as an already written and politically understood
value that all reasonable persons would approve.[58] It was an attempt
to imagine, in almost Rawlsian fashion, an ideal original position even
in the face of a recently agreed contract that made no mention of such
understanding.

On the face of it, therefore, the ECJ's interpretation might suggest
a belated but at least worthy integration of a fundamental value into
EU law. But although an example of creative jurisprudence it was also
an indication of a tepid approach. Respecting human rights was not
the primary aim.[59] Human rights per se were not the root of the general principle. The value of respect was contingent upon the approach
towards fundamental rights held by individual Member States. It was

---

[57] See Case 29/69 *Stauder* v. *City of Ulm* [1969] ECR 419–30 at 422. It would perhaps have
been more appropriate for the Court to have said, 'yet to be written' rather than
'unwritten'.

[58] This remains a solution for Constitutional Courts of more recently admitted
Member States. See, for instance, Judgment of the Polish Constitutional Court,
11 May 2005, K 18/04, online, available at: www.trybunal.gov.pl/eng/summaries/
documents/K_18_04_GB.pdf.

[59] The now classic critique offered by Jason Coppell and Aidan O'Neill, 'The European
Court of Justice: Taking Rights Seriously', *Common Market Law Review* 29 (1992) 669–92
has maintained that respect for human rights were merely used as a means to
developing integration. But whatever the underlying purpose, my argument is that
human rights were not deployed in accordance with a clearly understood substantive
appreciation of their content or effect.

not formed through an appreciation of the discourse of international human rights. Despite the declaration in *Costa* v. *ENEL* and *van Gend en Loos* that the new legal order created was 'of international law' it was only in *Nold* in 1974 that the Court saw fit to look for specific inspiration in the European Convention on Human Rights, along with other specified 'international treaties'.[60] A plausible conclusion is that the Court relied on Member States' traditions as a priority because they were the ones to be feared. They were the ones most likely to resist the authority of EU law. The ECJ's goal was to remedy the threat rather than to import human rights per se or *tout court*. Human rights discourse as a means to judge the nature and validity of the EU was based on consequence rather than value.

Internationale Handelsgesellschaft made this more explicit by holding that the protection of fundamental rights was to be 'ensured within the framework of the structure and objectives of the Community'.[61] Hence in *Opinion 2/94 on Accession by the Community to the ECHR*, it was held that '[n]o Treaty provision confers on the Community institutions any general power to enact rules on human rights'.[62] A value was ascribed that possessed contingent attributes, rendering it much less a value and more a principle (in line with my definitions).

The way in which respect for human rights were introduced into EU law intimates, therefore, that its foundations were particularly unstable. Since then, various moments have occurred when the cause of fundamental rights have appeared to be expanded. In areas of combating sexual discrimination, in the rights of the defence, in issues of equality, the ECJ has at least recognised the relevance of specific rights. But this recognition hardly amounts to a value-laden interpretation. The Court's approach remains very much in line with the general philosophy initially adopted towards them. Their respect is necessary if the EU is to avoid fundamental challenges through law. The scope of their application is to be determined by the preservation of the EU and, in particular, the constructed internal market. The desire to establish the application of fundamental rights is tempered with the need to ensure the preservation of the autonomy of the Union. There is little room for human rights to be allowed to address suffering other than that which might be experienced, as Damian Chalmers points out, as a result of

---

[60] Case 4/73 *Nold* v. *Commission* [1974] ECR I 491–516.

[61] Case 11/70 *Internationale Handelsgesellschaft* v. *Einfuhr- und Vorratstelle fur Getreide und Futtermittel* [1970] ECR II 1125–55.

[62] *Opinion 2/94 on Accession by the Community to the ECHR* [1996] ECR I-1759, at para. 27.

'external' or 'antithetical' impacts on the EU 'market society'.[63] The approach to asylum seekers and third state nationals, for instance, is 'subject to a managerialist approach' that emphasises the needs of the market above the needs of the individual.[64] Even with the cases of *Omega*[65] and *Schmidberger*[66] and other decisions appearing to favour human rights, there has hardly been a fundamental reappraisal of the role of human rights. The only principle (or in my terms 'virtue') that these cases advanced was that of proportionality, as Chapter 4 set out.

The contingent nature of the ECJ's attitude towards human rights continues to reflect, therefore, their secondary importance as a value.

Similar stories were told with the other values examined. In Chapter 6 we saw that liberty was barely conceived as an independent concept at the EU's inception. Like peace, the pooling of resources was supposed to ensure its preservation and strengthening. But it was not an aim in itself. It was rather a purported, even axiomatic, consequence of the construction of a common market. There was no coherent appreciation of liberty beyond the freedom to fulfil the market-oriented goals of the EU. That made it a very restricted value and hardly one to legitimate the whole EU enterprise and its development beyond market related matters. Whenever the idea of freedom appeared before the ECJ in its initial period it was in the context of the four freedoms that were necessary to give effect to the single market. The economic context was fundamental, not the value of freedom per se. Freedom was to be encouraged *in so far as* it related to achieving the aim of a common market. It had no independent meaning beyond that as an underlying value.

Some commentators suggest that this does not do justice to the unspoken understanding of liberty in the construction of the European vision. This had its roots, so it has been claimed, in the Western liberal imagination of the importance of the autonomy of the individual. Law and society are understood through this individualistic prism. Von Bogdandy has asserted rather grandly that this understanding is by no means imposed by nature, but is rather the 'most important artefact of European history, fundamental for the self-understanding of most

---

[63] Damian Chalmers, 'Political Rights and Political Reason in European Union Law in Times of Stress', in Wojciech Sadurski (ed.), *Political Rights under Stress in 21st Century Europe* (Oxford: Oxford University Press, 2006) 55–83 at 80.

[64] *Ibid.* at 82.

[65] Case C-36/02 *Omega* v. *Bonn* [2004] ECR I-9609.

[66] Case C-112/00 *Schmidberger* v. *Austria* [2003] ECR I-5659.

individuals in the Western world'.[67] The principle of direct effect, as established through *van Gend en Loos*, is offered as a representation of this value introduced into the EU's legal order. But that would be to recognise a very partial picture. That decision was particularly paternalistic if not dictatorial in character. The ECJ noted that,

[t]he nationals of the States brought together in the Community are called upon to cooperate in the functioning of this Community through the intermediary of the European Parliament and the Economic and Social Committee.[68]

It might be suggested that this was a promotion of 'political liberty', emerging from individual participation in the public sphere. But the Court could not seriously have meant this. Reference to the Parliament and the Committee as meaningful participatory processes for nationals in 1963, when *van Gend en Loos* was decided, would have been ironic at best. Even the Parliament at this early stage doubted its own role and validity, as we saw in Chapter 5 when I discussed the issue of democracy.

How else might liberty be interpreted? The Court went on to claim, 'Community law therefore not only imposes obligations on individuals but is also intended to confer upon them rights which become part of their legal heritage'.[69] We might detect from this a different sense of liberty of the individual. But the designation of obligations first and rights second hardly accords with a more libertarian notion. Admittedly it infers that individuals should be free of governmental interference. And in a national context the admission of obligations would flow reasonably naturally from that position, at least in so far as it related to the need for cooperation in the application of coercive laws to guarantee freedom. But this reciprocity was not so apparent when it came to the EU. A political society was not being constructed where participation in governance could ensure that these coercive laws were the product of the peoples of Europe. Liberty could be interpreted as the freedom to act so as to enforce the introduction of a single market, whether this accorded to one's political views or not. The concept was contained not by any appreciation of the wider socio-political context. It would be hard on this basis to see the value of liberty as anything other than a convenient means by which the EU could be policed on a day-to-day basis, enabling individuals to use the four freedoms to implement the single market through litigation.

[67] Bogdandy, 'Constitutional Principles' at 13.
[68] *van Gend en Loos* [1963].   [69] *Ibid.*

This interpretation was further supported when considering other possible attributes of a liberal conception of freedom. The principle of non-discrimination would appear as a vital precondition for the exercise of equal liberty. But although we might be more ready now to see the value of non-discrimination as recognised in EU law, it certainly did not hold such a fundamental place at first. Article 141 EC Treaty (now Article 157 TFEU) may have been the trigger for promoting equal treatment between men and women as regards pay, which has led to significant changes in the reality of equality, but this was constructed for economic reasons not some overarching commitment to a value of non-discrimination. We only have to recall that discrimination on the basis of race or other matters had no part in the original interpretation of *any* provision of the Treaties. Even now that the EU has accepted the need to tackle race discrimination it has not given itself the tools to act effectively in this regard.[70]

Similarly with the four freedoms, it was the 'body of values to be promoted through the creation and regulation of a single market' that were the inspiration for some form of value-orientation in the EU's early period.[71] This does not mean that individuals have not benefited extensively from provisions enabling them to move freely between the Member States to pursue their occupation or business. But to extrapolate from this a value of liberty that possesses deeper ideological connotations would be difficult to sustain. There was no attempt to follow national political notions of the value of freedom. So although the decisions of *Dassonville*[72] and *Cassis de Dijon*[73] may have allowed national interferences with the free movement of goods, for instance, this could only occur in limited and controlled circumstances. As we saw in Chapter 6, political decisions made at a national level through parliamentary processes regarding restrictions to the internal market were only allowed as *exception*. Even then, these exceptional circumstances would only be accepted if the ECJ was convinced that national measures were 'applied in a non-discriminatory manner', were 'justified

---

[70] Bob Hepple, for instance, has criticised the Race Directives by which the Union has set such great store as being 'incapable of redressing collective racial disadvantage', which in turn represents an acute obstruction of freedom of groups such as the Roma. See 'Race and Law in Fortress Europe', *Modern Law Review* 7:1(2004) 1–15 at 4.

[71] M. Poiares Maduro, *We, the Court: The European Court of Justice and the European Economic Constitution* (Oxford: Hart, 1998) at 167.

[72] Case 8/74 *Dassonville* [1974] ECR 837.

[73] Case 120/78 *Cassis de Dijon* [1979] ECR 649.

by imperative requirements in the general interest', were 'suitable for securing the attainment of the objective which they pursue' and would 'not go beyond what is necessary to attain it'.[74] These were all objective tests, ensuring that it was the ECJ which would ultimately decide the validity of the original interest that the Member State sought fit to protect. And the ECJ made clear that it would interpret any derogation from the free movement principles strictly 'so that its scope cannot be determined unilaterally by each Member State without any control by the Community institutions'.[75] The exception of nationally identified 'public policy' could only be relied on 'if there is a genuine and sufficiently serious threat to a fundamental interest of society'.[76] Although diverse interests have been protected on a case-by-case basis the underlying demand for justification demonstrates the way in which the freedom to determine the public good has shifted to the centre. Arguments may be made that are nationally constructed. But it is for the ECJ in the interests of the EU to decide whether they are truly acceptable.

Liberty thus remains fundamentally unconceptualised to any depth in EU law. Even when developing the rhetoric of an 'area of freedom, security and justice' little progress has been made. Claims by the Commission that freedom meant more than the free movement of peoples and included the 'freedom to live in a law-abiding environment in the knowledge that public authorities are using everything in their individual and collective power ... to combat and contain those who seek to deny or abuse that freedom' hardly clarified the matter.[77] Indeed, when it went on to address immigration, asylum and the integration of non-Union nationals under the heading of freedom, the thinness of the concept in the EU's hands became more apparent. There is little plausible philosophical underpinning offered here that would assist in the development of a clearer notion of this value.

The same could be said for the value of democracy but with significantly greater emphasis. We have seen how the ECJ was very willing to assume that the identification of a Parliament and other institutions was sufficient to consider the EU as imbued with some kind of

---

[74] Case C-55/94 *Gebhard* v. *Consiglio dell'Ordine degli Avvocati e Procuratori di Milano* [1995] ECR I-4565 para. 37.

[75] See *Omega* para. 30. See also Case 41/74 *Van Duyn* v. *Home Office* [1974] ECR 1337 para 18 and Case 30/77 *Bouchereau* [1977] ECR 1999, para. 33.

[76] See for instance Case C-54/99 *Église de Scientologie* [2000] ECR I-1335, para. 17.

[77] Commission, Communication 'Towards an Area of Freedom, Security and Justice' COM (1998) 459 final at 5.

democratic credentials. This was an assumption without substance. It was only in *SA Roquette Frères* v. *Council* in 1980, after the political endorsement of universal suffrage for the Parliament, that the Court began with any conviction to refer to 'the fundamental democratic principle that the peoples should take part in the exercise of power through the intermediary of a representative assembly'.[78] Chapter 5 showed that before then, the integration of the value of democracy was largely rhetorical. Although the EU could talk politically of the necessity of democracy as a value adhered to by all its Member States, and which would be a necessary condition for accession to the EU, this did not translate into a meaningful application of any but the most minor democratic processes.

Now we are faced with vaguely desperate attempts either to read democratic principles that are of any note into notions of EU citizenship or to support some kind of public space based on the twin notions of participation and transparency. In both cases the Court's attempts to develop the value has been weak. And in both cases the only plausible, if not effective, approach has been through individual rights. Even then matters of participation and transparency largely depend on highly controlled methods of interaction between public and institutions, as we saw in Chapter 5, or, at best, rights possibly enforceable through expensive, restricted and time-consuming individual litigation. And as for citizenship, rights are determined on an exclusionary basis so that only nationals of Member States can enjoy their protection.[79] The ECJ may be developing a 'sensitivity towards collective identity as part of individuals' lives' through the EU as *gemeinschaft* but those cases, allowing access to welfare benefits and supporting free movement provisions, hardly offer a new form of meaningful participatory or representative democracy, one that would suggest people are more than superficially engaged in the construction of policy at the European level.[80] Rather, the development of citizenship through jurisprudence

---

[78] Case 138/79 *SA Roquette Frères* v. *Council of the European Communities* [1980] ECR 3333 para. 33.

[79] See, for instance, Case C-184/99 *Grzelczyk* [2001] ECR I-6193 at para. 31. Samantha Besson and André Utzinger claim that 'the progressive shift from nationality to residence *qua* criterion of European citizenship rights has entrenched undue discriminations between nationals, European non-nationals, and non-European non-nationals in each Member State'. See 'Toward European Citizenship', *Journal of Social Philosophy* 39:2 (2008) 185–208 at 201.

[80] See Ulrich Haltern, 'On Finality', in A. von Bogdandy and Jürgen Bast (eds.), *Principles of European Constitutional Law* (Oxford: Hart, 2006) 727–64 at 759.

is a way of compensating individuals for the lack of democratic opportunity and perhaps even accountability evident in the EU.

What then of the rule of law? Might this be presented as possessing more substance? Chapter 3 demonstrated that although there were areas where the ECJ was able to develop a thicker conception, invariably there remain fields in which it has no jurisdiction to enter. One may be able to sustain an argument that virtues associated with the rule of law (separation of powers, right to judicial review for instance) were inherent in the EU legal system. However, huge gaps in jurisdiction mean that this is a highly contestable claim. At the very least, a contradiction between those virtues adopted and those such as consistency, clarity, etc., which were ignored for political reasons, is apparent. The implication is that the rule of law was again initially conceived as a process of ordering in the EU not as the expression of a value. Its content was only explored as an afterthought, and one that was even then poorly explored through the limited opportunities presented to the ECJ.

In sum, although one can demonstrate an improvement in the application and appreciation of values through EU law over time, in general there remains a significant and debilitating ambivalence towards each of them. They have all suffered from a foundation and application that has denied their specific applicability and development. Subsequent value articulation, bereft generally of political and constitutional definition as well as variable and contingent support, has meant that these salient values remain incapable of providing any form of plausible ethical core that would counter the debilitating indeterminacy inhabiting the EU terrain. In particular, there is little to suppose that EU law operates as an effective restraint on power, whether that is exercised by sovereign Member States *or* the institutions constructed by them. None of the values are sufficiently solid in their legal expression to provide such a bulwark. Zygmunt Bauman comments that 'one of the most conspicuous features of European identity was always the tendency to run after identity, while it stays stubbornly well ahead of its pursuers'.[81] This is the same for the pursuit of values both generally and through law. The only difference is that the pursuers operate with halters around their necks, which drag them down each time to a functional rather than inspirational or emancipatory appreciation of

---

[81] Zygmunt Bauman, *Europe: an Unfinished Adventure* (Cambridge: Polity Press, 2004) at 124.

the EU they intend to promote. Values cannot turn the EU into a project that owns a deeper meaning or a more attractive identity in such an environment. They are too constrained and too indeterminate to enhance any sense of public or general political loyalty. The argument that such indeterminacy represents a means by which diversity can be accommodated is naïve. If the very values are so contingent as a matter of policy then claims to commonality and community through those values have to be suspect.

Proposition 4: the current philosophy of EU law and the absence of 'justice'

This brings me to my *fourth* proposition. The central condition of indeterminacy with contingent and weak value definition and application suggests that the existing philosophy of EU law as apparent in the ECJ's jurisprudence rests upon a *theory of interpretation* which excludes anything other than a weak or diaphanously thin notion of justice. The varying political climate and structure of the Union is interpreted through a very narrow prism so as to give effect to the Treaties. But what the Treaties are supposed to achieve remains subject to constant political negotiation. Conscious of this, the ECJ has displayed an approach of applying the best possible interpretation so as to avoid conflict and preserve the primacy of EU law as a means of ensuring the EU's continuing existence. I suggest one can go so far as to propose that a virtue has been made of *indeterminacy* in EU law through the adoption of a second order of principles such as those of subsidiarity, respect for diversity, flexibility and multi-level governance. It has only peripherally become imbued with a defined and understandable ethical framework.

   This underlying philosophy accepts the environment that has been created on the basis that it is not for law to interfere with the political settlement. Law's role is to give effect to the Treaties that brought it into being without attempting to impose some presumed scheme of original common values that might in turn affect the contracted aims of the EU. Interpretation is the nature of law's response, a reflection of indeterminacy. How indeed can European law impose values upon a politically agreed construction that continues to change over time, remaining fundamentally ill-defined, without in effect altering the nature of those politics? Fearful of affecting the delicate political balance evident in the EU, the ECJ has reacted by focusing on a common denominator; the simple reading of the texts as they appear without imputing any strong version of values that, ironically, are otherwise used in political rhetoric. Those values that have been recognised as fundamental (at least for the purpose of membership of the Union) are interpreted as principles and constrained accordingly. They are also interpreted narrowly so as to preserve the one substantive and constant aim to construct and maintain a common market.

How might this approach be assessed? It is plausible to suggest that this philosophy is based on a rather strange interpretation of *grundnorm*. Hans Kelsen proposed that all legal systems operated with a basic norm as its foundation. He judged that a legal order was

a system of norms whose unity is constituted by the fact that they all have the same reason for their validity. And the reason for the validity of a normative order is a basic norm … from which the validity of all norms of the order are derived.[82]

Trevor Hartley has argued strongly against assuming that the Treaties can in any way provide that *grundnorm*.[83] Without following Kelsen, he notes that the Treaties are based on an agreement between states that is subject to international law. The *grundnorm*, therefore, does not rest within the Treaties but with the norms that underpin international law (the most prominent of which for Hartley being state sovereignty). Indeed, the case of *Humblet* in 1960 identified the principle of *pacta sunt servanda* as a good reason for developing the primacy of EU law.[84] Contrary to this view, however, I argue that EU law has been developed jurisprudentially on the *assumption* that the Treaties are a political representation of a different *grundnorm* having been created for the purposes of bringing into being a new legal order. That basic norm was a presupposed original constitution that saw the survival of Europe (in particular the sovereign states of France and what was left of Germany) through one lens: the preservation of a capitalist economic system. This positively ignored any sophisticated sense of justice on the basis that other interpretations would have moved the EU away from survival to the adoption of a (potentially) contradictory theory of society, something which might have jeopardised that survival provoking as it no doubt would have done the very ideological conflict it was in part

---

[82] Hans Kelsen, *Pure Theory of Law* (New Jersey: The Lawbook Exchange, 2002) at 31.

[83] Trevor Hartley, 'The Constitutional Foundations of the European Union', in Paul Craig and Richard Rawlings (eds.), *Law and Administration in Europe: Essays in Honour of Carol Harlow* (Oxford: Oxford University Press, 2003) 175–95.

[84] Case 6/60 *Humblet v. Belgium* [1960] ECR 559.

designed to resist. The EC Treaty, validated by this necessity of survival *in extremis* through the mechanism of a common market was thus a product of the perceived basic norm.

Whether plausible or not, the *grundnorm* of survival through economic integration provided the basis for the legal system to develop accordingly. So although EU law may well have been devised under the understanding that Member States are the ultimate guarantors of whatever constitution one might infer from the Treaties, a legal system has been constructed with the clear determination that sovereignty has been given up, albeit only in restricted areas, for the purposes of fulfilling the basic norm. The latter is indeed the presupposition of the former.

The implication of this condition is that a new legal system has been created. Much as we would look at a basic norm constructed for the law of a new state, for instance one emerging after the trauma of world war or colonial rule, we could do the same for the EU. The ECJ's proclamation of a new legal order of international law, since transformed in its eyes into a constitutional order in *Les Verts* thus dropping the international label,[85] suggests that an independent system that has its own *grundnorm* has been erected. The theory of interpretation underpinning the philosophy of EU law, therefore, requires all values adopted to inform but not override the *grundnorm*.

A highly constrained interpretation of values in EU law becomes understandable in this light. In an attempt to impose certainty on an otherwise volatile environment (which incidentally does not necessarily reflect a *political* appreciation of the *grundnorm* of the legal system), EU law, as developed by the Court, has kept strict control over all those values that have emerged as necessary elements of a legitimate polity in the contemporary era. Whether these have been identified through the amendment of the Treaties or from an awareness of values purportedly held in common amongst Member States' legal systems, all have been adopted with the *grundnorm* as the contingent delineator. We see this no more spectacularly than in the case of respect for fundamental rights, though we could make an equivalent example of freedom, democracy, the rule of law, or any other value expression. In each case, values have been re-interpreted as limited principles or even virtues that do not challenge or undermine the *grundnorm*. Any tensions have been resolved by ensuring these values are developed with

---

[85] Case 294/83 *Les Verts* v. *Parliament* [1986] ECR 1339.

limited meaning. Consequently, the philosophy of EU law presents a very muted appreciation of justice through values.

We might also discern in this current philosophy some Austinian characteristics. For it adheres to an approach that sees law as a tool of government, the aim of which is to impose order so as to achieve some form of common 'good'. The underlying assumption is that this common good is fundamentally structured around the establishment of a common market. That has always been the certainty deemed apparent in an otherwise uncertain environment. Everything, therefore, revolves around that postulate notwithstanding strong rhetoric suggesting additional aims such as the preservation of peace. And whether explicitly or implicitly in all questions that law is asked to resolve this is accepted as the essential fact of the EU. No substitute has been provided despite all the language and practice associated with the discovery and implementation of values. When ethical issues are addressed in EU law, they are always constrained by this assumption. What is considered 'just' is determined ultimately by reference to the *grundnorm*. Even where the Court decides to put aside the interests of the internal market for the benefit of a general principle, this is only done by way of exception. And the exception is defined invariably by reference to the internal market *not* to other values.

The most important consequence of such a diagnosis is the evaluation that whatever else the ECJ may have done, particularly through its development of general principles, it has singularly failed to countenance 'justice' as a clear ethical commitment in its own right. Its absence as a principle in Article 6(1) TEU and the tepid reference to it in the Constitutional and Lisbon Treaties confirms an underlying reluctance politically and legally to debate and define what justice might mean in and for the EU. By avoiding a correlation between its project, justice and law, any confrontation with the EU's capacity both to do justice and to be unjust has been largely avoided. The philosophy of EU law is conditioned accordingly.

This is not a matter confined to public law issues. We can see the same problems surface in recent attempts to construct a 'Draft Common Frame of Reference (DCFR) for Principles, Definitions and Model Rules of European Private Law'.[86] Reinhard Zimmerman *et al.*

---

[86] C. von Bar, E. Clive and H. Schulte-Nölke and H. Beale, J. Herre, J. Huet, P. Schlechtriem, M. Storme, S. Swann, P. Varul, A. Veneziano and F. Zoll, 'Principles, Definitions and Model Rules of European Private Law: Draft Common Frame of Reference: Interim Outline Edition' (Munich: Sellier, 2008).

heavily criticised the 'vague' approach to values within this document, suggesting that it 'contains a hotchpotch of diverse aims and underlying values which are neither precisely defined individually nor as regards their relation to one another'.[87] But the drafters were perhaps no more than reflecting the general philosophy of EU law that I have described above.[88]

Proposition 5: the prospects of philosophical regeneration through adjudication

We might despair of the future for the EU if the above sequential argument is accepted. For surely, a polity governed by a legal system based on a philosophy that eschews justice in its formulation will be unlikely to survive in the long term, particularly when faced with extreme tensions. Then the ethical hollowness of the enterprise may be exposed. But is it possible to change this philosophical condition? My *fifth* proposition responds negatively but only in so far as it claims that the ECJ is *not* capable of re-directing its own philosophy through a process of adjudication. Although rights might be taken seriously within the jurisprudence of the Court (and this is a dubious claim in itself), it does not have the will to do the same for other values. Support for this argument can be found by a brief demonstration of how change is unlikely to materialise from jurisprudence. The case of *Kadi* not only illustrates how deep the appreciation of the supposed *grundnorm* has infected the philosophy of EU law (again in the particular area of fundamental rights) but also demonstrates the limited resistance to it and, ultimately, the way in which it is reinforced.[89]

Kadi concerned the Council's imposition of a regulation (Council Regulation No 881/2002) implementing certain resolutions of the UN Security Council in applying specific restrictive measures to the applicant, amongst others, purportedly associated with Usama bin Laden, the Al-Qaeda network and the Taliban. The applicant claimed that this

---

[87] Reinhard Zimmermann, Horst Eidenmüller, Florian Faust, Hans Christoph Grigoleit, Nils Jansen and Gerhard Wagner, 'The Common Frame of Reference for European Private Law – Policy Choices and Codification Problems', *Oxford Journal of Legal Studies* 28:4 (2008) 659–708.

[88] I would like to thank Ewan McKendrick for bringing this particular issue to my attention and also to Hugh Beale for comments on the process by which this element of the DCFR came about.

[89] Conjoined cases C-402/05 P and C-415/05 P *Yassin Abdullah Kadi and Al Barakaat International Foundation* v. *Council* Judgment of the Court (Grand Chamber) 3 September 2008.

regulation breached fundamental rights under European law. We have already seen earlier in this chapter that Advocate General Maduro suggested that the priority of the ECJ was 'to preserve the constitutional framework created by the Treaty'.[90] He then went on to state that 'the Court cannot, in deference to the views of those institutions, turn its back on the fundamental values that lie at the basis of the Community legal order and which it has the duty to protect'.[91] The standards of review should still apply and should not be changed merely because certain extreme circumstances were purportedly in place. AG Maduro's opinion both reaffirmed the sanctity of the EU legal order whilst at the same time promoting the importance and predominance of the application of fundamental values. On the face of it, this might suggest an alteration in the philosophy of EU law. At least it could be used as the basis both for greater respect being paid to values and for how they should be considered when they conflict with each other. But such an optimistic interpretation fails to resolve the fundamental conditions of EU law that I have described. There are still significant constitutional restrictions on the application of values. The Court is not free to develop them. AG Maduro recognises this by inference in the following passage of his Opinion:

There is no reason … for the Court to depart, in the present case, from its usual interpretation of the fundamental rights that have been invoked by the appellant. The only novel question is whether the concrete needs raised by the prevention of international terrorism justify restrictions on the fundamental rights of the appellant that would otherwise not be acceptable. This does not entail a different conception of those fundamental rights and the applicable standard of review. It simply means that the weight to be given to the different interests which are always to be balanced in the application of the fundamental rights at issue may be different as a consequence of the specific needs arising from the prevention of international terrorism. But this is to be assessed in a normal exercise of judicial review by this Court. The present circumstances may result in a different balance being struck among the values involved in the protection of fundamental rights but the standard of protection afforded by them ought not to change.

In other words, the current restrictions on the interpretation of fundamental rights should pertain. We find this condition reaffirmed in

---

[90] *Kadi* v. *Council and Commission* Opinion of AG Maduro at para. 24. See, also *Opinion 2/94* [1996] ECR I1759 para. 30, 34 and 35.

[91] *Kadi* v. *Council and Commission* Opinion of AG Maduro para. 44.

the ECJ's subsequent ruling. It re-established the EU's legal system as autonomous, stating

an international agreement cannot affect the allocation of powers fixed by the Treaties or, consequently, the autonomy of the Community legal system, observance of which is ensured by the Court by virtue of the exclusive jurisdiction conferred on it by Article 220 EC, jurisdiction that the Court has, moreover, already held to form part of the very foundations of the Community.[92]

It went on to conclude that any of

the obligations imposed by an international agreement cannot have the effect of prejudicing the constitutional principles of the EC Treaty, which include the principle that all Community acts must respect fundamental rights, that respect constituting a condition of their lawfulness which it is for the Court to review in the framework of the complete system of legal remedies established by the Treaty.[93]

The integrity of the EU legal system remained the paramount consideration. Any systemic problems, vis-à-vis values as applied through principles, could not be satisfactorily addressed by the Court alone. So for all the significance of the Court's ruling in *Kadi*, that rights had been infringed, there has been no real substantive change. What else could the Court have done given its philosophical approach to date? The only indication of a possible shift towards values occurs almost in an oblique fashion. The ECJ stated that Article 297 EC Treaty (now Article 347 TFEU), which allows for Member States to take measures interfering with the functioning of the common market (on restricted grounds including 'to carry out obligations … for the purpose of maintaining peace and international security') cannot 'authorise any derogation from the principles of liberty, democracy and respect for human rights and fundamental freedoms enshrined in Article 6(1) EU as a foundation of the Union'.[94] The consequences of such a preference for values were certainly not explored by the Court. And it is doubtful whether the implications were really considered. Although we might be able to privilege respect for human rights accordingly, how would, for instance, 'democracy' (given the vague and ambiguous relationship EU law has with such a concept) be protected by the

---

[92] Conjoined cases C-402/05 P and C-415/05 P *Yassin Abdullah Kadi and Al Barakaat International Foundation* v. *Council* Judgment of the Court (Grand Chamber) 3 September 2008 para. 282.

[93] *Ibid.* para. 285.   [94] *Ibid.* para. 303.

Court in any reasonably foreseeable circumstances? Was this merely a rhetorical flourish that in practice would produce little in the way of adjudicated justice?

The Court's determination to reinforce principles of human rights in the highly charged and politicised arena of anti-terrorism activity may suggest a willingness to place this particular value closer to the heart of the system but ultimately, the judicature is not in a position to alter the current systemic dynamics through individual decisions such as this. EU law, even with respect for certain values noted within it, cannot be amended judicially from within given the predominant operative philosophy. Without really coming to grips with how justice can be framed within a scheme of values (something that is unlikely to arise without a radical constitutional settlement I would suggest) the whole EU edifice will remain affected by the unresolved condition of ethical indeterminacy. The likelihood of the Court addressing this condition on its own initiative is slim. One cannot really expect otherwise given the history of its apparent philosophy of EU law.

Conclusion

The purpose of this chapter has been to provoke a reconsideration of why the EU's institutional ethos (and its integral philosophy of EU law) appears incapable of a meaningful appreciation of values. My approach has been to consider the nature of both so as to demonstrate a plausible reason why this is so. The conclusion I reach is ultimately condemnatory. It is that any meaningful sense of justice (beyond a narrow form of 'economistic justice') has been, in large part, ignored and at best maintained as a secondary matter in the construction of both the institutional ethos and EU law. There may be very good reasons for this. But whatever those reasons may be the implications for the development of the EU and its law are significant. Without any developed notion of justice underpinning the philosophy of EU law I suggest this cannot change. Legitimacy will continue to be elusive thus undermining even the limited aims for systemic survival that have developed. Certainly at times of crisis, whether in relation to issues of security or economic hardship (as we are discovering), there is little to fall back on through law to guide the EU's decision-making. By relying on a functional interpretation of purpose, values have not been taken seriously.

The question now is whether an alternative approach as a first step towards constructing a more just institution, can be achieved in the context of the EU and its current law? This is the great constitutional question for the EU today and one which the study of EU law should not ignore. The ECJ's judgment in *Kadi*, as well as other recent jurisprudence, suggests that the Court is not averse to considering such a move. It might even welcome it. But EU law in general and the Court in particular remain too constrained by the historically developed philosophy to effect any change in their own right. That is not to say EU law cannot be used as a conduit for change. But this will require consideration of how a revised philosophy of EU law can be developed to reflect a 'moral politics' that takes values and justice more seriously and thus alter the nature of the institutional ethos as a whole. How this might be done is the subject of my final two chapters.

8 Towards the EU as a just institution

Introduction

The book has been largely diagnostic up to this point. It has examined those salient values declared as fundamental in the EU. It has analysed how they have been applied and articulated institutionally. And it has provided an interpretation of the philosophy of law and the institutional ethos in this context. The conclusion I reached in the previous chapter was that an indeterminacy of value definition and appreciation prevails. Justice is absent as a coherent institutional theme. And the EU has suffered in any claim to being a 'just institution' as a result.

Of course, I have taken it as axiomatic that the EU *should* become (or improve as) a 'just' institution. But this seems to me a reasonable inference when we contemplate the extent to which the EU assumes sovereign powers from its Member States, how its law impacts upon its constituents, and how its policies and actions affect the lives and expectations of a multitude of people within and outside its borders. So long as this remains the case we cannot reasonably ignore questions of justice in relation to the EU. By extension, we cannot avoid assessing the Union in terms of its qualities as a just institution-in-being or in-the-making. If we do, its legitimacy will always be in question. The threat of an institution developing that is predisposed to tyranny (or at best a disregard for justice in its operations) will embed itself as a severe and perhaps debilitating critique. Despite this apparent danger, one which in truth has been recognised by numerous individuals in the EU institutions over the years, my analysis suggests there has been a persistent failure to take values seriously. No clear understanding of how values may be adopted and applied has been evident either in political or legal judgment. And no coherent account of justice has been adopted institutionally. Even with all the rhetoric emanating from the EU and extensive academic good will towards the Union, such failure suggests the EU is presently *not* a sufficiently just institution. This, in turn, can only serve to undermine any claims as to its moral legitimacy whatever evidence of political or economic effectiveness or efficiency there may be.

How might this condition be remedied? The remainder of the book is devoted to this question. My starting point is to focus on resolving the present inadequate account of justice, which I claim is apparent in the philosophy of EU law and the institutional ethos as a whole. If the EU is to address the indeterminacy of its fundamental values there needs to be clarity about how they can be incorporated into a plausible theory of justice. For we need to know on what basis the EU can be reconstructed to ensure justice becomes a cohering and directing institutional theme. In other words, how the institutional ethos can be altered so as to place an acceptable notion of justice at its core.

This does not require, at least initially, a complete theory of justice for the EU to be presented. However, it does necessitate clarity about some of the groundwork that might be required for such a theory to be negotiated, politically adopted and publicly accepted. What are the basic premises, in other words, which need to be endorsed institutionally to underpin a consensus about justice in the EU? The particular purpose of this penultimate chapter, therefore, is to put forward a series of assumptions upon which, I argue, agreement will be necessary if a more substantial appreciation of justice within the institutional ethos is to be realised. Providing a vision of how that might be achieved I then leave to the final chapter.

Nine assumptions for an account of justice for the EU

What key assumptions, then, are necessary to construct a plausible account of justice for the EU? My approach to this question is to conjoin the philosophical methods of considering the matter in the abstract *and* in the particular context of the EU in its evolved form. By doing so, my aim is to appreciate the possible application of general principles of justice that might plausibly be applicable for a regional inter-state cooperative enterprise *and* to recognise the importance of building on the specific normative practices and understandings of the 'community' that the EU represents. This is a balance intended, on the one hand, to avoid charges of ethnocentrism that might easily arise if we only talk about the shared values of 'Europe',[1] and, on the other, to acknowledge that justice will only take root if it finds some connection with a community's moral understanding.[2] It also responds to Philip Allott's diagnosis that a vital task for the future of the EU is to 'integrate the philosophical and practical problem of the self-constituting of European society with the philosophical and practical problem of the globalising of human society'.[3] This seems to me to be an appropriate means by which we can usefully begin to talk about justice in the EU context.

With this in mind, I propose nine inter-related assumptions upon which a coherent account of justice for the EU might be constructed. I will state each briefly before addressing them individually in greater detail. The nine assumptions are:

First, some form of *cooperation* between states and peoples (beyond the simple coordination of activities) within a proximate geographical area for the purpose of attaining some common good and solving particular common problems is a plausible and desirable venture to pursue. The EU as currently formed represents one such venture.

Second, the construction of some form of institutional framework would be a plausible and reasonable response to manage such a regional cooperative venture. The EU currently possesses such a framework. This is *sui generis* in character, neither a super-state nor a pure international agreement between states.

Third, any regional cooperative venture and accompanying institutional framework, including the EU, is a proper and plausible location for substantive as well as formal (or procedural) justice to apply.

Fourth, any regional cooperative venture should possess the characteristics of a *primary* as well as a *secondary* agent for justice. The EU has already taken on characteristics of both.

Fifth, the expression of a suitable and coherent account of substantive justice, outlining how chosen values, principles and virtues should govern the actions of any regional cooperative venture, would be a

---

[1] This is a particular danger highlighted by Onora O'Neill in *Bounds of Justice* (Cambridge: Cambridge University Press, 2000).

[2] David Miller's work in particular is relevant here. See, in particular, 'Two Ways to Think about Justice', *Politics, Philosophy and Economics* 1 (2002) 5–28 where Miller argues that a contextual approach does not necessarily mean a form of relativism should be applied to justice.

[3] Philip Allott, *The Health of Nations: Society and Law Beyond the State* (Cambridge: Cambridge University Press, 2002) at 262.

plausible means by which any adopted institutional framework could operate. Although this book has revealed a wealth of rhetoric emerging from and about the EU with regard to values and principles, the institutional ethos has, however, failed so far to reflect a coherent narrative of justice applicable to the EU's operations.

Sixth, any plausible account of justice should accept that it is not feasible for all and every value promoted by the multiple constituents of any regional cooperative venture to be realised. A selection of appropriate values has to be made, something the EU has failed to do effectively.

Seventh, any plausible account of justice should adapt rather than revolt against any existing institutional ethos that may exist where, as in the case of the EU, a regional cooperative venture has already been in operation for some time and, at least rhetorically, has accepted the applicability of values that might reasonably be associated with justice.

Eighth, any plausible account of justice for a regional cooperative venture such as the EU should, by its very nature, be both outward and inward looking, capable of reflecting internal and external demands for justice. The institutions of the EU have embraced this demand through its constitution and practice but in an incoherent and contradictory (if not ironic) way.

Ninth, where any regional cooperative venture deploys law as a means of coercion in achieving and maintaining that cooperation, a philosophy of law should be adopted (in adjudication and legislation) that reflects the need for justice to be the predominant theme in decision-making. Given the relationship between the EU's philosophy of law and the institutional ethos it would be reasonable to suppose that a re-conceptualisation of such philosophy will help induce a re-conceptualisation of the ethos.

I will now examine each of these in a little more detail whilst relating them explicitly to the EU as I go.

First assumption: the EU as a regional cooperative inter-state venture

It cannot, of course, be a universal truth that the invention of the EU was and remains a necessary, let alone desirable, development of cooperation in the history of Europe. Many commentators and politicians would dispute my first assumption on this basis. Those who have examined the EU and berate its distant bureaucratic tendencies, its undemocratic credentials, its potential for corrupt practices,[4] its relentless emphasis on market economics, its capacity to appear impotent in the face of crises,[5] its technocratic impersonal nature, and its ability to interfere in the lives of individuals in apparently petty and irrational ways, have some cause to argue that this entity is not inherently a 'good thing'. But whatever the strength of these critiques, and indeed whatever the strength of my own critical judgment throughout this book, it remains a reasonable assumption that some kind of cooperative venture in Europe, which constructs a continental regime transcending the nation-state and playing on the principle that 'we' should live together cooperatively rather than in various states of isolation, is a plausible and desirable enterprise to pursue.

A distinction needs to be made here between an international 'cooperative' and 'coordinated' venture. The former I take to arise when we move from 'merely socially coordinated activity', as John Rawls has termed it, to a deeper association between peoples and states.[6] In other words, once we extend simple international agreements for mutual benefit to more sophisticated arrangements designed to achieve a 'common good', the venture represents an engagement with ethical commitments.[7] Cooperation then implies the development of an international *community* or even society which recognises and accepts a sense of solidarity transcending borders. We do not have to adopt a cosmopolitan account here to make this claim. Rather, it reflects those varied theories of global justice which prioritise a 'conception of the purpose of social cooperation that focuses on fellowship as well as on mutual advantage'.[8] A moral dimension stretching across national boundaries and designed to embrace a certain responsibility for those beyond one's immediate community is, therefore, presupposed in this meaning of cooperation. It assumes a notion of justice that is not contained by its social form, meaning that applied within a community

---

[4] The classic account of this possibility, if not reality, is Bernard Connolly, *Rotten Heart of Europe: the Dirty War for Europe's Money* (London: Faber and Faber, 2001).

[5] Internally, the lack of cohesion when faced with de Gaulle's absent chair policy, the Jorge Haider affair in Austria, the BSE crisis, and the complicity in extraordinary rendition have been charted in various places in this book. Similarly, externally, the Balkans wars, Iraq, Georgia, and the Israeli–Palestinian conflict have all exposed failures to act in concert when such an approach might have been expected of a suitably functioning cooperative enterprise.

[6] See John Rawls, *Political Liberalism* (New York: Columbia University Press, 2005) at 16.

[7] *Ibid.*

[8] Martha Nussbaum, *Frontiers of Justice: Disability, Nationality, Species Membership* (Cambridge, MA: Harvard University Press, 2007) at 227.

(even of states), but also incorporates its global form, where some sense of responsibility for the 'other' is acknowledged.

Of course, this understanding does not accord with some definitions of international cooperation. Robert Keohane, for instance, has maintained that 'altruism, idealism ... common purposes, internalized norms, or a shared belief in a set of values embedded in a culture' are not necessary for international cooperation to occur.[9] But this is a matter of terminology. It does not mean that an association adopting these characteristics is undesirable. Indeed, my use of the term 'cooperation' is to signify, contrary to Keohane, a position where a 'society of peoples or states' is constructed with an ethical dimension. This is not to say that political or economic coordinated arrangements could not achieve various acceptable forms of harmonious relations between states and peoples. These may well aim only to fulfil the particular interests of individual states. A strong case could be made that the originally constructed EEC was one such arrangement, in so far as it focused on an initially weak market-regulatory system rather than addressing non-economic factors of well-being. But my assumption is that cooperation beyond the level of the state, which entails the adoption of a moral dimension requiring the construction of appropriate moral principles, is welcome.

The central idea of European union, as articulated by one strand of European political philosophy stretching back at least to Abbé de Saint Pierre, Immanuel Kant, Jean-Jacques Rousseau and others and reflected in the contemporary neo-functionalists,[10] is based implicitly on this appreciation. The building of an enduring peace through a community of economic and wider integration from which would flow a deeper social, cultural, and political interdependence for the benefit of constituent states and peoples, has endured as a general vision for the EU. One cannot doubt, however, that this vision may be deemed *undesir-able* for all sorts of reasons. Many ideological perspectives recoil from any moral commitment other than to one's own citizens or community. But that does not make the idea of a European cooperative venture implausible. The key claim that the attainment of mutual benefit with corresponding mutual responsibilities beyond the economic (with peace at the forefront of this expansive ambition) should be a goal for

[9] Robert Keohane, *International Institutions and State Power: Essays in International Relations Theory* (Boulder, CO: Westview Press, 1989) at 159.

[10] The idea of European union has been charted in, for instance, Denis de Rougemont, *The Idea of Europe* (New York: Macmillan, 1966).

relations between states and their peoples, remains a reasonable, if not necessary, proposition. Whether the reality of economic crisis, environmental degradation and climate change, the impoverishment of many throughout the world, fears over security, crime, or drugs, demand a cooperative venture is perhaps beside the point. These factors may enhance the assumption but they are not strictly necessary to support it.

It is, however, another matter whether such a cooperative venture should be geographically defined. There is always a danger that global justice demands, for instance, may be threatened by regional cooperation as a result of those manifestations of exclusion that can accompany such a venture. Even though internal social justice issues may be adequately addressed, any moral commitment beyond borders could be ignored. Critiques of 'fortress Europe', for instance, speak to this possibility, engaging fears not only of 'keeping people out' but also of the projection of values that alienate those who are not deemed 'European' even though they live there. The dangers also extend to a failing to appreciate the impact of collective action on those outside the cooperative arrangement.

Nonetheless, it is plausible that a regional entity need not necessarily contravene the moral commitment I presuppose for cooperation. Indeed, it would seem plausible to recognise that if local variation and plurality in general is to be respected within an efficient and effective supranational enterprise then some form of geographical limit is at present inevitable. It does not follow that global institutions are either unnecessary or undesirable. Rather, as we have not reached such an advanced stage of social and political development that global institutions can fulfil all the demands of justice placed upon them, regional cooperative ventures have much to contribute. Constructing a cooperative venture to cope with the potential burdens and benefits of justice within and beyond a defined geographical area, such as Europe (or any other area for that matter), seems justifiable in this context. Various practical constraints will influence the efficacy of any particular arrangement but the identification of benefits will also determine its desirability.

This first assumption can be supported from a number of perspectives of political philosophy. These vary between ideal visions and empirical observations of European cooperation. Often the two forms of argument are fused if not confused. The ideal is often inferred from the realisation of what has already been achieved. The empirical is frequently assessed in comparison to what more could be achieved. In both respects, certain 'facts' that purportedly reflect original aims are deduced as indicators of current and future value. Invariably they focus on the absence of war between the Member States of the Union *and* the development of the economy of the EU since its inception. Of course, these 'facts' of peace and prosperity are not indisputably down to the existence of the EU.[11] But they are presented as strong indicators to suggest that it has had an important role to play in both. Other value-based arguments, such as efficiency (of markets or even international relations), effectiveness (in delivering policies that are transnational in character or coordinating collective actions in response to actual and perceived threats that relate to economic or societal security), or those that might attach to the values considered in this book, are also premised on the idea that the EU as a cooperative venture has enhanced those value positions and can continue to do so.[12]

Other more ideologically-led justifications for the EU are also prevalent. Many of these appear in the guise of cosmopolitanism. Here we see an approach to political philosophy that attempts to construct an ideal set of general principles for a cooperative vehicle for inter-state relations and see in the EU their potential application. It is perhaps best summed up by Ulrich Beck and Edgar Grande who recount their approach in terms of the 'reality of Europe' and advocate for 'a cosmopolitan union of Europe, in opposition to the false normativity of the national'.[13] 'Cosmopolitan Europe' they continue, 'is a Europe which struggles morally, politically, economically and historically for *reconciliation*'.[14] It incorporates 'a cosmopolitan legal ethics' that 'completely inverts relations of priority, so that the principles of cosmopolitan law *trump* national law'.[15] The argument that Beck and Grande advance supports the contention that the EU as a cooperative venture is plausible *and* desirable whether or not it adequately takes that form at present.

---

[11] See J.H.H. Weiler, *The Constitution of Europe* (Cambridge: Cambridge University Press, 1999).

[12] Samantha Besson considers some of the claims for the EU as an institution of global justice in 'The European Union and Human Rights: Towards a New Kind of Post-National Human Rights Institution', *Human Rights Law Review* 6:2 (2006) 323–60.

[13] Ulrich Beck and Edgar Grande, *Cosmopolitan Europe* (Cambridge: Polity Press, 2007) at 167.

[14] *Ibid*. at 168.   [15] *Ibid*. at 170.

Equally, the proposition would be supported by some philosophers who have adopted a Kantian perspective. Seyla Benhabib is a notable advocate in this respect.[16] And it is no surprise that she has used the example of the EU to provide a concrete demonstration of how aspects of cosmopolitan vision might be realised in practice.[17]

Of course, as I have indicated, counter-arguments can be, and have been, raised. Many have been fashioned along the lines of the EU's failure to establish a convincing account of its own legitimacy beyond the economic. But invariably these arguments do not deny the possibility of *a* European union with governing institutions as an ethical enterprise of some kind capable of addressing demands of justice. Rather, the talk is of institutional 'transformation' that is formulated once agreement is reached 'on the spirit of a future Europe'[18] or patience in waiting for Europe to develop a *demos* that will eventually create the basis for federation.[19] All of these critiques are still premised on the value of a regional cooperative venture of some description. They are in turn reflected in the EU's institutional rhetoric which has emphasised a principle of solidarity. This is based on the conceit that states have agreed to cooperate to achieve common goods and to operate within some ethical constraints (even if state self-interest might be a key motivating issue for that agreement).

Despite the philosophical and institutional support for my first assumption there can be no doubt that serious arguments against any move of power away from the local to some central authority may be antithetical to other plausible theories of justice. It is by no means certain, however, that the two perspectives are incompatible. Indeed, it is implicit in my remaining scheme of assumptions that any plausible theory of justice for the EU must consider the plural possibilities of justice across the region as well as beyond.

Second assumption: an institutional framework for the EU

My second assumption avoids the enduring wrangling over defining what the EU is,[20] claiming instead that it is sufficient to operate on the

---

[16] Seyla Benhabib, *Another Cosmopolitanism* (Oxford: Oxford University Press, 2006).

[17] Benhabib refers in particular to the EU's 'remarkable evolution of the norms of hospitality' thus working towards fulfilling one of Kant's requirements for perpetual peace. See Benhabib, *Another Cosmopolitanism* at 36.

[18] See Tzvetan Todorov, *The New World Disorder* (Cambridge: Polity Press, 2005).

[19] See Larry Siedentop, *Democracy in Europe* (London: Penguin, 2000) at 231.

[20] Erik Eriksen has provided an indication of the range of possible definitions. He suggests we could consider a pure market regime, a '*regulatory entity* based on

basis that it is plausible and desirable that as a regional cooperative venture of some kind it should adopt an *institutional* form in order to manage its business. Its structures and nature will, of course, require some definition even if that remains contested and volatile. But this should be determined by the values (taken seriously) which frame the cooperative venture. If not, then in all likelihood an institutional framework will be constructed that is aimless and incapable of addressing effectively the varied demands of justice.

The desirability of an institutional form for a regional cooperative venture is hardly alien to accounts of justice. Andrew Hurrell sums up the general reasons for treating institutions as important by noting their value as 'a means of helping to secure a framework for mutually intelligible moral debate; as a way of securing the stable implementation of shared rules; and in terms of the potential for the progressive development of a global moral community'.[21] Martha Nussbaum similarly promotes the value of institutions as necessary for the achievement of justice (in her case in promoting human capabilities).[22] Her reasons, however, have more to do with the effective realisation of personal ethical responsibility *through* institutions. 'Collective action problems', she declares, benefit from the delegation of ethical responsibilities to institutions to avoid poor coordination of individual effort and thus probable failure.[23] Institutions also enable individual duties to others to be fairly distributed through appropriate taxation systems. And they provide a higher degree of capacity, bringing together relevant skills and resources. At a more functional level, Robert Keohane has also argued that international institutions, in particular, have importance because they 'make it possible for states to take actions what would otherwise be inconceivable'.[24] They may, further, assist in determining 'how interests are defined and how actions are interpreted'.[25] All in all, institutions have the capacity to facilitate the application and evolution of justice provided, of course, they are committed to that end.

---

transnational structures of governance', 'a *value-based polity* premised on a common European identity', or a '*rights-based post-national union* – a federation – based on a full-fledged political citizenship'. See Erik Eriksen, 'Introduction' in Erik Eriksen (ed.), *Making the European Polity: Reflexive Integration in the EU* (London: Routledge, 2005) at 2.

[21] Andrew Hurrell, *On Global Order: Power, Values, and the Constitution of International Society* (Oxford: Oxford University Press, 2007) at 308.

[22] Martha Nussbaum, *Frontiers of Justice: Disability, Nationality, Species Membership.*

[23] *Ibid.* at 309.

[24] Keohane, *International Institutions and State Power* at 5.

[25] *Ibid.*

I should make plain that the meaning ascribed to institutions here is not as expansive as that which I expressed in Chapter 1. It relates to the formal construction of an organisational structure that is 'deliberately set up and designed' to encompass 'explicit rules and specific assignments of rules to individuals and groups'.[26] Law in its various forms, both 'hard' and 'soft', is central here. Ensuring that there is a correlation between the values of an institution and the philosophy of its law seems axiomatic in this context. This all speaks to the creation of systems of bureaucracy, decision-making, and acting that provide a rational and efficient means of delivering the goals of a cooperative venture. As I have argued, institutionalised behaviour will develop within these institutions and indeed an ethos *of* the institution is still inevitable whatever the constitutive arrangements. But it is the structure that I am referring to in this second assumption.

None of this is to say, of course, that shared institutions are naturally just. Simon Caney, for instance, is representative of a cosmopolitan philosophical approach that advocates for the plausibility of political institutions beyond the state *but* only in so far as they reflect certain values.[27] Much hangs then on the values and attendant principles of justice that are accepted as governing these institutions. But the central desirability of an institutional formation designed to coordinate and enforce a cooperative venture remains unaffected in theory by this condition. Even if such an institution is justified only in terms of efficiency or effectiveness in achieving certain self-interests, this assumption remains plausible.

When we look at the EU in this light we can see that, whatever the confusion over its nature, we can at least attest to its institutional form. Richard Bellamy and Dario Castiglione have charted the 'in-between' nature of the EU, falling in-between a polity and a regime and developing a variety of applicable norms and institutional forms. But it still represents an institutional response to its position.[28] It does not simply coordinate the activities of states or other political entities. Indeed, it transcends the state at the same time as making the state an integral part of its organisation. It has developed strong political and legal

---

[26] *Ibid.* at 4.
[27] Simon Caney, *Justice Beyond Borders: a Global Political Theory* (Oxford: Oxford University Press, 2005) 148–82.
[28] Richard Bellamy and Dario Castiglione, 'Legitimizing the Euro-"Polity" and its "Regime": the Normative Turn in EU Studies', *European Journal of Political Theory* 2:1 (2003) 7–34.

roles for itself which serve to administer if not govern its cooperative aspects. These have operated so as to have considerable impact on the lives of people within and outside its jurisdiction. This fact alone makes reflection about the nature of 'justice' within its domain a necessary endeavour.

Third assumption: the EU as a plausible site for justice

My third assumption is that any regional cooperative venture (constructed through some institutional form) is a plausible and necessary site for considerations of justice to be applied. My definition of such a venture entails that the construction and implementation of policy, law and action designed to affect the lives of people, directly or indirectly, within and often outside its borders, means that we cannot escape the demands of justice. At the very least it makes imperative an evaluation of the institution in justice terms.

One school of thought, which might oppose this assumption, should be considered. It relates to a philosophical argument concerning the correlation between (socio-economic) justice and sovereignty. Thomas Nagel has been at the forefront of this thinking.[29] He has proposed that what 'creates the link between justice and sovereignty is something common to a wide range of conceptions of justice' that 'all depend on the coordinated conduct of large numbers of people, which cannot be achieved without law backed up by a monopoly of force'.[30] Those institutions 'that have a pervasive effect on the shape of people's lives' need to operate through 'some form of law, with centralized authority to determine rules and a centralized monopoly of the power of enforcement'.[31] He proposed that without 'the enabling condition of sovereignty to confer stability on just institutions, individuals however morally motivated can only fall back on a pure aspiration for justice that has no practical expression'.[32] 'Justice', Nagel argues, 'applies only to a form of organization that claims political legitimacy and the right to impose decisions by force and not to a voluntary association or contract among independent parties concerned to advance their common interests'.[33] By extension this would suggest the EU, as an association from which states can legitimately remove themselves, could not be the location for the application of justice.

[29] Thomas Nagel, 'The Problem of Global Justice', *Philosophy and Public Affairs* 33:2 (2005) 113–47.
[30] *Ibid.* at 115.   [31] *Ibid.* at 116.   [32] *Ibid.*   [33] *Ibid.* at 140.

But it seems to me that this scheme of Nagel's is too restrictive to be useful in the light of the condition of sovereignty in the contemporary world. It also seems counter-intuitive. For it suggests that justice beyond the mere procedural can only truly be attained through a state possessing a monopoly of law-making and law enforcement powers. But such an absolute position fails to acknowledge the seepage of power away from the state to other institutions and other forms of governance. The experience of globalisation has demonstrated how porous contemporary sovereignty has become.[34] It would be strange if, as a point of philosophical and political departure, justice was denied or unduly restricted on the basis that absolute sovereignty no longer pertained in any one location. As Charles Beitz argued some thirty years ago, 'international relations is coming more and more to resemble domestic society in several respects relevant to the justification of principles of (domestic) social justice'.[35] The scale of interdependence, which has further developed since Beitz first provided his view, has meant that the requirements of justice crossing state frontiers cannot be easily dismissed. My assumption, therefore, is that the construction of an international cooperative venture, which involves the creation of institutions and law amidst the transfer of (some) sovereign powers, must engage the application of justice at a primary level. The potential impact on people's lives through consequent institutional activity and decisions *has* to provoke a moral dimension if they are to be accepted as legitimate. Otherwise justice becomes redundant as a meaningful concept for judging the actions of institutions beyond the state. That seems wrong to me.

Nonetheless, this still leaves open the task of agreeing what 'justice' means in the EU context. The possible scope of regional cooperation could encompass different demands at different locations and at different times. But at the very least it presupposes consideration of the needs, hopes and actual conditions of life for people individually or through associated communities who are affected by the EU's practice. Inevitably, I suggest, this requires deliberation on the scope and depth of substantive *as well as* simply procedural justice.

It follows from the above that if we accept the EU as a regional cooperative venture with an institutional form, howsoever that may

---

[34] The global economic crisis of 2008 onwards has provided a dramatic example.
[35] Charles R. Beitz, *Political Theory and International Relations* (Princeton: Princeton University Press, 1979) at 128.

be described now or in the future, it is plausible that it represents in theory and practice an appropriate site to consider the questions of justice posed *in spite of* Nagel's thesis. The 'normative turn in European Union studies' over the last decade has in truth arisen with this assumption very much in mind.[36] Indeed, the EU has variously, for good or ill: become a site for reaching decisions that possess the force of law and impact on the lives of those living within as well as outside its 'territory'; developed sophisticated and plural structures of governance whereby those decisions are processed through legally enforceable rules and less formal persuasive measures; legally adopted norms to influence the behaviour of its institutions; and overseen the surrender of some sovereignty by states in return for a collective examination of, and solution to, particular problems. We must surely conclude, therefore, that it is plausible, indeed necessary, to consider issues of substantive and procedural justice.

Before proceeding, though, a further counter-argument to my third assumption should be considered. This is based on a presumption that the fundamental legal environment of the EU is international *not* municipal. A traditional faultline between these two domains has been expressed on the basis that 'domestic systems strive to promote justice, but international systems only seek order and compliance'.[37] From this realist perspective the EU as a regime governed by international law might only need to pay attention to the construction of order amongst states and achieving the compliance of states in that enterprise. Justice conceived in terms of deeper responsibilities to individuals *by* states beyond (or even within) their borders does not possess much weight in such an environment. However, this is a tenuous argument in the context both of the contemporary development of international law in general and EU law in particular.

As far as the former is concerned there is ample precedent for suggesting that highly restricted interpretations of international justice are no longer credible. This is not to say necessarily that the Westphalian focus of international law has been lost. There remains a methodological as well as ideological preference for states to be seen as the primary focal point for international law and relations. It *is* to say, however, that the individual has been brought into this domain as a

---

[36] See Bellamy and Castiglione, 'Legitimizing the Euro-"Polity" and its "Regime": the Normative Turn in EU Studies'.

[37] Fernando R. Teson, *A Philosophy of International Law* (Boulder, CO: Westview, 1998) at 1.

subject as well as an object. The development of international human rights law and of international criminal law in particular indicates that international law is not now so hidebound by the statist precept.[38] Concepts of individual responsibility and intervention in the internal affairs of states are well-established exceptions to the presumption of state sovereignty. This progression of international law would not now support so readily the idea of a very restricted sense of justice applying to an international scheme of inter-state cooperation such as the EU. It may still be limited in comparison to nationally located conceptions, of course. But the scope for developing an understanding of justice that necessitates greater obligations towards people and peoples who are not citizens has expanded.

The gradual maturation of EU law provides both a particular and general support to this more recent progression of international law. The construction of rights and responsibilities of individuals is an illustration of how inter-state law can be deployed to extend more sophisticated notions of justice beyond the state. Of course, this general acceptance does not determine the nature of those norms that should apply. We might move from a very narrow conception, which saw only the most limited conditions required, to a fully-blown value-based constitution. For the former, justice could take the form of an administrative code that restricted institutional behaviour only in procedural terms. What I have already termed 'virtues' in the previous chapter would reflect this approach. Basic standards required of any public body (such as honesty, efficiency, capability, etc.) would ensure that actions were 'properly' conducted without dictating in any way the value of the policy to be implemented. Much of the recent discourse of global administrative law has this flavour. Alternatively, justice could take on a much thicker content that suggested the EU's activities were determined by a conception of the 'good' as well as those controls on how that might be attained.

Of course, there may be some who suggest that an adequate form of justice is already evident within the EU. Despite the structural and philosophical confusion, the aim for economic freedom to be established through the instigation and maintenance of a common market might be said to provide the foundations of a particular form of just

---

[38] For an account of the development of international law along these lines see, Martti Koskenneimi, *The Gentle Civilizer of Nations: the Rise and Fall of International Law 1870–1960* (Cambridge: Cambridge University Press, 2004).

regime. Subsequent commitment to virtues of governance (general principles of law) have re-enforced this interpretation so as to ensure that even with a limited aim the method of operation would accord with qualities perceived as worthy.

Such a narrow theory of justice, however, particularly one focused on the achievement of a market condition rather than the establishment of a modus vivendi for states, peoples and individuals (both within and outside the EU territory), simply fails to adhere to any objectively conceived and appreciated sense of justice. Although the EU might undertake operations that do not offend principles of justice, as they might be agreed through say some form of overlapping consensus, and although it might enhance particular values in particular economic-focused circumstances, this is insufficient to conclude that the institution as a whole is a sufficiently just one or is based on a theory of justice that can maintain political and popular support in the long term. The fact that the EU's pursuit of values is haphazard, sporadic, contradictory, and generally economistic in nature suggests ultimately those same values may well be threatened rather than supported. It remains plausible to assume, therefore, that the EU *should* be a site for substantive justice whilst accepting that its current form requires a thicker concept to be adopted. Indeed, it would be strange to suggest that an institution such as the EU, which possessed the power attributed to it, should *not* address some demands associated with notions of justice beyond the procedural. Given its assumed role as a cooperative venture as I have defined, justice must surely be engaged so as to question the purpose as well as processes adopted. I will return to this issue in my fifth assumption.

Fourth assumption: the EU as primary as well as secondary agent of justice

My fourth assumption is inspired by Onora O'Neill's categorisation of agents of justice.[39] She distinguishes between the primary agent 'with capacities to determine how principles of justice are to be institutionalized within a certain domain' and 'other, secondary agents of justice'.[40] The latter are defined by O'Neill only by the fact that they are not primary in nature. This is not entirely satisfactory. However, she

---

[39] Onora O'Neill, 'Agents of Justice' in Andrew Kuper (ed.), *Global Responsibilities* (London: Routledge, 2005) 37–52.
[40] *Ibid.* at 38.

does proceed to give some greater conceptual clarity when she outlines the role of the primary agent.

Primary agents of justice may construct other agents or agencies with specific competencies: They may assign powers to and build capacities in individual agents, or they may build institutions – agencies – with certain powers and capacities to act. Sometimes they may, so to speak, build from scratch; more often they reassign or adjust tasks and responsibilities among existing agents and agencies, and control and limit the ways in which they may act without incurring sanctions. Primary agents of justice typically have some means of coercion, by which they at least partially control the action of other agents and agencies, which can therefore at most be secondary agents of justice. Typically, secondary agents of justice are thought to contribute to justice mainly by meeting the demands of primary agents, most evidently by conforming to any legal requirements they establish.[41]

I use this extract *not* as an authoritative statement but rather a good point of introduction. If we followed O'Neill's description we might have to conclude that the EU, in terms of its original formation at least, could only be considered as a secondary agent. It was designed to operate in accordance with the responsibilities delegated to it by the Member States. In so far as any objective of justice may have been adopted (and my claim in the last chapter is that only a very weak version at best was assigned) the EU only operated according to state agreement. The responsibility to reply to any perceived substantive demands for justice was clearly confined not only by powers specifically bestowed on the EU but also by political practice. Even if the EU had the legal authority to act it could have been (and was) prevented from doing so by the interference of one or more Member State. This was made evident in the 1960s when the Commission's attempts to act autonomously in a number of initiatives, designed to establish its independent presence, encountered strong resistance particularly from France and its then President, Charles de Gaulle.

Since that period the EU and its law has become increasingly a centre of power rather than a peripheral player on the European political stage. Much of integration theory has attempted to understand and explain this. There may remain strong theoretical interpretations that argue the EU has not removed the intergovernmental character of its institutionalisation. But there are equally powerful presentations that maintain the EU has become a polity in its own right. The impact of

[41] *Ibid.*

its law, its policy formation *and* implementation, its budget, its increasingly powerful institutions beyond the Council, its construction of networks of influence that emanate from its own resources, and its evolving ability to dictate political agendas rather than simply implement those assigned by the Member States, all suggest that we are no longer dealing with a classic secondary agent in O'Neill's terms. The evidence suggests we now have an institution that merits analysis in terms of assumed as well as delegated responsibilities towards 'justice' howsoever that might be defined.

This means that a purely procedural justice approach is unlikely to be sufficient to reflect the power, position and responsibilities that now attach to the EU. Wherever the ultimate power and authority lies, this is, I maintain, a plausible assumption. The EU is in a position whereby it can operate as an independent agent for justice (through its various internal schemes of governance and its external activities in its development, security, defence and foreign policies) *and* perhaps more importantly as an agent for *in*justice.

We can still argue strongly that the EU remains a creature of its Member States, that it can be disbanded merely by the exercise of will of those constituents. This might imply that the EU can never be a primary agent. It always has to rely on the Member States for its existence. But the prospect of a mass 'exit', as it were, represents a state of exception that perhaps we should be wary about adopting as useful when deciding the extent of responsibility to be assumed or transferred to the EU whilst it remains in existence. It seems reasonable to seek to develop an institutional ethos that is appropriate to its current and probable future status rather than an extreme and unlikely possibility. In any case, few analysts see the EU as losing its political purchase in Europe in the foreseeable future. If anything its expansion of influence and power seems more of a credible option. The whole 'new institutionalist' and even social constructivist approaches in international relations theory confirm the power of 'path dependency' and Europeanisation respectively.[42] They attempt to explain why it is that despite seemingly great political and public opposition the EU has continued to grow and exercise influence as an independent entity of some kind.

[42] See, for instance, Paul Pierson, 'The Path to European Integration: a Historical Institutionalist Analysis', *Comparative Political Studies* 29 (1996) 123–63 and Jeffrey Checkel, 'Social Construction and Integration', *Journal of European Public Policy* 6:4 (1999) 545–60.

By observing that the EU operates as a primary and not just second-ary agent, notwithstanding its constitutional status, the construction of a substantive theory of justice for the EU has to be preferred. It allows us to consider the ideal for the institution as it has developed. Clearly, this requires a certain amount of flexibility in order to cater for future development. But one of the purposes of looking towards a theory of justice, as the basis for a philosophy of law and an institu-tional ethos, is to provide a value-based scheme of direction.

To a great extent this assumption also relies upon seeing the EU as potentially crossing the divide between 'social' and 'global' justice for-mulations.[43] As already noted, the former has been seen by some as the preserve of the nation-state.[44] Here rights of participation and welfare provision, for instance, are reserved for national citizens or those res-iding in the territory concerned rather than being on offer to all peo-ples whatever their location. Global justice on the other hand relates to responsibilities assumed for the plight of those beyond one's borders, those removed from one's national territory. Here rights associated with citizenship are not so readily transferable. There may be argu-ments for the distribution of wealth internationally but these do not correspond to the broader and deeper range of obligations that might be considered as justly assumed by a particular nation-state. Rights of participation and welfare provision do not find commensurate expres-sion globally.

If a distinction between social and global justice is accepted, then where does the EU fit in? Is the justice to be embraced focused on the social or global dimension? My fourth assumption is that if the EU is a primary *and* secondary agent, elements of *both* should be adopted. The EU has not only become a focus for matters of social justice, in so far as a pseudo-national form of citizenship with attendant rights has been constructed, but its institutions have also operated with a view to a very limited redistribution of wealth (particularly through regional development policy and varying budgetary contributions from dif-ferent Member States).[45] This is also evident where the application of

---

[43] In parallel, it would also cross the divide between national and international law.

[44] A strong argument of this position in the European context can be seen in Claus Offe, 'Is There, or Can There Be, a "European Society"?', in Aleksander Koj and Piotr Sztompka (eds.), *Images of the World: Science, Humanities, Art* (Krakow: Jagellonian University, 2001) 143–59.

[45] Cohesion policy represents this dimension as was seen in Chapter 6, notwithstand-ing its grave inadequacies.

general principles (particularly with regard to discrimination) is strong. Whether it *should* adopt a role in the internal social justice dimension is of course a topic of much debate. However, any discourse of solidarity that might attach to the peoples of Europe would have little meaning if it did *not* embrace some aspects of social justice that were otherwise deemed the preserve of the nation-state.

Parallel to this internal aspect, the EU also assumes responsibility on the global stage for issues such as human rights and democracy through its foreign policy and practice. Its development policies provide evidence that the EU has operated with increasing influence in matters of trade and aid. Here we can see a fairly rich history of EU activity that cannot be disaggregated from questions of global justice.

On these bases, the assumption that the EU is a primary as well as secondary agent is plausible and reasonable in theory *and* as a reflection of practice. It also serves as a reasonable precondition for a suitable account of justice to be constructed.

Fifth assumption: substantive justice as necessary and desirable

Given the previous assumptions, it would seem reasonable that the development of an account of justice would be an appropriate means to guide, if not govern, the determination of obligations assumed, the decisions made on policy and practice, and the adjudication of value conflicts. Whether such an account would underpin a constitution of some kind, or be represented by such a document, we can leave to one side for the moment. My fifth assumption is merely that an account of substantive justice is, at least, a plausible approach to take. This entails an appreciation of justice that is similar to that expressed by Zygmunt Bauman. He suggested justice is 'the one value that guards the common good (that is, from everyone's point of view, the good of others) against the inroads of egoistic self-promotion'.[46] The common good is a plausible aim for the EU as a cooperative venture.

No doubt the adoption of such an account for the EU may be considered a dangerous or unwelcome development. Although formal justice might be supported, whereby the application of rules was considered a necessary and desirable condition for the efficient management of inter-state relations, more substantive accounts incorporating broader

---

[46] Zygmunt Bauman, *Europe: an Unfinished Adventure* (Cambridge: Polity Press, 2004) at 127.

redistributive responsibilities and notions of obligations to 'others' will be opposed. Some arguments are predictable.

First, the political: if an account of justice is agreed or imposed this would suggest that the EU was evolving as a centre of European political society directly threatening the autonomy of the Member States. In particular, it might interfere unreasonably with states' ability to construct plural visions of societal organisation and the principles that would underpin them. For if a strong theory of justice were proposed at the European level then this might challenge one adopted at a national level. The concern here would be a loss of moral and political power whereby the EU would attain too significant a presence in shaping people's lives. Given the lack of democratic legitimacy, such a transfer of power might be unwelcome in principle. Nation-states, which it might otherwise be assumed were the most effective polities to articulate and adopt deeper and particular notions of justice, would be undermined in their representative role. But such an argument would be presuming that an account of justice could not be constructed that accepted a plural environment.

A European theory of justice could, of course, be fashioned so as to take into account the multi-levelled nature of the European political mix. Whether this would mean watering it down to a point whereby it ceased to operate except in procedural justice terms is a possibility. Indeed, that is how I have interpreted the current state of the philosophy of EU law and the institutional ethos as a whole. However, if my previous assumptions are accepted then it is surely plausible that a suitable account of justice could be constructed that avoids such critique.

Second, the pragmatic: the argument could be raised that the resources required to reach consensus on a theory of justice would deflect from the very real and important business that the EU has to conduct. We have already seen that much political energy has been expended on a constitution for Europe without being able to attract obvious support from its peoples. What chance would something as esoteric as a theory of justice have of being more widely accepted? The pragmatic or realist approach would counsel against such theoretical discussions. But again this would be an error. A suitable theory of justice could be instrumental in forming a polity that was able to articulate clearly what its future direction should be, what values were to be pursued and how, and what principles would provide guidance in that endeavour. It would not necessarily deflect the Union from its business. Instead it would help define and clarify it.

Third, the legal: it could be argued that the construction of an account of justice to underpin, specifically, a philosophy of EU law would unduly politicise the European Court of Justice and drive it into confrontation with both the legal systems of the Member States and the EU's other institutions. Critiques ranged against the ECJ over the past half century have frequently attacked its willingness to meddle in the political direction of the EU. Trevor Hartley has condemned the 'over-zealous judges and lawyers who believed they were laying the foundations of a new superstate'.[47] Would an account of justice explicitly guiding a philosophy of EU law suggest an enhancement of such zealousness? Would it empower the judiciary to reduce those institutional restraints limiting its ability to resolve questions that are really the domain of politics? Not necessarily. Where values and principles are more clearly defined it will be inevitable that some political decisions will be challenged through the law. That is indeed one of the possible purposes of an applicable account of justice. It is to constrain the political on the grounds of values that are considered immutable, and principles that are believed to be non-negotiable. This does not mean that there cannot be recognition of the right of decision-makers to act in the public interest and to favour one particular principle or value over another in certain circumstances. Indeed, there will always be conflicts that require resolution. The fact that a judgment on that resolution might give reasonable preference to the political appreciation of any circumstance does not mean that the account of justice will naturally unseat politics. It might even support it albeit within boundaries. The case of *Kadi* is an illustration of the possibility. The ECJ accepted the need for governments to identify threats to public security and to restrict liberties and rights accordingly. But what it did not accept was that those governments acting through the EU institutions would be free to act *without* any restraint. The question in this book has been whether those restraints evident in the philosophy of EU law have been sufficient. My conclusion in Chapter 7 was that they have not. A suitable account of justice would provide the basis for remedying this condition.

Fourth, the efficient: Claus Offe has maintained for some time that the EU is too big to be capable of operating as an effective site for distributive justice, which we might take to be a possible interpretation

---

[47] Trevor Hartley, 'The Constitutional Foundations of the EU', in Paul Craig and Richard Rawlings (eds.), *Law and Administration in Europe: Essays in Honour of Carol Harlow* (Oxford: Oxford University Press, 2003) 175–95 at 195.

of substantive justice in this context.[48] He argues that the nation-state represents the limits for a social group to see redistribution as a reasonable sacrifice to make. Even if this were true before the creation of the EU, such a claim could not logically preclude a *larger* social grouping acquiring sufficient public loyalty *in all circumstances*. Jürgen Habermas suggests there is no reason why the social learning process that enabled the nation-state to attract popular support to the extent of sacrifice, could not be widened to an even broader level.[49] It seems reasonable to suppose, in any event, that given that the EU is in theory and practice a plausible site for making decisions that will have outcomes impacting on the well-being of people in a number of societies (including beyond its borders) then some kind of guidance on an appropriate idea of substantive (including distributive) justice is needed. This would follow Beitz's observation that 'it would be a mistake to think that distributive justice pertains only to policies involving direct transfers of income'.[50] It also relates to matters of trade, environment, development cooperation, security, migration, technology, and numerous other areas. As the EU has attained a degree of prominence in each of these fields, accepted by Member States as an appropriate location for cooperation and even power, Offe's objection now seems ill-founded.

These four arguments, taken separately or collectively, therefore, do not obviate the desirability or indeed necessity of a plausible account of justice for the EU. They might have an impact on the scope and depth of that account but they do not make it anathema to the Union. Indeed, given the *fact* of the EU's power and agency in so many different fields and, in particular, the force and relative autonomy of EU law, an account of justice that attracts popular and political support could operate to provide the very core of legitimacy and determinacy that has been so lacking over the past half century.

Sixth assumption: the necessity of a selection of values

My sixth assumption tries to give greater clarity to the notion of justice applicable to any inter-state cooperative venture. It builds on certain

---

[48] Claus Offe, 'The Democratic Welfare State in an Integrating Europe', in Michael T. Greven and Louis Pauly (eds.), *Democracy Beyond the State? The European Dilemma and the Emerging Modern Order* (Lanham, MD: Rowman and Littlefield, 2000) 63–89.

[49] Jürgen Habermas, *The Postnational Constellation: Political Essays* (Cambridge: Polity Press, 2001) at 102.

[50] Charles Beitz, 'International Liberalism and Distributive Justice: a Survey of Recent Thought' 269–96 at 271.

observations of John Rawls, reflecting in turn the views of Isaiah Berlin. Both note that a choice has to be made when it comes to the adoption of values within institutions. My claim is that, as with any 'system of social institutions', a plausible just supra-international polity must recognise that there is a limit to 'the values it can admit'.[51] A 'selection must be made from the full range of moral and political values that might be realized'.[52]

In the case of the EU, it is not difficult to imagine that a great deal of competition might arise in this respect. With every additional acceding state the picture will become even more complex. If we accept Rawls' injunction, it would be foolish to suppose that such complexity should result in a never-ending acceptance of values rather than a selection. The current preference to list a multiplicity of values needs to be questioned from this perspective. If there is evidence of a selection having been undertaken then the number does not necessarily cause difficulty. However, if the list in the latest constitutional texts is accompanied by little substantiation then there is a danger of overstepping what Rawls called 'limited social space',[53] to say nothing of limited political space. There is simply insufficient room for the EU to pursue all the values mentioned in the Lisbon Treaty (and perhaps extractable from constitutional traditions of the Member States current and future) with equal vigour. A choice has to be made.

Although neither Rawls nor Berlin were contemplating notions of an international society when considering this aspect, this does not devalue the relevance for the EU. But we need to be clear about what relevance it does have. By noting, in effect, that the EU cannot realistically adopt every value and every interpretation of every value across the nations within its domain, does not mean (a) that it must only promote those values held by *all* without dispute or (b) focus on one value at the expense of all others or (c) avoid the issue of value definition altogether so as to retain the status quo. Each of these options would be divisive. The first suggests a lowest common denominator approach that would be unlikely to reflect the complexity of values chosen and their contextual nature. There would be a danger of values becoming unrecognisable, a watered down version that pleased few if any. Conflict would remain likely as the search for commonality produced little substance to promote a sense of popular allegiance. The second

---

[51] Rawls, *Political Liberalism* at 57.
[52] *Ibid.*   [53] *Ibid.*

would also be undesirable. If a value, say security or prosperity, were chosen to the exclusion of others then there would be a real possibility of other values being seriously and perpetually threatened. The third is a close representation of the current institutional ethos, where values are largely under-defined and the economic and institutional status quo is maintained. Those problems of indeterminacy rehearsed throughout this book would remain unaddressed.

Any selection, therefore, has to be undertaken with care. It does not mean the problems are insurmountable, only that when the inevitable selection of value(s) has to be made it is done with due regard for the dangers present. This will require a more sophisticated philosophy of EU law than currently evident.

Seventh assumption: an incremental rather than revolutionary theory of justice

My next assumption might seem to infer a tepid response to the state of the existing institutional ethos. And it must indeed be true that changing an ethos of an institution and reconstructing a new philosophy of its law is extremely difficult when set against attitudes and customs that have become entrenched over a protracted period.

This does not, however, imply that only the overthrow of a 'regime' is appropriate to obtain significant change. Rather, it is prudent to adopt Immanuel Kant's approach when he sought perpetual peace. In looking to develop a constitution the rules for which 'cannot be derived from the experience of those who have hitherto found it most to their advantage' but rather 'derived a priori by reason from the ideal of a rightful association of human beings under public laws as such', Kant advocated that change 'should not be made by way of revolution, by a leap, that is, by violent overthrow of an already existing defective constitution (for there would then be an intervening moment in which any rightful condition would be annihilated)'.[54] In other words, we should not throw out 'good' aspects of EU law, practice and policy in the hope of a reconstructed constitution. For all the apparent inability to grapple with a theory of justice that might acquire the support of its constituency the EU has, over its history, still demonstrated a capacity for embracing principles that one would associate with a liberal conception of justice. Starting from scratch would seem to be counter-productive, in the sense that the basic premise of the

[54] *Ibid.*

cooperative venture between the states and peoples of Europe remains a desirable invention.

Kant's call for 'gradual reform in accordance with firm principles' would therefore be a plausible response to the vagueness and confusion vis-à-vis values and principles that I have traced in this book.[55] This requires an understanding of the relative position of those values, principles and virtues (however weak) that can be seen as framing the EU's institutional ethos and the current philosophy of EU law *in order* to assess how that framework can be reformed. I assessed this in Chapter 7.

My seventh assumption, then, is that reform rather than revolution is a plausible way to proceed. In this one respect it accords with Thomas Nagel's comment that 'the path from anarchy to justice must go through injustice'.[56] If we are to create just institutions, Nagel suggests, we have to first create 'patently unjust and illegitimate global structures of power that are tolerable to the interests of the most powerful current nation-states'.[57] Only then, he claims, will we see 'institutions come into being that are worth taking over in the service of more democratic purposes'.[58] Without accepting Nagel's proposition, we could embrace this political realism but on the basis that we have already been through the initial unjust and illegitimate stage with the EU. The powerful states of Europe *have* been persuaded that the EU is 'tolerable' to their interests on balance. And an institution *has* been created that was initially and remains unjust and illegitimate according to many perspectives. We have, therefore, reached the point when justice *can* and *should* emerge from the development of this unjust institution.

Has this not been tried already? The deliberations over a Constitutional Treaty were surely an attempt, in part, to fix some sounder value-based character for the EU. But this only gives support to my assumption. For it suggests there is a general perception that a re-*evaluation* was and remains necessary. Of course, my argument has been that the deliberations did not succeed in identifying a suitably convincing framework for justice that would lead to effective reform. The provisions on principles and values (replicated in the Lisbon Treaty) are simply too vague and weak to address the institutional ethos that has become engrained.

---

[55] *Ibid.* at 492.   [56] Nagel, 'The Problem of Global Justice' at 147.
[57] *Ibid.* at 146.   [58] *Ibid.*

Nor has the constitutional condition been addressed in EU jurisprudence. There has been a judicial refusal to progress much beyond what might be interpreted as a perception of the 'technical good'. The ECJ has looked to achieve the most efficient way in which the end of the EU can be achieved. And it has determined that end by restricting its vision to the express aims of the Treaties. This is, in turn, based on an underlying neoliberal belief that the 'market economy' is in a position to meet any plausible claims for substantive justice, particularly one associated with the redistribution of wealth. Of course, the global economic crisis of 2008 onwards might indicate the folly of looking to the market to resolve any such claims.

The question, then, is whether the changes introduced by the Lisbon Treaty actually open the door for EU jurisprudence to look beyond its current identification of ends. My assumption is that, alone, they do not. However, they might be used as a springboard for revision. That would be preferable to a wholesale reorganisation that did not begin from a base of already agreed principles. It accords with the potential for a more radical politics *for* justice in the EU even though emerging from a site of hegemony.

Eighth assumption: an inward and outward looking account of justice

This brings me to my eighth assumption. Any appropriate theory of justice for the EU *must* reflect the EU's unique nature. This possesses three different characteristics none of which are predominant but all of which must be incorporated if the theory is to have practical application.

First, the EU is akin to a state in so far as it interferes in the lives of individuals within its borders. Second, it appears as an international agreement affecting the policies and behaviour of its Member States. And third, it operates collectively in relation to peoples and states *outside* the EU. Given these dimensions I suggest that any theory must reflect the *prudential* aspects of states (and peoples within those states) in so far as they represent values designed to fulfil needs deemed to be serving 'self-interests'. But it must also reflect the *moral* aspects in so far as they represent the commitment to the *other* within and outside the EU.[59]

---

[59] This might be described as a recognised ethical responsibility to care about the 'third party' in Emmanuel Levinas' terms. See, Levinas, *Otherwise than Being or Beyond Essence* (Pittsburgh: Duquesne University Press, 1998).

The 'other within' I take to include all those who do not, or do not feel they, qualify as EU citizens. The concept would also incorporate the recognition that even amongst EU citizens there will be basic local- ised distinctions made between those who emanate from EU states other than 'one's' own and one's compatriots (however mythically con- structed). This reflects the moral possibility of obligations owed to all of those in other states within the EU, something which is not neces- sarily appreciated by political or public constituencies. Do national gov- ernments and peoples really *care* about those who live far away across the EU territory? Should they care? Some commentators have asked whether there is any feeling such that individuals will fight and die for the EU as a means of determining the loyalty of Europeans to this venture. But perhaps of greater moment would be whether Europeans would sacrifice anything for those in other Member States from the ones they inhabit? If so, what would be the extent of such an assumed obligation? It is in this sense that the 'other within' would include those treated as different in Member States' societies on grounds of race or culture or religion, and *all* those beyond one's own national borders but still within the EU.

The 'other outside' may also be seen as warranting the assumption of similar but different obligations of an ethical character. Collectively, the question is: what is owed to the world as Europeans engaged in a project *projecting* Europe to the world as an entity imbued with moral worth? Undoubtedly, the limited responsibility assumed by the EU in this respect should be acknowledged. But we still need to compare the efforts made through the EU purportedly for the benefit of others (through aid, peacekeeping or making interventions, trade conces- sions, representation at international organisations) with those efforts that *could* be made. It is in the difference between the actual and the possible that any evaluation of justice beyond the EU's borders will be relevant.

It is in this context that I dispute Nagel's determination that justice is 'something we owe through our shared institutions only to those with whom we stand in a strong political relation'.[60] As mentioned previously, Nagel presupposes a clear line between the internal and external dimensions, which in the case of the EU as a polity does not apply. This is not to say that the demands of justice will always be the same, but it will require a theory of justice for the EU that will address

[60] Nagel, 'The Problem of Global Justice' at 121.

the conditions of the 'self' (both individual and state), the internal regarded 'other' and the external 'third party'. Indeed, the juxta-position of these three categories is ultimately the stuff from which justice is forged, particularly given my first assumption. A coopera-tive venture that does not operate on the basis of *both* rational and reasonable choice would, I suggest, be self-contradictory. The rational would emanate from the recognition that peoples' (or 'governments of peoples' in Rawls' phrase)[61] idea of 'the good' must be incorporated in a cooperative scheme if the continuing support of those peoples or governments for cooperation is to be obtained. The reasonable would reflect the understanding that the ideas of other peoples or govern-ments of peoples must also be recognised. Making the two compatible is, I suggest, *the* basic task for constructing an account of justice for a cooperative venture.[62] Otherwise, we would have a process of simple coordination, which lacked the ability to address any issues of justice or injustice in any meaningful way and operated through some form of autocratic decision-making.[63] Neither would be palatable if the EU continues to be engaged in anything beyond the most mundane mat-ters of relationship between states.

From this perspective, the current reference to 'justice' in terms of an 'area of freedom, security and justice' represents the term's palp-able conceptual limitations currently apparent in the EU. For in this designation, justice appears generally restricted by territory and in practice is limited to a narrow field of operations, mostly associated with criminal justice issues. Such a restraint can only undermine the nature of justice as a governing value for both law and policy. It is too selective and ultimately contradictory to the rhetoric of justice that is otherwise proffered by the EU, particularly in its global affairs. Of course, one might be able to say that the Union already operates such an approach to justice. Many of its external policies are designed

---

[61] Rawls, *Political Liberalism* at 16.

[62] Although this assumption adopts the language of justice as applied by political liber-alism to 'societies' and one can accept that the EU does not represent such a society, I am assuming that the basic principles espoused still have relevance. Indeed, some recent social theory has begun to talk about a European society of some form. See, for instance, Gerard Delanty and Chris Rumford, *Rethinking Europe: Social Theory and the Implications of Europeanization* (Abingdon: Routledge, 2005).

[63] Rawls uses the example of 'merely socially coordinated activity' to help distinguish what he means by 'social cooperation'. Again I am arguing that this has resonance for the EU particularly given the empirical evidence available to show that it has engaged in far more than coordination. See Rawls, *Political Liberalism* at 16.

to promote abroad the values discussed in this book with considerable rhetorical if not practical vigour. But the failure to articulate this with constitutional exactitude means that there is little guidance for decision-makers as well as judges to rely upon where the issues may lack clarity. A suitable theory of justice underpinning a philosophy of law for the EU must, therefore, encompass explicitly the dimensions of 'self' and 'other' mentioned above if it is to be convincing. Any attempt to limit responsibility for the EU as a polity to EU citizens or even those residing within the region occupied by the EU Member States will only produce a discriminatory approach that will undo any reasonable notion of justice that might be applied.

Ninth assumption: the importance of law as a conduit of change

My ninth and final assumption is simple. It rests on the understanding that where any regional cooperative venture deploys law as a means of coercion in achieving and maintaining that cooperation, a philosophy of law should be adopted (particularly in adjudication) that reflects the need for justice to be the predominant theme in decision-making. If this does not take place, then there is a danger of law becoming an agent for resistance to, or distortion of, a devised theory of justice. The critiques levelled against law, its 'complexities and hidden antinomies' in Lon Fuller's words,[64] its judicial activism or, perhaps more appropriately, its conservatism, accentuate this problem. And, indeed, my evaluation of EU law as developed through jurisprudence would suggest that it has been complicit in the establishment of the institutional ethos that does not take justice or values sufficiently seriously.

Nonetheless, law remains a powerful force, whether negatively or positively, in the development of justice. We cannot realistically separate the two. One can be undone or made whole by the other. Hence, we have no choice but to consider the role of law in the construction of an account of justice for the EU. This will require some appreciation of the pragmatic implications. Given the dynamic and influential relationship between the EU's philosophy of law and the institutional ethos, as described in Chapter 7, it would be reasonable to suppose that a re-conceptualisation of such philosophy would be a sensible focus for achieving a re-conceptualisation of the institutional ethos as a whole. In other words, law's importance in the cooperative venture of the EU should be recognised and provide the basis for action.

[64] Lon L. Fuller, *Anatomy of the Law* (Harmondsworth: Penguin Books, 1971) at 13.

This does not mean we can rely on an active judiciary to achieve this change. As I maintained in Chapter 7, the likelihood of breaching the perimeters of the current ethos and philosophy from within is slim. There are simply too many institutional constraints to expect radical change from legal adjudication alone. Rather, a politically agreed and imposed interpretative regime focused on justice, supported by an enthusiastic judiciary committed to developing a new philosophy with justice at is centre, would be necessary. It may not be sufficient but it would be necessary. At the very least it will provide a plausible point of departure in the development of justice in the EU. This is the main theme I take forward to my final chapter.

Conclusion

The nine assumptions I have offered provide a suitable basis for undertaking my final task for this book. This is to consider *how* we might develop a philosophy of EU law that will in turn prompt an alteration in the institutional ethos. My chosen route for change has the potential to build on existing ethical thinking at the same time as developing more substantial accounts of justice for the EU. The modest claim is that this will make the reformulation of the EU as a just institution more likely rather than less. I appreciate it cannot achieve all we might desire for the Union but it represents a step forward in terms of justice.

9 Concluding proposals

Introduction

The previous chapter provided some of the groundwork for constructing a plausible account of justice for the EU. Parameters were set so as to think more carefully about the way in which values, law, and justice might coalesce in the institution of the Union.

But there is one more assumption that I should introduce. In truth, it has been largely present, albeit unspoken, throughout this book. It is that the EU will *not* become a state in the foreseeable future. Politically, such a transformation has too many opponents and too few powerful advocates to be considered feasible. And culturally, there is insufficient cause to believe that the peoples of Europe are forming significant ties that would lead to acceptance of the 'monopoly of violence' becoming concentrated in some European state. Despite some sociological work claiming a 'European society' is emerging, at present the forces against any form of federation being constructed are far too strong. There is little point, therefore, in looking to such a transformation to provide the impetus for redesigning the EU as a more just institution.

Given this, and my other nine assumptions, what reasonable ambitions can be entertained for an account of justice to take hold within the EU's institutional ethos? If the issue were forced, I suppose at the very least, consensus might be achieved around the proposition that the institutions of the EU, whether acting autonomously or by the manipulation of states (or indeed any other entity), should do no 'harm'. Such an injunction might be considered reasonable although imprecise. What might constitute harm and what might connect the EU with such harm are complex questions with labyrinthine possibilities. Issues of suffering, causation, and responsibility

develop, hydra-like, so as to make a seemingly simple proposition pro-
foundly difficult to realise or assess. When we then add into the mix a
desire that the EU should not only do no harm but should also act so
as to achieve some conception of the 'good', the ensuing complexity
becomes immense.

It would be churlish to suggest that the EU institutions have failed to
confront this Herculean task. Although I have condemned the relative
absence of justice in the institutional ethos and the philosophy of EU
law, there has been an appreciation that constraints should be placed
on the institutions so as to avoid doing harm to certain limited interests. The stories of those salient values in this book reflect this basic
commitment. There are also reasonably strong indicators showing that
the EU institutions have made positive attempts to do 'good' for people
both within and outside the Union. Of course, by the same measure,
there is likely to be evidence to the contrary on both accounts. No
doubt harm has been caused directly or indirectly through the application of certain policies and/or the failure to take action within its
power to prevent harm being undertaken by others.

The purpose of this book, however, has not been to construct a cost–
benefit analysis, to assess whether on balance the EU has done more
harm than good. This will always be a fluctuating calculation often
dependent on the political perspective one might adopt. We are likely
to see and interpret the information available to suit our prejudices.
Undertaking such an assessment then was never the point of my analysis. Instead, the aim has been to understand how, and to what degree,
values may influence decision-making both to avoid doing harm and
achieve some 'good'. In short, what is the institutional ethos that
appears to guide policy and judgment? This has been an essential prelude, if not precondition, for considering what ethos *should* be in place.
For too long, institutional discourse has taken shelter behind economic success so as to avoid determining the nature of values which
should govern action within the EU. But complacency can no longer be
afforded in this respect. At times of stress, some clarity of values and
their association with justice is essential if the EU as an institution is to
preside legitimately over decisions of harm avoidance and the achievement of the 'good'. Without that, the Union's capacity to retain public
and political support to enhance its usefulness or even sustain its survival will be severely undermined. The need to attain some determinacy of values and incorporate a plausible sense of justice is acute.

But I cannot hope to provide a complete response to this demand here, however. That will require a substantial work in its own right. Attention will need to be paid to the values to be adopted, the principles that will give them greater definition and the practical arrangements that will bring them into effect. My list of assumptions is the first step on this path. But, by way of conclusion, I would like to make some tentative proposals as to how we might proceed from here. My aim in this respect is to build on the assumptions outlined and, in particular, consider how a reconfiguration of the philosophy of EU law might be undertaken as a vital contribution to making the EU a more just institution. As I claimed in the previous chapter, taking such a route is justified on the basis that if the current philosophy has, in part, constituted as well as reflected the institutional ethos of the EU, then its reformulation to take values and justice more seriously should have a positive and significant impact on that ethos. In the absence (and unlikely emergence) of a discernible *volksgeist*, or public consciousness erupting, this, I suggest, might be the only viable route open for effective change.

My concluding (and tentative) proposals, then, are made in two parts. In the first, I promote two basic propositions. One identifies the need for a constitutional re-settlement that makes much more explicit the importance and institutional influence of (selected) values. The other then argues for instituting the fulfilment of *human rights* (as opposed to fundamental rights) as a plausible means by which *all* salient values can be provided with sufficient definition so as to govern EU law and the EU's decision-making as a whole. I contend that it is through this value-medium that the current philosophy can be re-constituted and justice better defined. In particular, the indeterminacy attached to values can be addressed.

The second part then begins to explore how these propositions might be put into effect. It does so by outlining an agenda for further research and political debate (and perhaps activism) to establish the fundamental principles necessary to construct an account of justice based on the assumptions I have offered. These principles would provide the foundations for a revised philosophy of EU law and institutional ethos. Considerably more work will be required, as I have said, to put flesh on these bones. In particular, the institutional re-construction that will be required will be significant. But this is a task I can leave to future enquiry.

Two proposals for justice

I have already suggested in the previous chapter that the constitutional debates over the past few years have implied an institutional accept-ance that a revision of the EU's institutional ethos is necessary and desirable. My first proposal builds on this appreciation. Specifically, it looks to the change in the aims of the EU originally announced in the Constitutional Treaty and repeated in the Lisbon Treaty. For here, I believe, there is the potential to unlock justice for the EU.

The provision, the new Article 3(1) TEU, sets the aim of the Union to 'promote peace, its values, and the well-being of its peoples'. This is an inspired but flawed amendment to the TEU. It is inspired because it suggests a radical departure vis-à-vis an institutional approach to values. Previously, their attainment was not explicitly recognised as an objective of the Union. The only relatively unambiguous commitment was to respect fundamental rights under the original Article 6(2) TEU. Even so, we have to remember that the ECJ made clear in *Opinion 2/94* that no 'Treaty provision confers on the Community institutions any general power to enact rules on human rights'.[1] There was an 'absence of express or implied powers for this purpose'.[2] By making the promo-tion of values the aim of the EU, a strong argument can be made that the power to create rules so as to achieve this aim will be adopted as the Lisbon Treaty becomes operational. But what responsibility would be provoked by the requirement to 'promote'?

This is where the provision is flawed. It is ambiguous, even inde-terminate, as regards the commitment generated. For 'promotion' might only mean the adoption of practices and standards to endorse and encourage the nominated values. The possibility of this replicat-ing the rhetorical devotion to values without any specific increase in institutional responsibility might be politically very tempting. There is significant danger, indeed, that the current institutional ethos would remain unaffected. If values are to be taken more seriously, this exist-ing provision has to be revised. My proposal is that the provision should instead commit the Union not only to 'promote' but also *respect*, *protect* and *fulfil* certain defined values.

Before turning to the nature of these values, a matter for my second proposal below, we need to register the differences between these four

[1] *Re the Accession of the Community to the European Human Rights Convention (Opinion 2/94)* [1996] 2 CMLR 265 para. 27.
[2] *Ibid.* at para. 28.

commands of promotion, respect, protection and fulfilment. Any distinction may at first sight seem to be slight. Nonetheless, it is surely important for any constitutional text to be as clear as possible about the commitment adopted for its institutions. Although we might accept that constitutions should provide sufficient space for political deliberation, to enable the process of democratic debate to have meaning, this will not obviate the need to establish reasonably determinate ethical parameters. Of course it has been my critique of the EU's institutional ethos that such parameters have been so porous as to undermine fundamentally any discernible moral or legal commitment. Consequently, if we were to distinguish between promotion, respect, protection and fulfilment then some definition should be sought.

There are a number of reasonable precedents to which we could look. Two in particular are apposite. They may already be in the mind of the reader. First, although we have to be circumspect about adopting any national constitutional precedent in case this promotes an unnecessary suspicion of federalism, the South African Constitution of 1993 possesses particular relevance. Second, the 1997 Maastricht Guidelines regarding violations of economic, social and cultural rights also has potential value.[3] Both precedents may focus on human rights but, as we will see, this will be very apposite for my proposed scheme.

First, then, the South African Constitution. This has provoked considerable attention given the tendency of the South African Constitutional Court to acquire a reputation for radical decision-making over the past decade. Lying at the heart of the juridical development has been the Constitutional commitment in section 7(1) that '[t]he state must respect, protect, promote and fulfil the rights in the Bill of Rights'. It has been made clear in various judgments that such a declaration, with emphasis on the demand for 'fulfilment', has enabled the Constitutional Court to adopt a 'reasonableness review' for determining whether the South African state has satisfied its obligations in this respect particularly as regards socio-economic rights.[4] In conducting that review, the Court must adhere to section 39(1)(a) of the Final Constitution which obliges it to 'promote the values that underlie an open and democratic society based on human dignity, equality and freedom'. The Court, therefore,

---

[3] See Maastricht Guidelines on Violations of Economic, Social and Cultural Rights 1997. For a commentary see, for instance, Sandra Fredman, *Human Rights Transformed* (Oxford: Oxford University Press, 2008).

[4] For a debate on this jurisprudence see Stu Woolman and Michael Bishop (eds.), *Constitutional Conversations* (Cape Town: Pretoria University Law Press, 2008).

has the role of interpreting the actions of government vis-à-vis these constitutional demands. In much the same fashion it seems plausible that a similar scheme could be transplanted to the EU. The particular values deemed essential for fulfilment would need to be specified in detail and those that *framed* judicial interpretation of action taken by the EU to that end would need to be kept to a reasonable minimum. It follows that the explosion of values articulated by the Lisbon Treaty would fall foul of this demand (and my sixth assumption).

Second, as we saw in Chapter 4 the Maastricht Guidelines also advocated for the need for respect, protection and fulfilment (although not promotion) to be given differing meanings vis-à-vis rights. Their particular emphasis was on the economic, social and cultural rights set out in the UN Convention of 1966.[5] 'Respect' was taken as refraining 'from interfering' with the enjoyment of these rights. 'Protection' required the prevention of 'violations of such rights by third parties'. And 'fulfilment' required states 'to take appropriate legislative, administrative, budgetary, judicial and other measures towards the full realization of such rights'.[6] Guideline 19 also imposed a duty on all states 'to ensure that the policies, programmes and activities' of international organisations of which they are members 'are constantly reviewed with a view to ensuring that violations' of rights do not occur and 'their operations are consistent with respect and protection' of those rights.

With these precedents very much in mind, I suggest that adopting the same terminology would set a legislative and practical framework that the EU institutions would be required to implement and against which their actions could be judged.

Realistically, I recognise, however, that it is most unlikely that the provision will be so altered. The political will to revisit *any* of the contents of the Lisbon Treaty whilst it still remains alive must be weak. In which case, an interim, although unsatisfactory, strategy might have to be adopted. This would focus on the desirability of pursuing the Lisbon Treaty's proposals as possessing potential interim value vis-à-vis an alteration in the philosophy of EU law. Despite its vagueness, as I have noted, the planned commitment to 'promote' values could be interpreted judicially as encompassing each of the demands for respect, protection and fulfilment recommended above. Indeed, following the pronouncement of the ECJ in *Kadi* that the EU's institutions cannot

[5] UN Convention on Economic, Social and Cultural Rights 1966.
[6] Maastricht Guidelines at para. 6.

'authorise any derogation from the principles of liberty, democracy and respect for human rights and fundamental freedoms enshrined in Article 6(1) EU as a foundation of the Union',[7] as we saw in Chapter 7, it would be possible to develop this judicial reasoning so as to increase the legal commitment beyond injunction. The requirement to respect human rights, equality, aspects of democracy and the rule of law is, at least, already enshrined in EU law and it would not be stretching the point too far to suggest that the new obligation to *promote* these and other values, expressed in terms of human rights, should include a positive as well as negative obligation. In other words, the Court would be entitled to expect the EU institutions to act so as to protect *and* fulfil the constitutional values if the aim of the Union was to have any meaning at all. Further, the absence of the maintenance of the internal market *as an aim* rather than an objective in the Lisbon Treaty, would also suggest that the values should not be solely interpreted through an economic lens. The ECJ would be released from the straightjacket of translating justice in purely market-based terms.

Of course, the recommendation for this interpretation would require a revision in the adjudicative aspect of the philosophy of EU law that might also seem unlikely. I have already doubted the ability of the ECJ to adopt a different philosophy *so long as there is no constitutional change*. But the seeds of such a move have been planted by the opinions of Advocate General Maduro and an ECJ apparently more willing to contemplate an enhanced value appreciation in EU law, as I explored at the end of Chapters 4 and 7. I will return to the specific potential in this respect in my second proposal below. But I must emphasise that the preferred and longer term strategy, nevertheless, would still be the revision and adoption of the constitutional provision. A clear commitment by all the EU institutions in respect of identified and defined values would be preferable politically and functionally. Otherwise, conflict between the Court and the other organs of the EU will likely ensue.

But this still leaves the problem of my consistent critique; the indeterminacy of values. Surely, this condition is not resolved merely by empowering the EU institutions to promote a vast array of indistinctly defined values? This takes me to my second proposition.

In order to address the failure of values, and most importantly the failure to identify a plausible account of justice for application within

---

[7] Conjoined cases C-402/05 P and C-415/05 P *Yassin Abdullah Kadi and Al Barakaat International Foundation* v. *Council* Judgment of the Court (Grand Chamber) 3 September 2008, para. 303.

the institutional structure of the EU, I propose that the change in (or interpretation of) the provision recommended above would only lead to meaningful change if the values identified are provided with greater substance. My argument is that the most suitable and plausible means of resolving this is through a human-rights-based interpretation. In other words, rather than attempt to provide a constitutional definition of democracy, liberty, the rule of law, peace, etc., as independent concepts applicable to the EU, each should be shaped according to a human rights foundation. This obviously requires an expanded conception of human rights to reduce the uncertainty of, give greater substance to, and frame the direction of, the salient values. It will require both a revised Bill of Rights for Europe *and* a revised institutional structure capable of monitoring and enforcing such rights effectively. And before that, it will require a clearer understanding of what is meant by 'human rights' in this institutional context.

How can this proposal be justified? Some preliminary points can be made whilst recognising that a deeper and more prolonged investigation into the theoretical and practical dimensions will be required. But as a starting contention I suggest that in comparison with the other expressed values, *human rights* possess sufficient normative substance and legal appreciation together with sufficient commonality and sufficient moral weight to acquire support amongst the people and legal systems of Europe and frame practical initiatives for the achievement of justice both internally and externally. None of the other values, I argue, has satisfied these requirements alone or as a composite whole. This is not to say they should be discarded or ignored in the EU's constitutional order. Far from it. But it is to acknowledge that they should be defined primarily through and by human rights. There is, indeed, good cause to suggest that human rights reflect persistent and convincing social (and legal) appreciations of how to attain those other values.

Of course, this claim is bound to cause concern for those who advocate for (a) a balanced approach to values, or (b) the pre-eminence of one particular value (other than respect for human rights),[8] or (c) bare notions of procedural justice, as the basis for acquisition of legitimacy. Each of these approaches, which have dominated the landscape

---

[8] Bellamy and Castiglione suggest 'freedom' as an overarching aim. See, Richard Bellamy and Dario Castiglione, 'Legitimizing the Euro-"Polity" and its "Regime": the Normative Turn in EU Studies' *European Journal of Political Theory* 2:1 (2003) 7–34. J.H.H. Weiler advocates for tolerance in 'In Defence of the Status Quo: Europe's Constitutional *Sonderweg*', in J.H.H. Weiler and Marlene Wind (eds.), *European Constitutionalism beyond the State* (Cambridge: Cambridge University Press, 2003).

of European studies, is, however, less than satisfactory. I have already dismissed (c) by assuming that an account of substantive justice precludes reliance on procedural aspects alone to govern the EU (my fifth assumption). Alternatives (a) and (b) require further discussion.

The problem with a balanced approach is that rarely, if ever, has a scheme been promoted to show *how* some form of value-equilibrium might be operated. Either the kind of general vagueness amounting to a debilitating indeterminacy, which has beset the EU since its institution, afflicts the proposals or we end up with a scheme that replicates the existing attitude to general principles, which I found wanting in Chapter 7. The multiple expression of values without any coherent understanding of how they should and do interact, how they should be and are treated when there is conflict between them, and even what substantive account of normative content they possess, has resulted in a lightweight approach to *how* some form of ethically governed decision-making can be effected. It is this practical dimension to a stated scheme of values coupled with an indeterminate understanding of the nature and scope of those same values that has infected the institutional ethos. As I have argued, this results in an incapacity of the EU to act as a conduit or source of governance through values other than perhaps in potential reaction to exceptional circumstances (for example, if faced with a clear and massive breach of a value such as respect for fundamental rights). Even then, the structures that have been put in place, as I examined in Chapter 3 in relation to Article 7 TEU and its failure of deployment in the case of Iraq, are constructed in such a way as to make action severely restricted. Instead of a balance being operated to give effect to values through the EU, the exigencies of the market have provided a sort of surrogacy for values. Economic issues have been the dominant factors determining the EU's direction. This remains the undermining feature of the EU.

Those approaches that have attempted to prefer one value (other than with regard to human rights) over others also suffer from significant weaknesses. It is not self-evident that any other value has the capacity, reasonable normative stability, or political support to produce an ethical framework that does justice to the EU's *sui generis* nature and position *and* will evoke sufficient public allegiance.[9] Indeed, I have tried to

---

[9] For some support for this contention see the Eurobarometer results for spring 2008 where peace, human rights and respect for human life were the three most significant values preferred. See results at http://ec.europa.eu/public_opinion/standard_en.htm.

show in the first part of this book how the identified values have failed to acquire significant conceptual purchase in the EU. The claims that could be made for the predominance of one of these as institutionally developed are, therefore, weak. Although each occupies in name an important place in the modern liberal state, none has acquired sufficient substantive content in EU discourse or practice to be useful as the governing principle for a polity at this level. The best that they have achieved is a safety net, again, reserved for exceptional, perhaps even extreme, circumstances. Their content is likely to remain indeterminate and to be limited to simple matters of formality.

It is worth reviewing briefly each of the key values addressed in the previous chapters to support my contention.

With democracy, there is a growing recognition that achieving some commonly appreciated understanding of this value is simply not feasible.[10] Rather, looking to better development of some of the associated virtues, as I have termed them, such as transparency and participation, has been the trend. But my enquiry suggests that this will do nothing substantial to the quality of ownership felt by citizens towards the EU. Representative participation remains distant, ineffectual and fundamentally un-involving. There has been precious little evidence that the role of the European Parliament or any of the other institutions has been, or will be, able to induce any feeling of patriotic association, constitutional or otherwise. More likely than not there will always appear to be a demonstrable and dis-engaging gap between individuals and social groups and those decision-making institutions. Technical consultation, through various media, is unlikely to produce any democratic fulfilment. The idea that a 'public space' can be manufactured that truly absorbs the commitment of people to power is unrealistic if not fundamentally flawed in today's indeterminate Europe. Again, this is not to say that the democratic virtues have no place in the EU. Rather, my claim is that respect for, and promotion, protection and fulfilment of, human rights will necessitate a continuing commitment to establish participation, consultation and transparency as worthy and natural elements of a plausible account of human rights for the EU. This would involve positive as well as negative consequences. Individuals should be able to take action where these democratic virtues are substantially

---

[10] See Deirdre Curtin, 'Accountability in Europe's Accumulated Executive Order', in Beate Kohler-Koch and Fabrice Larat (eds.), *Efficient and Democratic Governance in the European Union* CONNEX Report series No. 9 (Mannheim, 2008) 163–72 at 173–4.

breached. Similarly, the institutions should be enjoined to commit themselves to adopting whatever participatory processes are reasonably practicable, depending on available technology and resources.[11] Any greater commitment, say through a European Parliament given the power to govern, may suggest democratic rule but it would also mean the imposition of a federal state. That would seem to be the natural consequence of preferring democracy as a constituting value. But that is not an option that commands sufficient popular support at present. It may become a palatable outcome in the future but an enhanced commitment to the value of democracy at this stage may produce, ironically, undemocratic institutions, at least in the minds of a significant proportion of the people of Europe. In the meantime, Boaventura de Sousa Santos' assessment that 'the hegemonic model of modern democracy is tied up with national time-space and state action' means that its extension 'to transnational or local time-spaces' is 'highly problematic', remains a pertinent reading of the EU's predicament vis-à-vis this value.[12] Protecting democracy through human rights, however, could result in achieving reasonably applicable democratic processes that are acceptable, effective and enforceable. They would also provide a focal point for expressing when institutional decisions and policies impact upon people's lives to their detriment. And they would provide the language for articulating differing visions of justice that reflect democracy as 'for' people as well as 'of' people.[13]

As to the rule of law, this value also may have support as a basic framing condition in so far as that term expresses the need for non-arbitrary decision-making and the existence of effective means of judicial review. But thicker conceptions that attempt to impose a more complete social theory through law lose their attraction at the European level so long as a legal system that allows plural processes subsists. In other words,

---

[11] Admittedly the issue of resources and available technology could be used to restrict any institutional commitment here. But this reflects the current approach to the 'right' to participation. We cannot expect a continual process of referenda or large-scale acquisition of public opinion across twenty-seven states and their 450 million inhabitants for every issue arising. A reasonable approach can be expected but that is probably as far as one needs to go in theory. What is reasonable will change from time to time. Adjudication can protect the remainder of the right. A failure to undertake reasonably meaningful public consultation could be determined by the Courts.

[12] Boaventura de Sousa Santos, *Toward a New Legal Common Sense: Law, Globalization, and Emancipation*, 2nd edn (London: Butterworths, 2002) at 205.

[13] See Carol Gould on this point, *Globalizing Democracy and Human Rights* (Cambridge: Cambridge University Press, 2004) at 215.

to attempt to impose a social vision through law without the necessary consent of the people of Europe would again smack of the tyranny that Immanuel Kant warned would be a natural consequence of any form of 'world government'. The limited set of procedural virtues associated with the rule of law would remain appropriate but again they are best expressed through the actionable discourse of human rights. Access to justice and judicial review as a conjoined theme encapsulates the connection provided that the fulfilment of human rights is central to the institutional ethos *and* the legal philosophy of the EU.

With liberty there is also a failure to offer a coherent value that could underpin the EU enterprise. The central inability to appreciate the possible dimensions of freedom for individuals and states has ensured that a blurred sense of liberty persists. It is difficult to imagine how it might be reconstructed so as to provide a practical governance of the ethical framework of the EU *without* mediation through the discourse of human rights. Indeed, human rights present a much more plausible means by which both liberty and liberties can find expression, protection and fulfilment. Otherwise the concept becomes an amorphous and largely incoherent value to organise the governance of the EU with any seriousness. Equality is burdened by the same problems and released through the same medium of human rights, provided we are not hidebound by the EU's existing restrictive approach to rights.

In this latter respect, for 'fundamental rights', as currently realised by the EU institutions, and very much in contrast to '*human* rights', there is a similar failure. Chapter 4 made clear the irony permeating their presence in the EU. The internal and external bifurcation continues to plague the development of a human rights conception. There is such discrepancy even at the level of recognition of rights to suggest an incompatibility with justice. For how can a just institution operate a conception of rights that makes a distinction between those recognised internally and those externally and indeed provides greater powers in the latter domain? This represents a complete reversal of the common experience of modern liberal states. There, internal robust attitudes to human rights are often accompanied by contingent and pragmatic approaches when confronted with external human rights concerns. For the EU institutions, however, the lack of clarity, application and enforcement *internally* undermines the authority of any claim that fundamental rights in their present formulation could provide a suitable basis for an appropriate account of justice for the EU.

Other values, such as peace, tolerance and solidarity, have also been preferred but none have acquired any strong support in the EU beyond the rhetorical. They all remain too abstract and lacking in practical content to direct governance in any meaningful ethical way. They certainly do not provide the constitutional environment within which a philosophy of EU law might otherwise draw useful inspiration. Nor do they possess the qualities to suggest that a commitment to substantive justice can become entrenched in the EU. Their application cannot alone render the EU a just institution.

In sum, therefore, all these salient values not only fail to find effective form in the EU at present but individually they suffer when they are considered beyond the state. They do not have the capacity to operate across national borders with sufficient clarity to govern the operations of this regional cooperative venture with justice as a central motif.

By contrast, I suggest, the power of the *language* and *practice* of human rights rests in their exceptional ability; to draw people together in community; to channel social aspirations; to address fundamental fears; to provide a means of expressing claims for social change; to guide and frame those in authority in their policy and decision making; to impose significant control on the exercise of power; to provide respect for one's identity as an individual human being *and* as a member of differing and interlocking communities. They attach to individual demands to be seen as individuals and respected as individuals and to be treated as socially associated with others. Dignity requires this correlation between the collective and the individual within community. And human rights discourse brings these dimensions together to provide both the means and the ends of a cooperative project with justice at its core. Their value is appreciated with extraordinary ubiquity.[14]

But if we are really to draw on this dual-focused power, a reformulation of current institutional thinking about *human* rights in the EU will be required. We must envisage them as more transformative in nature than simply the protection of individuals from arbitrary interference with their autonomy by acts of EU institutions or their agents. Human rights must be conceived as possessing dimensions and effects that are altruistic as well as serving particular interests. If not, my assumption that the EU is a reasonable venture to enable people to live together in

---

[14] In political philosophy those voices promoting human rights as a core moral theme abound. For two recent works see Allen Buchanan, *Justice, Legitimacy, and Self-determination* (Oxford: Oxford University Press, 2004); and David Miller, *National Responsibility and Global Justice* (Oxford: Oxford University Press, 2007).

cooperation across national borders would be severely undermined (my first assumption). For if there is only self-interest at work in the construction and operation of the EU, which is the underlying claim of those who see the EU as an enterprise to be determined by the rational choice of Member States, then it would be hard to see how it could fulfil any moral demands made of it that are not arbitrarily and indeterminately decided. I have contested that this is an undesirable state of affairs and counter-intuitive to deeper notions of peace and the sense of people's appreciation of the value of living in community with others. It also fails to accord with the perceived need to establish institutions capable of contributing to the fulfilment of notions of justice through cooperation rather than simply coordination of largely economic activities.

A research agenda for a just institution

My proposed emphasis on the constitutional prominence of human rights in the EU will necessitate fundamental strategic changes. As I have said, I cannot hope to provide the detail here. Indeed, I believe that it would require considerable collective enquiry that is perhaps best framed through a research (if not political) agenda. The basic parameters of such a programme I *can* propose, however. These would need to focus upon constructing the governing principles required to: (a) reconceptualise *human* rights in the context of the EU; and (b) determine the distribution of responsibilities for their fulfilment. Of course, much also will depend on the resources made available to the EU institutions and the practical imagination that might be used to build a structure capable of realising my preferred value. But if agreement can be reached in these two key areas of concept and responsibility then the work needed to construct the necessary institutional framework can begin. The means by which human rights could be understood, reviewed and realised could follow. At the very least, it would inspire the EU institutions to develop a philosophy of EU law through both adjudication and legislative practice to give best effect to the primary value of human rights.

Without attempting to do any more than sketch some of what might be contemplated, I will briefly assess these two crucial issues.

Re-conceptualising human rights for the EU

If we are to move away from, and beyond, the market as a cohering theme for human rights we need to understand what is going to be the replacement. This will require some philosophical and practical enquiry. Intellectual consistency as to what is meant by 'human rights' would be essential. Clearly, as I have already suggested, the current understanding of fundamental rights in the EU is insufficient. A conception of *human* rights is needed as a replacement. Given the acknowledgement that whatever the EU may become it is presently not a state and that legal norms associated with human rights are predominantly exercised and defined by reference to individuals who belong to a specific legal community (invariably as citizens of nation-states) a human rights conception will be required that acknowledges these states of affair and seeks allegiance across the EU constituent communities. We could, of course, create a parallel legal community through the EU and provide rights through a notion of European citizenship. That is, indeed, how some limited political rights have been incorporated into the EU's legal system. But this has not and will not capture public commitment to the EU. Nor does it provide sufficient conceptual grounding to address the depth of impact that EU law and practice continues to exercise on people's lives within and beyond Europe. By definition it excludes too wide a range of people to serve the interests of *human* rights. If a constitutional and institutional commitment to human rights is to be fulfilled, therefore, then a more coherent and expansive conception has to be adopted. A plausible correlation between the internal and external manifestation of human rights will be required (in line with my eighth assumption).

But can we really expect a European popular appreciation of human rights throughout the Union, and beyond to be agreed and, in to the bargain, accord with the assumptions set out in the previous chapter?

My argument is that it remains plausible that a basic conception of the *purpose* of human rights could unite differing visions across the EU even though agreement might not be possible on *all* aspects and dimensions of this value. This purpose can, in the words of Thomas Pogge, be identified as to 'work for an institutional order and public culture that ensure that all members of society have secure access to the objects of their human rights'.[15] The 'object of a human right is whatever this human right is a right to'.[16] Once we accept that the EU

---

[15] Thomas Pogge, *World Poverty and Human Rights: Cosmopolitan Responsibilities and Reform* (Cambridge: Polity Press, 2002) at 65.

[16] Thomas Pogge, 'Human Rights and Human Responsibilities', in Andrew Kuper (ed.), *Global Responsibilities: Who Must Deliver on Human Rights?* (London: Routledge, 2005) 3–35 at 15.

represents an institutional attempt, however weak, to order a form of European society through law as its coercive means, then we must conceptualise human rights in the EU accordingly. It does not mean that the EU should replace the national obligation or indeed supplant the position of national societies. Rather, it means we have to find a sense of commonality to realise agreed human rights that will focus institutional behaviour as an inter-state operation.

This normative demand, currently unsatisfied in the EU's constitutional structure, seems more likely to be met by looking beyond European fundamental rights parochialism. In other words, limiting the sense of human rights to those European legal texts on the subject appears to be distinctly inadequate. Rather, if we are attempting to determine an understanding of human rights that transcends particular locations and speaks to people across borders (both within and outside 'Europe'), any Eurocentric interpretation simply cannot serve. For this reason there would have to be serious enquiry into the underlying meaning behind the language of human rights. I have suggested elsewhere that it is the promise of a response to 'suffering' that provides this core meaning.[17] I do not intend to advocate for this further here but suffice to say that the emotional as well as rational appeal of human rights should not be ignored. And this appeal has to be conceived by reference to material that better represents a connection between the internal and external sense of 'others' as well as 'our own' objects of human rights.

It seems sensible, therefore, that if we are to find some expression of rights that might provide a focus of enquiry we would be wise to look to those key instruments of *international* human rights norms. For these surely provide a better point of departure for constructing a basic set of norms for the EU to follow so as to respond to the prudential and moral values that a cooperative venture should pursue. We could still draw on the common constitutional traditions of Member States but from a methodological perspective internationally agreed standards created through the auspices of the UN (as well as the Council of Europe) must surely provide a more solid means of identification of norms that would satisfy my eighth assumption regarding the internal and external aspects of the EU's institutional

---

[17] Andrew Williams, 'Human Rights and Law: Between Sufferance and Insufferability', *Law Quarterly Review* 122 (2007) 132–57. The theoretical project this article represents has application to the EU. However, this is a task for further research.

concerns. The initial focus could be those documents all Member States have signed. We do not need to be restricted to the European Convention on Human Rights, which is a highly constrained document in general human rights ambitions in any case. Those conventions addressing various subject matters of human rights offer a considerably more expansive normative base that should underpin both internal policies of the EU and its external affairs. They would specifically include the conventions adopted through the UN structures.[18] Other instruments that have been embraced by a substantial majority of Member States should also be considered. This would prevent one state, for instance, from vetoing what would otherwise be a moral consensus.

On this basis, it would be possible to work towards a consolidated institutional Bill of Rights of significantly greater value than offered by the EU Charter of Fundamental Rights. The EU Charter may have gone some way to produce a coherent vision of human rights captured by the EU but it remains an incomplete document. Not only does it fail to address collective rights (and in turn collective notions of suffering) in greater detail (minorities are not expressly addressed) but more importantly it avoids determining the scope of rights recognised by the EU. So, for instance, those 'rights' described in terms of 'principles' would need to be redrawn to make the commitment more visible. Examples would include references to the environment (currently Article 17), aspects of discrimination relating to the elderly (Article 25) and those with disabilities (Article 26). Definite statements of rights to ensure that the EU was committed to undertaking 'reasonable' measures to prevent pollution and promote conservation etc. would be considerably more empowering than the present muted requirement to 'integrate' environmental concerns into Union policies. With the rights of the elderly and the disabled, a greater commitment than recognition and respect for such persons 'to lead a life of dignity and independence' would be more conducive to adopting positive measures. At the moment, the Charter represents a constrained approach to human rights, reflecting the thin conceptualisation adopted. My proposition requires a significant adjustment in favour of rights for groups and

---

[18] Key conventions would include: the Universal Declaration on Human Rights; the International Conventions on Civil and Political Rights and on Economic Social and Cultural Rights; the Convention for the Elimination of Discrimination Against Women; the Convention for the Elimination of Racial Discrimination; the Convention Against Torture; the Declaration on the Right to Development.

individuals the precedents for which already exist in part within the Council of Europe and UN systems.[19]

It is within this Bill of Rights that other values could then find their more deliberate expression and definition. Democracy, liberty, the rule of law, equality, could all be represented in terms of human rights. This already happens to a certain extent through the application of general principles of EU law. But the political as well as legal embrace of such rights would be a necessary corollary of my location of human rights as the primary value. And their judicial interpretation would have to be framed by a *human* rights perspective *not* one constructed from the aim of achieving a common market.

Would these normative standards then have application in the external realm? Given what I have said about the need to fuse the EU's institutional approaches to human rights in both the interior and exterior dimensions (my eighth assumption) then it would make sense that a full Bill of Rights would also provide the basis for directing external policies. It would incorporate those economic, social and cultural rights that have been identified as so vital for those who suffer poverty in particular. The normative standards would thus remain consistent. Indeed, if we are to retain the label of 'human' this is essential. And, of course, we would have to countenance seriously the prospect of external affairs becoming justiciable in human rights terms.

Establishing the responsibility towards human rights

If the EU represents a regional cooperative venture (my first assumption), any revised normative scheme as suggested above would need to be reflected in the responsibilities assumed by its institutions. What form these might take would need to be carefully constructed. The internal and external realms have differing demands but they are, nevertheless, related by a sense of duty of assistance that can be expressed in terms of global justice, something that I have already indicated has some resonance for the EU's institutions.

As far as the internal realm is concerned, the requirement of promotion, respect, protection and fulfilment suggests a progression at work. We already have a constitutional commitment for the EU not to

---

[19] The various conventions and charters that exist under the auspices of the Council of Europe are already generally accepted as applicable by all Member States. It would be sensible therefore for these to be enshrined in the EU along with the ECHR.

violate human rights. There may be practical failures in such commitment but the principle is robust. But the more we move from 'respect'
to fulfilment both as regards fundamental rights and my expanded
notion of human rights (to encompass other salient values) the more
we encounter the influence if not claim of politics. For any suggestion
that the EU should adopt positive duties in relation to human rights in
its Member States may be met by forceful counter-argument. This can
be represented in the form of the following syllogism:

Positive duties only emerge legitimately from a society's collective recognition
of responsibility to and for its members' well-being. Europe is not yet a society in any meaningful or coherent way. Thus, Europe's responsibility to adopt
positive duties in relation to the fulfilment of the purpose of human rights
cannot be justified.[20]

Such a logical argument could conclude that the only proper place
for the allocation of duties remains with the state. So long as the EU
fails in any attempt to re-constitute itself as a state, this will not alter.
It might accept that the EU could still have a role to respond positively
to any catastrophe or crisis but this would be exceptional and by definition would be reactive and would not entail any imposition of a
European vision of social justice. It would deny the appropriateness of
distributive justice being practised by the EU.

But we have already seen that the EU has embraced some ideas about
social and distributive justice despite its non-state form. On matters
of discrimination, consumer protection, the environment, social welfare, regional development, evidence has emerged of a willingness to
go beyond the reactive and move to the proactive response. But as I
have charted, initiatives have tended to be focused around the market,
which it has held as its limited preserve. How then might responsibility be developed to fulfil my proposal for human rights as a framing
value for adjudication and governance?

If we accept that the EU has dual status as primary as well as secondary agent (my fourth assumption) then the nature of responsibility would have to follow. EU law would have to be developed so as to
ensure that all its institutions respected human rights in its dealings.
Of course, that is no more than currently expected, at least as regards

---

[20] This, in essence, is the argument of Claus Offe, 'The Democratic Welfare State in
an Integrating Europe', in M.T. Greven and L. Pauly (eds.), *Democracy Beyond the State?
The European Dilemma and the Emerging Modern Order* (Lanham, MD: Rowman and
Littlefield, 2000) 63–89.

fundamental rights. The review of acts and omissions of EU institutions and Member States when implementing EU law would remain the core activity but it would not limit it. An additional requirement would need to be designed so that the ECJ would take into account the consequences of those acts and omissions. If the effects of EU institutional activities and policies were to fail to respect human rights then this would have to be the subject of institutional review and response.

The EU's duty regarding human rights, however, would then have to shift focus onto the behaviour of Member States. In other words, its responsibility would be to take action that could be 'reasonably calculated to realise the enjoyment' of those rights *through* the Member States.[21] Although the fundamental principle must be that in the absence of a European society, particular visions of social justice through human rights should remain to be constructed at the level of the nation-state, the role of human rights at the EU level would be to support that development *but* within a general appreciation of human rights. Even if another society wishes to manage its vision of justice in a particular way, Europe as a whole would still review that development in order to ensure that human rights were protected. This is something that is already recognised when it comes to examining the conduct of third-party states.

Paradoxically perhaps, the Member States would have to remain key players in the construction of this responsibility, albeit subject to independent review. They would, in this respect, be bound by an obligation akin to Guideline 19 of the Maastricht Guidelines on economic, social and cultural rights. As I have mentioned already, this imposes a duty on states 'to ensure that the policies, programmes and activities' of international organisations of which they are members (here the EU) are monitored so as to ensure violations of rights do not occur and 'their operations are consistent with respect and protection' of those rights. Running parallel with this obligation would be one requiring the EU to act reasonably in both *supporting* Member States in *their* primary responsibility and *judging* Member States in the exercise of their attendant duties.

The process of adjudication would then need to be both political and legal. The former suggests a means by which the EU would be obliged to assess the extent to which Member States were acting reasonably in the protection and fulfilment of human rights. What would be considered

---

[21] This is the formula adopted by the Maastricht Guidelines at 4.

reasonable would *not* then be considered in the light of a 'minimum core' (as considered in the context of the assessment of economic social and cultural rights under international standards)[22] but rather the context of all other Member States. A European standard should be possible to identify. There is already reasonable consensus, for instance, on the determination of poverty in the European context. Other appropriate measures must be possible on health, education, the environment, etc. If failure was adjudged to have taken place in the light of these standards, the EU's responsibility would then be triggered in the first instance so as to *support* those states through collective measures. The prospect of enforcement would also have to be present. For these purposes at least, the EU would act as the institutional conduit for the internal development of a form of distributive justice *through* human rights.

This, in part, would be a more complete fulfilment of one of the historic purposes of the EU outlined in the original EEC Treaty, namely to 'strengthen the unity of [Member States] economies and to ensure their harmonious development by reducing the differences existing between the various regions and the backwardness of the less favoured regions'.[23] Of course, my notion of responsibility in this respect has more to do with seeing disparity as a systemic *injustice* that can and should be remedied rather than a state of affairs that is the product of uncontrollable market forces. The consequence of this is *not* to view the purpose of, for instance, cohesion/regional policy as a means of ironing out some of the more notable imbalances resulting from the single market and economic and monetary union. Such a focus would inevitably reinforce the economistic nature of justice in the EU. Instead, a human rights approach would place values ahead of efficiencies, determining distribution in order to address problems *of* human rights. These may well emerge from economic variations but that does not mean the solutions are always to be found in the economic realm, in growth and economic performance.[24]

---

[22] See Limburg Principles on the Implementation of the UN Convention on Economic Social and Cultural Rights UN doc. E/CN.4/1987/17, Annex.

[23] Preamble para. 5 EEC Treaty.

[24] Some appreciation of this perspective has been evident in the recent *Barca Report* on cohesion policy. See, Fabrizio Barca, 'An Agenda for a Reformed Cohesion Policy: a Place-based Approach to Meeting European Union Challenges and Expectations' April 2009. He notes the importance of devoting attention to the 'equitable distribution of well-being' in reforming cohesion policy (at 28) and of addressing issues of social inclusion (at 29 et seq.). Barca still feels the need to rely on an economic justification however, which reinforces the current institutional ethos.

The dual nature of the EU is, therefore, implicit here, as both secondary agent for Member States, and primary agent in its own right (thus following my fourth assumption). Internally, the responsibility would have connection with (but not subsume) traditional notions of *social* as well as *global* justice. In the external realm, the terrain of global justice arguments would come more to the fore. But in this latter respect we would need to ask, what should the EU as an institution owe to the world? More pertinently, perhaps, what should the EU owe to the world's poor? Again, if we accept the immanent universality of human rights this would suggest that the EU owed a great deal. If the EU's promise was to respect, protect and fulfil human rights then it would be false to restrict the responsibility to within its own boundaries. It would be morally questionable if the universalism deemed appropriate to activate responsibility across internal national frontiers was then denied when looking beyond its collective external boundaries. By its very definition, justice requires acknowledgement of those distant factors that will, through consequences intended or unintended, impact on one's own life-experience. Similarly, it acknowledges the impact of domestic decisions on the lives of distant others, something that Charles Beitz, for one, rightly demands to be acknowledged.[25]

We would have to question, then, what the relationship should be between the responsibility assumed internally (which would include that owed to the impoverished *in* the EU) and externally. Here the dilemma of resources will have to be faced. No doubt, the argument could be made that the internal responsibility to human rights could well use up all means reasonably available through the EU. For instance, if the reasonable level required to fulfil human rights in Europe on European standards necessitated significant redistribution of wealth, then it would be possible to imagine that there would be nothing substantial left to address external conditions of human rights. But such an argument should be addressed in the same way that the individual ethical argument that self-sacrifice to the point of 'devourment' has been countered. It is a self-defeating position.[26] And it can be resolved by the understanding that institutions should be searching for a 'fair' distribution that acknowledges the demands of the internal and external in tandem. The whole discourse of 'development' has, indeed,

---

[25] See Charles Beitz, 'International Liberalism and Distributive Justice: a Survey of Recent Thought', *World Politics* 51:2 (1999) 269–96.

[26] See, for instance, Martha Nussbaum, *Frontiers of Justice: Disability, Nationality, Species Membership* (Cambridge, MA: Harvard University Press, 2007) at 309.

assumed that the wealthy countries of Europe owe a significant (but still limited) duty to the poor *elsewhere* no matter what the economic conditions prevalent internally. That may have had more purchase when the EU consisted of the richer nations of Europe. With the enlargement to incorporate Ireland and Greece and then those states of Central and Eastern Europe, the EU ceased to be an exclusively rich-country club. Nonetheless, the EU has not reduced its mandate or its practical commitment to those outside the EU. The argument really has only been about the amount of external aid rather than whether it should be provided or not. Would it be fair to say, in this case, that it would be 'unjust' to have a system that would reduce commitments to the world's poor because of the need to address variations in European standards of living, even at a time of economic difficulty if not crisis in Europe?

Perhaps an answer can be found in the nature of human rights I am proposing. It would presume (in accordance with my eighth assumption) that the external and internal dimensions of the EU must be considered as part of a single commitment. So, if the value of human rights is to be primary then the determination to attend to poverty (and related issues such as climate change) on a global scale *must* capture the EU's attention and be fully integrated into its governing precepts. There should be no borders when it comes to fulfilling this ethical commitment. But this does not mean that the 'scope' of commitment remains the same whatever the location of the problem.[27] When assessing what is reasonable *internally* both in terms of what a Member State is doing to fulfil human rights within its domain and what the EU as a collective can do to support that state, an evaluation should be made of the collective demands that existed *externally*. It would not necessarily mean that exterior claims would 'trump' internal ones but it might well mean that in addressing human suffering on a global scale, resources must be allocated more equitably to distant sufferers. The institutional competences would have to be developed accordingly. It would also mean that practices under the control of, or passing through, the EU institutions would have to be properly assessed for their impact on human suffering and altered or amended accordingly.

The seeds of recognition of this responsibility (although not competences) can be seen in the EU's recent approach to children's rights.

---

[27] See David Miller, *National Responsibility and Global Justice* for a convincing account of the varying degrees of responsibility in issue.

Policy initiatives have accepted that there is a conjoined duty to act here for a specific set of rights.[28] But this needs to be extended to encompass (a) the relative demands of all accepted human rights internally and externally, and (b) the relationship between policies and actions of the EU and its constituents and human rights conditions *outside* its legal regime. It would entail, in particular, that the legal restraints on what may be undertaken by the EU would need to be removed (overturning the competence restriction of *Opinion 2/94*) so that the false double dichotomy between the internal (restricted but justiciable) and external (unrestricted but unjusticiable) activities can be ended. And it would require the EU institutions to recognise the potential implications for human suffering of its (and its Member States') policies and practices, particularly with regard to those relating to trade, the environment, agriculture, migration, and all those matters which transcend internal and external borders.[29] An obligation to institute a fair system of international trade to 'combat excessive inequalities' as the philosopher David Miller suggests, would be reasonable to expect in these circumstances.[30] The detriment caused to the developing world of action taken by or through EU institutions would need to be assessable.

There would also need to be a determination of a proper process for perceiving the suffering of others as articulated by them and not just through bureaucratic human rights impact assessments.[31] Enquiry into the notion of accountability, in the sense of broadening the rules of *locus standi* and institutionalising a more effective and coordinated means of monitoring human rights matters is an absolute necessity in

---

[28] See Commission, Towards an EU Strategy on the Rights of the Child COM (2006) 367 4 July 2006.

[29] The injunction not to be involved in an unjust institution is a starting point for this latter issue but it is insufficient if we are looking for ways in which the responsibility for human rights I propose for the EU is to be discharged. The obligation may well expand to review corporations located within the EU as well. At the very least it would suggest that where Member States exercise authority through law over corporations registered in their domain, they should institute processes for reviewing the behaviour of corporations *wherever* they operate. The EU's responsibility could then be to oversee and coordinate the nature of these national processes to ensure that differing legal systems throughout the Union were not exploited by corporations to reduce their commitment to human rights.

[30] Miller, *National Responsibility and Global Justice* at 267.

[31] This would open up the possibility of what Santos calls the 'subaltern cosmopolitan perspective' whereby the 'transnational community of suffering' is enabled to communicate their condition through avenues of participation at the EU level. See Santos, *Towards a New Legal Common Sense* at 14.

this respect. Current attitudes towards access to justice are so limited in EU law that reconstituting the EU as a just institution demands that the debate about this issue is fully embraced. Otherwise, the dislocation between the principle of the primary value and its realisation will further undermine the venture.

Again this will have resource implications. But without measures and processes designed to hear the voices of suffering (and those who represent them) and engage them in the decisions to be made in response (an appropriate development that the current principle of participation surely reflects) the demand for a more just institution will be difficult if not impossible to realise.

There are numerous other matters that would need to be confronted and addressed if my two main proposals are to be followed. But the issues of conceptualisation and responsibility are, I suggest, of paramount importance. Their thorough investigation through research and political debate is essential if any constitutional and practical change is to be achieved. And their ingestion as fundamental principles in a revised philosophy of EU law, to guide legislative formation and judicial interpretation, would be crucial in the reconfiguration of the institutional ethos that I have advocated.

Final thought

The proposals and two lines of enquiry suggested in this chapter are clearly insufficient alone to transform the EU into a more just institution. But I suggest they provide a plausible point of departure particularly for informing a new philosophy of EU law designed to give effect to my proposed primary value. Even then, change will only be possible if there is a practical realisation of the vision advanced *and* a constitutional amendment to the aims of the EU is adopted. The Commission, the Parliament and most notably the Court might then be encouraged to make the fulfilment of human rights internally *and* externally their fundamental responsibility. The devil may be in the detail, as I have attempted to show in the disparity between the robust institutional rhetoric about values and the reality of practical action. But it is a devil that may be harnessed through a more coherent account of justice based on a plausible set of assumptions and principles. This has been the purpose of this and the preceding chapter. By building on an existing institutional ethos through a reinvigorated philosophy of EU law founded on a constitutional clarification, I have tried to map a route forward. This is both theoretically plausible and conscious of the practical applications that would have to be entertained. I suggest that this basic ethical scheme provides a path towards an account of justice appropriate for the EU. In such a way law, values and justice might merge so as to make the EU a more just institution. That, at least, is the ambition. And it is one that desperately needs to be fulfilled. It may not create a 'soul' for Europe but it might entail the construction of an ethos that will enhance justice (as, in Bauman's words, a 'pang of conscience')[32] rather than see it ignored or diminished. Then perhaps we can talk about the value of the European Union with greater confidence.

[32] Zygmunt Bauman, *Europe: an Unfinished Adventure* (Cambridge: Polity Press, 2004) at 126.

Bibliography

Allan, Pierre and Keller, Alexis, 'The Concept of Just Peace, or Achieving Peace through Recognition, Renouncement, and Rule', in Allan, Pierre and Keller, Alexis (eds.), *What is a Just Peace?* (Oxford: Oxford University Press, 2006) 195–215.

Allan, T.R.S., 'The Rule of Law as the Rule of Reason: Consent and Constitutionalism', *Law Quarterly Review* **115** (1999) 221–44.

Allen, David and Smith, Michael, 'External Developments', *Journal of Common Market Studies* **42** Annual Review (2004) 95–112.

Allott, Philip, 'The Crisis of European Constitutionalism: Reflections on the Revolution in Europe', *Common Market Law Review* **34** (1997) 439–90.

Eunomia; New Order for a New World (Oxford: Oxford University Press, 1990).

The Health of Nations: Society and Law Beyond the State (Cambridge: Cambridge University Press, 2002).

Alston, Philip and Weiler, J.H.H., 'An "Ever Closer Union" in Need of a Human Rights Policy: the European Union and Human Rights', in Alston, Philip, Bustelo, Mara and Heenan, James (eds.), *The EU and Human Rights* (Oxford: Oxford University Press, 1999) 3–97.

Alter, Karen, *Establishing the Supremacy of European Law: the Making of an International Rule of Law in Europe* (Oxford: Oxford University Press, 2001).

Althusser, Louis, *Montesquieu, Rousseau, Marx: Politics and History* (London: Verso, 1982).

Anderson, Benedict, *Imagined Communities: Reflections on the Origin and Spread of Nationalism* (London: Verso, 1991).

Anderson, Malcolm, Den Boer, Monica, Cullen, Peter, Gilmore, William C., Raab, Charles D. and Walker, Neil, *Policing the European Union: Theory Law and Practice* (Oxford: Clarendon Press, 1995).

Anderson, Perry, 'Depicting Europe', *London Review of Books,* **20** September 2007.

'Under the Sign of the Interim', in Gowan, Peter and Anderson, Perry (eds.), *The Question of Europe* (London: Verso, 1997) 51–71.

Arendt, Hannah, *On Violence* (London: Allen Lane, 1970).

Arnull, Anthony, 'The Rule of Law in the European Union', in Arnull, Anthony and Wincott, Daniel (eds.), *Accountability and Legitimacy in the European Union* (Oxford: Oxford University Press, 2002) 239–55.

Balibar, Etienne, *We, The People of Europe: Reflections on Transnational Citizenship* (Princeton: Princeton University Press, 2004).

Bañkowski, Zenon and Christodoulidis, Emilios, 'The European Union as an Essentially Contested Project', *European Law Journal* **4:4** (1998) 341–54.

Bar, Christian von, Clive, Eric and Schulte-Nölke, Hans et al., 'Principles, Definitions and Model Rules of European Private Law: Draft Common Frame of Reference: Interim Outline Edition' (Munich: Sellier, 2008).

Barnard, Catherine, *The Substantive Law of the EU,* 2nd edn (Oxford: Oxford University Press, 2007).

Bartels, Lorand, *Human Rights Conditionality in the EU's International Agreements* (Oxford: Oxford University Press, 2005).

Bauman, Zygmunt, *Europe: an Unfinished Adventure* (Cambridge: Polity Press, 2004).

   Modernity and the Holocaust (Cambridge: Polity Press, 2000).

   Postmodern Ethics (Oxford: Blackwell, 1993).

Baxi, Upendra, 'The "War *on* Terror" and the "War *of* Terror": Nomadic Multitudes, Aggressive Incumbents and the "New" International Law', *Osgoode Hall Law Journal* **43:1** (2005) 7–43.

Beck, Ulrich, *Cosmopolitan Vision* (Cambridge: Polity Press, 2006).

Beck, Ulrich and Grande, Edgar, *Cosmopolitan Europe* (Cambridge: Polity Press, 2007).

Beitz, Charles, 'International Liberalism and Distributive Justice: a Survey of Recent Thought', *World Politics* **51:2** (1999) 269–96.

   Political Theory and International Relations (Princeton: Princeton University Press, 1979).

Bellamy, Richard and Castiglione, Dario, 'Legitimizing the Euro-"Polity" and its "Regime": the Normative Turn in EU Studies', *European Journal of Political Theory* **2:1** (2003) 7–34.

Benhabib, Seyla, *Another Cosmopolitanism* (Oxford: Oxford University Press, 2006).

   'Toward a Deliberative Model of Democratic Legitimacy', in Benhabib, Seyla (ed.), *Democracy and Difference: Contesting the Boundaries of the Political* (Princeton: Princeton University Press, 1996) 67–94.

Berlin, Isaiah, *Four Essays on Liberty* (Oxford: Oxford University Press, 1969).

Besson, Samantha, 'The European Union and Human Rights: Towards a New Kind of Post-National Human Rights Institution', *Human Rights Law Review* **6:2** (2006) 323–60.

Besson, Samantha and Utzinger, André, 'Toward European Citizenship' *Journal of Social Philosophy* **39:2** (2008) 185–208.

Bignami, Francesca, 'Creating European Rights: National Values and Suprantional Interests', 2005 Duke Law School Working Paper Series.

Bogdandy, Armin von ,'Constitutional Principles', in Bogdandy, Armin von and Bast, Jürgen (eds.), *Principles of European Constitutional Law* (Oxford: Hart, 2006) 3–52.

'The European Union as a Human Rights Organization? Human Rights and the Core of the European Union', *Common Market Law Review* **37** (2000) 1307–38.

'The European Union as Situation, Executive, and Promoter of the International Law of Cultural Diversity: Elements of a Beautiful Friendship', *European Journal of International Law* **19:2** (2008) 241–75.

Booth, Ken, *Theory of World Security* (Cambridge: Cambridge University Press, 2007).

Brandt, Peter and Tsatsos, Dimitris, 'From the Constitutionalisation of Europe to a European Constitution', in Albers, Detlev, Haseler, Stephen and Meyer, Henning (eds.), *Social Europe: a Continent's Answer to Market Fundamentalism* (London: Europe Research Forum, 2006) 9–31.

Brandtner, Barbara and Rosas, Allan, 'Human Rights and the External Relations of the European EU: an Analysis of Doctrine and Practice', *European Journal of International Law* **9:3** (1998) 468–90.

Buchanan, Allen, *Justice, Legitimacy, and Self-determination* (Oxford: Oxford University Press, 2004).

Buzan, Barry and Waever, Ole, *Regions and Powers: the Structure of International Security* (Cambridge: Cambridge University Press, 2003).

Buzan, Barry, Waever, Ole and de Wilde, Japp, *Security: a New Framework for Analysis* (Boulder, CO: Lynne Rienner, 1998).

Caney, Simon, *Justice Beyond Borders: a Global Political Theory* (Oxford: Oxford University Press, 2005).

Castoriadis, Cornelius, *The Imaginary Institution of Society* (Cambridge: Polity Press, 1987).

Chalmers, Damian, 'Constitutional Reason in the Age of Terror', Global Law Working Papers 06/04 Hauser Global Law Programme.
  'Political Rights and Political Reason in European Law in Times of Stress', in Sadurski, Wojciech (ed.), *Political Rights under Stress in 21st Century Europe* (Oxford: Oxford University Press, 2006) 55–83.

Charillon, Frédéric, 'The EU as a Security Regime', *European Foreign Affairs Review* **10** (2005) 517–33.

Checkel, Jeffrey, 'Social Construction and Integration', *Journal of European Public Policy* **6:4** (1999) 545–60.

Cohen, G.A., *History, Labour, and Freedom* (Oxford: Oxford University Press, 1988).
  'Where the Action is: on the Site of Distributive Justice', *Philosophy and Public Affairs* **26** (1997) 3–30.

Cohen, Joshua and Sabel, Charles, 'Directly-Deliberative Polyarchy', *European Law Journal* **3:4** (1997) 313–42.

Connolly, Bernard, *Rotten Heart of Europe: the Dirty War for Europe's Money* (London: Faber and Faber, 2001).

Cooke, B. and Kothari, U. (eds.), *Participation: the New Tyranny?* (London: Zed Books, 2001).

Coppell, Jason and O'Neill, Aidan, 'The European Court of Justice: Taking Rights Seriously', *Common Market Law Review* **29** (1992) 669–92.

Craig, Paul, 'Constitutional Foundations, the Rule of Law and Supremacy',
  Public Law (2003) 92–111.
Curtin, Deirdre, 'Accountability in Europe's Accumulated Executive Order',
  in Kohler-Koch, Beate and Larat, Fabrice (eds.), *Efficient and Democratic
  Governance in the European Union,* CONNEX Report series No. 9 (Mannheim,
  2008) 163–72.
  'Emerging Institutional Parameters and Organised Difference in the
  European Union', in de Witte, Bruno, Hanf, Dominik and Vos, Ellen
  (eds.), *The Many Faces of Differentiation in EU Law* (Antwerp: Intersentia,
  2001) 347–77.
  'European Legal Integration: Paradise Lost?', in Curtin, Deirdre M., Smits,
  Jan M., Klip, André and McCahery, Joseph A. (eds.) *European Integration and
  Law* (Antwerp: Intersentia, 2006) 1–54.
de Búrca, Gráinne, 'Beyond the Charter: how Enlargement has Enlarged the
  Human Rights Policy of the European Union', *Fordham International Law
  Journal* **27** (2004) 679–714.
  (ed.), *EU Law and the Welfare State: in Search of Solidarity* (Oxford: Oxford
  University Press, 2005).
  'Fundamental Rights and the Reach of EC Law', *Oxford Journal of Legal Studies*
  13 (1993) 283–319.
Dehousse, Renaud, *The European Court of Justice: the Politics of Judicial Integration*
  (Basingstoke: Macmillan, 1998).
Delanty, Gerard and Rumford, Chris, *Rethinking Europe: Social Theory and the
  Implications of Europeanization* (Abingdon: Routledge, 2005).
Derrida, Jacques, *The Other Heading: Reflections on Today's Europe*
  (Indiana: Indiana University Press, 1992).
de Rougemont, Denis, *The Idea of Europe* (New York: Macmillan, 1966).
Deutsch, Karl, Burrell, Sidney A., Kann, Robert A. et al., *Political Community
  and the North Atlantic Area: International Organization in the Light of Historical
  Experience* (Princeton: Princeton University Press, 1957).
de Witte, Bruno, 'The Nature of the Legal Order', in Craig, Paul and de Búrca,
  Gráinne (eds.), *The Evolution of EU Law* (Oxford: Oxford University Press,
  1999).
  'Politics Versus Law in the EU's Approach to Ethnic Minorities', EUI
  Working Paper (2000) RSC No. 2000/4.
Dougan, Michael, 'Free Movement: the Work Seeker as Citizen', in Dashwood,
  Alan, Hillion, Christophe, Spencer, John and Ward, Angela (eds.),
  Cambridge Yearbook of European Legal Studies, Vol. 4 (Oxford: Hart, 2002)
  93–133.
Douglas-Scott, Sionaidh, 'The Rule of Law in the European Union – Putting
  the Security into the Area of Freedom, Security and Justice', *European Law
  Review* **29:2** (2004) 219–42.
Doyle, Michael, 'Kant, Legacies, and Foreign Affairs', *Philosophy and Public
  Affairs* **12:3** and **12:4** (1983) 205–35 and 323–53.
Duchêne, François, 'Europe's Role in World Peace', in Mayne, Richard (ed.),
  Europe Tomorrow (London: Fontana, 1972) 32–47.

Dupre, Catherine, 'After Reforms: Human Rights Protection in Post-communist States', *European Human Rights Law Review* **5** (2008) 621–32.

Dworkin, Ronald, *Sovereign Virtue: the Theory and Practice of Equality* (Cambridge, MA: Harvard University Press, 2000).

Eilstrup-Saniovanni, Mette and Verdier, Daniel, 'European Integration as a Solution to War', *European Journal of International Relations* **11:1** (2005) 99–135.

Ellwood, David W., *Rebuilding Europe: Western Europe, America and Postwar Reconstruction* (Harlow: Longman, 1992).

Endicott, Timothy, 'The Impossibility of the Rule of Law', *Oxford Journal of Legal Studies* **19** (1999) 1–18.

Eriksen, Erik (ed.), *Making the European Polity: Reflexive Integration in the EU* (London: Routledge, 2005).

Eriksen, E.O. and Fossum, J.E., 'Europe at a Crossroads: Government or Transnational Governance?', in Joerges, Christian, Sand, Inge-Johanne and Teubner, Günther (eds.), *Transnational Governance and Constitutionalism* (Oxford: Hart, 2004) 115–46.

Erskine, Toni (ed.), *Can Institutions Have Responsibilities? Collective Moral Agency and International Relations* (Basingstoke: Palgrave, 2003).

Esteban, Maria Luisa Fernandez, *The Rule of Law in the European Constitution* (The Hague: Kluwer Law International, 1999).

Estébanez, M.A.M., 'The Protection of National, or Ethnic, Religious and Linguistic Minorities', in Neuwahl, N. and Rosas, A. (eds.), *The European Union and Human Rights* (The Hague: Kluwer Law International, 1995).

Estella, Antonio, *The EU Principle of Subsidiarity and its Critique* (Oxford: Oxford University Press, 2002).

Falk, Richard, *On Human Governance: Towards a New Global Politics* (Cambridge: Polity Press, 1995).

Fitzpatrick, Peter, 'New Europe, Old Story: Racism and the European Community', in Ireland, Paddy and Laleng, Per (eds.), *The Critical Lawyers' Handbook 2* (London: Pluto Press, 1997) 86–95.

Fletcher, Maria, 'Schengen, the European Court of Justice and Flexibility Under the Lisbon Treaty: Balancing the United Kingdom's "Ins" and "Outs"', *European Constitutional Law Review* **5** (2009) 71–98.

Foley, Michael, *The Silence of Constitutions: Gaps, 'Abeyances' and Political Temperament in the Maintenance of Government* (Abingdon: Routledge, 1989).

Fredman, Sandra, *Human Rights Transformed: Positive Rights and Positive Duties* (Oxford: Oxford University Press, 2008).

Freeman, Heather Berit, 'Austria: the 1999 Parliamentary Elections and the European Union Members' Sanctions', *Boston College International and Comparative Law Review* (2002) 109–24.

Fuller, Lon, *Anatomy of the Law* (Harmondsworth: Penguin Books, 1971).

The Morality of Law (New Haven: Yale University Press, 1964).

Gadamer, Hans-Georg, *Truth and Method* (London: Sheed and Ward, 1979).

Gaddis, John Lewis, *The Cold War* (London: Penguin, 2007).

Galtung, Johan, *The European Community: A Superpower in the Making* (London: George Allen & Unwin, 1973)

'Peace and the World as Inter-civilizational Interaction', in Väyrynen, Raimo (ed.), *The Quest for Peace: Transcending Collective Violence and War among Societies, Cultures and States* (London: Sage, 1987) 330–47.

Garbagnati Ketvel, Maria-Gisella, 'The Jurisdiction of the European Court of Justice in Respect of the Common Foreign and Security Policy', *International Comparative Law Quarterly* **55** (2006) 77–120.

Gardner-Feldman, L., 'Reconciliation and Legitimacy: Foreign Relations and Enlargement of the European Union', in Banchoff, T. and Smith, M. (eds.), *Legitimacy and the European Union: the Contested Polity* (London: Routledge, 1999) 66–90 at 67.

Gearty, Conor A., 'The Internal and External "Other" in the Union Legal Order: Racism, Religious Intolerance and Xenophobia in Europe', in Alston, Philip *et al.* (eds.), *The EU and Human Rights* (Oxford: Oxford University Press, 1999) 325–58.

Giddens, Anthony, *Europe in the Global Age* (Cambridge: Polity Press, 2007).

Giubboni, Stefano, 'Free Movement of Persons and European Solidarity', *European Law Journal* **13:3** (2007) 360–79.

Glover, Jonathan, *Humanity: a Moral History of the Twentieth Century* (London: Pimlico, 2001).

Gould, Carol, *Globalizing Democracy and Human Rights* (Cambridge: Cambridge University Press, 2004).

Rethinking Democracy: Freedom and Social Cooperation in Politics, Economy, and Society (Cambridge: Cambridge University Press, 1988).

Gray, John, *Enlightenment's Wake* (Abingdon: Routledge, 2007).

Griffin, James, *On Human Rights* (Oxford: Oxford University Press, 2008).

Guliyeva, Gulara, 'Lost in Transition: Russian-speaking Non-citizens in Latvia and the Protection of Minority Rights in the European Union', *European Law Review* **33:6** (2008) 843–69.

Haas, E., *Beyond the Nation State: Functionalism and International Organization* (Stanford: Stanford University Press, 1968).

Habermas, Jürgen, *Between Facts and Norms* (Cambridge: Polity Press, 1997).

The Divided West (Cambridge: Polity Press, 2006).

The Inclusion of the Other: Studies in Political Theory (Cambridge: Polity Press, 1998).

The Postnational Constellation: Political Essays (Cambridge: Polity Press, 2001).

'Three Normative Models of Democracy', in Benhabib, Seyla (ed.), *Democracy and Difference: Contesting the Boundaries of the Political* (Princeton: Princeton University Press, 1996) 21–30.

Haltern, Ulrich, 'On Finality', in Bogdandy, Armin von and Bast, Jürgen (eds.), *Principles of European Constitutional Law* (Oxford: Hart, 2006) 727–64.

'Pathos and Patina: the Failure and Promise of Constitutionalism in the European Imagination', *European Law Journal* **9** (2003) 14–44.

Hamburg, David and Holl, Jane, 'Preventing Deadly Conflict: from Global Housekeeping to Neighbourhood Watch', in Paul, Inge, Grunberg, Isabelle and Stern, Marc (eds.), *Global Public Goods: International cooperation in the 21st Century* (Oxford: United Nations Development Programme/ Oxford University Press, 1999) 366–81.

Harlow, Carol, 'Global Administrative Law: the Quest for Principles and Values', *European Journal of International Law* **17** (2006) 187–214.

Hartley, Trevor, 'The Constitutional Foundations of the European Union', in Craig, Paul and Rawlings, Richard (eds.), *Law and Administration in Europe: Essays in Honour of Carol Harlow* (Oxford: Oxford University Press, 2003) 175–95.

Hayek, Friedrich, *The Constitution of Liberty* (London: Routledge and Kegan Paul, 1963).

Held, David, *Democracy and the Global Order* (Cambridge: Polity Press, 1995).

Hepple, Bob, 'Race and Law in Fortress Europe', *Modern Law Review* **7:1** (2004) 1–15.

Hill, Christopher and Smith, Karen (eds.), *European Foreign Policy: Key Documents* (London: Routledge, 2000).

Hirschmann, Nancy, 'Toward a Feminist Theory of Freedom', *Political Theory* **24:1** (1996) 46–67.

Hobsbawm, Eric, *The New Century* (London: Abacus, 2000).

Hoffman, Stanley, 'Europe's Identity Crisis: Between the Past and America', in Hoffman, Stanley, *The European Sisyphus: Essays on Europe 1964–1994* (Boulder, CO: Westview Press, 1995) 9–50.

'Europe's Identity Crisis: Between the Past and America', *Daedalus* **93:4** (1964) 1244–97.

Hooghe, Liesbet and Marks, Gary, *Multi-Level Governance and European Integration* (Lanham, MD: Rowman & Littlefield, 2001).

Horne, Alistair, *The Price of Glory* (London: Penguin, 1993).

Hughes, James, Sasse, Gwendolyn and Gordon, Claire, *Europeanization and Regionalization in the EU's Enlargement to Central and Eastern Europe: the Myth of Conditionality* (Houndmills: Palgrave Macmillan, 2004).

Hurrell, Andrew, *On Global Order: Power, Values, and the Constitution of International Society* (Oxford: Oxford University Press, 2007).

Hurrelmann, Achim, 'European Democracy, the "Permissive Consensus" and the Collapse of the EU Constitution', *European Law Journal* **13:3** (2007) 343–59.

Ifestos, Panayiotis, *European Political Co-operation: Towards a Framework of Supranational Diplomacy* (Aldershot: Avebury, 1987).

Jacobs, Francis G., *The Sovereignty of Law: The European Way* (Cambridge: Cambridge University Press, 2007).

Jaspers, Karl, *The Question of German Guilt* (New York: Capricorn Books, 1961).

Judt, Tony, *Postwar: a History of Europe Since 1945* (London: Pimlico, 2007).

Jünger, Ernst, *Storm of Steel* (London: Penguin, 2004).

Kadelbach, Stefan, 'Union Citizenship', in Bogdandy, Armin von and Bast, Jürgen (eds.), *Principles of European Constitutional Law* (Oxford: Hart, 2006) 453–99.

Kagan, Robert, *Of Paradise and Power: America and Europe in the New World Order* (New York: Alfred A. Knopf, 2003).

Kant, Immanuel, 'Toward Perpetual Peace: a Philosophical Project', in Gregor, Mary J. (trans. and ed.), *Immanuel Kant: Practical Philosophy* (Cambridge: Cambridge University Press, 1996) 315–51.

Kelsen, Hans, *Pure Theory of Law* (New Jersey: The Lawbook Exchange, 2002).

Kenner, Jeff, 'The Paradox of the Social Dimension', in Lynch, P., Neuwahl, N. and Rees, W. (eds.), *Reforming the European Union: from Maastricht to Amsterdam* (London: Longman, 2000).

Keohane, Robert, *International Institutions and State Power: Essays in International Relations Theory* (Boulder, CO: Westview Press, 1989).

Khaliq, Urfan, *Ethical Dimensions of the Foreign Policy of the European Union: a Legal Appraisal* (Cambridge: Cambridge University Press, 2008).

Khanna, Parag, *The Second World: Empires and Influence in the New Global Order* (London: Penguin, 2008).

Kingreen, Thorsten, 'Fundamental Freedoms', in Bogdandy, Armin von and Bast, Jürgen (eds.), *Principles of European Constitutional Law* (Oxford: Hart, 2006) 549–84.

Koskenneimi, Martti, 'Constitutionalism as Mindset: Reflections on Kantian Themes about International Law and Globalization', *Theoretical Inquiries in Law* **8:1** (2007) 9–36.

   The Gentle Civilizer of Nations: the Rise and Fall of International Law 1870–1960 (Cambridge: Cambridge University Press, 2004).

Kostakopoulou, Dora, 'On the Move: Ideas, Norms and European Citizenship: Explaining Institutional Change', *Modern Law Review* **68:2** (2005) 233–67.

Kymlicka, Will, *Multicultural Citizenship: a Liberal Theory of Minority Rights* (Oxford: Oxford University Press, 1995).

Lacroix, Justine, 'For a European Constitutional Patriotism', *Political Studies* **50** (2002) 944–58.

Lasok, Paul, 'The Rule of Law in the Legal Order of the European Community', in Economides, Kim, Betten, Lammy, Bridge, John, Shrubsall, Vivian and Tettenborn, Andrew (eds.), *Fundamental Values: a Volume of Essays to Commemorate the Seventy-Fifth Anniversary of the Founding of the Law School in Exeter 1923–1998* (Oxford: Hart, 2000) 85–114.

Lauterpacht, Hersch, *The Function of Law in the International Community* (Oxford: The Clarendon Press, 1933).

Layne, Christopher, 'Kant or Cant: the Myth of the Democratic Peace', in Brown, Michael, Lynn-Jones, Sean and Miller, Steven (eds.), *Debating the Democratic Peace* (Cambridge, MA: MIT Press, 1996) 157–201.

Lenaerts, Koen, 'Fundamental Rights in the European Union', *European Law Review* **25:6** (2000) 575–600.

Leonard, Mark, *Why Europe will run the 21st Century* (London: Fourth Estate, 2005).

Levinas, Emmanuel, *Otherwise than Being or Beyond Essence* (Pittsburgh: Duquesne University Press, 1998).

Levy, Daniel, Pensky, Max and Torpey, John (eds.), *Old Europe, New Europe: Transatlantic Relations after the Iraq War* (London: Verso, 2005).

Lewis, C.I., *The Ground and Nature of the Right* (New York: Columbia University Press, 1955).

Lindahl, Hans, 'Acquiring a Community: the *Acquis* and the Institution of European Legal Order', *European Law Journal* **9:4** (2003) 433–50.

Lindberg, Leon. N. and Scheingold, Stuart A., *Europe's Would-be Polity: Patterns of Change in the European Community* (Englewood Cliffs, NJ: Prentice-Hall, 1970).

Lipschutz, Ronnie, 'Reconstructing World Politics: the Emergence of Global Civil Society', *Millennium* **21:3** (1992) 389–420.

Lord, Christopher and Harris, Erika, *Democracy in the New Europe* (Basingstoke: Palgrave, 2006).

Luhmann, Niklas, *Social Systems* (Stanford: Stanford University Press, 1995).

Lyotard, Jean-François, *Europe, the Jews and the Book* (London: UCL Press, 1993).

MacCallum Jr., Gerald C., 'Negative and Positive Freedom', *The Philosophical Review* (1967) 312–34.

MacIntyre, Alasdair, *After Virtue: a Study in Moral Theory*, 2nd edn (London: Duckworth, 1985).

Maduro, Miguel Polares, 'The Importance of Being Called a Constitution: Constitutional Authority and the Authority of Constitutionalism', *International Journal of Constitutional Law* (2005) 332–56.
  'Striking the Elusive Balance Between Economic Freedom and Social Rights in the EU', in Alston, Philip *et al.* (eds.), *The EU and Human Rights* (Oxford: Oxford University Press, 1999) 449–72.
  We, the Court: the European Court of Justice and the European Economic Constitution (Oxford: Hart, 1998).

Magnette, Paul, *What is the European Union? Nature and Prospects* (Basingstoke: Palgrave, 2005).

Majone, Giandomenico, 'Europe's "Democratic Deficit": The Question of Standards', *European Law Journal* **4** (1998) 5–28.

Mayall, James, 'The Shadow of Empire: the EU and the Former Colonial World', in Hill, Christopher and Smith, Michael (eds.), *International Relations and the European Union* (Oxford: Oxford University Press, 2005) 292–316.

Mill, J.S., *On Liberty* (Oxford: Blackwell, 1946).

Miller, David *The Liberty Reader* (Edinburgh: Edinburgh University Press, 2006) 58–79.
  (ed.), *National Responsibility and Global Justice* (Oxford: Oxford University Press, 2007).
  'Two Ways to Think about Justice', *Politics, Philosophy and Economics* **1** (2002) 5–28.

Milward, Alan, *The European Rescue of the Nation State* (London: Routledge, 1992).

Mitrany, David, *A Working Peace System* (Chicago: Quadrangle Books, 1966).

Moravcsik, Andrew, 'In Defence of the "Democratic Deficit": Reassessing Legitimacy in the European Union', *Journal of Common Market Studies* **40:4** (2002) 603–24.
  'Europe Without Illusions' *Prospect*, July (2005) 25–6.

Mouffe, Chantal, *On the Political* (London: Routledge, 2005).

Nagel, Thomas, 'The Problem of Global Justice', *Philosophy and Public Affairs* **33:2** (2005) 113–47.

Neumann, Franz, 'Rechtsstaat, the Division of Powers and Socialism', in Kirchheimer, Otto and Neumann, Franz, *Social Democracy and the Rule of Law* (London: Allen & Unwin, 1987) 66–74.

Nicolaidis, Kalypso and Lacroix, Justine, 'Europe's Competing Paradigms', in Foot, Rosemary, Gaddis, John Lewis and Hurrell, Andrew (eds.), *Order and Justice in International Relations* (Oxford: Oxford University Press, 2003) 125–54.

Nowak, Manfred, 'Human Rights Conditionality in the EU', in Alston, Philip *et al.* (eds.), *The EU and Human Rights* (Oxford: Oxford University Press, 1999) 687–98.

Nugent, Neill, *The Government and Politics of the European Union,* 3rd edn (London: Macmillan, 1994).

Nussbaum, Martha, *Frontiers of Justice: Disability, Nationality, Species Membership* (Cambridge, MA: Harvard University Press, 2007).

Offe, Claus, 'The Democratic Welfare State in an Integrating Europe' in Greven, Michael T. and Pauly, Louis (eds.), *Democracy Beyond the State? The European Dilemma and the Emerging Modern Order* (Lanham MD: Rowman and Littlefield, 2000) 63–89

'Is there, or can there be, a "European Society"?', in Koj, Aleksander and Sztompka, Piotr (eds.), *Images of the World: Science, Humanities, Art* (Krakow: Jagellonian University, 2001) 143–59.

O'Neill, Onora, 'Agents of Justice' in Kuper, Andrew (ed.), *Global Responsibilities* (London: Routledge, 2005) 37–52

Bounds of Justice (Cambridge: Cambridge University Press, 2000).

Peterson, John, 'Europe, America, Iraq: Worst Ever, Ever Worsening?', *Journal of Common Market Studies* **42** (2004) 9–26.

Peterson, John and Blomberg, Elizabeth, *Decision-Making in the European Union* (Basingstoke: Macmillan, 1999).

Pettit, Philip, *A Theory of Freedom: from the Psychology to the Politics of Agency* (Cambridge: Polity Press, 2001).

Pierson, Paul, 'The Path to European Integration: a Historical Institutionalist Analysis', *Comparative Political Studies* **29** (1996) 123–63.

Pijpers, Alfred E., 'European Political Co-operation and the Realist Paradigm', in Holland, Martin (ed.), *The Future of European Political Co-operation* (London: Macmillan, 1991) 8–35.

Pinder, J., *The Building of the European Union,* 3rd edn (Oxford: Oxford University Press, 1998).

Pogge, Thomas, 'Human Rights and Human Responsibilities', in Kuper, Andrew (ed.), *Global Responsibilities: Who Must Deliver on Human Rights?* (London: Routledge, 2005) 3–35.

World Poverty and Human Rights: Cosmopolitan Responsibilities and Reform (Cambridge: Polity Press, 2002).

Pound, Roscoe, *Interpretations of Legal History* (Gloucester, MA: P. Smith, 1967).

Preuss, Ulrich K., 'The Iraq War: Critical Reflections from "Old Europe"', in Bartholomew, Amy (ed.), *Empire's Law* (London: Pluto Press, 2006) 52–67.

Radcliffe, J. 'The Scott Inquiry, Constitutional Conventions and Accountability in British Government', *Crime, Law and Social Change* **26:3** (1997) 239–52.

Radielli, Claudio, 'The Open Method of Coordination: a New Governance Architecture for the European Union?', *Swedish Institute for European Policy Studies* Reports 2003:1.

Technology in the European Union (London: Longman, 1999).

Raepenbusch, Sean van and Hanf, Domink, 'Flexibility in Social Policy', in de Witte, Bruno, Hanf, Domink and Vos, Ellen (eds.), *The Many Faces of Differentiation in EU Law* (Antwerp: Intersentia, 2001).

Rawlings, Richard, 'The Eurolaw Game: some Deductions from a Saga', *Journal of Law and Society* **20:3** (1993) 309–40.

Rawls, John, *The Law of Peoples* (Cambridge, MA: Harvard University Press, 1999).

Political Liberalism (New York: Columbia University Press, 2005).

Raz, Joseph, 'The Rule of Law and its Virtue', in Cunningham, Robert L. (ed.), *Liberty and the Rule of Law* (College Station: Texas A&M University Press, 1979) 3–21.

Rechel, Bernd, 'What Has Limited the EU's Impact on Minority Rights in Accession Countries?', *East European Politics and Societies* **22** (2008) 171–91.

Rehn, Olli, *Europe's Next Frontiers* (Baden-Baden: Nomos, 2006).

Ricoeur, Paul, 'Reflections on a New Ethos for Europe', in Kearney, Richard (ed.), *The Hermeneutics of Action* (London: Sage, 1996) 3–13.

Rittberger, Berthold and Schimmelfennig, Frank, 'The Constitutionalization of the European Union: Explaining the Parliamentarization and Institutionalization of Human Rights', May 2005 Institution of Advanced Studies Vienna Political Science Series.

Rorty, Richard, *Contingency, Irony and Solidarity* (Cambridge: Cambridge University Press, 1989).

Rosenau, James, *Distant Proximities: Dynamics Beyond Globalization* (Princeton: Princeton University Press, 2003).

Sacerdoti, Giorgio, 'The European Charter of Fundamental Rights: from a Nation-State Europe to a Citizens' Europe', *Columbia Journal of European Law* (2002) 37–52.

Sadurski, Wojciech, '"Solange, Chapter 3": Constitutional Courts in Central Europe – Democracy – European Union', *European Law Journal* **14:1** (2008) 1–35.

Said, Edward, *Culture and Imperialism* (London: Vintage, 1994).

Santos, Boaventura de Sousa, *Towards a New Legal Common Sense: Law, Globalization, and Emancipation,* 2nd edn (London: Butterworths, 2002).

Sarooshi, Danesh, *The United Nations and the Development of Collective Security* (Oxford: Oxford University Press, 1999).

Scharpf, Fritz W., 'The European Social Model: Coping with Diversity', *Journal of Common Market Studies* **40** (2002) 645–70.

Scheler, Max, *Formalism in Ethics and Non-Formal Ethics of Values* (Evanston: Northwestern University Press, 1973).

Scott, Colin, 'The Governance of the European Union: the Potential for Multi-Level Control', *European Law Journal* **8:1** (2002) 59–79.

Sen, Amartya, *Development as Freedom* (Oxford: Oxford University Press, 1999).
'Elements of a Theory of Human Rights', *Philosophy and Public Affairs* **32:4** (2004) 315–56.
Rationality and Freedom (Cambridge, MA: Harvard University Press, 2002).

Senden, Linda, 'Soft Law, Self-Regulation and Co-Regulation in European Law: Where do They Meet?', *Electronic Journal of Comparative Law* **9:1** (2005).

Shäuble, Wolfgang and Phillips, David L., 'Talking Turkey: is Europe Ready for a Muslim Member?', *Foreign Affairs* **83:6** (2004) 134–7.

Shore, Cris, 'The Cultural Policies of the European Union and Cultural Diversity', Research Position Paper 3 Council of Europe 2003.

Shuibhne, Niamh Nic, 'The European Union and Minority Language Rights', *MOST Journal on Multicultural Societies* **3:2** (2001).

Siedentop, Larry, *Democracy in Europe* (London: Penguin, 2000).

Smith, Adam, *An Inquiry into the Nature and Causes of the Wealth of Nations* (London: Greenland and Norris, 1805).

Smith, Anthony D., 'National Identity and the Idea of European Unity', in Gowan, Peter and Anderson, Perry (eds.), *The Question of Europe* (London: Verso, 1997) 318–42.

Smith, Karen, 'The EU, Human Rights and Relations with Third Countries: Foreign Policy with an Ethical Dimension', in Smith, Karen and Light, Margot (eds.), *Ethics and Foreign Policy* (Cambridge: Cambridge University Press, 2001).

Snell, Jukka, '"European Constitutional Settlement", an Ever Closer Union, and the Treaty of Lisbon: Democracy or Relevance?', *European Law Review* **33:5** (2008) 619–42.

Špidla, Vladimir, 'Some Reflections on the European Social Model', in Albers, Detlev, Haseler, Stephen and Meyer, Henning (eds.), *Social Europe: a Continent's Answer to Market Fundamentalism* (London: European Research Forum, 2006) 111–16.

Stolke, Verena, 'Talking Culture: New Boundaries, New Rhetorics of Exclusion in Europe', *Current Anthropology* **36:1** (1995) 1–24.

Stuart, Lord Mackenzie, *The European Communities and the Rule of Law* (London: Stevens & Sons, 1977).

Styan, David, *France and Iraq: Oil, Arms and French Policy Making in the Middle East* (London: I.B. Tauris & Company, 2006).

Summers, Robert, 'Evaluating and Improving Legal Processes – A Plea for Process Values', *Cornell Law Review* **60** (1974) 1–52.

Teson, Fernando R., *A Philosophy of International Law* (Boulder, CO: Westview, 1998).

Todorov, Tzvetan, *The New World Disorder* (Cambridge: Polity Press, 2005).

Tomkins, Adam, 'Responsibility and Resignation in the European Commission', *Modern Law Review* **62:5** (1999) 744–65.

Toth, A.G., 'The European Union and Human Rights: the Way Forward', *Common Market Law Review* **34** (1997) 491–529.

Tridimas, Takis, *The General Principles of EU Law,* 2nd edn (Oxford: Oxford University Press, 2006)

Trubek, David M., Cottrell, Patrick and Nance, Mark, '"Soft Law," "Hard Law," and European Integration: Toward a Theory of Hybridity', *Jean Monnet Working Paper* (2005) 02/05.

Trybus, Martin, *European Union Law and Defence Integration* (Oxford: Hart, 2005).

Ullman, Richard H., 'Redefining Security', *International Security* **8** (1983) 129–53.

Van Bossuyt, Anneleen, 'Is there an Effective European Legal Framework for the Protection of Minority Languages? The European Union and the Council of Europe Screened', *European Law Review* **32:6** (2007) 860–77.

Wakefield, Jill, 'BSE: a Lesson in Containment? Avoiding Responsibility and Accountability in the Compensation Action', *European Law Review* **27** (2002) 426–44.

Walker, Neil, 'Europe's Constitutional Momentum and the Search for Polity Legitimacy', *International Journal of Constitutional Law* **3:2** (2005) 211–38.

'Flexibility within a Metaconstitutional Frame: Reflections on the Future of Legal Authority in Europe', in de Búrca, Gráinne and Scott, Joanne (eds.), *Constitutional Change in the EU: from Uniformity to Flexibility* (Oxford: Hart, 2000) 9–30.

'In Search of the Area of Freedom, Security and Justice: A Constitutional Odyssey', in Walker, Neil (ed.), *Europe's Area of Freedom, Security and Justice* (Oxford: Oxford University Press, 2004) 3–37.

Walzer, Michael, *Just and Unjust Wars,* 3rd edn (New York: Basic Books, 2000).

Ward, Ian, 'A Decade of Europe? Some Reflections on an Aspiration', *Journal of Law and Society* **30** (2003) 236–57.

Weeramantry, Lucian G., *The International Commission of Jurists: the Pioneering Years* (The Hague: Kluwer Law International, 2000).

Weiler, Joseph, *The Constitution of Europe* (Cambridge: Cambridge University Press, 1999).

'In Defence of the Status Quo: Europe's Constitutional *Sonderweg*', in Weiler, J. and Wind, M. (eds.), *European Constitutionalism Beyond the State* (Cambridge: Cambridge University Press, 2003) 7–23.

Un'Europa Cristiana: un saggio esplorativo (Milan: BUR, 2003).

'Federalism without Constitutionalism', in Nicolaïdis, Kalypso and Howse, Robert (eds.), *The Federal Vision* (Oxford: Oxford University Press, 2001).

Weiler, Joseph, Haltern, Ulrich R. and Mayer, Franz C., 'European Democracy and its Critique', *West European Politics* **18:3** (1995) 4–39.

Weiler, Joseph and Wind, Marlene (eds.), *European Constitutionalism Beyond the State* (Cambridge: Cambridge University Press, 2003).

Wessels, Wolfgang, 'EPC after the Single European Act: Towards a European Foreign Policy via Treaty Obligations', in Holland, Martin (ed.), *The Future of European Political Co-operation* (London: Macmillan, 1991) 143–60.

Wilkinson, Michael A., 'Civil Society and the Re-imagination of European Constitutionalism', *European Law Journal* **9:4** (2003) 451–72.

Williams, Andrew, *EU Human Rights Policies: a Study in Irony* (Oxford: Oxford University Press, 2004).

'EU Human Rights Policy and the Convention on the Future of Europe: a Failure of Design?', *European Law Review* **28:6** (2003) 794–813.

'Human Rights and Law: between Sufferance and Insufferability', *Law Quarterly Review* **122** (2007) 132–57.

'The Indifferent Gesture: Article 7 TEU, the Fundamental Rights Agency and the UK's Invasion of Iraq', *European Law Review* **31** (2006) 4–28.

Wolfers, A., *Discord and Collaboration* (Baltimore: Johns Hopkins University Press, 1962).

Woolman, Stu and Bishop, Michael (eds.), *Constitutional Conversations* (Cape Town: Pretoria University Law Press, 2008).

Youngs, Richard, 'Normative Dynamics and Strategic Interests in the EU's External Identity', *Journal of Common Market Studies* **42:2** (2004) 415–35.

Zeitlin, Jonathan, 'Social Europe and Experimentalist Governance: Towards a New Constitutional Compromise?', in de Búrca, G. (ed.), *EU Law and the Welfare State: in Search of Solidarity* (Oxford: Oxford University Press, 2005), 213–41.

Zielonka, Jan, *Europe as Empire: the Nature of the Enlarged European Union* (Oxford: Oxford University Press, 2006).

Zimmermann, Reinhard, Eidenmüller, Horst, Faust, Florian, Grigoleit, Hans Christoph, Jansen, Nils and Wagner, Gerhard, 'The Common Frame of Reference for European Private Law – Policy Choices and Codification Problems', *Oxford Journal of Legal Studies* **28:4** (2008) 659–708.

Index

CAMBRIDGE STUDIES IN EUROPEAN LAW AND POLICY

Books in the Series